Library of
Davidson College

Also in the Variorum Collected Studies Series:

JEAN-CLAUDE MARGOLIN
Erasme dans son miroir et dans son sillage

JEAN-CLAUDE MARGOLIN
Erasme: le prix des mots et de l'homme

E. WILLIAM MONTER
Enforcing Morality in Early Modern Europe

D. P. WALKER
Music, Spirit and Language in the Renaissance

ALLEN G. DEBUS
Chemistry, Alchemy and the New Philosophy, 1550–1700

CHARLES B. SCHMITT
The Aristotelian Tradition and Renaissance Universities

WALTER PAGEL
Religion and Neoplatonism in Renaissance Medicine

WALTER PAGEL
From Paracelsus to Van Helmont
Studies in Renaissance Medicine and Science

E. J. ASHWORTH
Studies in Post-Medieval Semantics

DONALD R. KELLEY
History, Law and the Human Sciences
Medieval and Renaissance Perspectives

J. S. CUMMINS
Jesuit and Friar in the Spanish Expansion to the East

BRIAN TIERNEY
Church Law and Constitutional Thought in the Middle Ages

JOHN W. O'MALLEY
Rome and the Renaissance: Studies in Culture and Religion

JACQUES HEERS
Société et économie à Gênes (XIVe–XVe siècles)

VINCENT ILARDI
Studies in Italian Renaissance Diplomatic History

PAUL GRENDLER
Culture and Censorship in Late Renaissance Italy and France

J. Russell Major

The Monarchy, the Estates and the Aristocracy in Renaissance France

VARIORUM REPRINTS
London 1988

British Libary CIP data

Major, J. Russell (James Russell)
 The monarchy, the estates and the aristocracy in Renaissance France. — (Collected studies series; CS279).
 1. France. Social life, 1420-1650
 I. Title
 944'.026

ISBN 0-86078-227-1

Copyright © 1988 by   Variorum Reprints

Published in Great Britain by   Variorum Reprints
20 Pembridge Mews London W11 3EQ

Printed in Great Britain by   Galliard (Printers) Ltd
Great Yarmouth Norfolk

VARIORUM REPRINT CS279

The Monarchy,
the Estates and the Aristocracy
in Renaissance France

Professor J. Russell Major

CONTENTS

Introduction   ix-xii

Acknowledgements   xiii

THE RENAISSANCE MONARCHY

I   The Renaissance Monarchy: A Contribution to the Periodization of History   112-124
The Emory University Quarterly XIII.
Atlanta, Ga., 1957

II   The Renaissance Monarchy as Seen by Erasmus, More, Seyssel and Machiavelli   17-31
Action and Conviction in Early Modern Europe: Essays in Memory of E.H. Harbinson, eds. Theodore K. Rabb and Jerrold E. Seigel. Princeton, N.J.: Princeton University Press, 1969

III   Popular Initiative in Renaissance France   27-41
Aspects of the Renaissance: A Symposium, ed. Archibald R. Lewis. Austin, Texas: University of Texas Press, 1967

THE ESTATES GENERAL AND THE PROVINCIAL ESTATES

IV   The Third Estate in the Estates General of Pontoise, 1561   460-476
Speculum XXIX.
Cambridge, Mass., 1954

V   The Assembly at Paris in the Summer of 1575   701-715
Post Scripta: Essays on Medieval Law and the Emergence of the European State, in Honor of Gaines Post, eds. Joseph R. Strayer and Donald E. Queller *(Studia Gratiana XV).* Rome, 1972

VI	The Electoral Procedure for the Estates General of France and its Social Implications, 1483-1651 *Medievalia et Humanistica X.* *Boulder, Col., 1956*	131-150
VII	The Payment of the Deputies to the French National Assemblies, 1484-1627 *The Journal of Modern History XXVII.* *Chicago, Ill., 1955.*	217-229
VIII	The Loss of Royal Initiative and the Decay of the Estates General in France, 1421-1615 *Album Helen Maud Cam, vol. II (Studies presented to the International Commission for the History of Representative and Parliamentary Institutions XXIV).* *Louvain-Paris: Editions Nauwelaerts, 1961*	247-259
IX	Henry IV and Guyenne: A Study concerning the Origins of Royal Absolutism *French Historical Studies IV.* *Cincinnati, Ohio, 1966*	363-383
X	French Representative Assemblies: Research Opportunities and Research Published *Studies in Medieval and Renaissance History I.* *Lincoln, Nebraska, 1964*	183-219

THE ARISTOCRACY

XI	The Crown and the Aristocracy in Renaissance France *The American Historical Review LXIX.* *Washington, D.C., 1964*	631-645
XII	Noble Income, Inflation, and the Wars of Religion in France *The American Historical Review LXXXVI.* *Bloomington, Indiana, 1981.*	21-48

XIII	"Bastard Feudalism" and the Kiss: Changing Social Mores in the Late Medieval and Early Modern France *The Journal of Interdisciplinary History XVII.* *Cambridge, Mass., 1987*	509-535
XIV	The Revolt of 1620: A Study of Ties of Fidelity *French Historical Studies XIV.* *Cincinnati, Ohio, 1986*	391-408
Index		1-9

This volume contains xiii + 285 pages

PUBLISHER'S NOTE

The articles in this volume, as in all others in the Collected Studies Series, have not been given a new, continuous pagination. In order to avoid confusion, and to facilitate their use where these same studies have been referred to elsewhere, the original pagination has been maintained wherever possible.

Each article has been given a Roman number in order of appearance, as listed in the Contents. This number is repeated on each page and quoted in the index entries.

INTRODUCTION

Forty years ago when I began research on my doctoral dissertation on the Estates General of 1560, the prevailing wisdom was that the Renaissance monarchs, in alliance with the middle class, forged centralized absolute monarchies in most European states. In achieving this self-conscious goal they were aided by the decline of the feudal nobility provoked by the partial substitution of a "bastard feudalism" for the traditional lord-vassal relationship, the invention of gunpowder, and inflation on the one hand, and the rise of the middle class, the growth of nationalism, the development of standing armies and large bureaucracies, and the revival of Roman law on the other. Neat and persuasive as this scenario was, it seemed to me from the first to be filled with unproved assumptions and questionable generalizations. From an early date I have tried to discover the true nature of the Renaissance monarchy, to learn why representative government failed to triumph in France as it did in England, and to find out how the French nobility managed to adapt itself to changing circumstances and remain the dominant social class in spite of a long assumed challenge by the middle class. The essays that follow concern these three interests. They were written as much as thirty-five years ago and reflect my groping for a new and more satisfactory interpretation of Renaissance history. Several, including the studies of the estates of Pontoise and the assembly of 1575, have never to my knowledge been cited by any historian, although the former is based on the previously undiscovered manuscript journal of the third estate and the meeting itself was of exceptional importance. By bringing these and some less obscure articles together in a single volume I hope that a coherent picture of the three topics is presented. I need hardly say that if I were writing these articles today, I would do some things differently; but, in spite of over-simplifications and occasional errors, I remain convinced that the basic thrust of these essays is essentially correct and that the views that prevailed in the 1940s have been substantially altered as a result of the work of many historians.

In the first article I suggest that the Renaissance monarchies were dynastic, legitimate, and therefore of necessity decentralized. Kings had neither the military power nor the bureaucracy to impose their wills. Rulers were strong only when they won the support of substantial segments of their subjects, and the passion for uniformity — for centralized, rational, and ordered states — was not characteristic until the seventeenth century. Erasmus, More, Seyssel, and Machiavelli substantially agreed with this view as did many other contemporary thinkers. Since rulers lacked the bureaucracy to attend to many aspects of government, the people seized the initiative. The third article explores how the Catholic clergy, the Huguenots, the provincial estates, the towns, and the villages became increasingly able to govern themselves.

The second group of articles explores the question of why the Estates General and some of the provincial estates failed to survive in France. In resolving this problem it is pertinent to ask what use these institutions were to the crown and to the vocal elements of the population. The refusal of the secular estates to vote funds in 1560, 1561, and 1575, to say nothing of later meetings, must have dampened any enthusiasm the crown may have had for such assemblies. The clergy, on the other hand, was frightened into making a generous gift in 1561. This led to the formation of the assembly of the clergy which met periodically until the Revolution to vote taxes that its agents collected, to submit petitions of grievance, and to look after its affairs. Chancellor L'Hôpital offered the same opportunity to the secular estates, but they refused.

If meetings of the Estates General accomplished little from the standpoint of the king, it is equally true that they were not much more successful in winning the affection of his subjects. There was some competition to be elected, but the desire to be a deputy was almost never strong enough to cause anyone to offer to serve without compensation as became the rule in England. There was often hope when the Estates General was summoned, but meetings generally ended in disappointment and the people were often reluctant to reimburse their representatives.

If we turn to the question of why the Estates General did not satisfy the needs of either the kings or the people, we are struck by the fact that the former failed to ask that deputies be given full powers to deal with financial matters in 1560 and 1575. Judging by the electorate's response in 1561 the crown might have been unsuccessful if it had. Nevertheless, it seems clear that royal officials did not know how to manage the electoral process or to control the deputies' deliberations once they did meet. The use of bailiwick elections and the separation of the orders into three chambers further increased the difficulties of royal officials and put obstacles in the way of the deputies developing a common initiative. As a result, by the end of a meeting officials, deputies and the electorate were disillusioned.

The introduction of bailiwick elections in 1484 provides an opportunity for studying some neglected aspects of French society. One is struck by the extension of suffrage in northern France to include the villages and their parish priests. Small towns often sought to be included, but the extension of suffrage to the villages must be attributed primarily to the local royal officials who were motivated in part by the Roman law principle of *quod omnes tangit* but more by their desire to replace the municipal oligarchy as leaders of local society. The conflict between town and local royal officials, who often came from the same social class, was one of the most complex and least understood in France. It was more apparent in the elections than friction between the second and third estates, this despite the fact that there was a tendency for the three estates to abandon the frequent medieval practice of deliberating and voting as a single house.

The Estates General died relatively painlessly, but many local notables were deeply attached to their provincial estates which they saw as the bulwarks of their privileges. Sully's decision to replace the tax collectors of the estates with *élus* threatened their ability to limit royal taxes and to make levies for their own purposes. His frank admission to the Agenais deputy that he wanted "the *taille* to be levied in all of France in the same fashion" amounted to a declaration of war against the provincial estates. Sully succeeded in establishing *élections* in Bugey, Bresse, and Gex, but Guyenne's long resistance caused him to halt his initial moves against Languedoc and Burgundy. Immediately after his dismissal in 1611, the *élus* were abolished in Guyenne. The 1620s saw an effort to revive Sully's design of creating a uniform system of tax collection based on the *élus*, but strong provincial reaction led Richelieu to abandon the effort after the Day of Dupes, November 11, 1630. Ultimately the *élus* with their venal offices proved no more reliable than the officials of the estates, and the crown found in the non-venal intendants the solution to their fiscal administrative problems.

The third group of articles are part of an on-going effort to show how nobles adapted themselves to changing circumstances and managed to remain the dominant social class. In the first and more general article I emphasize the nobles' financial status and the patron-client relationship. The remaining three articles are based on years of further research and explore the same questions in greater detail. Historians who have argued that noble income declined in the inflationary period of the sixteenth century have generally compared income to grain prices. Nobles, however, produced nearly all their food and the prices of things they actually bought increased only about half as fast as grain prices. Their real income, therefore, increased rapidly until the Wars of Religion and held its own thereafter, if they were able to avoid alienating their lands and these lands escaped the depredation of troops. Nobles sought to compensate for the decline of the feudal relationship by inventing a "bastard feudalism" that evolved into a patron-client relationship. Homage was dropped because the kissing and kneeling aspects of the ritual became unpopular, and not because patrons wanted or anticipated less loyalty. At first the new relationship was cemented by indentures, but later verbal oaths or less formal understandings may have sufficed. As late as 1620, however, written agreements were still sometimes used. In the revolt of that year some patrons and clients behaved in the approved fashion, but others did not. The patron-client relationship had become as fragile as the feudalism of three centuries before. This change helped to open the way to the establishment of an absolute monarchy.

Emory University J. RUSSELL MAJOR
June 1987

ACKNOWLEDGEMENTS

Grateful acknowledgement is made to the following for their kind permission to reproduce the essays in this volume: Prof. Thomas H. English for *The Emory University Quarterly* (I); the Princeton University Press (II); the University of Texas Press (III); the Medieval Academy of America (IV); Cardinal Alphons Stickler and the Editrice LAS (V); Mrs Rosamund D. Thomson (VI); The University of Chicago Press (VII); Editions Nauwelaerts (VIII); the editors of *French Historical Studies* (IX, XIV); the University of Nebraska Press (X); the American Historical Association (XI, XII); the editors of *The Journal of Interdisciplinary History* and the MIT Press (XIII).

I

The Renaissance Monarchy:
A Contribution to the Periodization of History

THE CONCEPT OF A RENAISSANCE has been defended and attacked ever since Burckhardt published his *Civilization of the Renaissance* in Italy nearly a century ago. There are those who see in the fifteenth and sixteenth centuries a definite period of European history. Others recognize in these years only a continued growth that had begun well back in the Middle Ages. Still others look on the two centuries as witnessing the decline of the medieval civilization. The attitude of the scholar is determined in part by his field of research. The art historian, for example, is usually a strong supporter of the thesis that there was a Renaissance and that it constituted a definite historical period. The economic historian often prefers to see the real change as taking place around the eleventh century with the revival of trade and the growth of towns. The devout Catholic, on the other hand, interprets the period as being one of a decline beginning with the false teachings of William of Occam and ending in the horrible tragedy of Luther and Descartes. Students of literature, science, philosophy, and political theory have added their ideas to further confuse the concept of the Renaissance; but although there are political histories aplenty, little effort has been made to interpret the period from the standpoint of the nature of the state, this in spite of the fact that Burckhardt saw in the peculiar political situation in Italy one of the principal causes of the Italian Renaissance.

The purpose of this paper is to explore the nature of monarchies to the north and west of Italy, paying particular attention to France. It is my hope to add support to Burckhardt's thesis that the state of this period differed enough from what had gone before and what was to come after, to constitute a definite period in history, but to deny that the Swiss scholar's bold characterization of the Renaissance city-state as being a work of art, that is, "the fruit of reflection and careful adaptation," has any validity for the monarchies at that time.

In developing the concept of a Renaissance Monarchy for France, we miss the dynastic changes that make such convenient, though not entirely accurate, marks of delineation for England, yet it seems undeniable that there was considerable difference between the monarchies of, let us say, Philip IV, Francis I, and Louis XIV, between the Medieval, the Renaissance, and the Baroque. The system of government typified by Francis I had its formative period during the reigns of Charles VII and Louis XI and its period of decline during the reigns of Henry IV and Louis XIII.

The first and most pronounced characteristic of this monarchy was its dynastic structure and motivation. Foreign and domestic policy centered around the question of marriages, for it was by marriages that states were enlarged. Wars of conquest were undertaken to secure a claimed inheritance, not strategic borders. The national and economic considerations that loom so large in modern statecraft were ignored, and we find Charles VIII surrendering land in what is now southern France to Spain and what is now northern France to the Habsburgs in order to buy their neutrality before he embarked on an expedition to conquer Naples, for which he had a dynastic claim. Not until the reign of Louis XIV did the French kings abandon their desire to win Italy and adopt as their goal the achievement of their natural boundaries of the Pyrenees and the Rhine. Before one condemns this type of diplomacy, however, it should be remembered that it was by marriage that the Habsburgs built the mighty empire of Charles V. His lands were more extensive than those of Napoleon or Hitler and his empire was to endure far longer.

Internal policy also depended largely on marriage. Nobles were sometimes able to amass enough land to become threats to one or even two monarchs. The Burgundian dukes brought together so many duchies and counties in France and the Empire that they posed a serious problem to both the Valois and the Emperor. The House of Foix-Navarre won huge estates on both sides of the Pyrenees.

I

Other families did likewise, but if a noble house could build its power by dynastic arrangements, the kings could profit by the extinction of a great family, for when there was no heir, feudal territories escheated back to the crown. It was by this process that the French monarchy added so much to its domain, and a large part of the internal policy of the Valois was designed to further the work of nature and chance. Louis XI married his crippled daughter, who could have no children, to the Duke of Orléans in order to insure the eventual acquisition of his lands, while two French kings sought and won the hand of Anne of Brittany to keep her highly prized duchy united with the crown.

Since territorial aggrandizement at the expense of foreign states and the local nobility depended on dynastic claims and feudal law, legality had to be stressed to an unusual degree. The Renaissance prince has often been pictured as a highly individualistic ruler with little respect for aught save wit and power, but in fact even the Italian potentate was ever anxious to find legal justification for the authority he wielded, and elsewhere rulers were still less subject to challenge on this score.

This stress on legitimacy and legality by the Renaissance Monarchs was not limited to their own rights, it involved a respect for the rights of their subjects. When a new king came to the throne, he invariably confirmed the privileges of individuals, towns, provinces, and other corporate groups in his kingdom. When a princely or feudal domain fell to a king, he at once recognized the privileges its inhabitants had been granted by their previous rulers. Indeed, the people of the newly incorporated territories were as apt to accept the orders of their new sovereign by virtue of his being Count of Provence or Duke of Brittany as king of France.

The acceptance of the idea of legitimacy and privilege and the existence of strong provincial loyalties made necessary a decentralized form of government. Not only were the customs, laws, and privileges of each and every territory recognized, but the kings established sovereign law courts in the larger provinces. Thus *Parlements* or courts of justice, and several types of financial courts were organized in Burgundy, Languedoc, Brittany, Provence,

Dauphiné, and elsewhere from which there was no appeal to any higher court at Paris. The decisions of these courts were based on law, custom, and tradition, and not until the mid-seventeenth century is there evidence that any universal principles of reason and morality were applied. The judges could and did render decisions against royal officials and the crown itself, although the king, as the fountain of justice, was able to overrule their objections by a personal appearance. The existence of these courts provided assurance that the three hundred odd local customs in France would be preserved until the Revolution.

The legal decentralization described above was paralleled by the decentralization of administration. There was a governor in each of the dozen or more great provinces of France who, with or without royal approval, assumed the various regalian powers. In addition, about two-thirds of the provinces had representative assemblies that voted, and often collected taxes and attended to other administrative matters. Beneath the provinces were the bailiwicks and seneschalries. These jurisdictions were ruled by the bailiff or seneschal and a host of lesser officials who, like the governors, were as apt to follow their own desires as to obey the directives of the king.

Alongside the hierarchy of the royal officials there existed the seigneury and the town. The seigneurs were still a power in the villages, and it has often been pointed out that the peasant rarely came into contact with royal authority except to pay taxes. The towns were largely self-governing, with their own elected officials, independent systems of taxation, and militia to defend their fortified walls. Thus, the land the kings won by their dynastic policies did not point to a consolidation of power in the hands of the central government as much as to the acceptance of the diversified, decentralized conglomeration of provinces, duchies, counties, seigneuries, and towns that was the Renaissance Monarchy.

Closely associated with the decentralization of the Renaissance Monarchy was the confusion of boundaries, privileges, rights, and jurisdictions only too apparent in every branch of the government. The sea provided the only clearly defined boundary of the Renaissance state. Elsewhere much land was in dispute. Territories, inde-

I

pendent, or with strong claim to independence, such as the duchy of Bouillon, the principalities of Montbéliard, Bidache, and Salm, the republics of Mandure and Mulhouse, the counties of Sarrverden, Venaissin, and Sault, to say nothing of the papal state of Avignon and the principality of Orange existed along the borders and even in the interior of the country. Many of these enclaves owned smaller enclaves in France, while France, in turn, was sometimes in possession of parishes surrounded by these enclaves. There is ample evidence to show that often neither the French king, the foreign ruler, nor the local magistrates could agree on what they owned. Foreigners held fiefs in France, and in the bailiwick of Gex they sought to vote in the elections to the Estates General of 1789. Ecclesiastical boundaries rarely coincided with those of the nation and the dioceses of many foreign archbishops and bishops included parishes in France. Two of these foreign prelates were actually elected deputies to the Estates General in 1789.

More serious was the confusion about the boundaries of the administrative subdivisions of the kingdom. Nearly every bailiwick had jurisdiction over parishes completely surrounded by neighboring bailiwicks. Frequently parishes and even towns were claimed by rival royal authorities. It was impossible for any magistrate to know exactly what territory he was to administer. As late as 1789 there were no less than 1800 divided or contested parishes in France. Many secondary bailiwicks claimed independence from the principal bailiwick to which they had been traditionally considered to be attached. There were quarrels about the extent and nature of the justice in countless seigneuries. Each town possessed its special privileges, which more often than not differed from those of its neighbor. Royal officials sometimes had only the vaguest idea of the rights of each. The resultant confusion was so great that it was difficult for officials to govern or the law to operate. Disobedience could safely become commonplace, and one is not surprised to find one aristocrat writing after the Revolution that before 1789 people enjoyed "the most complete liberty. One was free to speak, to write, to act with the greatest independence, and one could even defy the authorities in perfect security." Certainly Burckhardt's description of the Italian city-state as being "the fruit of reflection and careful adaptation" has no validity for the monarchies of that time.

Why did the Renaissance Monarchs of France and other countries permit so much decentralization and confusion? Why did they respect the privileges of their subjects? The answer to these questions lies partly in the fact that the rulers were products of the climate of opinion of their age. They had been taught that a king was responsible for the well-being of his subjects, that to deprive them of their long-recognized privileges was to become a tyrant, and tyranny was as hateful in their age as it had been in the medieval period. Nowhere does this fact show more clearly than in the decisions rendered by the king in council. These invaluable records provide the most trustworthy evidence we have for the motives behind the actions of the kings and their principal advisors. They prove that the crown had even greater respect for privilege and tradition than the regular law courts, and give direct contradiction to any theory that the Renaissance Monarchs sought to increase their authority at the expense of the legitimate rights of their subjects. Indeed, the most frequent type of dispute to be brought before the council resulted from the encroachments of local royal officials in the name of the king on the prerogatives and privileges of individuals and corporate groups, but almost invariably the decision of the councillors favored the privileged to the discomfiture of the over-zealous local officials. There was, of course, the possibility that a ruler would recklessly break the bonds of tradition or that he would be so self-righteous as to interpret every questionable royal prerogative in his own favor; but if there were such kings, their weakness in character was checkmated by their weakness in power.

It has been generally assumed that the establishment of standing armies on the continent in the late fifteenth and sixteenth centuries furthered the growth of royal absolutism. However, the most casual examination of the size and composition of the new armies dispels any illusion of their being an effective instrument against the people. The troops in the peacetime army and militia of France seldom numbered more than one and a half modern divisions. Even with the rapid transportation and communication of today coupled with the immense superiority of the arms and training of the modern soldier over the civilian population, such a force could hardly subject an unwilling population of fifteen million persons. Witness the recent difficulties of the Russians in Hungary. Furthermore, the system of livery and maintenance or clientage gave the great noble a military force of his own. The Duke of Montmorency came to court in 1560 with a retinue of 800 horsemen, and he could have mustered a larger force had there been any need. Fortified towns the size of Troyes and Amiens had 3000 militiamen equipped with artillery and munitions. Thus, while the king could have captured the castles of a Montmorency and taken any single town in the kingdom, it was cheaper and easier for a ruler to avoid offending his subjects, and any sort of an attack on the privileges of the nobility or towns as a whole was clearly impossible.

It is true that in time of war the Renaissance Monarchs sometimes had armies of 40,000 or 50,000 men, but these troops were raised and paid by their officers, and not the state. They therefore obeyed their commanders and not the king. As late as the Thirty Years War both the French king and the Emperor were often more endangered by their own disobedient troops than by the troops of the enemy. Some of these forces were officered by mercenaries, but the bulk were commanded by the native nobility, who could hardly be expected to turn on their fellow nobles or even the towns on the directives of the king.

If the Renaissance Monarchs lacked the military power to suppress their subjects, they also lacked the bureaucracy to govern them. In 1505 there were only 12,000 royal officials in France, a nation of 15,000,000 inhabitants and 480,000 square kilometers, or one official for each 1,250 inhabitants and one for each 40 square kilometers. In 1934 there was one official for each 70 inhabitants and 56 for each 40 square kilometers. Furthermore, it was impossible for the Renaissance Monarch to control the limited number of officials he possessed. In the first place, whereas the Washington bureaucrat is armed with a typewriter, a mimeograph machine, the government printing office, and rapid means of communication, the Renaissance Monarch had only a limited number of scribes to record his orders.

When he wanted to send a directive to the bailiffs, he had to have it copied by hand a hundred times, for there were a hundred bailiffs. As a result, orders from the central government were few and brief, leaving local officials very much to their own devices. The printing press was, of course, known, but as late as 1600 it was used only to print important ordonnances, and not for normal administrative correspondence.

In the second place, the financial difficulties that beset the Renaissance Monarchs led them to sell government posts, and once an office became venal, its holder could not normally be discharged without financial reimbursement. He was left free to obey or disobey the few brief directives he received with little likelihood that the king would ever know the difference, or that if he did, he could do anything about it.

If, then, the Renaissance kings lacked a strong, loyal army and an adequate, obedient bureaucracy, what was the basis of monarchical power? The answer seems clear. Kings were obeyed only because, or rather when, the bulk of the population supported their cause. The devotion of the French people to their king was described by a Venetian ambassador as "a unique thing in the Christian world." The purpose of Machiavelli's *The Prince* was to teach how power could be won and maintained, and no one was more certain than the author that it was more important for a ruler of his day to satisfy the people than the military, because "the people are the more powerful." To secure the support of the people, the prince was advised to appear to have all the traditional virtues, to tax lightly, and when great feudal dependencies were won back, to alter neither the laws nor the taxes of the inhabitants. The more experienced Commynes likewise advised kings to secure the affection of their subjects. Even Cardinal Richelieu wrote that "love is the most powerful motive which obliges one to obey."

The Renaissance kings were supported by their subjects for a number of reasons. They were the restorers of order after a long period of warfare marked by all the horrors of pillaging and murdering by undisciplined soldiers. There was no safe, logical alternative to their rule, however much town and noble might be opposed to further increases in royal power. They accurately sensed the feelings of the people and, as we have seen, were ever ready to support and protect their privileges even against their own officials. They kept in intimate contact with the people by wandering from one part of their kingdom to another, receiving everyone without barriers of rigid formality. Indeed, there was a degree of intimacy between the kings and their people that surprised the ambassadors of republican Venice. In 1561 one of them attributed the devotion of the French people to the crown to "the familiarity which exists between the monarch and his subjects all of whom he treats as his companions. No one is excluded from his presence. Lackeys and people of lowest condition dare to enter the private office of the king in order to see everything that happens and to hear all that is said. If one wishes to speak of something important, he must have the patience to find a place where there are not a great many people and then speak in a low voice in order not to be heard. This great familiarity, it is true, makes the subjects insolent, but at the same time it makes them faithful and devoted to their kings." We would do well to picture the Renaissance Monarch as being the "first gentleman" of France rather than the "Sun King." The removal of the court to Versailles by Louis XIV was symbolic of the separation of the crown from the people during his reign, and the return of the court to Paris in 1789 could have had equal importance had an abler man been the head of the state.

A more tangible way of winning support also lay in the power of the kings. They controlled a vast system of patronage. Most of the highest offices of the church lay at their disposal and the wealthiest bishoprics and abbeys went to their faithful supporters. Government positions, one of the most lucrative of all forms of employment during the period, found their way into the same hands. Fiefs, patents of nobility, and nearly every type of privilege could be granted by the monarch. He who served the crown loyally and ably could hope for untold riches. Montmorency, Wolsey, and Richelieu were only the most famous of those who won wealth and power through loyalty. Thousands of lesser names could be added.

One last way of winning popular support was through the use of representative institutions. It may seem strange that kings encouraged and developed assemblies of the estates, but since neither the medieval nor the Renaissance Monarchs had ever heard of representative government, they could have foreseen no reason to fear or destroy representative assemblies. They regarded these institutions as tools for their use, like their councils and their judicial and financial courts. It is true that representative assemblies sometimes got out of hand, but did not the council also check the king upon occasion? As long as no one thought that either the council or the assembly could govern alone, the one was no more dangerous than the other, and both could prove of value upon occasion. The uses of the estates were discovered during the Middle Ages, and strong monarchs, as Edward I of England and Philip IV of France, did not hesitate to summon large assemblies.

The practice of holding national assemblies declined in most countries in the fourteenth century, but was revived by the Renaissance Monarchs. These kings were faced with problems growing out of two great changes. One was the influx of precious metals from the New World which led to a rapid rise in prices. Higher prices, in turn, necessitated higher taxes and led to social unrest. The second great change was the Protestant Revolt. Sooner or later nearly every European dynasty had to deal with a rebellious religious minority. The kings had neither the bureaucracy nor the army to cope with the new situation. Their only hope was to win the support of the people for whatever action they determined to take. This they could best do by summoning the deputies of the people and explaining to them their policy and needs. It was not often that the burgher from the town or the seigneur from the manor mustered sufficient courage to resist the crown on these occasions, and once a Parliament or Estates General had committed itself to the desired course, the king had a powerful propaganda weapon. He could claim that he had won the sanction of the people in the ordonnance he issued, and in the deputies he had valuable agents who explained the royal policy to their constituents when they returned to their homes.

The kings had no fear of the assemblies of the estates because these institutions were generally not considered to have any inde-

I

pendent power. Indeed, the prevailing argument, perhaps put forth by the kings themselves, was that representative assemblies served to increase royal power by enabling them to extend their influence into fields of activity ordinarily denied to them. This attitude is illustrated by Philippe de Commynes when, in writing of a proposed invasion of the continent in 1474 by England, he said: "But things move very slowly there because the king cannot undertake such work without assembling his parliament, which is like our three estates, and, consisting of sober and pious men, is very serviceable and a great strengthening to the king. When these estates are assembled, he declares his intention and asks his subjects for an aid."

To Commynes the English Parliament did not decrease the power of the king by preventing him from levying an aid without consent. Rather Parliament increased his power by making it possible for him legally to obtain money beyond his ordinary revenue. In the same spirit Henry VIII declared to the Commons in 1543: "We at no time stand so highly in our estate royal as in time of Parliament, wherein we as head and you as members are conjoined and knit together in one body politic."

Henry III of France stated that "holding the estates is a means ... to reaffirm the legitimate authority of the sovereign rather than to disturb or diminish it." Jean Bodin wrote: "We conclude, therefore, that the sovereignty of the monarch is neither altered nor diminished by the presence of the estates. On the contrary, his majesty is much greater and more illustrious seeing his people acknowledge him as their sovereign."

Statements such as these could be multiplied without end, and nearly all the Renaissance Monarchs put theory into practice by endeavoring to use representative institutions as a means of winning popular support for their program. In every country from Spain to Sweden rulers turned to their representative institutions for additional taxes, and in England, Denmark, and Sweden the kings successfully used their estates or Parliaments to introduce Protestantism. In the Empire, Scotland, the Low Countries, and France the monarchs also went to the estates to solve the religious problem, but with less success. Civil wars broke out, and it was only then that the theory began to develop that the representative institution had an authority separate from the crown. It was only then that the kings began to dread the meetings of the estates.

I have described the Renaissance Monarchy as being a decentralized state with confused boundaries and jurisdictions, but motivated by the forces of dynasticism, legality, and tradition. Its strength lay not in the size or loyalty of its army or bureaucracy, but rather in the support it received from the people. It remains to be shown that the nature of this state differed enough from what had gone before and what was to come after to give support to the thesis that the Renaissance constitutes a separate period in history.

The medieval state had also been dynastic, traditional, decentralized, and confused. It had relied on popular support, but it nevertheless differed from that of the Renaissance. Medieval decentralization was derived largely from the activities of the great feudal nobles and their vassals. Renaissance decentralization was essentially bureaucratic. Thus in the Middle Ages the duchy of Burgundy was governed by her duke, in the Renaissance it was ruled by a royal governor and subordinate officials; there were several types of sovereign courts to administer justice and provincial estates to negotiate with the crown. It was not the individual rights of the Duke of Burgundy that were stressed in regard to the crown, but rather the collective privileges of the inhabitants of the duchy.

A combination of time and degree also separates the medieval from the Renaissance. The thirteenth-century monarchs had been strong, those of the fourteenth and early fifteenth centuries were weak, but the kings of the sixteenth century were again men of ability. A Henry VI provides a break in the continuity between Edward I and Henry VIII. Furthermore, the Renaissance Monarchs were able to do bigger things. The medieval king helped open trade in the Mediterranean; the Renaissance king aided in the discovery of the water route to India and the New World. The medieval king encouraged an economic revival characterized by merchant and craft guilds, the Renaissance king sparked a commercial and industrial revolution. The former exercised a minor influence in arts and letters, the latter were the greatest patrons of their age.

I

The break between the Renaissance Monarchy and that of the late seventeenth and eighteenth centuries is more pronounced. Dynastic politics did not completely disappear, but national and economic considerations became more important. Armies became larger and the kings won effective control over them. Commanders in the wars of Louis XIV did not change sides at will as they had done during the Thirty Years War. The bureaucracies became larger and more efficient. The intendant of Louis XIV and the carefully trained officials of the Great Elector of Brandenburg were only the finest examples of what was a general European phenomenon. The popular-consultative aspects of the Renaissance Monarchy were abandoned. Kings ceased to wander from place to place, but preferred to remain in one or two favorite palaces. Elaborate court etiquette shut them off from all but their most favorite subjects. The official press replaced the representative assembly as the means to control public opinion. It is no coincidence that the reign of Louis XIII saw the last meeting of the Estates General until the Revolution, and the appearance of a government-controlled newspaper and an official annual news journal. Gradually the rational and ordered conceptions of the seventeenth century with the preference for the simple over the complex permeated governments. Judicial decisions came to be rendered in the name of the universal principles of justice rather than being based on custom alone. The decentralized conglomerations of duchies and counties so characteristic of the Renaissance Monarchy became abhorrent, and officials consciously sought to weld them into the centralized, well-ordered state. The new approach was clearly expressed by a minister of Philip IV of Spain when he said: "The most important task that confronts your Majesty is to make yourself King of Spain; by which I mean, Sir, that your Majesty should not rest content with the titles of King of Portugal, King of Aragon, King of Valencia, and Count of Barcelona, but that your majesty should labor and plan, with careful and secret consideration, to reduce all these realms of which Spain is now composed, to the fashion and laws of Castile, without any difference." When a royal advisor could make this statement, the state had indeed become "the fruit of reflection and careful adaptation." Our modern age had finally been born.

II

THE RENAISSANCE MONARCHY AS SEEN BY ERASMUS, MORE, SEYSSEL, AND MACHIAVELLI*

FOR a long time it was commonplace to find the origins of the modern state in the "New Monarchies" of the Renaissance. It was argued that the Renaissance monarchs, aided by a rising middle class and the growth of nationalism, created absolute, centralized states in which they governed with the aid of large bureaucracies and in which they stifled all opposition with armies plentifully supplied with artillery.

Recently, nearly every aspect of this interpretation has been challenged. The typical Renaissance monarchy, in the view of the present writer, was dynastic, not national; decentralized, not centralized; and constitutional, not absolute, in that there were laws, customs, and institutions which checked the authority of the ruler. The dominant class was the aristocracy, not the middle class, and the monarchy itself was inherently weak because neither the bureaucracy nor the army was large or loyal enough to insure orderly government without a wide measure of popular support. To secure this support, kings rewarded their most important subjects with titles, positions, land, and economic opportunities; held representative assemblies and enlarged meetings of their councils to explain their policies and to become better acquainted with the problems of their subjects; and traveled about the countryside to obtain firsthand knowledge of local conditions and to maintain closer contact with the people.[1]

The above interpretation has been developed from the study of society and institutions, especially those of France, but to date little effort has been made to relate it to contemporary political thought. This essay is intended to fill partially this gap by briefly exploring

* I should like to express my appreciation to Professor J. H. Hexter of Yale University for reading and criticizing this article while in manuscript form.

[1] For short essays by various historians and a selected bibliography, see Arthur J. Slavin, *The "New Monarchies" and Representative Assemblies—Medieval Constitutionalism or Modern Absolutism?* (Boston, 1964). In addition to the essay included in this work, I have outlined my conception of the Renaissance monarchy in *Representative Institutions in Renaissance France, 1421-1559* (Madison, Wis., 1960), pp. 3-20, and in "The French Renaissance Monarchy as seen through the Estates General," *Studies in the Renaissance*, IX (1962), 113-125.

II

books by Erasmus, More, Seyssel, and Machiavelli written between 1513 and 1517. Neither the choice of authors nor the choice of works has been entirely arbitrary. The period 1513-1517 comes after the Renaissance monarchies had become fully established but before the Protestant Reformation had created new political and religious issues. The authors selected provide a cross section of opinion in that they differed in their country of origin, education, and experience. Erasmus was a citizen of the Holy Roman Empire who had been educated as a theologian and humanist. More was an Englishman who coupled law with a humanistic background. Seyssel was a Savoyard who, because he spent most of his adult life in the service of the French king, may be considered as representing France; he had been trained in Roman and canon law but was also interested in humanistic activities. Machiavelli was the product of an Italian city-state who had been educated more as a man of affairs than as a scholar. Both Machiavelli and Seyssel wrote their principal works after long years of experience in government, while More wrote *Utopia* just before he embarked on a distinguished public career. Erasmus never had practical political experience.

A man whose interests were as narrowly centered on Christian morality and good literature as Erasmus's was not likely to be a penetrating observer of the political scene. His writings, including the book-length *Education of a Christian Prince*, are full of the pious platitudes so common in the "mirror of princes" literature. He knew little about the problems of government, and even the political views he derived from his study of antiquity came more from equally inexperienced moral philosophers or early Christian teachers than from the politically minded Roman historians to whom Machiavelli owed so much. Erasmus's conception of what was and what ought to be was deeply influenced by his residence in the Low Countries, the Rhineland cities, France, England, and Italy; by his personal contacts with kings, emperors, popes, ministers, bishops, scholars, and less exalted persons in many walks of life; and by the basic precepts of Christian humanism. Under such circumstances the value of his writings lies less in their originality than in the manner in which they reflect the scholar's attitude in that age.[2]

[2] Essays on Erasmus's political and social thought may be found in Augustin Renaudet, *Études Erasmiennes* (Paris, 1939), pp. 65-121, and in the introduction of Lester K. Born's translation of *The Education of a Christian Prince* (New York, 1936). The quotations below are taken from the Born translation, except

II

Erasmus admitted that "it is the consensus of nearly all wise-thinking men that the best form [of government] is monarchy.... If a prince be found who is complete in all good qualities," he added, "then pure and absolute monarchy is the thing. (If that could only be! I fear it is too great a thing even to hope for.) If an average prince (as the affairs of men go now) is found, it will be better to have a limited monarchy checked and lessened by aristocracy and democracy. Then there is no chance for tyranny to creep in, but just as the elements balance each other, so will the Commonwealth hold together under similar control. If a prince has the interests of the Commonwealth at heart, his power is not checked on this account, . . . but rather helped. If his attitude is otherwise, however, it is expedient that the state break and turn aside the violence of a single man."[3]

Thus Erasmus's conception of a monarchy was essentially contractual. The good prince, he felt, should not only recognize the rights of towns and provinces but should also convoke representative assemblies to consent to taxes and to advise on laws and ordinances. By doing so, he would increase his authority because he would have secured the support of the people. And, like his subjects, the prince should obey the laws he had made.

Although *The Education of a Christian Prince* was intended for the future emperor Charles V, Erasmus did not hesitate to point out that "even the greatest dominions prospered without a prince; for example, the republics of Rome and Athens. But a prince cannot exist without a commonwealth. . . . What is that which alone makes a prince, if it is not the consent of his subjects?"[4]

Such a state was not an unattainable Utopia. In Erasmus's view, it actually existed in the Netherlands and elsewhere. If in later years he strayed from this ideal, it was not in the direction of absolute monarchy, for even his limited trust in princes waned; rather, he increasingly admired the republican institutions of the Swiss cantons.

Erasmus recognized the dynastic character of the monarchies of his day, but he bitterly regretted that this situation existed and counseled princes to confine their marriage alliances within the limits of their own kingdoms. Part of his objection came from his sympathy for brides "who are sometimes sent away into remote places to [marry] men who

---

that, where he translated *res publica* and *patria* as "state," I have used "commonwealth" and "fatherland," respectively.

[3] Born, pp. 173-174.
[4] *Ibid.*, p. 233.

have no similarity of language, appearance, character, or habits, just as if they were being abandoned to exile."[5] But he also argued that foreign marriages weakened that close bond that should exist between the royal family and the people, because "it could hardly be expected that the fatherland would whole-heartedly recognize children born of such alliances, or that such children would be lastingly devoted to the fatherland."[6] Furthermore, foreign marriages are "the cause of making wars more frequent and more atrocious; for while one kingdom is allied to another through marriage, whenever anyone is offended he uses his right of relationship to stir up the others."[7]

Erasmus also noted the dominant position of the European aristocracy, although once more he was not pleased with what he saw. "Nature created all men equal," he declared.[8] "I should not strip the well-born of their honors if they follow in the footsteps of their forefathers and excel in those qualities which first created nobility. But if we see so many today who are soft from indolence, effeminate through sensual pleasures, with no knowledge of any useful vocation, . . . I ask you, why should this class of persons be placed on a higher level than the shoemaker or the farmer?"[9] Among the charges Erasmus leveled against the nobility was that those of their number "who are more lavish than their private means allow, when the opportunity is presented, stir up war in order to replenish their resources at home even by the plunder of their peoples."[10]

One should not expect Erasmus and his fellow observers to have referred to the Renaissance monarchs as being inherently weak, for in spite of their lack of power these rulers were much stronger than their fifteenth-century predecessors. Erasmus, however, did hold that a king's strength depended less on his army and bureaucracy than on whether he had won the love of the people. "He does not lose his prerogatives, who rules as a Christian should," he declared. "The following arguments will make that clear. First, those are not really yours whom you oppress in slavery. . . . But they are really yours who yield obedience to you willingly and of their own accord. Secondly, when you hold people bound to you through fear, you do not possess them even half. You have their physical bodies, but their spirits are estranged from you. But when Christian love unites the people and their prince, then everything is yours that your position demands, for a good prince

[5] *Ibid.*, p. 243.   [6] *Ibid.*, p. 242.   [7] *Ibid.*   [8] *Ibid.*, p. 177.
[9] *Ibid.*, p. 226.   [10] *Ibid.*, p. 252.

does not demand anything for which service to his country does not call."¹¹ In short, "the king rejoices in the freedom of his people; the tyrant strives to be feared, the king to be loved."¹²

To win the love of his people the prince must be worthy of their love. He should make every effort to get to know his kingdom. "This knowledge is best gained from [a study of] geography and history and from frequent visits through his provinces and cities. Let him first be eager to learn the location of his districts and cities, with their beginnings, their nature, institutions, customs, laws, annals, and privileges. No one can heal the body until he is thoroughly conversant with it. . . . Next, the prince should love the land over which he rules just as a farmer loves the fields of his ancestors or as a good man feels affection toward his household."¹³ He should reside in his kingdom, for "nothing so alienates the affections of his people from a prince as for him to take great pleasure in living abroad, because then they seem to be neglected by him to whom they wish to be most important."¹⁴

The prince himself should be kindly, clement, and courteous and should choose ministers with similar virtues. He must make every effort to increase the prosperity of his people and to avoid taxation by governing honestly, living frugally, and avoiding wars. Were taxes to become necessary, the rich, not the poor, should bear the brunt of the burden. A prince should not shut himself up in a palace, like the Persian kings, but ought to travel about to see and be seen by the people. On public occasions "the prince should not be extravagant or lavish, but splendid. . . . In those matters which pertain to him as an individual, he should be more frugal and moderate. . . ."¹⁵ In this manner foreigners and subjects were to be impressed on great occasions, but the prince ought normally to live a simple life in order to avoid expense and to maintain contact with his people.

It is not surprising that More's evaluation of the Renaissance state and society was essentially the same as that of his friend, Erasmus. Yet the medicine he prescribed in *Utopia* was much more potent.

More's *Utopia* is divided into two books. The first consists of a dialogue between three persons in which a somewhat exaggerated picture of the evils of European, and especially English, society is drawn. The second consists of Raphael Hythlodaye's account of life on the island of Utopia, a country whose size and geographical location near

¹¹ *Ibid.*, pp. 179-180.   ¹² *Ibid.*, p. 164.   ¹³ *Ibid.*, p. 205.
¹⁴ *Ibid.*, p. 208.   ¹⁵ *Ibid.*, p. 247.

II

a continent were similar to England's but whose institutions and social structure were almost the exact opposites.[16]

In the first book More leaves no doubt that he recognized the dynastic nature of the European states, a situation he decries because wars have resulted from conflicting dynastic claims. Even when dynastic wars are successful, further difficulties result—a point More makes by having Hythlodaye tell a story about the Anchorians who lived on the mainland to the southeast of Utopia. "Once upon a time they had gone to war to win for their king another kingdom to which he claimed to be the rightful heir by virtue of an old tie by marriage. After they had secured it, they saw they would have no less trouble over keeping it than they had suffered in obtaining it. The seeds of rebellion from within or of invasion from without were always springing up in the people thus acquired. They realized they would have to fight constantly for them or against them and to keep an army in continual readiness. In the meantime they were being plundered, their money was being taken out of the country, they were shedding their blood for the little glory of someone else, peace was no more secure than before, their morals at home were being corrupted by war, the lust for robbery was becoming second nature, criminal recklessness was emboldened by killings in war, and the laws were held in contempt—all because the king, being distracted with the charge of two kingdoms, could not properly attend to either."[17] As a result, the Anchorians finally insisted that their king give his new kingdom to a friend "who," Hythlodaye remarked pointedly, "was driven out soon afterwards."[18] In Utopia itself there were no dynastic problems because the cities were presided over by elective, not hereditary, princes.

Equally clear was More's recognition of the predominance of the European aristocracy, which derived much of its power from bastard feudalism and used its position to provoke wars and to exploit the poor. "Now there is the great number of noblemen who not only live idly themselves like drones on the labors of others, as for instance the tenants of their estates whom they fleece to the utmost by increasing

---

[16] For the genesis of *Utopia*, see J. H. Hexter, *More's Utopia: The Biography of an Idea* (Princeton, 1952). For a description of the government of Utopia, see Marie Delcourt, "Le Pouvoir du roi dans l'Utopia," *Mélanges offerts à M. Abel Lefranc* (Paris, 1936), pp. 101-112.

[17] This and other quotations are from Edward Surtz's translation of *Utopia* (New Haven, 1964), pp. 42-43.

[18] *Ibid.*, p. 43.

the returns, ... but who also carry about with them a huge crowd of idle attendants who have never learned a trade for a livelihood."[19] These idle retainers are permitted to rob the countryside in the vain hope that they will prove useful as soldiers in time of war. English "noblemen, gentlemen, and even some holy abbots ... leave no ground to be tilled, they enclose every bit of land for pasture; they pull down houses and destroy towns, leaving only the church to pen the sheep in."[20] Because of their behavior, More placed neither an aristocracy of birth nor an aristocracy of wealth in Utopia and saw to it that society there was predominantly urban rather than rural.

More recognized that a constitutional and legal structure existed in the European states, but he thought that rulers were often encouraged by their advisors to abuse their positions. In describing the methods that were used to obtain money, More unconsciously revealed the inherent weakness of the European monarchs. Instead of raising taxes, as a strong king would logically do if he wanted additional funds, these Renaissance rulers were often advised to alter the quantity of precious metal in the currency, to have make-believe wars as a pretext to raise money, to fine persons for breaking "old and moth-eaten laws, annulled by long non-enforcement, which no one remembers being made and therefore everyone has transgressed,"[21] and to take other stopgap measures. The crown's reliance on popular support is revealed when Hythlodaye suggests "that these counsels are both dishonorable and dangerous for the king, whose very safety, not merely his honor, rests on the people's resources rather than his own."[22]

It might be argued that More's decision to give Utopia a decentralized government consisting of semi-autonomous city-states was a reaction against the centralizing efforts of the Renaissance monarchs. It is more likely, however, that Utopia's city-state structure was borrowed from the much admired ancient Greeks. More does not accuse the Renaissance monarchs of centralizing their states in Book One of *Utopia*; indeed, in Book Two he gives the Utopian government the right to transfer children from one family to another and to regulate the lives of the people to a degree that no Renaissance king would have dared imitate. In this respect, at least, More's criticism of the European monarchies was that they governed too little, not too much. On the whole, the picture he painted of the Europe of his day was done in the same colors that Erasmus had used in his work. The writings of

[19] *Ibid.*, p. 21. [20] *Ibid.*, pp. 24-25. [21] *Ibid.*, p. 44.
[22] *Ibid.*, p. 45.

both point to the need to revise the traditional interpretation of the Renaissance monarchy.

Claude de Seyssel was the illegitimate offspring of a distinguished Savoyard family.[23] After a brief period on the law faculty at Turin, he entered the service of the Duke of Savoy and, later, of Louis XII of France. He participated in numerous diplomatic missions, helped organize the French government in the newly conquered duchy of Milan, and was made Bishop of Marseilles as a reward for his services. After the death of Louis XII in January 1515, he wrote *La Monarchie de France* to show the new king, Francis I, why France was the best-ordered monarchy and how this monarchy "could be preserved and increased."

In Seyssel's opinion, the French monarchy owed its superiority to kingship being hereditary in the male line, to three reins that checked royal authority, and to the harmony that existed between the social classes. The three reins were religion, justice, and *la police*. Since the French were Christians, it was necessary for the kings of France to be good Christians also in order to have "the love and complete obedience of the people. . . ."[24] Almost by definition, a Christian king could do nothing tyrannical. Justice was a check because it was administered by judges of *Parlement* and other sovereign courts who were appointed for life and could not be removed by the king. *La police* consisted of the basic laws, ordinances, and customs which had been kept for such a long time that kings did not attempt to change them. There were three social classes: the nobles, who were primarily a military order; the *peuple gras*, consisting of merchants, important public officials, and lawyers; and the *peuple menu*, consisting of farmers, craftsmen, and minor officials. Harmony between these classes was facilitated by the relative ease with which an able man could rise from one class to another, a situation which removed much of the desire of one class to conspire against the other two. In Seyssel's view, the clergy was not a separate estate because its members came from all three classes, a circumstance which also contributed to greater social harmony and mobility.[25]

---

[23] For the life of Seyssel, see Alberto Caviglia, "Claudio di Seyssel," *Miscellanea di Storia Italiana*, 3rd ser., XXIII (1928). For a study of his political thought, see William F. Church, *Constitutional Thought in Sixteenth-Century France* (Cambridge, Mass., 1941), pp. 22-42.

[24] Claude de Seyssel, *La Monarchie de France*, ed. J. Poujol (Paris, 1961), p. 117. For the three reins, see esp. pp. 112-119, and pp. 143-166.

[25] *Ibid.*, pp. 120-128.

The bulk of *La Monarchie de France* was devoted to showing how the kingdom "could be preserved and increased." Here, even more clearly than in the brief description of France itself, support may be found for this writer's interpretation of the Renaissance monarchy. Its dynastic character was assumed. Wars of conquest were to be undertaken only if the justice of the cause could be sustained "before God and before the world."[26] Although Seyssel gave no specific examples, one may rest assured that dynastic claims were the most likely type to be placed on the approved list. The three reins on royal authority were specifically designed to provide a constitutional check, but the king was told that he must support them "to secure the conservation and augmentation of the state."[27] The nobles were recognized as constituting the preeminent estate, but instead of counseling their destruction Seyssel advised the king to help maintain their position, although he was to take care that they "did not become too insolent."[28] Decentralization was assured by Seyssel's insistence not only that the customs and privileges of French provinces and social classes be preserved but also that the same consideration be extended to newly acquired territories. Only after the affection of new subjects had been won were they to be drawn slowly and gently toward "the manners and laws of the Prince, so that they would forget their old ones and dwell better with the other subjects of the said Prince...."[29]

The inherent weaknesses in the monarchy and the need of the prince to win popular support are everywhere apparent. For Seyssel, the strength of the kingdom was determined by the wealth, unity, and obedience of the people, the quality of the army, and the fortifications of cities, towns, and castles—all of which "depend on good counsel and government."[30] To secure this good counsel and government, the French kings had small, medium, and large councils to consult. Seyssel did not mention the Estates General or, more surprisingly, the provincial estates, but he pointed out that "it is sometimes expedient to summon a small number of people from the principal cities and towns of the kingdom."[31] In addition, the king was advised to visit all his provinces, including those on the frontier, "in order to see and hear . . . how the people are governed and how officials conduct themselves, . . . giving ready audience and prompt judgment to subjects who come with complaints."[32] In this manner Seyssel preserved the consultative nature of the monarchy, although he

[26] *Ibid.*, p. 204.   [27] *Ibid.*, pp. 142-143.   [28] *Ibid.*, p. 156.
[29] *Ibid.*, p. 217.   [30] *Ibid.*, p. 167.   [31] *Ibid.*, p. 136.   [32] *Ibid.*, p. 168.

II

assigned little or no role to representative institutions. The need to instill harmony between social classes, to provide justice, to keep taxes low, and to promote prosperity were all advocated, not only as a moral duty but also as a means of winning popular support. On the other hand, Seyssel devoted many pages to the problem of how to control the army, whose loyalty could not be counted on and whose services were evidently designed to be used against a foreign enemy, not against the liberties and privileges of the people.[33] No more than Erasmus and More did he envisage a centralized, absolute, national, bourgeois monarchy.

But can the same be said of Machiavelli? Surely the man who has been accused of writing a textbook for tyrants and praised for devising a plan to achieve the "unity of his Italian motherland,"[34] the man who has been acclaimed as the founder of *raison d'état* and the father of political science—surely this man must have anticipated the modern state. There is, of course, a vast literature that says he did, but our suspicions are aroused by Professor J. H. Hexter's discovery that, although Machiavelli no longer used *lo stato* to mean a "state of mind" or a social class, he did not employ the term to mean a dynamic living organism in whose service men should live and die. Rather, *lo stato* nearly always found itself in the position of being the subject of a passive verb or the object of an active one. Hence, to Machiavelli, "*lo stato* is not a matrix of values, a body politic; it is an instrument of exploitation, the mechanism the prince uses to get what he wants. . . ."[35] True, the Florentine had abandoned the medieval definitions of *lo stato*; yet he did not adopt the modern one. Between the Middle Ages and modernity lay the Renaissance, an age that was indebted to its parent and contributed to its child, but also an autonomous age in which the state in theory and in fact can be classified as being neither medieval nor modern.

It has often been pointed out that the organization of *The Prince*[36] resembled the "mirror of princes" literature, but it has not been sufficiently stressed that, in spite of different moral overtones, the author's conception of the nature of the state was similar to that of Seyssel,

---

[33] *Ibid.*, pp. 169-187.

[34] A phrase used by Pasquale Villari.

[35] J. H. Hexter, "The Loom of Language and the Fabric of Imperatives: The Case of *Il Principe* and *Utopia*," *American Historical Review*, LXIX (1964), 958.

[36] In view of the numerous editions of *The Prince*, references will be made to the pertinent chapter. With one or two minor changes, I have quoted from the translation of Luigi Ricci, as revised by E.R.P. Vincent.

Erasmus, and More. Machiavelli opened *The Prince* in the customary manner by defining the different types of states. Monarchies, which he alone planned to treat in this work, "are either hereditary in which the rulers have been for many years of the same family, or else they are of recent foundation. The newly founded ones are either entirely new, as was Milan to Francesco Sforza," or else they are mixed, consisting of an hereditary state like Spain and a newly acquired one like Naples.[37] "The difficulty of maintaining hereditary states accustomed to a reigning family is far less than in new monarchies; for it is sufficient not to transgress ancestral usages, and to adapt one's self to unforeseen circumstances.... In as much as the legitimate prince has less cause and less necessity to give offence, it is only natural that he should be more loved...."[38]

It was to new and mixed monarchies, however, that Machiavelli devoted most of his attention, because their problems were most pertinent in Italy. Military might was not enough to hold a new territory, for, "however strong your armies may be, you will always need the favour of the inhabitants to take possession of a province."[39] It is easy to win this favor if the newly annexed inhabitants have "the same nationality and language." To possess them securely it is necessary to "bear in mind two things: the one, that the blood of their old rulers be extinct; the other, to make no alteration either in their laws or in their taxes...."[40]

"But when dominions are acquired in a province differing in language, laws, and customs, the difficulties to be overcome are great, and it requires good fortune as well as great industry to retain them; one of the best and most certain means of doing so would be for the new ruler to take up his residence there.... Being on the spot, disorders can be seen as they rise and can quickly be remedied.... Besides which, the province is not despoiled by your officials, the subjects being able to obtain satisfaction by direct recourse to their prince, and wishing to be loyal they have more reason to love him, and should they be otherwise inclined they will have greater cause to fear him."[41] Another method of holding a newly acquired state is to plant colonies in it, but garrisons are useless because the cost of maintaining them will "consume all the revenues of that state, ... so that the acquisition will result in a loss, besides giving much greater offence, since it injures every one in that state...."[42]

[37] Ch. I. [38] Ch. II. [39] Ch. III. [40] *Ibid.*
[41] *Ibid.* [42] *Ibid.*

II

THE RENAISSANCE MONARCHY

In view of the stress he had placed on the difficulty of holding newly acquired territories, Machiavelli felt it necessary to devote the next chapter to explaining why Alexander the Great and his successors had been able to hold so much of Asia. "Kingdoms," he declared, "have been governed in two ways: either by a prince and his servants, ... or by a prince and by barons, who hold their positions not by favour of the ruler but by antiquity of blood."[43]

"Examples of these two kinds of government in our own time are those of the Turk and the King of France. All the Turkish monarchy is governed by one ruler, the others are his servants, and dividing his kingdom into 'sangiacates,' he sends to them various administrators, and changes or recalls them at his pleasure. But the King of France is surrounded by a large number of ancient nobles, recognized as such by their subjects, and loved by them; they have their prerogatives, of which the king cannot deprive them without danger to himself. Whoever now considers these two states will see that it would be difficult to acquire the state of the Turk; but having conquered it, it would be very easy to hold it. In many respects, on the other hand, it would be easier to conquer the kingdom of France, but there would be great difficulty in holding it."[44]

For Machiavelli, then, the dominant class in France—and, by implication, in most other Western European monarchies—was the nobility. Bureaucratic government, so often associated with the Renaissance monarchies, he found in the ancient kingdom of Darius and the Ottoman empire of his day. One need only read the first four chapters of *The Prince* to see that Machiavelli recognized the importance of dynasticism and unconsciously accepted the inherent weakness of monarchs that made it advisable for them to win support by leaving laws and taxes as they were, respecting the privileges of the aristocracy, and making themselves available to their subjects. These basic presumptions underlie the remainder of *The Prince* and all of his relevant political writings.

So much has been written concerning Machiavelli's recommendations that a prince disregard moral laws that this topic must be investigated further. In the first place, it should be pointed out that Machiavelli recognized that it was advantageous for a ruler to govern within a basic institutional framework, because he would lose popular support if he did otherwise.[45]

[43] *Ibid.*, ch. IV.   [44] *Ibid.*
[45] *Ibid.*, chs. II and XII. In *The Discourses* Machiavelli warned princes to

II

"I conclude, therefore, that a prince need trouble little about conspiracies when the people are well disposed, but when they are hostile and hold him in hatred, then he must fear everything and everybody. Well-ordered states and wise princes have studied diligently not to drive the nobles to desperation, and to satisfy the populace and keep it contented, for this is one of the most important matters that a prince has to deal with."

"Among the kingdoms that are well ordered and governed in our time is France, and there we find numberless good institutions on which depend the liberty and security of the king; of these the chief is the *parlement* and its authority, because he who established that kingdom . . . [recognized the need for] a third judge that, without direct charge of the king, kept in check the great and favoured the lesser people. Nor could any better or more prudent measure have been adopted, nor better precaution for the safety of the king and the kingdom."[46]

It is true that a prince must be prepared to lie and deceive, "for how we live is so far removed from how we ought to live, that he who abandons what is done for what ought to be done, will rather learn to bring about his own ruin than his preservation." Nevertheless, mindful of the prince's need for popular support, Machiavelli added that "he should be prudent enough to avoid the scandal of those vices which would lose him the state. . . ."[47]

Even a man who acquires a state through villainy "must arrange to commit all his cruelties at once, so as not to have to recur to them every day, and so as to be able, by not making fresh changes, to reassure people and win them over by benefiting them."[48] It is true that, if a choice has to be made, "it is much safer to be feared than loved"; nevertheless, "every prince must desire to be considered merciful and not cruel."[49]

Machiavelli advised that "a prudent ruler ought not to keep faith when by so doing it would be against his interest, and when the reasons which made him bind himself no longer exist." But, aware of the

---

remember "that they begin to lose their state from the moment when they begin to disregard the laws and ancient customs under which the people have lived contented for a length of time" (Bk. III, ch. V).

[46] *The Prince*, ch. XIX. For other comparable statements concerning the role of law in France, see also *The Discourses*, Bk. I, chs. XVI, XIX, LV, LVIII, and Bk. III, ch. I.

[47] *The Prince*, ch. XV.   [48] *Ibid.*, ch. VIII.   [49] *Ibid.*, ch. XVII.

29

THE RENAISSANCE MONARCHY

need of the prince to have popular support, he added that "it is well to seem merciful, faithful, humane, sincere, religious, and also to be so. . . ."[50] "The prince," in short, "must . . . avoid those things which will make him hated or despised. . . ."[51]

On a more positive side, Machiavelli suggested that the prince "ought, at convenient seasons of the year, to keep the people occupied with festivals and shows; and as every city is divided either into guilds or into classes, he ought to pay attention to all these groups, mingle with them from time to time, and give them an example of his humanity and munificence, always upholding, however, the majesty of his dignity, which must never be allowed to fail in anything whatever."[52]

Machiavelli's preference for native troops over mercenaries has often been commented upon, but it should be equally stressed that his evaluation was based on the presumption that the former would be more loyal, a loyalty that could be ensured only if the prince had won the support of his subjects. "Fortresses may or may not be useful according to the times; . . . a prince who fears his own people more than foreigners ought to build fortresses, but he who has greater fear of foreigners than his own people ought to do without them. . . . Therefore the best fortress is to be found in the love of the people, for although you may have fortresses they will not save you if you are hated by the people."[53]

The chief difference between Machiavelli's and Erasmus's contributions to the "mirror of princes" literature lies in the fact that the former advised the prince to commit immoral acts in case of necessity while the latter never abandoned the Christian code; but many of their underlying presumptions concerning the nature of the Renaissance monarchy were essentially the same.

Of the characteristics so long associated with the Renaissance monarchy, only one, nationalism, seems to have really played an important role in the thought of any of our four thinkers, and among them it is most apparent in Machiavelli. Yet, even in regard to the Italian, one must be cautious. Most contemporary scholars have abandoned the theory that Machiavelli sought a prince who would unite Italy and form a territorial monarchy like those in the North. Rather, they interpret the last chapter of *The Prince* as a call for a temporary alliance between the various Italian states to drive out the foreigners.[54] Na-

[50] *Ibid.*, ch. XVIII.   [51] *Ibid.*, ch. XIX.   [52] *Ibid.*, ch. XXI.
[53] *Ibid.*, ch. XX.
[54] See, e.g., Felix Gilbert, *Machiavelli and Guicciardini: Politics and History*

tionalism, for Machiavelli, was essentially a negative force that provoked cooperation against the outsider, rather than a positive force that would bring unity to long-separated kingdoms, duchies, and provinces. Although Machiavelli saw that it was easier for a prince to acquire and hold a province in which his language was spoken, he never suggested that a prince should try to conquer only those lands where his tongue was used or that he should attempt to unite all his fellow nationals in one state.

The medieval concept of the Empire had died, and even the cosmopolitan Erasmus avoided publishing an edition of Dante's *De Monarchia* when requested to do so by Charles V's great chancellor, Gattinara.[55] But our four observers were equally far removed from seeing in nationalism the cohesive force that it became in the nineteenth century. They were men of the Renaissance, and the dynastic, decentralized, constitutional, aristocratic monarchy, as they saw it, was neither medieval nor modern: it was the monarchy of the Renaissance, a monarchy whose power rested neither on its army nor on its bureaucracy but on the degree of support it received from the people.

---

in Sixteenth-Century Florence (Princeton, 1965), pp. 182-184; 325-326. Allan Gilbert, however, still holds to the older view. See his translation of *Machiavelli: The Chief Works and Others* (Durham, 1965), I, 8-9.

[55] Renaudet, *Études Erasmiennes*, pp. 95-97.

From: Theodore K. Rabb and Jerrold E. Seigel, eds., Action and Conviction in Early Modern Europe: Essays in Honor of E.H. Harbison. *Copyright © 1969 by Princeton University Press. Excerpt, pp. 17-31, reprinted with permission of Princeton University Press.*

III

Popular Initiative in Renaissance France[1]

JACOB BURCKHARDT FOUND in the peculiar political situation in Italy one of the principal causative forces of the Renaissance, but instead of emphasizing the virtues of republican Florence and Venice, his book leaves the reader with the impression that the tyrant was the typical figure on the scene. Burckhardt attributed the growth of individualism to the struggle for power, and to this individualism, combined with the revival of antiquity and the genius of the Italian people, he attributed "the discovery of the world and of man," a phrase which he thought summed up the very essence of the Renaissance. Recent historians put more emphasis on the economic and social situation, but the picture of Italy as a land of petty tyrants remains in the popular mind.

Most of those who study the kingdoms to the north during the late fifteenth and sixteenth centuries stress the formation of territorial states and the growth of royal absolutism. With a few exceptions they avoid the use of the words "tyrant" and "despotism," but they leave the reader with the impression that the Renaissance saw the substitution of royal initiative and royal government for popular initiative and self-government. If this substitution actually took place, it becomes necessary to attribute the creative energy that led to new advances in the European civilization and that carried it far beyond the confines of the tiny peninsular continent primarily to the kings and not to the people.

During the late nineteenth century there emerged in Germany a group of historians known as the corporative school, who advanced a completely contrary theory of the nature of the state and society, although, so far as I know, students of the idea of the Renaissance have blissfully ignored their existence.[2] According to the corporative historians[3] the

---

[1] I am indebted to my colleague Professor George P. Cuttino for reading and criticizing this article.

[2] Neither the school nor its most important members are mentioned in Wallace K. Ferguson, *The Renaissance in Historical Thought* (Boston, 1948).

[3] For an essay on the writings of the corporative school see Émile Lousse, *La*

Reprinted by permission of the publisher from Archibald R. Lewis, ed., Aspects of the Renaissance: A Symposium. *Copyright © 1967 by the University of Texas Press.*

III

feudal age was essentially individualistic because it was characterized by contracts between lord and vassal. From the dawn of the thirteenth century, however, men began to organize themselves into corporative groups, such as guilds, universities, and towns, and later, especially during the breakdown of monarchical authority in the fourteenth century, into local leagues of clergymen, nobles, towns, and other groups, that were called orders, or estates. These estates sent deputies to assemblies that met on their own initiative when the occasion demanded. Both the corporation and the estate were largely self-governing and they reached the peak of their independence during the first half of the fifteenth century.

The revival of royal and princely power in the late fifteenth century led not to the destruction of the estates, but rather to a new constitutional arrangement. In Germany, the corporative historians argue, the princes persuaded their subjects to abandon their narrow provincialism by creating single representative institutions for all their lands to be used as instruments for welding into territorial states the haphazard conglomerations of estates, smaller corporative groups, and surviving feudal lordships. What emerged in Renaissance Germany, therefore, were not little absolute states ruled by the princes, but rather dualistic states, in which the power of the prince was balanced by the power of the estates as expressed by their deputies in their *Landtage,* or Estates-General. Only in the last half of the seventeenth century were the *Landtage* weakened or destroyed by the princes; only then did princely absolutism emerge in Germany.

This interpretation of German history has become so widely accepted that it has found its way into such general surveys as those of Barraclough[4] and Fay.[5] Recently Carsten[6] has published two excellent books, which, while eschewing most of the theoretical apparatus of the corpora-

---

société d'ancien régime: Organisation et représentation corporatives (Louvain, 1943), I, 1–62. The remainder of the volume interprets medieval Europe from the standpoint of the corporatists. More recent writings of this school are often included in *Studies Presented to the International Commission for the History of Representative and Parliamentary Institutions* (Louvain, 1938). *Album Helen Maud Cam* (Louvain, 1961), II, contains a list of the contents of the first twenty-four volumes published in this series.

[4] Geoffrey Barraclough, *The Origins of Modern Germany* (Oxford, 1947).

[5] Sidney B. Fay, *The Rise of Brandenburg-Prussia to 1786* (New York, 1937).

[6] Francis L. Carsten, *The Origins of Prussia* (Oxford, 1941); *Princes and Parliaments in Germany* (Oxford, 1959).

tive school, provide conclusive proof of the widespread influence of representative institutions in Renaissance Germany.

The corporatists have been less successful in imposing their interpretation on other countries, perhaps because when their influence reached its height in the late 1930's a new and perverted form of the corporative state was being established in many European countries. Nevertheless, the corporatists won some support outside Germany and count among their numbers such men as Émile Lousse, a Belgian who includes among his credentials the presidency of the International Commission for the History of Representative and Parliamentary Institutions.[7] The corporative school has found no adherents in the Anglo-Saxon world. English historians have been especially belligerent toward the attempts of the corporatists to force the facts of their country's history to fit into their theoretical pattern. Sir Maurice Powicke felt it necessary to remind the readers of the *English Historical Review* in 1946 that the corporatists were not "seers or prophets," but rather "distinguished historians" in their own countries.[8]

Since the end of World War II many studies of representative institutions have appeared. Few of them have adopted the theoretical framework of the corporative school, but they have clearly indicated that popular initiative was not lacking in the various European states. Histories revealing the role of the citizenry in municipal government also have appeared. The most significant of these works from the standpoint of the Renaissance was Hans Baron's *The Crisis of the Early Italian Renaissance*.[9] Baron dared to argue that liberty, not tyranny, was the mother of culture and that in the active civic careers led by the citizenry, including the humanists, is to be found one of the principal motivating forces of the Italian Renaissance.

Thus two conflicting approaches to the Renaissance confront each other. In one view the Renaissance is depicted as an age when tyrants in Italy and absolute monarchs in the north dominated the scene. In the other the Renaissance is seen as a period when the people themselves, through their representative, municipal, and other institutions

---

[7] Leading French historians who have accepted many of the ideas of the corporatists are Georges de Lagarde, François Olivier-Martin, and Étienne Delcambre.

[8] *The English Historical Review*, LXI (1946), 251.

[9] Hans Baron, *The Crisis of the Early Italian Renaissance* (Princeton, 1955), 2 vols.

and through their individual deeds were the principal creative force. I suggest that the latter interpretation more nearly fits Renaissance France, a period which I see as lasting from the mid-fifteenth until the early seventeenth century.

At first glance France appears to have been the country *par excellence* of the monarch because no Estates-General emerged as a permanent institution through which the people could act at the national level as a balance to the desires of the crown. But when one searches for the explanation of this failure he finds it not in the desires of an all-powerful ruler to destroy representative assemblies, but rather in the strength of provincial and local institutions through which the people preferred to exercise their initiative.

Indeed, in several periods the French kings made sincere efforts to create an Estates-General just as the German princes and other Renaissance rulers were doing. Charles VII, for example, during the early part of his reign frequently summoned the deputies of the three estates from all or most of his kingdom in spite of the protests of the outlying provinces, but he abandoned this practice around 1440 because in the crucial matter of taxation he found large assemblies to be of propaganda value only. Time and again he had persuaded the deputies to vote large sums to combat the English invaders only to find that the provincial loyalties of the people were so strong that they refused to recognize the validity of a grant made in the national assembly. Before he could secure the money he had to win the consent of the provincial estates, for consent at the provincial level was not automatic. Indeed, Charles could rarely induce a locality to vote its share of the levy granted by the Estates-General. Thus, the three estates of La Marche voted only 2,500 of the 12,000 livres levied on the province as a result of a grant made by the larger assembly in 1425, and the three estates of Auvergne voted only 30,000 of the 45,000 livres levied on them as a result of a grant made to the King in 1431.[10]

The Estates-General did not meet to vote taxes between 1440 and 1483, but in 1484 the deputies assembled at Tours and consented to a taille of 1,500,000 livres. Once more the provincial estates had to be consulted before the money could be collected. The Burgundian delegates were so fearful that their constituents would accuse them of granting concessions to the king that they obtained a letter from him stating that they had not given final consent to any tax while at the Estates-

[10] J. Russell Major, *Representative Institutions in Renaissance France, 1421–1559* (Madison, 1960), pp. 21–39.

Popular Initiative in Renaissance France 31

General and that all levies had to be approved by the three estates of the province. Their unwillingness to recognize the taxing authority of the national assembly was reinforced when the provincial estates met shortly thereafter and refused to vote a single livre of its share of the levy consented to at Tours. In 1485 when the king levied a larger tax than that which had been agreed upon by the Estates-General none of the provincial estates protested, and when he failed to convoke the national assembly to vote taxes thereafter they were equally indifferent. Thus the French people's loyalty to their provincial institutions, not the enmity of the crown, was the principal cause for the failure of the Estates-General to become an effective institution during the fifteenth century.[11]

In 1560 the crown renewed its efforts to make the Estates-General a useful institution, but the deputies who assembled at Orléans refused to vote a tax. The humanist chancellor, L'Hôpital, sent them home with instructions to consult their constituents on how the king should raise money to pay his debts, and a second assembly was ordered to hear their replies. The crown promised that the three estates could appoint a committee to supervise the collection of any tax they decided to vote, but even this concession brought no change of heart. When the deputies assembled again some months later at Pontoise the nobility and the third estate were once more recalcitrant. The clergy, frightened by their colleagues' suggestion that the king should solve his difficulties by helping himself to their revenue and temporal goods, proved more cooperative and voted a large sum. From that time until the Revolution the clergy were assembled periodically to consent to taxation. In return, the king gave them the right to collect the taxes that they granted, to have permanent syndics to look after their privileges, and to submit petitions for redress.[12] In short, the clergy became as nearly a self-governing body as the estates did in Germany. Other orders would probably have won similar privileges if they had been more cooperative. Once more the people's preference for exercising their initiative at the provincial level had cost them the opportunity to make a permanent place for the Estates-General.

Taxation was not the only matter that the crown consulted the people about, for the kings wanted to receive their subjects' advice and to associate them with their policies. Assemblies for such political purposes

---

[11] *Ibid.*, pp. 94–116.
[12] J. Russell Major, "The Third Estate in the Estates General at Pontoise," *Speculum*, XXXIX (1954), 460–476.

rarely required a full meeting of the Estates-General; a group of specialists on the matter under discussion was sufficient. The towns were often asked to send deputies to advise the crown on economic and currency matters, the *Parlements* on judicial affairs, and mixed groups of notables on more general subjects. These meetings, especially frequent during the early stages of the Renaissance monarchy, lent a popular flavor to the government, but as no fixed composition or procedure was ever established they never became institutionalized.[13]

The Huguenots were the only other group that established a self-governing institution at the national level. They had two types of representative institutions, the synod and the political assembly, both being organized at the national and local levels. At the base of the synod was the consistory of the individual churches; above the consistories were the colloquies; above the colloquies were the provincial synods; and above the provincial synods was a national synod. Each type of assembly was composed of both ministers and elders. The lay-dominated political assemblies were organized in a similar manner and became the governing institutions of this religious denomination that truly formed a state within a state. They provide a signal proof of the initiative and self-governing capabilities of the French people of the Renaissance.[14]

Thus two groups in Renaissance France, the Catholic clergy and the Huguenots, formed effective national representative institutions over their local institutions because they felt threatened—the clergy by the laity and the Huguenots by the Catholics. Most of the population never felt that their privileges were in sufficient danger to warrant such action and they were unwilling to cooperate with the crown in forming an effective Estates-General even when offered the privilege of controlling the taxes that they voted, a practice which lay at the heart of the dualism of the German principalities so often described by the corporative historians.

This situation gives rise to several questions. Why did the mass of the French people feel so secure in its privileges? The answer seems obvious: because the kings never threatened them. But why did the kings respect the privileges of their subjects? Why did they not break the power of the

[13] Major, *Representative Institutions*, pp. 47–49, 52–53, 117–120, 127–130.
[14] There is no recent study of sufficient length on either Huguenot institution, but for two recent articles see Marcel Reulos, "Synodes, assemblées politiques des réformés français et théories des états," *Anciens pays et assemblées d'états*, XXIV (1962), 97–111; and Robert M. Kingdon, "Calvinism and Democracy: Some Political Implications of Debates on French Reformed Church Organisation, 1562–1574," *The American Historical Review*, LXIX (1964), 393–401.

Popular Initiative in Renaissance France

provincial estates, the municipal governments, and the other local institutions through which the people exercised their initiative to the point of transgressing the royal will? The answer, I think, lies in the fact that the kings lacked the power to take such action even if they had so desired.[15]

During the Renaissance the French army and militia rarely reached 25,000 men in time of peace and twice that number in time of war. Even with the rapid transportation and communication of today and with the immense superiority of the arms and the training of the modern soldier, such a force could hardly subject a population of 15,000,000 or more persons. This fact was doubly true at that time because the great nobles and towns could still put in the field armies that were nearly as well armed and well trained as those of the king. Furthermore, the king could not count on the obedience of his own troops. Mercenaries were notoriously unreliable, and the French contingents were officered by nobles who had no intention of making war on the privileged members of society. As late as the Fronde royal armies still changed sides at the beckoning of a Condé or a Turenne. The king might force a few individual nobles and towns or even several provinces to obedience, but he could not launch a successful frontal attack on the privileges of his subjects.

A second factor that prevented the kings from destroying the people's role in government was that the royal bureaucracy was as inadequate as the royal army. Around 1505 about one Frenchman in 1,250 was a royal official. Today about one American in 20 works for the federal government. Each of us, therefore, claims 62.5 times as much of an official's time as the Renaissance Frenchman. Furthermore, in spite of shorter working hours and numerous coffee breaks, the American bureaucrat, with the aid of the telephone, typewriter, and numerous other machines, can do far more work in one day than the most conscientious official of four centuries ago. The historian is sometimes surprised at the minor affairs that occasionally claimed a Renaissance officeholder's attentions, but the documents concerning such activities should be weighed against the obvious fact that many details must have escaped the worker's notice. Montaigne was correct when he said that the average Frenchman did not have contact with royal authority more

---

[15] For a general discussion of the nature of the Renaissance monarchy see Major, *Representative Institutions*, pp. 3–20; and J. Russell Major, "The French Renaissance Monarchy as Seen through the Estates General," *Studies in the Renaissance*, IX (New York, 1962), 113–125. The discussion in the two following paragraphs is taken from these works.

than once or twice in a lifetime[16] and Cardinal Richelieu was equally near the truth when he declared that the authority of the king was scarcely known in Languedoc.[17]

If the king left his subjects to their own devices to a degree that is difficult for the modern man to imagine, it becomes evident that the people must have had institutions through which they governed themselves. The most important of these institutions were the provincial estates.

The first provincial estates were formed in the thirteenth century, but not until the Hundred Years' War were they established in most parts of France. In some instances the initiative seems to have emanated from the crown or the local royal officials; in others it came from the great feudal nobles who established representative assemblies in their fiefs or from the local inhabitants who bound themselves together for their mutual protection.[18]

At the close of the Hundred Years' War Charles VII ceased to convoke regularly a few of the provincial estates, but the crown never adopted a general policy of opposition to these institutions. Louis XI actually revived some of the provincial estates in the early part of his reign and from that time until the end of the Renaissance they met regularly in about two thirds of France and occasionally elsewhere.[19] Although kings and royal officials must have been frequently irritated by the actions of the provincial estates, their overall attitude was friendly. In 1556 the leading inhabitants of the southwest pointed out to Henry II that although a number of local estates existed in their part of France, no general assembly was organized in which the estates in the entire region could meet and deal with their common problems. Henry, in keeping with the Renaissance attitude toward representative institutions, wrote his lieutenant general in Guyenne telling him to have

[16] Cicely V. Wedgwood, *Richelieu and the French Monarchy* (New York, 1950), p. 133.

[17] Cardinal Richelieu, *Testament politique,* ed. Louis André (Paris, 1947), pp. 233–234.

[18] On the diverse origins of the provincial estates see H. Prentout, "Les états provinciaux en France," *Bulletin of the International Committee of Historical Sciences,* I (July, 1928), 632–647; Gustave Dupont-Ferrier, "De quelques problèmes relatifs aux états provinciaux," *Journal des Savants* (August–October, 1928), pp. 315–357; Étienne Delcambre, *Les états du Velay des origines à 1642* (Saint-Étienne, 1938), pp. 5–10.

[19] Major, *Representative Institutions,* pp. 39–45, 50–52. Later Louis XI may have become disillusioned about the estates (see Helmut G. Koenigsberger, "The Parliament of Piedmont during the Renaissance, 1460–1560," *Studies Presented to the International Commission for the History of Representative and Parliamentary Institutions,* XI [Louvain, 1952], 98, n. 1).

Popular Initiative in Renaissance France 35

the estates of every diocese and province in his government name one deputy from each order to attend an assembly to be held at a time and place of the lieutenant general's choosing.[20] Between 1556 and 1605 the estates of Guyenne met over sixty times.[21] Thus a Renaissance monarch had created a representative institution at his subjects' request, the deputies of which were drawn from a territory larger than any other in France with the possible exception of Languedoc.

Most of these estates consisted of the leading clergymen, the nobles with fiefs, and the deputies of the principal towns of the province, but there were many exceptions. Only the bishops and twenty-two noblemen were permitted to participate for their orders in the estates of Languedoc during the Renaissance. At the opposite extreme there were some local assemblies to which only villages and small towns sent deputies. During the sixteenth and early seventeenth centuries the suffrage was decidedly extended. The parish priest, the noble without a fief, and the village peasant won voices in many of the assemblies of the estates from which they had formerly been excluded. In Languedoc, where no significant extension of the suffrage occurred during this period, the disfranchised elements of the population nevertheless demanded to be heard. Only the towns, where the bourgeois patricians, royal officials, and lawyers held control, generally failed to increase the suffrage, and even here the disorders of the Wars of Religion enabled the lower classes to win temporary recognition in many localities.[22]

This extension of the number of people who participated in representative institutions by attending the assemblies or by voting for deputies to attend was accompanied by an actual increase in the number of functions performed by the estates. We are often led to believe that their only important duty was to vote the taxes that the king requested, but this is not so. Through the petitions that they submitted to the crown they exercised an influence on royal policy in regard both to the nation as a whole and to their particular province. Within the individual provinces the estates were the dominant influence in law, legislation, and administration. During the Renaissance the customs of nearly every jurisdiction in France were codified. This codification was done in as-

[20] Archives départementales, Haute-Garonne, C 3796, No. 3.
[21] The estimate of the number of meetings is based on research in the archives of southwestern France, especially at Agen. The provincial estates of Guyenne enjoyed a brief revival after the death of Henry IV, but the last known meeting was in 1635.
[22] J. Russell Major, *The Deputies to the Estates General of Renaissance France* (Madison, 1960).

semblies of the three estates. Thus, what we would now call private law as well as some aspects of public law were actually determined by the people, not by the king. If it became necessary to revise or clarify the custom, new assemblies were held for this purpose.[23]

Equally important was the administrative role of the estates. This role was exercised in several ways. In the first place, while the estates rarely appropriated all the money that the king requested, they levied additional sums to support a bureaucracy of their own. All the estates had permanent officials who acted for them during the period that the estates were not in session. In some of the smaller assemblies the municipal officials of the principal towns served by right as syndics or principal executives. Thus the consuls of Agen were also the syndics of the estates of Agenais. In all the larger estates and in many of the smaller ones syndics who served as administrators and permanent representatives were elected. Much of their time was spent at court on the affairs of the province, but even when at home they were ever watchful to protect local privileges and to carry out the administrative decisions of the estates. Often the estates appointed clerks and established archives to keep their records. The documentation that has come down to us from the estates of Burgundy and Languedoc is vastly superior to that of the English Parliament during the Renaissance. In most localities where provincial estates were active, the officials of the estates, not those of the king, apportioned and collected the taxes.[24]

The provincial estates used their power to tax and to hire officials to undertake projects that they conceived to be in their interests. They voted money to build roads, bridges, and canals, to establish postal services, and to support other activities that would help the economy. They raised and equipped armies, they built and repaired fortifications, they constructed buildings to house convents and hospitals, and they undertook to relieve the needs of the poor, although in the field of social welfare they lagged behind modern legislatures. Educational activities did not fail to receive their attention.[25] In 1535 the estates of Languedoc

[23] Major, *Representative Institutions*, p. 6.

[24] For a discussion of the sources and secondary works on the provincial estates see J. Russell Major, "French Representative Assemblies: Research Opportunities and Research Published," *Studies in Medieval and Renaissance History*, I (1964), pp. 181–219.

[25] The introduction to the inventory of the archives of the estates of Burgundy provides an indication of the varied activities of such institutions. See Joseph Garnier, *Archives départementales de la Côte-d'Or, inventaire sommaire, série C, introduction aux tomes III et IV*, pub. Jean Rigault (Dijon, 1959); Roger Doucet, *Les institutions de la France au XVIe siècle* (Paris, 1948), I, 347–359.

Popular Initiative in Renaissance France 37

rejected the petition of the faculties of the Universities of Toulouse and Montpellier for exemption from the taille, and in 1579 the estates sought legal action from *Parlement* to prevent the faculties of these institutions from cutting classes so often. But if the estates were guilty of this all-too-modern legislative attitude of insisting that members of university faculties pay taxes and attend classes, they were also capable of a more helpful approach. In 1542 the estates of Languedoc sought the assistance of the king and the Catholic Church in increasing the salary of the faculty at Toulouse.[26] By the late Renaissance the estates of Quercy appropriated annually 1,100 *écus* for the support of the University of Cahors and 1,000 *écus* for those persons instructing the youth in the smaller towns of the little province.[27]

Individual faculty members and scholars occasionally received financial support from the estates if their projects seemed practical. A member of the medical faculty of Montpellier was given 60 *écus* by the estates of Languedoc in 1547 in recognition for his efforts to grow plants that had medicinal value.[28] It was not an age, however, when financial support was given only to scientists, for the work of the historian won monetary recognition from the representatives of the people. When the estates of Languedoc learned that the royal historiographer was going to write a description of their province, they voted him 100 *écus* and promised him an additional sum upon completion of his work if his book proved to be "useful," that is, if it supported their privileges.[29] Financial support for historians who defended the rights and liberties of Languedoc increased rapidly during the second quarter of the seventeenth century, when the estates seemed threatened the most, but on the whole only after the close of the Renaissance did the estates display much interest in specific academic activities, and not until the Enlightenment did the artist and the humanist receive recognition. The Renaissance was an age of popular initiative, but in France this energy was not directed toward humanistic and artistic activities.

The control that the provincial estates exercised over taxation also

---

[26] André Baudouin and Felix E. C. Pasquier, *Archives départementales de l'Haute-Garonne, inventaire sommaire, série C* (Toulouse, 1903), II, 28, 89, 35–36.

[27] Archives départementales, Gironde, C 3979. Bibliotèque Nationale, MS. Clairambault 360, fols. 12–14v.

[28] Baudouin and Pasquier, *Archives départementales de l'Haute-Garonne*, II, 149.

[29] J. Russell Major, "The Crown and the Aristocracy in Renaissance France," *The American Historical Review*, LXIX (April, 1964), p. 643.

enabled them to influence the actions of royal bureaucracy. It was usually their task to vote and collect the taxes to pay the salaries of the governor, the lesser officials, and the troops located in their respective provinces. Failure to vote the necessary sum was exceptional, but the possibility of such denial of funds was always present and made officials hesitant to offend local susceptibilities even in the interest of the king. Furthermore, the estates often voted sums in addition to those requested by the crown in spite of the efforts of the Renaissance monarchs to check the practice. Part of the additional money appropriated was used to supplement the income of the governor and the other officials. In 1620 the three estates of Languedoc not only voted their governor and members of his family their usual salaries and gifts, but also granted him 30,000 livres in consideration of his extraordinary expenses, 132,000 livres to reimburse him for recent military expenses, and 10,800 livres for "his great services." The king's secretary of state who handled the affairs of Languedoc was voted 1,500 livres and his assistant, 300. Other officials were often remembered. Thus the governor and the principal royal officials in the province were as much the representatives of the people as they were of the king, and to a lesser extent the secretaries of state and other officials at court were brought within their orbit. Under such circumstances a governor who could influence the king was more valuable to a province than one who could not. For this reason the three estates of Brittany asked the king to make Cardinal Richelieu their governor. Who else was in a better position to protect their liberties and further their petitions at court? Provence sought the services of the Cardinal's demented brother.[30]

A governor or other official who failed to cater to vocal elements of the population or who proved unable to influence royal decisions relative to a province could expect no special emoluments. Indeed, the estates of Provence failed to vote the ineffectual duke of Guise his salary or the money to pay his troops in 1629 or 1630. Thus the right to vote and collect taxes not only made it possible for the provincial estates to give the king less than he requested, as they usually did, but also enabled them to pay royal officials to persuade the king to accept their decision.[31]

The provincial estates were not the only institutions through which Renaissance Frenchmen exerted their initiative in government and administration. Numerous towns throughout France possessed charters giving them considerable control over their internal affairs. In spite of

[30] *Ibid.*
[31] *Ibid.*

Popular Initiative in Renaissance France 39

statements to the contrary, the towns held their own, or nearly so, against the encroachments of royal authority during the sixteenth century. Indeed, some towns like Le Puy and Dijon actually increased their privileges, while many new towns won charters for the first time. This continued strength of the towns should come as no surprise when we remember that the French Renaissance was marked by economic prosperity and population growth.[32]

Within their own jurisdictions the towns were even more active than the provincial estates were in theirs. They levied and collected taxes for their own needs and those of the king. The amount of the king's taxes was not as narrowly subjected to his will as has usually been supposed. Deputies from the various towns frequently journeyed to court to negotiate for reductions; rarely did they return home without some success. Lyons thought that it could confront the crown better alone than in conjunction with the small, neighboring towns and villages. By refusing to cooperate with the outlying districts in such matters Lyons contributed to the failure of provincial estates to meet periodically in Lyonnais.[33]

The towns were active in regulating economic matters, in enforcing law and order, and in rendering justice. They built fortifications, bought artillery and munitions, and employed troops that were normally used in self-defense but during troublous times were sometimes dispatched on military missions elsewhere. In the fields of health, education, and welfare the towns were much more active than the provincial estates. The towns frequently financed and controlled primary and secondary schools, and occasionally financially aided universities.[34] Thus the towns provide an excellent example of the initiative exercised by the people of Renaissance France. The sharp distinction that has so often been drawn between them and the towns of Italy had been exaggerated. Lyons may have been less independent of the king of France than Florence was of the emperor, but her citizens nevertheless possessed many rights and liberties.

The vast majority of the inhabitants of Renaissance France still lived in the country. Here the seigniory, of course, has been depicted as dying in every century since the high Middle Ages, but the demands of the peasantry in 1789 suggest that it still had a considerable amount of life

---

[32] Doucet, *Les institutions*, I, 360–363. Doucet does not go as far as I would in denying that the French towns lost most of their authority to the kings during the Renaissance.
[33] *Ibid.*, pp. 386–391; Major, *Representative Institutions*, p. 42.
[34] Doucet, *Les institutions*, I, 380–393.

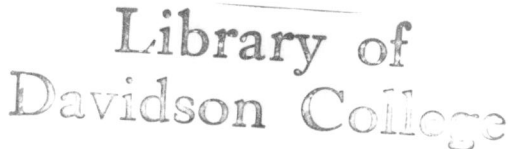

at that date. Indeed, the codification of the customs during the Renaissance contributed to the preservation of most of the judicial rights of the seigneur. What he lost was the controlling influence that he had once wielded in village administration. It was not the king, however, who replaced him at the local level, but the villagers themselves. By the dawn of the sixteenth century they had organized themselves into corporate groups that could sue and be sued. When matters arose that affected their common interest they held meetings after church. Every head of a household was permitted to attend even if that head happened to be a woman. Among the duties of the village assembly was the election periodically of a syndic or other official to carry out the group's decisions and to represent its interest.

These village communities attended to matters concerning the management of the common lands and the repairs of the church and the cemetery, and of other buildings. They defended their interests at court when they came into conflict with the seigneur, the curé, or other villages. In some instances the larger villages even operated schools for the young. During the course of the sixteenth century more and more of the villages were called upon to send deputies to *bailliage* assemblies to elect deputies to the Estates-General or to deal with matters concerning the *bailliage* itself. Most important of all, the village assemblies elected the official who assessed and collected taxes in the community. Thus even at the village level a wide degree of self-government was evident in Renaissance France and, if anything, the amount of self-government increased during the period.[35]

Popular initiative was less clearly felt in foreign matters than in domestic, but towns and representative assemblies were sometimes consulted before important actions were taken, or were asked to ratify treaties. The famous meeting of the Estates-General in 1439, for example, was summoned to advise the king on whether he should make peace with England. The invasion of Italy in 1494 was preceded by assemblies of prelates and nobles at Lyons on March 17 and of the deputies of the towns on April 7. The three estates at Troyes in 1420 ratified a treaty with England excluding the dauphin, Charles, from the throne. The treaties with Maximilian of Austria in 1482, with the Habsburgs, England, and Spain in 1492–1493, with England in 1525, and with Charles V in 1529 and 1544 were ratified by the provincial estates, by the towns, or by both. Sometimes the king joined the estates in break-

---

[35] *Ibid.*, pp. 396–402; Major, *The Deputies,* esp. pp. 124–127.

Popular Initiative in Renaissance France 41

ing a treaty. In 1506 Louis XII used the petition of the three estates of Tours as an excuse to break the treaty calling for the marriage of his daughter Claude to the future Emperor Charles V so that she could marry the count of Angoulême, afterwards Francis I. Francis I himself used the desires expressed by the three estates of Burgundy as an excuse not to cede the province to the Emperor as he had agreed to do by the tems of the Treaty of Madrid (1526).[36]

Thus popular initiative was still a prominent factor in Renaissance France and, I suspect, in other countries as well. This fact, more than the role of the monarchs, should be stressed when we seek to explain the creative energy of an age that began to lift Western civilization to heights far above those attained by the Islamic and Chinese worlds and that began to carry this culture to other parts of the world. To popular initiative, largely, we should attribute what has been called somewhat inacurately "the discovery of the world and of man."

[36] Major, *Representative Institutions,* pp. 45–47, 58–59, 120–125, 130–140. Both Louis XII and Francis I seem to have encouraged the estates to request that the treaties be broken, but it is nevertheless significant that the climate of opinion was such that a king could use his subjects' desires as an excuse to break his word.

IV

THE THIRD ESTATE IN THE ESTATES GENERAL OF PONTOISE, 1561[1]

ALTHOUGH the session of the Estates General at Pontoise in 1561 is of almost unparalleled interest to students of religious and constitutional history, it is certainly the least known of all the post-mediaeval assemblies of the estates. This may at first seem surprising since it has been the subject of two articles based on manuscript material.

Noël Valois, late archivist at the Archives Nationales, was the author of one of these articles. He concentrated his study on the elections and there found a Protestant conspiracy to capture the Estates General and establish a "kind of representative government." Protestants, he discovered, had been instructed by their leaders to appear at the electoral assemblies in the *bailliages* and to endeavor to put into the *cahiers* a specific program designed to further their religion and to try to bring about the election of persons friendly to their cause. The efforts of the highly organized religious minority brought success in many of the electoral assemblies and this fact, Valois believed, accounted for what he has termed the Protestant complexion of the Estates of Pontoise.

Another study of the Estates General of 1561 was made by Paul Van Dyke, who concentrated his attention on the *cahiers* prepared by the two secular estates at Pontoise. In them he found proof that "ideas in regard to the right of representatives of the nation to impose marked limits on the power of the crown were, before the beginning of the civil wars, very widespread among Frenchmen who possessed by ancient custom any voice in the government." "Some of these utterances cannot be paralleled from an English parliament until the grand remonstrance."[2]

But what happened at Pontoise when the estates were in session? Here neither Valois nor Van Dyke offer us more than the barest outline, since they had little information to rely on beyond copies of the *cahiers* of the secular estates and a few letters, speeches, and miscellaneous documents. It is the purpose of this article partially to fill this gap in our knowledge by a study of the activities of the third estate based primarily on Manuscript 379 (ancien 9183) in the Bibliothèque du Sénat (now Bibliothèque du Conseil de la République) rather than to duplicate or evaluate the work of Valois and Van Dyke. Manuscript 379 contains among other documents an authenticated copy of the *procès-verbal* and the original

---

[1] I wish to acknowledge assistance from a Fulbright Fellowship and from Emory University which made the research for this article possible.

[2] Noël Valois, "Les Etats de Pontoise," *Revue d'histoire de l'église de France*, xxix (1943), 237–256. Paul Van Dyke, "The Estates of Pontoise," *English Historical Review*, xxxviii (1913), 472–495. Henri Tartière's *Etats généraux de Pontoise, Cahier du tiers estat* (Mont de Marsan, 1867) consists of little more than the *cahier* of the third estate.

The Third Estate at Pontoise, 1561

cahier of the third estate. The *procès-verbal* is one of the most detailed and informative that we have on any assembly of the estates, being 74 folios in length written in a small but for the sixteenth century, rather legible hand. It covers the period 6 August to 26 August and provides considerable information hitherto unknown to historians. But before beginning to recount that which took place at Pontoise, it would be well, perhaps, to review briefly the events leading to the opening of the estates in August 1561.

In April 1559 France concluded the Peace of Cateau-Cambrésis, bringing to an end the long and costly Habsburg-Valois Wars. Foreign affairs became secondary to domestic concerns as the eyes of the government turned away from Italy and the Rhine. This shift in policy came none too soon, for Protestantism in France was growing at an accelerated rate. This fact, coupled with the criticism of the abuses of the Church by liberal and nominal Catholics, seriously threatened the existing ecclesiastical organization of the kingdom, if not the doctrine of the Universal Church. At the same time, economic and social unrest, occasioned largely by heavy taxation and the rise in prices, had reached alarming proportions. To make matters worse, many of the nobles and some towns found in this situation natural allies for the achievement of their own political desires, namely the restoration of that part of their privileges and political power which had been lost to the crown during a century's growth of monarchial power.

To meet these threats, the Valois had neither sufficient financial resources nor an effective governmental organization. The long wars with the Habsburgs, the rising cost of government, the luxurious life at court, had all served to put the government heavily in debt and had led the king to alienate or mortgage a large part of the domain and the usual sources of taxation. The crown had borrowed so heavily that it could hope for little more credit and was already having to pay interest at a rate as high as sixteen per cent. Although the royal council was composed of men of ability, proper liaison between central and local authority was lacking, for the Valois rulers had never really been able to solve the problem of local government. The growth of centralized authority which followed the close of the Hundred Years War had by no means destroyed all the power of the provincial estates, *bailliage* assemblies, sovereign courts, nobility, or town officials. Even royal appointees tended to behave in a surprisingly independent manner when removed from the eyes of the court. Only a strong and popular king could hope to control his own government. Unfortunately, France had no such man at the head of the state, for the experienced though none too intelligent Henry II was accidentally killed less than three months after the conclusion of the war. He was succeeded by his son Francis II, who, though legally of age, was too young to rule. Francis II died near the close of 1560, leaving the throne to his ten-year-old brother, Charles IX. Thus, during the critical years which followed the Treaty of Cateau-Cambrésis, France had no king who could personally control the state. It fell to the royal advisors to make an effort to bring internal peace and stability to France.

These advisors had the courage and the wisdom to develop a new program to meet the challenges of their revolutionary age, even though, as events were to prove, they lacked the authority, the prestige, and the popular following to force the peaceful acceptance of any solution. The new policy was first announced in the meeting of the king's council at Fontainebleau in August 1560. It involved a two-point program. The first was the restoration of religious unity by persuasion rather than by force. If the Pope proved unwilling to convoke a general council under conditions which offered some chance of bringing about religious unity, a national council was to be held in order to correct the abuses of the Church and to find a definition of doctrine acceptable to both Catholic and Protestant. The Cardinal of Lorraine made this aspect of royal policy his special province and his efforts were to lead to the Assembly of Poissy.

The second part of the program called for the convocation of the first full assembly of the estates since 1484. The crown intended to explain to the deputies the necessity of heavy taxation to meet the emergencies of the day, but, at the same time, was willing to act favorably on their complaints in hopes of quelling some of the discontent and of convincing the people of its sincerity. Thus the Estates General were to be revived to strengthen the monarchy by opening new sources of revenue and by influencing public opinion.

The hopes of the royal advisors were high when the Estates General opened in October 1560 at Orléans, but they were doomed to disappointment. The deputies proved willing enough to voice their complaints and to make recommendations concerning the Church or the government, but they refused to consider the problem of the king's debts, on the grounds that their constituents had given them no authority to discuss the question of finance. Nevertheless, the crown received graciously the *cahiers* of the deputies and promised a favorable reply.

The government remained determined, however, to get financial aid and on 14 February 1561, two weeks after the closing of the Estates General at Orléans, a new assembly was ordered. In the letter of convocation the royal advisors pointed out that the complaints and remonstrances of the people had been satisfied, that the deputies had been informed of the great debts inherited by the new king, and that additional taxation was necessary in order to redeem the mortgaged domain, *aides*, and *gabelles*. This money could be raised largely by a gift from the Church, but an increased tax on wine and salt was also suggested. The electoral assemblies were instructed to advise, deliberate, and make conclusions on the recommended taxation, or to suggest other means and expedients to aid the crown. The new assembly was to meet at Melun on 1 May.

The stage was thus set for one of the most significant of all the assemblies of the Estates. The crown had replied favorably to the complaints of the people at Orléans and was presumably preparing an ordonnance based on their *cahiers* to be registered and published by the *parlements*. In return, financial assistance was now requested and Chancellor l'Hôpital had even gone so far as to tell the deputies at Orléans that they themselves could name a committee consisting of the *échevins* of the towns and other responsible persons to see that the money was collected at a minimum cost. The crown thus offered the redress of grievances in return for financial aid. If the estates accepted, future requests were almost certain to be made and frequent convocations thereby assured. With the Estates

The Third Estate at Pontoise, 1561

General in control of the tax collecting machinery, it would indeed be difficult to weaken its position at a later time. Who can doubt but that one of the most critical points in French constitutional history had been reached?

The initial response of the voters to the overtures of the crown was disappointing. On 15 March the estates of the *prévôté* of Paris assembled as directed and the secular orders not only refused all financial assistance but even disavowed the deputies of the Estates at Orléans who had given recognition to Catherine de Médicis as regent. They sought to reconstitute the council without the Guises and the cardinals.

Catherine hesitated, but in a few days she decided to draw Navarre closer to her by making him lieutenant general of the kingdom and giving him powers nearly equal to her own. In return the princes recognized her as regent. Here was born the union and accord between the queen mother and the King of Navarre of which we are to hear so much during the meeting of the Estates General at Pontoise. But it was a precarious union, one that could be easily dissolved through the interference of an outside force — for example, the deputies of the three orders. On 25 March, therefore, Catherine postponed the Estates General until 1 August and ordered new elections. Electoral assemblies were instructed to discuss only the financial affairs of the crown and to ignore the question of the constitution of the government. It was not until 29 July that an order was issued changing the meeting place of the Estates General from Melun to Pontoise.

Meanwhile, plans for the national council had been slowly progressing. The prelates of France were instructed to meet at Poissy, a small town ten miles south of Pontoise. Arrangements had been made for Protestant leaders to be present during part of the assembly in hopes of bringing about an agreement on doctrine. The court was established at Saint-Germain-en-Laye, about three miles west of Poissy and twelve miles south of Pontoise on the left bank of the Seine. The situation had been laid for the two assemblies, the one religious and the other financial, whose failures were to leave France to the ravages of civil war for more than thirty-five years.[3]

Historians have always assumed that the Estates General of Pontoise began on 1 August, the day appointed in the letters of convocation, and that the usual opening assembly was held in which the king and the court participated.[4] This may have been the case, but there is some doubt, for neither the English, Venetian, nor Tuscan ambassadors reported any such ceremony, and few of the deputies could have been present, as the order changing the place of meeting from Melun to Pontoise had been issued at Saint-Germain only two days before, leaving little time for the notification of the deputies and their journey to the new location.

---

[3] For further details, see Lucien Romier, *Le Royaume de Catherine de Médicis*, 2 vols., (Paris, 1922), *La Conjuration d'Amboise* (Paris, 1923); and *Catholiques et Huguenots à la cour de Charles IX* (Paris, 1924); H. Outram Evennett, *The Cardinal of Lorraine and the Council of Trent* (Cambridge, England, 1930); Michel François, *Le Cardinal François de Tournon* (Paris, 1951); J. R. Major, *The Estates General of 1560* (Princeton, 1951).

[4] Romier cites Abbé Trou, *Recherches historiques et archéologiques sur Pontoise* (Pontoise, 1841) as proof, but Trou makes no such statement (*Catholiques et Huguenots* . . . , p. 180).

Nevertheless, enough deputies appeared at Pontoise during the first week in August for some basic decisions as to the organization of the assembly to be made. Some bishops found themselves in the difficult position of having been elected to meet with the estates at Pontoise, but at the same time ordered to assemble at Poissy with other ecclesiastical dignitaries in a national council to discuss affairs of religion. It is not surprising that the deputies of the clergy determined to meet at Poissy in spite of the orders of the king, so as to be better able to cooperate with their fellow ecclesiastics. They seem to have worked there under the presidency of the archbishop of Bordeaux, delegate from Guyenne, apart from the prelates summoned to the council.[5]

The two secular estates remained at Pontoise. They chose the refectory of the Cordeliers as their meeting place, and on 7 August we find the nobility assembling on one side of the room and the third estate on the other. Their sessions were held separately and seemingly more frequently in different rooms, but the third estate voted to inform the nobility of all their actions, and asked the same courtesy in return. Furthermore, they suggested that if their deliberations led to a common end, the two estates should submit a single *cahier*. Thus was born, on the initiative of the third estate, the close cooperation and mutual understanding between the two secular orders that was to characterize the assembly. On the other hand, the third estate voted not to inform the clergy of its activities and sharply condemned that order for its failure to assemble at Pontoise. Only on the persuasion of the nobility did they finally decide to send a deputation to Poissy to invite the first estate to join the other orders at Pontoise. On 11 August the clergy replied by protesting their desire to keep the unity which existed between the estates, but at the same time pointing out that some of their number were also a part of the colloquy then meeting at Poissy. Nevertheless, the clerical deputies promised to come to Pontoise the following day. This promise was kept, for on 12 August a deputation from the clergy informed the third estate that they had moved to the archiepiscopal residence in Pontoise to deliberate.[6]

We do not know how long the delegates of the clergy remained at Pontoise, but it is certain that they had returned to Poissy by 21 August and that their relationship with the third estate did not improve. The height of the bad feeling between the two orders was reached on 23 August, when several deputies of the clergy were seen to enter the assembly room of the nobility and then, after a time, leave in a manner which seemed to indicate that they wished to conceal themselves from the third estate. The desire, real or supposed, for secrecy on the part of the delegation aroused the worst apprehensions among the deputies of the third estate and they quickly asked the nobility to inform them of the nature of

---

[5] "Diario dell'assemblea de'Vescovi à Poissy," published by J. Roserot de Melin in *École française de Rome—Mélanges d'archéologie et d'histoire*, XXXIX (1921–1922), 96–99. B.N., ms. fr. 3953 ff. 6–8. This last appears to be an extract from the *procès-verbal* of the deputies of the clergy and has been overlooked by historians of the Assembly of Poissy.

[6] "Recueil et procès-verbal . . . du tiers estat . . . ," Bibliothèque du Sénat, ms. 379, ff. 170, 177v–178v, 189–189v, 195v–196. This document will hereafter be cited as *pv*.

the visit. The nobility indicated that the clergy had only given them the contents of their *cahier*. With a tone of injured innocence, the third estate now sent a delegation to the clergy complaining at not having been visited along with the nobility, but at the same time suggesting closer cooperation. The clergy excused themselves on the grounds that they have not desired to trouble the third estate. The whole episode was of little importance except that it indicated the deep distrust which existed between the two orders.[7]

The assembling of the nobility and the third estate in a single building, if not a single room, was facilitated by the fact that a change in electoral procedure had greatly reduced the number of deputies. The letters of convocation had instructed the electoral assembly in each *bailliage* to send three deputies, one from each estate, to the principal city of the *gouvernement* where in turn one deputy from each estate was to be chosen to attend the Estates General. This departure from the usual electoral procedure was not brought about by fear of large representative bodies, but, as a well-informed contemporary said, to avoid the confusion so prevalent in the more numerous assembly at Orléans and also to spare the people who paid their own deputies as much expense as possible.[8] Indeed, the procedure used in the elections of 1561 was far less of an innovation than might at first seem apparent, for in the other meetings of the Estates General the deputies of the *bailliages* of each *gouvernement* met in the Estates General and prepared a *cahier*. Then the *cahiers* of the *gouvernements* were combined to form the general *cahier* of the order. The electoral procedure of 1561 simply meant that *cahiers* of the *gouvernements* were prepared in the provinces rather than at the Estates General itself. Since the process of preparing all *cahiers* beyond the *bailliage* level was a mechanical one, carried out by carefully instructed deputies who could not legally ignore the wishes of their constituents, the crown had little more opportunity to influence the Estates of Pontoise than those of Orléans.

There were thirteen *gouvernements* in France in 1561, so one might expect to find thirteen, and only thirteen, deputies from each estate in the little town of Pontoise on 1 August ready to carry out their assigned task of advising the king on his financial needs. On 6 August, however, when our *procès-verbal* begins, we discover that the patience of the deputies from the eight *gouvernements* present was so exhasted that they determined to proceed to the verification of their powers on the following day at 7 A.M. without waiting longer for their absent fellows. Only gradually did the assembly become complete. The deputies from Lyonnais and the Ile-de-France made their appearance on 8 August and those of Languedoc and Provence on the following afternoon. The deputies from Brittany did not arrive until the afternoon of the fifteenth, five days after the date first set by the king for the completion of the *cahier*. It is difficult to understand why they were so late, as they had been elected by the estates of Brittany on 22 March. For some

---

[7] B.N. ms. fr. 3953, f. 6 *pv.* ff. 228–230v.

[8] Printed letters of the various royal orders convoking the estates may be found in the B.N., F 46821. Pierre de La Place, *Commentaires de l'estat de la religion et republic soubs les rois Henry II et François II et Charles IX* (1565), f. 169.

reason they delayed their departure from Brittany until 2 August and thereafter must have proceeded at a very leisurely rate.[9]

But the third estate showed its independence not only by the late arrival of many of its delegates, but also by electing more than the required number, for only seven of the *gouvernements* respected the direct orders of the king to send only one deputy. Two deputies were formally accepted for the third estate from Brittany, Dauphiny, Orléans and Berry, and Langudeoc though in the last two, the additional delegates were deputed by *baillaiges* within the *gouvernement* rather than by the assembly of the *gouvernement* itself. Burgundy was content with three, while from Guyenne came a deputy from each *sénéchaussée* since no agreement could be reached in the assembly of their *gouvernement*. As a result, no less than thirteen deputies appeared, for the most part late, under her banner. Thus the assembly of thirteen became an assembly of over thirty deputies.

Since the assemblies of the *gouvernements* had failed to obey the king's instructions to send only one deputy each, the procedure followed at Pontoise became complicated. It would be unfair to allow each of the deputies from Guyenne, for example, the same voice as the deputy, say of Normandy, who represented an entire *gouvernement*. It was therefore decided that one deputy would be chosen from each *gouvernement* to speak and vote in the assembly for the remainder. The extra deputies were, however, given seats in the rear of the chamber. Actually the presence of additional delegates proved to be of some value since they served as replacements for those regular delegates who were temporarily absent on missions or otherwise engaged.[10]

It might be supposed from the tardiness of so many of the deputies and from the haphazard way in which their elections had been carried out that they were not men of experience or responsibility. This was by no means the case, for almost without exception the representatives at Pontoise were men with a legal, governmental, or legislative background. Nearly half had been deputies to the Estates General at Orléans and still more had served in the provincial estates.

We need only to glance at the principal deputies to see how true this was. The voting member of the Burgundian delegation was Jacques Massol, lieutenant general from the chancellery of Beaune. Before the Estates had come to an end, however, the real leader of the delegation was Jacques Bretaigne, *vierg* or mayor of Autun and the holder of various other offices. Mathieu Poulaim, councilor of the town of Rouen, spoke, and voted for Normandy; Guillaume Le Blanc, advocate in the court of the *Parlement* of Bordeaux, for Guyenne; Jehan de Mesgrigny, president at the *siège présidial* of Troyes, for Champagne and Brie; Jehan de Heunegrams, attorney of the king at Montdidier, for Picardy; Claude du Verguer, advocate of the king at Bourges, for Orléans and Berry; Jehan Fallaiseau, advocate of the king at Tours, for Touraine, Anjou, and Le Mans; Michel Rodders, advocate of the king in Auvergne, for Lyonnais; Claude Berard, *assesseur* at Aix, for Provence; De Sayne, lieutenant general of the *bailliage* of Melun, for Ile-de-

---

[9] *pv.* ff. 169–181, 203. Charles de La Lande de Calan, *Documents inédits relatifs aux Etats de Bretagne de 1491 à 1589* (Rennes, 1908), I, 145, published in *Archives de Bretagne*, xv.

[10] *pv.* ff. 169v–170, 173–173v.

The Third Estate at Pontoise, 1561

France; Jehan Robert, doctor of law and attorney of the estates of Dauphiny, for Dauphiny; Jehan Rogier, seneschal of Ploërmel, for Brittany; and Claude Terlon, advocate in the *Parlement* of Toulouse, for Languedoc. During his sickness, Terlon was replaced by Guillaume Roque of Nîmes who had been deputed by the strongly Protestant *sénéchaussée* of Nîmes, no doubt to keep an eye on the less rabid deputy of the *gouvernement*. Robert Le Blanc, syndic of the estates of Languedoc, also replaced Terlon on several occasions, though apparently he had not been specifically elected by anyone and was never formally accepted as a delegate by the deputies at Pontoise. Probably his position as syndic was regarded as being sufficient to prove his right to speak for his province. Mesgrigny was elected president of the third estate; Poulaim served as clerk during the first part of the assembly and Heunegrams during the latter.

One of the first tasks undertaken by the assembly was that of the verification of the powers of the deputies. This was done on 8 August for those delegates then present, the powers of the tardy deputies being checked later upon their arrival. Of the deputies from *gouvernements* only De Sayne, from the Ile-de-France, found his right to sit in the assembly challenged at this time. He was at first refused a seat on the grounds that his powers had not been signed by François de Montmorency, the governor of the Ile-de-France, that the deputies of only six of the twelve *bailliages* in the *gouvernement* had signed the *cahier*, and that neither the provost of the merchants nor the *échevins* of Paris had been consulted. The queen mother, however, intervened on his behalf, and her assistance, plus a new document which bore the signature of Montmorency, was sufficient to give him a seat several days later. The deputies were no doubt justified in looking carefully into the powers of De Sayne, for it had been the troubles in the March elections in the *prévôté* of Paris which had led to the postponement of the Estates General. Members of the sovereign courts had been ordered to preside over the new assembly of the *prévôté* to insure order, but their presence led to protests that the liberty of the estates was being infringed upon. Perhaps, for this reason the *prévôté* had no delegation to the assembly of the third estate of the Ile-de-France and the town of Paris found it advisable to send a deputy to Pontoise with their *cahier*. Could the crown have decided that the best way to avoid troublesome complaints of the Parisians was simply not to convoke them with the rest of the *bailliages* of the Ile-de-France, or could the governor, François de Montmorency, have been responsible for the failure of Paris to participate? We know that he was not above such interference, for on 20 August Charles IX wrote him a letter to inquire why he had not permitted the substitute for the *bailli* of Vermandois, the deputy of the nobility, to make his appearance at Pontoise or at least to send his *cahier*. It seems most likely that if fault there was, it lay with him.[11]

On Thursday, 7 August, the first day the assembly was really in session, a messenger arrived from the king to inform the deputies of the nobility and the third estate assembled together that they were to bring their *cahiers* to Saint-Germain-en-Laye that Sunday. Mesgrigny replied for the third estate that they

---

[11] La Place, *op. cit.*, f. 196v. pv. ff. 175–184v, 201–204. B.N. ms. fr. 3183, f. 13.

would prepare their *cahier* as rapidly as possible in order not to give the people unnecessary expense or to delay the affairs of the king, but that they could not finish their work in so short a time. Le Blanc, Robert, and later Massol were elected to go to the king to ask for additional time and also to request that the royal replies to the *cahiers* of Orléans be sent to them so that they would not ask for things which had already been granted. If the replies of the king had already been sent to the *Parlement* of Paris, the Estates asked that a copy be prepared. The king was further requested not to permit *Parlement* to make any changes.[12]

On Saturday morning the legation reported that the crown had been willing to grant an extension of time. As for the *cahiers* of the Estates of Orléans, they had been sent to the *Parlement* of Paris in the form of an edict. The King of Navarre was to go to Paris to get them and they would be delivered to the estates in three days. Furthermore, no changes in the original replies to the *cahiers* would be made.[13]

Thus two problems of a constitutional and a practical nature were brought to the fore. The estates were by no means enthusiastic about the fact that *Parlement* claimed to review their acts before enregistering and publishing them, and they were anxious to prevent any possible changes. The nobility and the third estate went so far as to make a stipulation in their *cahiers* against submitting the ordonnance prepared on their advice to *Parlement*. Secondly, the interest in the *cahiers* expressed at the beginning of the assembly provided a hint to the crown that satisfactory action must be taken on this score before its financial needs would be considered. Here the nobility were much more blunt. In a speech, apparently to his fellow deputies, Nicolas de Beaufremont, Baron de Sennecy, pointed out that they had been assembled to provide the king with money, but that it would be expedient before doing so to insist that he give specific answers to their demands. Once the money was in royal hands, there would be no more assemblies of the estates or opportunities to make requests.[14]

Evidently the government had anticipated this attitude on the part of the deputies, for on 28 July and again on 29 July Catherine de Médicis had written to *Parlement* asking for the verification of the Ordonnance of Orléans without modifications. The king issued a similar order, but *Parlement* did not receive the royal letters accompanied by the ordonnance until 2 August. The following day was Sunday, so the court had no session as was its custom. By this time, the government, already impatient and also anxious to please the deputies, sent a messenger to *Parlement* with instructions that all other work should cease until the ordonnance was published, which should be done by the fifth. Speed was necessary because the estates refused to answer the royal request for funds before the ordonnance was published. On 5, 6, and 8 August *Parlement* received additional letters and messengers from both the king and the queen mother urging haste and relating the publication of the ordonnances with their financial demands on the estates. In spite of the royal pressure, *Parlement* was still discussing the first article on 9 August. That same day we find the King of Navarre, accompanied by several other nobles, appearing before *Parlement* to say that he

---

[12] *pv.* ff. 170–172v.   [13] *pv.* ff. 177–177v.   [14] B.N. ms. fr. 15494, f. 33v.

The Third Estate at Pontoise, 1561

was charged by the king to tell them not to debate each article but to verify the ordonnance as a whole without modification. This the court refused to do, arguing that they had not been present at the Estates General of Orléans as they had been at Tours in 1468 and 1483 and that some of the articles were schismatic, and therefore should be considered with care. Two causes for the procrastination of *Parlement* now became evident: jealousy of the Estates General and a hearty dislike for the anti-clerical articles in the Ordonnance of Orléans. The struggle between *Parlement* and the government continued and was to end in the house arrest of the president and in the publication of the ordonnance in spite of remonstrances by *Parlement* against many articles. The crown had successfully fought to give the delegates their desires. But what were the estates doing meanwhile, and what would they offer in return?[15]

It must be confessed that once the deputies began to meet, they worked diligently. Sessions generally began at 6 A.M. Even Sunday and feast days found them at their tasks. Only near the end of the sessions, when nearly all their work was done, did the deputies of the third estate relax sufficiently to begin their day at 7 A.M. and to forego a Sunday meeting.

The first action taken by the third estate after their chamber had been organized and their powers verified was not, however, to discuss the financial needs of the crown, but rather to ask the nobility to join with them in writing a letter to the king protesting the July Edict on religion just published by *Parlement* which had been prepared on the advice of a large assembly of notable personages. This edict was less strong than the *Parlement* and pro-clerical elements desired, but nevertheless, the deputies found it contrary to the *cahiers* of Orléans and they asked that it be suspended until after their own *cahiers* had been heard. Furthermore, they requested that all religious persecution should cease during the holding of the estates. The nobility joined in this petition and Poulain and Fallaiseau were named to bear it to the king.[16]

The deputies of the third estate never received a direct reply, but in a few days they decided to break further the royal commands to discuss only the problem of the debt by voting to place articles on religion in the *cahier*. This action was opposed by the deputies of Picardy, Orléans, Lyonnais, Ile-de-France, and Provence. The opposition of the last named deputy was especially strong, but he was finally persuaded to adhere to the will of the majority. The protesting deputies were, however, given the right to place their remonstrances at the end of the *procès-verbal*, and of this privilege they were to make full use. The majority asked that a national council be held, to be attended by Protestants as well as Catholics and presided over by the king and the princes of the blood. Here religious differences would be settled by the "word of God alone." Meanwhile, the deputies requested that religious persecution cease. Since it was not possible to prevent

---

[15] A.N. X1a 1598, ff. 118v–119, 156v–157v, 160v–162, 168v–169v, 173–173v, and scattered data ff. 214–422v. The extracts of the Register of the *Parlement* of Paris published in *Recueil de pièces originales et authentiques, concernant la tenue des Etats généraux* (Paris, 1789), IV, 345–367, are neither complete nor accurate.

[16] *pv.* ff. 179–180.

Protestants from worshipping as they pleased, the deputies asked that one church or other place in each town be assigned to them. Secret assemblies, massacres, and the growth of factions within the state would thereby be prevented. Other articles called for religious instruction in French and the removal of judicial duties from the ecclesiastics to give them greater time for their religious responsibilities. Thus the third estate advocated the reformation of abuses within the Catholic Church and the use of toleration and persuasion to bring about religious unity.

Of the five *gouvernements* that opposed, Lyonnais and Picardy did so on the grounds that they had not been empowered or instructed by their constituents to discuss religious problems. The deputies from the Ile-de-France and Provence were strong in their opposition and advocated what amounted to a continuation of persecution. We do not know on what grounds Orléans objected. The deputies from Brittany also had no instructions to deal with religion, but they had not arrived when this vote was taken. If the vote of the uninstructed delegations were ruled out, we find that a substantial majority of the *gouvernements* favored an even bolder policy of toleration and persuasion than the queen mother and Hôpital were then following. Whether the vote resulted from the intrigues of the Protestants during the elections as Valois argued, or whether it reflected the true opinion of the majority of Frenchmen is difficult to determine. In opposition to the weighty evidence offered by Valois, however, it could be pointed out that few of the delegations seem to have been dominated by men who can be specifically attached to the Protestant cause, and even here the evidence is by no means complete. When they returned home, the deputies from Burgundy had difficulty collecting money for their expenses, but the action of the Burgundian estates was taken only on the grounds that the deputies had asked for churches for the Protestants without specific instruction to do so. Apparently the rest of their actions were found acceptable. Furthermore, Terlon of Languedoc, who leaned to the Burgundian side in every vote recorded in the *procès-verbal* of the third estate, was nevertheless violently attacked by strongly Protestant Nîmes for his alleged failure to support the motion to give churches to the Protestants. His voting must therefore be considered that of at least a nominal Catholic. What was true of Terlon was in all probability true of others, so that the actions taken at Pontoise by the third estate may well have resulted as much from anticlericalism and religious indifference as from the Protestant conspiracy discovered by Valois.[17]

Be this as it may, the court was quick to hear of the debate within the third estate, and on 12 August, the day after the vote on the religious question, a delegation arrived at Pontoise to tell the three estates to discuss only the financial difficulties of the king. The third estate did not chose to reply directly to the

---

[17] *pv.* ff. 182v–186. The *cahier* of the third estate, Bibl. du Sénat, ms. 379, ff. 243–259v, original. There are many copies of this *cahier*, among them are B.N. ms. fr. 15494, ff. 48v–62; ms. Dupuy, 646; ms. fr. 3970. The copy published by Tartière varies slightly from the original. H. Abord, *Histoire de la réforme et de la ligue dans la ville d'Autun* (Paris, 1855), I, 140–141. Léon Ménard, *Histoire civile, ecclésiastique et littéraire de la ville de Nîmes* (Nîmes, 1873–1875), IV, 263–270, 283–290.

royal order, but, after consulting the nobility, simply stated that they would be ready to deliver their *cahier* on Monday, 18 August.[18]

A second issue which confronted the estates was whether recommendations should be made concerning the government of the kingdom. Most theorists conceded to the estates the right to name the government during the minority of a king, but on the other hand, the queen mother had forbidden the delegates to consider the problem. The question was first raised on 12 August, and immediately a long debate ensued. The deputies from Ile-de-France, Provence, Picardy, and Lyonnais said that they had been given no powers to discuss the question of the government by their constituents. Nevertheless, the last two felt that their instructions allowed them enough latitude to voice an opinion. The deputy from Picardy argued that the estates had to establish the council during the minority of the king and that this right must be maintained. However, he expressed his gratitude to the queen mother for her virtue and prudence and for the union and mutual understanding which existed between her and the princes of the blood. This general opinion was adhered to by the majority of the deputies and it was decided to include an article to the effect in the *cahier*.

If the discussion of the religious question had irritated Catherine de Médicis because it delayed consideration of the royal debts, the discussion of the question of the government infuriated her because she interpreted it as a challenge to her power, or at least a threat to the precarious unity she had achieved with Navarre. She must have learned of the developments within the third estate that same evening for on the following day Admiral Coligny arrived in Pontoise with a message from the king. The deputies of the three estates assembled together in refectory of the Cordeliers to hear him and were informed of the perfect union and accord which existed between the queen mother, the King of Navarre, and the Princes of the blood. Although Coligny assured the deputies that neither Catherine de Médicis nor the King of Navarre had any intention of infringing on the rights of the estates or on the ancient laws of the kingdom, he none-the-less gave them the royal order that they were not to concern themselves with the constitution of the government, but only with the subsidy for the king.

The estates then separated to confer on the new demands from the court. After some debate the third estate named Massol and Poulaim to go to the king and the queen mother and inform them exactly what they had put in their *cahier* for the conservation of the laws and ancient customs of France and the authority of the estates. They were also instructed to inquire about the exact financial position of the king. On 15 August Massol reported that the king had instructed his officers of finance to show his accounts to a delegation from the estates. No mention was made of the articles concerning the constitution of the government at this time.[19]

The dissatisfaction of the crown with the initial attempt of the third estate to deal with political questions by no means deterred them from further activity in this direction. On the 16th they voted to include articles in their *cahier*

[18] *pv.* ff. 195-195v.   [19] *pv.* ff. 191-202v.

which requested that ecclesiastics be excluded from the council on the grounds that they had taken an oath of fidelity to the Pope and that their presence was required in their churches. It was further requested that no offensive wars be undertaken and that no new taxes be imposed without the consent of the estates which should be assembled every two years. None of these articles aroused serious debate in the assembly and there is no evidence of any specific objections being raised except on the question of ecclesiastics in the council. On this matter the deputy from Normandy filed a protest at the end of the *procès-verbal* while several other delegations contented themselves with attacking in a more general way the articles on religion and government.[20]

This last deviation from the royal commands does not seem to have bothered Catherine, but she was still by no means willing to permit the third estate to tamper with the union she had achieved with Navarre and the other princes with so much difficulty. On Monday, the 18th, Poulaim reported that he had seen the queen mother and had found her very angry. She had pointed out that the clergy and the nobility had approved the present government and she supplied Poulaim with a copy of their article with a suggestion that the third estate do likewise. The proposed article praised and consented to the accord reached between the queen mother and the King of Navarre with the agreement of the princes and prayed them to continue to control the government until the king was of age — this without prejudice to the rights of the princes or estates should a similar occasion arise in the future.

That afternoon the Sieur de Mortier arrived from the queen to reinforce her request that the third estate accept the article of the nobility approving her government. Mortier was quick to point out that failure to do so might break the accord between the queen, the King of Navarre, and the princes, thereby threatening the peace of the kingdom. Apparently aware of the close cooperation which existed between the secular orders as well as the anti-clerical feeling within the third estate, he stressed the approval won from the nobility, but failed to mention the clergy.

A lively debate ensued in the chamber of the third estate when Mortier departed and no final agreement could then be reached. The argument continued the following day. Mesgrigny, president of the assembly, reported that he had been summoned to court and that there he had been given a memoir by the king's secretary which agreed in substance with that brought by Poulaim. This constant royal pressure, plus the example of the nobility, had its effect and a number of deputies began to waver. At length the article offered by Poulaim was definitely accepted. He and Verguer were named to inform the queen. Catherine de Médicis had won her first and only victory over the recalcitrant members of the chamber of the third estate.[21]

Ironically, Claude Berard of Provence, who had been absent that day, chose this moment to stalk into the assembly and announce that he was taking leave of the company on the grounds that the estates had been convoked only to dis-

---

[20] *pv.* ff. 207–207v, 234–239v. *Cahier* of third estate.

[21] *pv.* ff. 209–214. The *procès-verbal* does not indicate that the King of Navarre visited the deputies.

cuss the debts of the king and that there were articles included in the *cahier* on other matters that were directly contrary to the memoirs and instructions given him by his constituents. He left with no further explanations, taking care to give the *cahier* of Provence directly to the king with a statement to the effect that the secular estates were attempting to destroy the Catholic Church. The departure of the staunchest defender of Catholicism did much to strengthen the more radical element in the assembly at the very moment they had suffered a defeat in the recognition given to the government of Catherine de Médicis. Almost immediately they were to have an opportunity to show their new strength.[22]

While the argument with Berard ensued, Poulaim copied the article in the *cahier* touching on the government and administration of the kingdom. When he had finished, he attempted to leave, but was told to remain in the assembly until all the articles had been revised. At length he said that he wanted to speak to his valet and left. When he did not return, Verguer went to his lodging only to find him gone. It was apparent that Poulaim had departed for the court with the article on the government to show the queen mother without waiting for his fellow deputy. Until this point, Poulaim had been one of the most important figures in the third estate. He had served as clerk for a time and had been frequently chosen to represent his order at the court. To these honors must be added his recent election as speaker for his order. The recognition just given to the government of Catherine marked his greatest triumph — and now he rushed to Saint-Germain with his happy tidings for the queen without waiting for Verguer, no doubt in the hope of winning the credit for the turn of events for himself.

The reaction of the third estate was quick. The deputy from the Ile-de-France was named to accompany Verguer to the queen to present the article. The new delegation was to proceed as rapidly as possible in order to arrive before Poulaim. That same afternoon the two deputies returned and reported that they had shown the article to the queen mother and that she had given thanks to the third estate. The assembly then returned to the question of Poulaim and proceeded to revoke his election as their speaker when the *cahier* was presented to the king. In his place was named Jacques Bretaigne of Autun. Thus the moderate Poulaim was replaced by the fiery Burgundian whose name for centuries has epitomized the Estates General of Pontoise. Until this point Bretaigne had not played a very prominent role. Massol, not he, held the vote of Burgundy, and he had done little more than to rewrite the *cahier* in a more elegant manner.

Poulaim was by no means disposed to let this honor slip from his grasp without a struggle. On the afternoon of 21 August he appeared in the chamber of the third estate for the first time since his unannounced departure a few days before and complained that the clerk had refused to give him a copy of the *procès-verbal* or of the order revoking his election as speaker. The assembly was unsympathetic to this complaint, but in order to soften the blow, decided on the following day to permit Poulaim to resign from the office of speaker. Poulaim refused and departed from the assembly despite the request of his fellow deputies that he take his seat and sign the *cahier*. The delegate from Normandy must have turned to

[22] *pv.* ff. 214–215. Valois, *op. cit.*, fn. 45.

the court for help, for on the 23rd a messenger arrived at Pontoise with a letter from the queen mother asking that he be restored to his former position and pointed out that his fault was a small one and done only to please her. This the third estate refused to do and dispatched a delegation to the king, the queen mother, and the chancellor asking that the liberties of the third estate be preserved. It was the government's turn to bow. Bretaigne, and not Poulaim carried the word for the third estate.[23]

It must not be supposed that the third estate found no time at all to consider the debts of the king. As early as 11 August the deputies began their debate on this subject and what was to have been the most critical issue of the Estates General was quickly resolved. The third estate argued that the taxes levied in the past were so heavy that any further burden would be unbearable. In return for the sincere efforts of the crown to correct the abuses in the government and to please the deputies by forcing an unwilling *Parlement* to accept the Ordonnance of Orléans, the third estate wrote in their *cahier* that it had nothing to offer his majesty except "good will." Perhaps the deputies would have been more accurate if they had said "good will and advice," for article after article told the king how he could solve his financial difficulties. They recommended that the fiscal administrators be investigated, that all pensions be revoked and, except in the case of the queen mother, returned, and that the number of officials in the royal household be reduced. If the sums thus gained were not sufficient to pay the debts of the king, the third estate recommended that the king take the revenue of all ecclesiastical beneficies, offices, and dignities which were not actually administered by the holder, that a graduated income tax be levied on the possessors of other benefices, and that the surplus revenue of the monastic orders be confiscated. In addition to these measures, the third estate generously offered the king permission to confiscate part of the temporal goods of the clergy. So great a sum could be derived from this act that the king would have an excess of funds which could be applied for such worthy purposes as to encourage trade, fortify the frontier towns, and to reduce the *taille* to the amount levied during the reign of Louis XII.

None of the deputies seems to have realized that their failure to grant the king any of their own goods seriously imperilled their chances of being convoked again, or if any of them did recognize this fact, they were so tied by the instructions given them by their constituents that they could do nothing. The only serious disagreement between the deputies came on the question of the confiscation of the temporal goods of the clergy. On this matter the deputies of Ile-de-France, Dauphiny, and Provence found the actions of their colleagues unreasonable.[24]

How soon Catherine de Médicis learned of the decision of the third estate to offer nothing of its own is difficult to say. In other instances she had been informed immediately of the developments within that body, as is evidenced by the frequent messengers she sent to Pontoise. The same was probably true in this case. The later insistence of the queen mother that the third estate concentrate on financial matters can be explained by her desire to keep the minds of the deputies

[23] *pv.* ff. 215–218v, 220–223v, 231–233.
[24] *pv.* ff. 186–187v, 189–190v.

away from affairs on which she did not desire their opinion, and also to make certain that they had plenty of time available to make generous offers in regard to the goods of the clergy. Indeed, she had probably hoped for only a small amount of aid from the secular estates and may have consciously used them to frighten the clergy into making a large contribution. The rumor was so current that the temporal goods of the clergy were to be sacrificed that the Spanish ambassador protested to Catherine on 1 August against such an action. As further evidence, we note that as soon as the *cahiers* of the estates were submitted and their contents became generally known, increased pressure was put on the clergy at Poissy to come to terms.[25]

The third estate finished their *cahier* on 19 August, but it was not until 27 August that the final meeting of the Estates General was held at Saint-Germain-en-Laye in the presence of the king. The assembly got off to an inauspicious beginning for the Church when a quarrel broke out between the princes of the blood and cardinals over the question of precedence. The victory of the princes on this question caused the Cardinals of Tournon, Lorraine, and Guise to depart immediately, leaving the estates to continue without their presence.[26]

This matter being settled to the satisfaction of the princes, the chancellor suggested that the speaker of each estate propose freely what he thought to be good. The orator of the clergy promised the king a generous gift, but in return asked that the king protect the Catholic Church and enforce the July Edict, which called for a certain amount of religious persecution.

The speaker for the nobility, Nicolas de Beaufremont, Baron de Sennecy, pronounced a short but eloquent plea for the cessation of religious persecution and the restoration of uniformity by instruction. The *cahier* he submitted for his order was quite similar to that of the third estate except that it offered the king a contribution from both the other orders rather than from the clergy alone. The members of the nobility were no more willing than the third estate to assist the king in his financial difficulties with their own goods.[27]

By far the longest oration was that made by Jacques Bretaigne for the third estate. His speech followed closely the *cahier* of his order except that he permitted himself to be persuaded by his Protestant sympatheis to dwell overlong on the faults of the Catholic Church. There can be little truth in the charge so often made by historians, following the Venetian ambassador, that the speech did not reflect the will of those who elected him. What he said had been incorporated

---

[25] *Lettres de Catherine de Médicis (Collection de documents inédits)*, ed. H. de la Ferrière (Paris, 1880), I, 222. A. de Ruble, *Le Colloque de Poissy* (Paris, 1889), pp. 24–25.

[26] *pv.* f. 217. B.N. ms. fr. 15494, ff. 33v–34. L'Aubespine to Limoges, 29 Aug. 1561, B.N. ms. fr. 6618, ff. 4–10. Suriano to Doge, 29 August 1561, *Despatches of Michele Suriano and Marc' Antonio Barbero, Venetian ambassadors at the court of France, 1560–1563*, ed. Sir Henry Layard (Lymington, 1891). La Place, *op. cit.*, f. 216.

[27] La Place, *op. cit.*, f. 216v. B.N. ms. fr. 15494, ff. 95v–100, 57–59v. Extracts from the speech of Beaufremont have been printed in P. M. Baudouin, *Histoire du protestantisme et de la ligue en Bourgogne* (Auxerre, 1881), I, 180–182. There are many copies of the *cahier* of the nobility. Among them are B.N. ms. fr. 15494, ff. 66v–95v; ms. n.a. fr. 2794; ms. fr. 4763; ms. fr. 3970; Bibliothèque du Sénat, ms. 379. I have not yet been able to find the original.

into the *cahier* of his order, and even more significant is the fact that the *procès-verbal* reveals that he had submitted his oration to the third estate for approval. Only a minority of the deputies had objected. Nevertheless, the temper of the pronouncement was so anti-clerical that the old Constable of Montmorency suggested that the speaker should be hanged.[28]

With the speeches of the three deputies, the Estates General of Pontoise came to an end, and with it, the great experiment in the use of representative assemblies inaugurated at Fontainebleau the year before. The crown had been sincere in its desire to inform the people of its problems and, at the same time, to answer their grievances. In return, a certain amount of understanding, cooperation, and above all, financial assistance was required. The secular estates had asked for much, even to the point of threatening the position of the queen mother, but they had been willing to give nothing of their own. Small wonder Charles IX did not see fit to assemble them again during his reign. On the other hand, the clergy, thoroughly frightened by the attitude of its fellow estates and fearful of drastic action by the crown, signed the Contract of Poissy on 21 September which guaranteed the government about 17,000,000 *livres* over a period of years to pay the mortgage on the domain and some other debts. The ecclesiastical assembly had proved most fruitful. It is not surprising, therefore, that the clergy was frequently convoked thereafter to give money to the king. In return for these concessions the king gave the clergy such privileges as to collect the taxes it granted, to have permanent syndics to look after its privileges, and to make complaints. In short, the assembly of the clergy of France achieved a position comparable to that of the *pays d'états*.

If the deputies of the secular estates had done little for the king to warrant their convocation again, it is equally true that they had not done much for the people that would lead to a demand for further sessions. Following their request, the *cahiers* submitted were not made into an ordonnance to be registered and published by the *parlements*. Instead, copies of the *cahiers* with the royal replies were sent to each of the *gouvernements* to be displayed. Not having been sanctioned by the *parlements*, we are safe to assume that they were not enforced in the courts and hence were of little value. Even the resistance of the secular estates to taxation proved to be of no use for on 22 September the king proceeded to impose the proposed wine tax anyway. We need not look further to know why there was no strong popular demand for a meeting of the Estates General for a decade. An institution which served no better the king or his people could hardly expect a thriving existence.[29]

---

[28] The speech of Bretaigne was printed several times in 1561 and has since been published in such places as La Place, *op. cit.*, ff. 216v–230, and *Mémoires de Condé servant d'eclaircissement et de preuves à l'histoire de M. de Thou* (London and Paris, 1743), II, 437–454. Suriano to Doge, 29 August 1561 in Layard, *op. cit.*, *pv* f. 226–226v.

[29] Major, *op. cit.*, pp. 112–114. La Place, *op. cit.*, f. 235. The replies of the king to the *cahier* of the third estate were published by Tartière.

V

THE ASSEMBLY AT PARIS IN THE SUMMER OF 1575

" The majority of our Historians have not mentioned these estates... ", Georges de La Faille wrote over 250 years ago when he referred to the assembly of 1575 (1). His statement could be repeated with even greater fervor today. Georges Picot (2) was obviously ignorant of its existence and, more surprisingly, recent students of the period have failed to take note of this obscure meeting (3).

Two factors probably account for this situation: In the first place, *bailliage* elections with their wide publicity and broad participation were not used to choose the deputies. In the second place, nothing of importance was accomplished in the meeting. The man of 1575, like the historian, was content to ignore the whole affair. Unimportant as the meeting was, however, a study of what took place reveals something of the nature of the Renaissance monarchy and the attitudes of its leading citizens.

The estates of 1575 was summoned by Henry III. No king ever had greater reason to seek the support of his subjects and few kings were more willing to gamble on the outcome of an assembly. He had a high regard for his oratorical ability and persuasive powers, talents that could in normal times be put to good use in a meeting. Unfortunately for the young king, pas-

---

(1) GERMAIN DE LA FAILLE, *Annales de la ville de Toulouse* (Toulouse, 1701), II, 339.

(2) GEORGES PICOT, *Histoire des Etats Généraux* (Paris, 2nd ed., 1888), 5 vols.

(3) PIERRE CHAMPION died before he could complete his detailed study of Henry III. His *Henri III roi de Pologne* (Paris, 1943-1951), 2 vols. ends a few months before the assembly was held. PHILIPPE ERLANGER, *Henri III* (Paris, 7th ed., 1948); NICOLA M. SUTHERLAND, *The French Secretaries of State in the Age of Catherine de Medici* (London, 1962), and ALINE KARCHER, *L'Assemblée des Notables de Saint-Germain-en-Laye (1583)* in *Bibliothèque de l'École des Chartes*, CXIV (1956), 115-62, and *Recherches sur les tentatives de réforme du gouvernement de Henri III (1577-1584)* in *Position des Thèses de l'École des Chartes* (1956), 61-67; ignore the meeting. The assembly is not directly mentioned in the valuable edition of the correspondence of Henry III, *Lettres de Henri III roi de France*, ed. MICHEL FRANÇOIS (Paris, 1965), vol. II. A few historians, including PAUL VAN DYKE, have made vague and misleading references to the meeting, *Catherine de Médicis* (New York, 1922), II, 214; but on the whole only a handful of local historians have been aware of its existence.

sions were too aroused for the protagonists to alter their course because of mere words. In spite of two full meetings of the Estates General and a number of smaller assemblies that led to several great reforming ordinances, the position of the crown steadily deteriorated during his reign.

Henry III became king of France upon the death of his brother on May 30, 1574, but he did not fully assume the reins of government until his return from Poland in September. By that time the position of the crown was desperate. The Wars of Religion, which had raged intermittently since 1562, were taking a turn for the worse. The Politique faction led by the able and powerful Marshal Damville was in the process of forming a powerful alliance with the Protestants in southern France. The King of Navarre and the Duke of Alençon, Henry's brother, were prevented from joining the malcontents only by their semi-confinement at court, while actual imprisonment was regarded as necessary for Damville's older brother and Marshal Cossé. Only the Guise faction and the ultra Catholics provided substantial support for the crown, and their support was likely to be withdrawn if sufficient concessions were made to the Montmorencies and the Protestants to insure their good behavior.

On April 11, 1575 the Protestants and their Catholic allies presented Henry with a list of 91 articles. Anxious as he was to reestablish peace in his kingdom, he felt that he could not accept an article that provided for freedom of worship in the suburbs of every town. It is significant that he raised no objection to the proposal that the Estates General be called three months after peace was established, but this and other concessions were not enough to satisfy the Protestant-Politique union (4). Peace negotiations continued, but the likelihood that there would be a full scale civil war grew daily. The problem that faced Henry was where to find the money to support an army.

During the preceding decade and a half, royal revenue had increased by about 3,500,000 *livres*, but this gain had been wiped out by a devaluation of the currency. Since the buying power

---

(4) *Calendar of State Papers, Foreign Series, of the Reign of Elizabeth, 1575-77*, ed. ALLAN J. CROSBY (London, 1880), 50-51, 58-59. One of the concessions that Henry is reported to have been willing to make was that the estates could " set the taxes ", 55.

of precious metals had also declined during this period, Henry III actually received less income than his brother, Francis II, had when in 1560 he had convoked the Estates General to provide a solution to his financial difficulties (5). Henry was certainly needlessly extravagant at times, but even with the financial management of a Queen Elizabeth he would have been in difficulty.

The usual practice of having the towns borrow money for the king and pay the interest from revenues he assigned to them for that purpose no longer provided an adequate system of public credit. Henry had few remaining sources of revenue he could alienate and the towns were finding that the anticipated income fell short of expectations. By the winter of 1574-1575 the city of Paris could no longer meet its obligations and in July was forced to ask the king for permission to levy a tax on the sale of fish in order to pay its creditors. Direct borrowing at higher interest rates was clearly necessary (6).

Loans were sought from Venice, Florence, and the Pope. Internal sources were not neglected and it is reported that even the court nobility agreed to advance 50,000 francs in January 1575 to pay the wages of the royal guard. Few, however, willingly entrusted their wealth to the hardpressed monarch. The bankers of Lyon refused to advance 300,000 francs at 15 percent interest and the inhabitants of Paris were very slow to subscribe to a 600,000 *livres* loan that the city fathers had agreed to in March 1574, a few months before Charles IX had died (7).

Additional taxes were also sought. Arrangements were made for the French clergy to contribute 2,000,000 *livres*, although to raise such a large sum it was necessary to alienate part of the patrimony of the church (8). Some of the provincial estates

---

(5) JEAN J. CLAMAGERAN, *Histoire de l'impôt en France* (Paris, 1868), II, 197-202.

(6) BERNARD SCHNAPPER, *Les Rentes au XVIe siècle* (Paris, 1957), esp. pp. 156, 216, 267-69. *Registres des déliberations du bureau de la ville de Paris*, ed. FRANÇOIS BONNARDOT (Paris, 1893), VII, 223-26, 267-69, 277-80, 284-87.

(7) FÉLIX ROCQUAIN, *La France et Rome pendant les Guerres de Religion* (Paris, 1924), 179, 187. *Calendar of States Papers, Foreign...*, 10. VAN DYKE, II, 171-72. *Registres... Paris*, VII, 161-65, 190-91, 194-95, 219, 225, 266-68.

(8) LOUIS SERBAT, *Les Assemblées du clergé de France* (Paris, 1906), 68-71. Some of the printed edicts are in the Bibliothèque Nationale. See *Actes Royaux*, F. 46,847, (nos. 23, 25 and 28).

were asked for special contributions. Learning that the rebellious Damville had convoked the estates of Languedoc on his own authority, Henry summoned a rival assembly of the province to meet in his presence at Villeneuve-d'Avignon in December, 1574. The three estates, persuaded by Henry's logic and eloquence, granted special taxes to support the war in addition to voting their usual contribution (9). This early success undoubtedly contributed to his willingness to hold assemblies.

Henry departed from Avignon around January 11, 1575, and moved quickly up the Rhône River valley. At Romans he briefly attended the meeting in which the three estates of Dauphiné voted to support an army of 2,000 men to carry on the war in that province. By January 20, he was at Lyon to appear before the deputies of Lyonnais, Forez, and Beaujolais. What happened at this meeting escapes the historian, but it is possible that a loan of 16,000 *livres* was arranged (10).

It was, of course, impossible for Henry to participate in the meetings of all the provincial estates and others were called upon to act in his stead. The deputies of the estates of Guyenne assembled at Gimont on March 14 to hear the lieutenant general, La Valette, plea for financial assistance to support the war, a plea they attempted to counter by stressing the poverty of the province. The three estates of Burgundy met on May 15 and requested lower, not higher, taxes. The king did win a routine " free gift " of 50,000 *livres*, but those present took the precaution of directing the officers of the estates to make no gift or advance without their consent. When the king's lieutenant asked for money to raise four companies to retake a Protestant stronghold, these officials dutifully refused to provide the funds (11).

The three estates of Brittany were not called into session

---

(9) CLAUDE DE VIC and JEAN VAISSETE, *Histoire générale de Languedoc* (Toulouse, 1889), XI, 599-602.

(10) *Inventaire sommaire des archives communales antérieures à 1790, ville de Grenoble*, ed. MARIE-A. PRUDHOMME (Grenoble, 1886), I, BB27. An extract from the registers of the estates is in the Bibliothèque Municipale of Grenoble, ms. 2311. *Lettres de Henri III...*, II, 82, 83, 92, 98, 129-30.

(11) Archives Communales, Saint-Sever, II, 1 (1519-1789). *Inventaire sommaire des archives départementales antérieures à 1790, Côte d'Or*, ed. JOSEPH GARNIER (Dijon, 1886), ser. C., III, 74-75, 115.

The Assembly at Paris in the summer of 1575

that winter or spring. In June of the preceding year a special session had been held in which the estates had flatly refused to vote 90,000 *livres* to pay the costs of the war. The crown had promptly called a second special meeting in which a grant of 60,000 *livres* was finally obtained. As this precedent suggested that a special session in 1575 would be even more recalcitrant, Henry simply ordered that the necessary war taxes be collected without the consent of the estates. When the regular meeting of the three estates was held in September, a strong protest was made against this arbitrary act and their *procureur* and those of the towns were ordered not to levy any tax in the future without their consent (12). The three estates of Normandy had been asked for a special contribution in November, 1574, and for some reason the king decided to wait until the same time in 1575 to make a new request (13).

In spite of these efforts the results were disappointing. The English ambassador reported on March 30 that he could not learn of any money that had reached the king, and the Parisian diarist, Pierre de l'Estoile, emphasized the poverty of the court by saying that is was rumored that " le Roy n'avoit pas de quoi avoir à disner " (14).

Faced with this situation Henry sought another solution. In May 1575 he created an unprecedented number of new offices. The bureaucracy in the *eaux-et-forêts* was greatly expanded, the number of the *élus* was increased in the *élections*, and additional notaries were given to the *bailliages*, *sénéchaussées*, *prévôtés*, and other seats in the kingdom. June saw a substantial expansion in the number of appraisers and surveying personnel (15).

But even the French appetite for offices could be temporarily satiated. An additional source of revenue was necessary. Having tried to borrow from every likely prospect, having extracted what he could from the clergy and the provincial estates, and

---

(12) *Archives de Bretagne*, XV (1909), 34-73, and esp. 67, 71.

(13) *Cahiers des états de Normandie sous le règne de Henri III* ed. CHARLES DE ROBILLARD DE BEAUREPAIRE (Rouen, 1887), I, 196-206.

(14) *Calendar of State Papers, Foreign...*, 37. PIERRE DE L'ESTOILE, *Mémoires — Journaux*, eds. GUSTAVE BRUNET and others (Paris, 1889), I, 54.

(15) Printed copies of these edicts are located in the Bibliothèque Nationale, *Actes Royaux*, F. 46,848, nos. 8, 9, 11, and 16.

having made his appeal to the French love of offices, a tax on the inhabitants of the privileged towns was the most probable remaining recourse. Continual royal demands and the condition of the country made careful preparations necessary. As the first step towards establishing a new levy, the king ordered an assembly to be held in Paris on July 20.

The brief letters of convocation which were dispatched to the towns on May 23 gave no inkling of the purpose of the meeting beyond that those who attended were to hear some things that the king had to say concerning the state of his affairs (16). The town councilors of Rouen were disturbed by this nebulous statement and wrote one of their number who was then at court to see if he could discover the occasion for the meeting. Evidently his reply was unsatisfactory because on July 11, shortly before electing a deputy to attend the assembly, a similar request was made of the newly appointed *bailli* of Rouen. The *bailli* told them that he had heard that the meeting concerned the establishment of peace (17).

A prominent citizen of Troyes was also in Paris when the town council first considered the royal letter. The councilors decided to ask him to remain for the meeting, but, suspicious of the motives of the king, they instructed him to learn the will of his majesty, but to give neither advice nor consent to anything that would be proposed. For some reason our chance visitor to Paris escaped this assignment and one of the *échevins* was dispatched in his stead (18).

Lyon evidently believed that the best defense was a strong offense. Her councilors dispatched two deputies armed with a lengthy petition to the king setting forth the town's grievances. The document began with a description of their financial problems which should have created a certain community of spirit with the bankrupt monarch. To resolve their difficulties they asked for permission to tax foreign merchandise entering the town for six years. The councilors also requested that a Parlement be established in Lyon and shrewdly pointed out that substantial sums would be raised by the sale of offices which would auto-

---

(16) *Registres... Paris*, VII, 257.
(17) Archives Communales, Rouen, A19, fos. 372, 375-376v.
(18) Archives Communales, Troyes, A19, fols. 15v-16.

matically accompany the creation of a new sovereign court. Tempting as the idea must have been to the hardpressed Henry, he seems to have believed that the resulting difficulties with the Parlement of Paris, in whose jurisdiction Lyon lay, would more than outweigh any advantages of granting this request. Lyon had other problems growing out of its frontier position and banking establishments that could profit with royal assistance, but no article suggested anything that would increase royal revenue except the creation of a Parlement, and several would have the opposite effect. Clearly there was little hope for Henry here (19).

Amiens sought protection through influence. Her deputies made a point of visiting the lieutenant general of the government of Picardy on their way to Paris. That official gave them letters of recommendation to the king, to a prominent councilor, and to Villeroy, the influential secretary of state charged with the affairs of Picardy. Thus armed, they won audiences with the council and with the king, and used the opportunity to protest that they were good and faithful subjects (20).

Other town councils elected their deputies between the closing days of June and the middle of July without leaving records reflecting any doubts that they may have been held concerning the intentions of the king. In all, twenty-six sent deputies to the estates.

Little is known concerning the ecclesiastics and nobles who attended. In addition to members of the royal family and the chancellor, the deputies of Amiens specifically named three prelates and six great nobles who were present, but added that " several archbishops, bishops and deputies of the church, [and] several gentlemen and representatives of the nobility... " were there (21). The deputy from Toulouse was content to state simply that " all the estates of France were summoned " (22). Henry III is reported to have said that he had convoked " the deputies of the clergy elected by the provinces, some of the most prominent gentle-

---

(19) Archives Communales, Lyon, BB93, fols. 87, 115-119v.

(20) *Inventaire sommaire des archives communales antérieures à 1790, ville d'Amiens*, ed. GEORGES DURAND (Amiens, 1897), III, 39.

(21) *Recueil des monuments inédits de l'histoire du tiers état* ed. JACQUES AUGUSTIN THIERRY (Paris, 1853), II, 831.

(22) LA FAILLE, II, 339.

men " (23), and the representatives of the principal towns. These statements suggest there were elective elements among the clergy and possibly the nobility, but that most of the nobles who attended did so by virtue of receiving direct summons of the king.

After several postponements caused by difficulties raised by the council and the late arrival of some of the deputies (24), the ceremony opening the estates (25) was held on July 28 in the Louvre (26). One can imagine the impressive display the overdressed and yet largely untried king, his shy bride of less than six months, and his stout, power-hungry mother, Catherine de Médicis, must have made, surrounded as they were by many of the leading dignitaries of the kingdom. Conspicuously present were the Dukes of Mayenne and Aumale and the Marquis d'Elboeuf, leaders of the Guise faction who could be counted on to advocate war against the Protestants and their equally hated Politique allies. The Italians: Birague, the chancellor, the Duke of Nevers, the Cardinal of Ferrara, and Marshal Retz were also there. Like the queen-mother they probably preferred a compromise peace. A victorious war would leave them to the tender mercies of the Guise, but abject surrender was equally undesirable, for among the Protestant-Politique conditions for peace was a provision that they be dismissed from their posts. Among those present only the inexperienced King of Navarre could be counted on to favor peace, and he was more a prisoner than an active

---

(23) THIERRY, II, 832.
(24) *Inventaire... Amiens*, III, 39.
(25) Our knowledge of the estates of 1575 is derived entirely from the reports the deputies of the towns made to their respective councils when they returned home. The reports of the deputies of Amiens and Toulouse have been published: THIERRY, II, 830-34, and LA FAILLE, II, 339-41. The remaining three are located in the Archives Communales of Troyes, A19, fol. 21; Rouen, A19, fol. 380; and Lyon, BB93, fols. 131v-132v. I am indebted to the Archivists of these cities for locating the relevant materials in the municipal registers and having them microfilmed for me. I would also like to express my appreciation to those other archivists who sought in vain for references concerning this little- known meeting. The most detailed account is by the deputies of Amiens. I have followed it but have noted in footnotes where other accounts vary significantly.
(26) The Rouen account gives July 30 as the date of the opening meeting and the other three are not specific. I have preferred the Amiens version because the letter Henry gave the deputies when he dismissed them was dated August 4. The sequence of events at the estates probably took more than five days. Therefore, July 28 is the more likely date of the first meeting.

The Assembly at Paris in the summer of 1575

participant in the deliberations. His slippery ally, the Duke of Alençon, was probably not there. Whether they stood for peace or for war, these members of the court nobility probably favored a tax because a well-heeled monarch had more to give than one who did not have the wherewithal to dine.

The king opened the meeting by telling how he had made every effort to restore order and obedience to the crown when he had returned from Poland, but that there were those who continued to raise armies, seize towns, and pillage his loyal subjects. To compel their obedience it would be necessary to put several armies in the field at considerable expense. Since this would increase the suffering of his afflicted people, he would like to pacify his kingdom, but several difficulties stood in the way that he and his council had been unable to resolve. If God gave peace, he wanted the assembly to advise him how it could be maintained, as earlier pacifications had been shortlived. If the war continued, he wanted the assembly's advice on how to defeat his rebellious subjects. Especially did he seek the opinion of those present on how to raise promptly the money that would be necessary either to maintain peace or to wage war.

Chancellor Birague spoke next. His address was longer and dealt more specifically with the problems before the assembly, but he added nothing essential to what the king had said. Henry had won praise from the deputies of Amiens for his oratorical skill; the Italian-born chancellor received no such accolades.

The Cardinal of Bourbon, almost certainly following a prearranged plan, then asked that a delay be permitted to enable those present to decide what advice to give on these great and important matters. The king granted his request and ordered the assembly to meet again the following afternoon in order to learn more details concerinng the reasons for holding the assembly and to hear the proposals of his councilors (27). At that time they were to suggest means to raise money that would impose a minimum burden on the people.

The next morning all, or almost all of the deputies of the

---

(27) The Troyes, Toulouse, and Lyon accounts are so brief that they leave the impression that the work of the estates took place in a single day. The Rouen account specifically concurs with the Amiens on the duration of the assembly.

towns went to the *hôtel de ville* to discuss with the provost of the merchants and the *échevins* of Paris what course of action to follow during the assembly that afternoon. A decision was reached that the deputies would insist that they had been authorized only to hear what would be proposed to them in the assembly and to report back to their constituents. They mutually agreed not to exceed this response for fear that if anyone offered advice, it would obligate the town which had deputed him.

That afternoon the assembly met once more in the Louvre, but the king did not attend on this occasion. The chancellor, who presided in his stead, had evidently learned of the decision of the deputies of the towns, for he promised that those present could freely give their advice to the king without placing the province or town that had delegated them under any obligation. This comforting assurance was dispelled by the *trésorier de l'épargne* who reported that the revenue was 14,300,000 *livres* per year and that expenses were 20,600,000, leaving a deficit of 6,300,000 *livres* per year. Clearly the king wanted money (28).

This done, the clergy was asked to give its opinion. The Cardinal of Bourbon spoke of the loyalty of his order to the crown and of the need to support the king in his difficulties. The clergy had never refused to come to his aid. That same year it had given him 2,000,000 *livres*. The nobles asked to delay their reply until the following Monday as they had not yet reached a decision.

Bernard de Supersantis, who was then serving his third term as a *capitoul* of Toulouse, had been elected spokesman for the towns, presumably during the morning session at the *hôtel de ville*. Following the agreement that had been reached, he declared that they had powers only to hear what would be proposed in the assembly and to report back to their constituents, who, if the king so commanded, would give their advice. The chancellor then asked the deputies from Reims, Paris, Rouen, and perhaps other towns to express their opinions, but they concurred with the spokesman of Toulouse (29). Seeing that the deputies

---

(28) The Lyon account gives the income at 16,000,000 *livres* and the expenses at 22,000,000. Both accounts, and also that of Rouen, said that the deficit was about 6,000,000 *livres*.

(29) In their respective accounts the deputies of Lyon and Rouen both said that they spoke, although their participation was not mentioned in the other versions.

The Assembly at Paris in the summer of 1575

could not be divided, the chancellor terminated the meeting.

During the next few days some of the deputies asked the chancellor for permission to depart, but he refused to let them go until the nobles had given their advice. At some point in the negotiations the nobility authorized their spokesman to recommend that the king solve his financial difficulties by confiscating and selling all the possessions of the Huguenots and rebels, and by taking half the goods acquired by the officers of justice and finance (30). The first part of this advice was not very helpful as it could be implemented only after Henry had inflicted a decisive defeat on his foes, a thing that he could not do until he first obtained the money to raise the needed armies. Royal officials had already contributed something to the crown in one guise or another; to demand half their goods would risk alienating them completely. The nobles almost certainly knew this, but since they had had no intention of offering anything of their own, they could only hope to give the appearance of being helpful by offering someone else's possessions.

The deputies of the towns met once more, this time in a private home, but they would not budge from their initial position that they were only authorized to hear and report. On August 4, after notifying the chancellor, they presented themselves to the king on his return from mass and told him of their decision. Then, after protesting their devotion to his service, they asked to return home. Henry, who had probably anticipated the outcome of this adventure, graciously granted their request and gave them leave to depart on the following day bearing letters to their constituents. These letters stressed the mutual loyalty and obligations of prince and subject and informed their readers that the delegates had been fully briefed on the critical position in which the crown found itself.

The deputies of Troyes, Rouen, Lyon, and Amiens reported in person or by letter to their respective town councils between August 8 and 11, but those who had further to travel could not have been so prompt, the deputy from Toulouse delaying until

---

(30) Only the Toulouse account gives the reply of the nobility. This text suggests that their reply followed that of the clergy and that both took place on the opening day, but this was clearly not the case.

December 1, for what reason we know not. Judging by the account of the estates given by the deputies from Amiens, Henry had persuaded those who attended that he was a loyal Catholic who had the welfare of his subjects at heart, but that he had great need of financial assistance because of the heavy debts incurred during the past wars. Henry did not, however, wait for the towns to suggest a solution to his fiscal problems — perhaps he anticipated that each town would be content to explain why it could not contribute. On August 17 he issued letters levying a tax on the towns to support 50,000 foot soldiers (31).

Then began the interminable negotiations to collect the money. The towns of Brittany found a warm defender in the three estates of the province, but the more common approach was for each town to carry on its own negotiations, Amiens winning a reduction of its share of from 10,000 to 5,000 *livres* (32). Paris escaped the levy altogether. Perhaps Henry was having so much trouble collecting the 600,000 *livres* loan that had been granted him the preceding March that he felt that it would be useless to try. He did not hesitate to remind his capital of his generosity when he asked it for 133,334 *livres* in December to pay his Swiss troops. The citizens of Paris were unimpressed and Henry was still trying to finish collecting the tax twelve months later (33).

With such a record of lack of accomplishment there is little wonder that the estates of 1575 went almost unnoticed by its contemporaries and has been forgotten by their descendants. Yet an examination of this assembly does provide a better understanding of the Renaissance monarchy. Henry summoned the estates because the financial position of the crown was desperate. He sincerely wanted advice which, if given and followed, would be a powerful propaganda weapon when he began to negotiate with the towns and estates. Except for the impractical proposals of the nobility, he was unable to pry any recommendations from the assembly. The deputies of the towns saw through his plan and refused to make any suggestions concerning a tax, or even

---

(31) Bibliothèque Nationale, *Actes Royaux*, F. 46,849 (9). *Lettres de Henri III.*, II, 215.
(32) *Archives de Bretagne*, XV (1909), 67, 71. THIERRY, II, 830-31.
(33) *Paris, Registres*, VII, 309-328, 331-32, 334, 335, 338-63, 376, 378-79, 381, 392, 394, VIII, 7-8, 22, 39-40. Henry even had trouble getting a 20,000 *livres* loan requested on June 27, 1575, VII, 256-61, 270-72, 280.

on the question of whether there should be peace or war. Strongly Catholic, they could not recommend granting the concessions necessary for peace, but they knew that a recommendation of war would open the way for the king to demand financial assistance to implement their suggestion.

From Henry's point of view the assembly must have been disappointing, but it was not a complete failure. If we may judge by the reports that deputies carried back to their constituents, he had managed to persuade them of his sincerity and of his great financial distress, important preparatory steps in securing at least partial cooperation for the levy that followed. Seen in this light, the estates of 1575 was a direct descendant of a long line of medieval assemblies that were summoned more to persuade towns and provincial estates to accept a tax than to give actual consent for a levy. Its composition was similar to that of the medieval assemblies in that it consisted of clergymen and noblemen who for the most part were individually summoned, and of the deputies of the leading towns. In the procedures followed and in its brief duration it also followed earlier precedents (34).

The Estates General of 1484 was the first in which *bailliage* elections were used extensively (35). Modern historians have generally insisted that from this time only an assembly composed of deputies chosen in this fashion should be termed an " Estates General ". The continued existence of the older type of assembly has generally been ignored unless associated with some important event as in the meetings at Tours in May 1506, at Paris in January 1558, and at Rouen in November 1596-January 1597. Contemporaries recognized the differences between the two types of assemblies, but they referred to them interchangeably as an " assembly of the estates ", an " assembly of the three estates ", an " assembly of notable persons ", and, least frequently of all, as an " Estates General ".

How often assemblies with representative elements like that of 1575 were held during the Renaissance will never be ascertained

---

(34) J. RUSSELL MAJOR, *Representative Institutions in Renaissance France* (Madison, 1960), esp. 3-59.

(35) *Ibid.*, 66-68.

until the archives of the leading towns are fully exploited, a task that no individual historian could hope to accomplish. We do know that only seventeen months before the Paris assembly there had been a smaller meeting at Saint-Germain composed of representatives from Parlement and deputies from the provinces (36). Even Louis XIV did not scorn to hold an assembly of the towns, although the consultative aspect of the Renaissance monarchy clearly declined during his reign (37).

An examination of the estates of 1575 also provides a better understanding of the French people. The clergy had already contributed and could be expected to do nothing more. As a result of their generally cooperative attitude, however, an assembly of their order had come into being in 1561 that met periodically until the Revolution, not only to vote money for the king but also to look after their own interests. The nobility offered nothing except bad advice in 1575 and was no more generous on other occasions. As a result, their order was not periodically convoked. The non-cooperative spirit of the third estate doomed it to the same fate.

Henry was certainly poorly advised when he neglected to explain the reasons for the assembly and to request that full powers be given the deputies when he issued the letters of convocation, but it would nevertheless be incorrect to overemphasize the role the mandate system played in the failure of the towns to so much as offer advice. As far as can be ascertained Troyes alone considered giving its deputy the power only to hear and report. Rather, the deputies saw the loophole that the king had left open and decided to invoke the mandate system in the meeting in the *hôtel-de-ville* in the morning following the opening ceremony in which the king had made known his wishes (38).

---

(36) *Négociations diplomatiques de la France avec la Toscane*, ed. ABEL DESJARDINS (Paris, 1865), III, 899.

(37) WARREN C. SCOVILLE, *The French Economy in 1700-1701: An Appraisal by the Deputies of Trade* in *The Journal of Economic History*, XXII (1962), 231-52.

(38) In recent years there has been considerable interest in the study of the mandate system during the Middle Ages. Of especial importance are the articles GAINES POST has recently reprinted in *Studies in Medieval Legal Thought: Public Law and the State, 1100-1322* (Princeton, 1964). In contrast, the mandate system in the early modern period has been neglected. FRANÇOISE CAGNINACCI, *Le Mandat dans la doctrine française de l'ancien régime*,

The Assembly at Paris in the summer of 1575

The lack of a proper mandate was their excuse for not cooperating, not the cause of their failure to do so. Had the king asked for consent to lower taxes, they would have been very vocal indeed.

By not offering any advice the deputies of the towns abdicated any control they might have had over the size or the nature of the inevitable tax. When word of the levy was received, the towns and provincial estates resisted individually as best they could. In many instances they probably won substantial reductions as the example of Amiens suggests, but the non-cooperative spirit they exhibited in 1575 and on other occasions helped to prevent the development of a periodically convoked national assembly that could have influenced royal policy far more than any individual town could hope to do.

XIIIe-XVe siècles (Nancy, 1962), deals with the role of the mandate in private law only. Two recent works: J.-P. CHARNAY, *Naissance et développement de la ' verification des pouvoirs ' dans les anciennes assemblées françaises* in *Revue historique de droit français et étranger* (1962), 556-89, (1963), 20-56; and C. SOULE, *Les Pouvoirs des députés aux États généraux de France* in *Liber Memorialis Sir Maurice Powicke, Studies Presented to the International Commission for the History of epresentative and Parliamentary Institutions*, XXVII (Louvain and Paris, 1965), discuss the public law aspects of the mandate system but neither is based on an adequate knowledge of the theoretical background or on a thorough exploitation of the sources. For a very brief account and for a list of earlier studies see my *The Deputies to the Estates General in Renaissance France* (Madison, 1960), 4-9, 168-69.

VI

THE ELECTORAL PROCEDURE FOR THE ESTATES GENERAL OF FRANCE AND ITS SOCIAL IMPLICATIONS, 1483-1651 [1]

THE ELECTIONS to the Estates General are significant as part of the constitutional history of France. They provide opportunities to see French local government in action: to watch the activities of the *bailliage* officials in relation to the royal directives for holding the elections, the traditions of the particular *bailliage*, and the desires of the local inhabitants; to learn how balloting was conducted, how *cahiers* were prepared, and above all, to discover who spoke for the community of the *bailliage*, that is, who could vote.

The elections to the Estates General are of equal importance for the unparalled insight they provide into the structure of society, the relation between the social orders, and the policies of the crown. Here one has documents that record how the members of the three estates acted when brought together, what disputes occurred between and within the individual orders, and what actions were taken by the king to resolve any difficulties that might arise. These records indicate that while there was a hierarchical conception of society, there were few quarrels between the three setates. A conflict, hitherto rarely suggested except by the students of French local history, did rage from the middle of the sixteenth century between the two leading groups within the third estate: the local royal officials and the municipal leaders. The issue was in part a matter of precedence, but also involved was the control of the *bailliage* elections and even of the municipalities themselves. Our documents further reveal that the crown, far from supporting its own officials, threw its weight on the side of the traditional privileges of the municipalities. [2]

---

[1] The research for this article was made possible by generous assistance from a Fulbright Fellowship, a Guggenheim Memorial Foundation Fellowship, and Emory University during 1952-54.

[2] There have been several studies of French electoral procedure. The most detailed is that of Lalourcé and Duval, *Forme générale et particulière de la convocation et de la tenue des assemblées nationales ou États généraux de France* (Paris, 1789), 3 vols., hereafter cited as *Convocation*. This work, which consists of a discussion of electoral procedure and a volume of documents, suffers from having been hurriedly put together to meet the demand for information concerning the Estates General occasioned by the convocation of that body on the eve of the Revolution. Charles J. Mayer, *Des États généraux et autres assemblées nationales* (Paris, 1788-1789), VII, 273-444; Georges Picot, "Les Élections aux États généraux dans les provinces de 1302 à 1614," *Séances et travaux de l'académie des sciences morales et politiques*, CII (1874), 5-33, 209-21; "Le Droit électoral de l'ancienne France. Les Élections aux États généraux dans les provinces de 1302 à

There were not a large number of meetings of the Estates General. Only the Assemblies at Tours in 1484, at Orléans in 1560-61, at Pontoise in 1561, at Blois in 1576-77 and 1588-89, and at Paris in 1593-94 and 1614-15 can be thus classified prior to the most famous of all meetings in 1789. Elections were also held in 1649 and 1651 during the Fronde, but in each instance the Estates General was canceled.

Those large medieval gatherings so often called Estates Generals by modern historians were not so named by the people of that time. They were referred to as Assemblies of the Estates or as Assemblies of the Three Estates and were composed for the most part of individually summoned ecclesiastics and nobles and of the deputies of the town. The electoral history of these meetings, therefore, consists only of the activities of the municipalities. It was during the minority of Charles VIII that the new policy was inaugurated of using the *bailliage* and other local estates to name the deputies for all three orders to the national assembly and it was at about this point that the term Estates General came into use.

Our concern is with the meetings of the estates of the *bailliages*, *sénéchaussées*, and a few other jurisdictions as the town and the *prévôté* of Paris and the estates of Brittany, Dauphiné, and Provence that the crown ordered to name deputies. In the letters of convocation the kings gave few directives on how the election should be held. They were content to direct the *bailli*, seneschal, or the lieutenant general to assemble in the principal town of their jurisdiction "all those of the three estates... who are customarily called in similar cases..." [1] Thus the basic question of who should be summoned was decided not at Paris but in the provinces with only the proviso that past procedure be taken into consideration. The magistrate, clergyman, noble, and burgher were left relatively free to cooperate or differ, and royal interference occurred only when one of the parties to a dispute appealed to the king in council.

When those of the three orders who were summoned arrived at the local capital, they were assembled by the *bailli*, seneschal, or lieutenant general to hear the letters read convoking the Estates General and perhaps one or two long-winded

---

1614," *Revue des deux mondes* (June, 1874), 626-650; and *Histoire des États généraux* (Paris, ed. of 1888), V. 243-274; Paul Viollet, "Élections des députés aux États généraux réunis à Tours en 1468 et 1484," *Bibliothèque de l'École des Chartes*, XXVII (1866), 22-58; and Jacques Cadart, *Le Régime électoral des États généraux de 1789 et ses origines (1302-1614)* (Paris, 1952), should also be mentioned. The above studies of the elections were based on a very limited number of documents and only that of Viollet added significantly to the account of Lalourcé and Duval. The material for the present article was drawn from the manuscripts in various depositories at Paris and from about forty of the departmental and thirty of the municipal archives. Departmental archives not visited contained no important material listed in the published inventories that had not been printed. Sources published in the various local periodicals and histories have been used extensively. Complete documentation would be so voluminous that only the principal, primary source for each statement has normally been given and no attempt has been made to furnish references for general comments. It is my intention to publish in book form at a later date an account of the elections in each jurisdiction for which I have been able to find material. At that time full documentation and a complete bibliography will be included.

[1] *Convocation*, II, 49. See also, 24, 30, 34, and 43.

speeches. Then, after the attendance roll was called, the three orders either elected their deputies together or else separated and chose them apart. Voting was usually done by a voice ballot, but occasionally the secret ballot was used, especially in southern France. As might be expected, the local magnates sometimes insisted that the former method be employed in the hope of being better able to control the outcome of the election. In 1651 the pro-Mazarin bishop of Angers cowed the opposition by insisting that voting be done by voice rather than by written ballot. Two years earlier in Languedoc, the diocese of Toulouse complained that the bishop of Rieux had refused to permit voting by ballot in accordance with "the ancient and modern usage of this province." [1]

A plurality rather than a majority of votes was required for election. In 1576 the nobility of the duchy of Nevers gave thirty-five votes to the Sieur de Blanche--fort and thirty-eight to six other candidates, but Blanchefort was declared elected. In 1588 the provost of the merchants received only 139 of the 380 votes cast in the elections of the *prévôté* of Paris, but he was accepted as deputy although one of his nineteen opponents had received 105 votes [2]. No instance has been found where a run-off election was held to ensure the backing of a majority of voters for the chosen deputy. This is one of the few invariable rules that can be established for sixteenth and seventeenth century electoral procedure.

Sometimes a single *cahier* was prepared for the three orders to be taken to the Estates General. Just as often, each order prepared one of its own. This task might be performed by the group as a whole or by a committee, and the committee might or might not report back to the order or the entire eseembly for approval of its work. Occasionally no *cahier* was prepared at all, and this left to the deputy the decision as to the course he should follow once he had arrived at the national assembly.

With this general framework in mind, let us turn first to the problem of who was summoned for each order. The suffrage for the clergy varied widely in France from place to place and from one election to another. Every ecclesiastical corporation might be told to send a proctor and every holder of a benefice told to appear in person, as often happened in the north; or the bishop alone might be convoked, as in Languedoc, where only eight ecclesiastics voted in the large *sénéchaussée* of Carcassonne in 1614 and six in Toulouse in 1576 and in 1649. [3] Even where all or many of the abbots, priors, and deputies of the chapters and monasteries were summoned, the number who were present at the elections was apt to be exceedingly small. Six clergymen attended the assembly in Mâconnais in 1560 and nine in Blois and sixteen in Maine in 1576. [4] Only in those places where the

---

[1] A. Debidour, *La Fronde angevine. Tableau de la vie municipale au XVII siècle* (Paris and Angers, 1877), pp. 176-177. H. L., XIV, 237.
[2] Bibl. comm., Blois, ms. 89, fols. 12-13. *Convocation*, II, 265-266.
[3] *Convocation*, II, 204. Arch. dép., Tarn, C 230. H. L., XIV, 232.
[4] Arch. dép., Saône-et-Loire, C 505, no. 2. Bibl. comm., Blois, Municipal register for October 1, 1576. Th. Cauvin, *États du Maine, députés et sénéchaux de cette province* (Le Mans, 1839), pp. 13-47.

curés of the rural parishes were convoked was there a large attendence for the first estate. These relatively insignificant persons therefore claim our attention.

There is no known instance of the widespread convocation of the curés in any *bailliage* in 1484, but in 1560 and thereafter we can sometimes document their appearance in the elections in the governments of Picardy, the Île-de-France, Normandy and Champagne, though in several places in this northern and eastern tier of France we can be equally certain of their absence, as in the *bailliage* of Amiens in 1560 and 1561. [1] On leaving these four governments, one finds the convocation of the lower clergy less frequent and appearing at a later date. The first traces of the curés taking part in the elections elsewhere were on the border of this region and by 1614 the movement towards the increased representation of the first estate had spread eastward into the fringes of Burgundy to include the *bailliage* of La Montagne and southward into central France, though some places such as the *bailliage* of Blois resisted until the Revolution. [2] During the Fronde the parish clergy were consulted in Agenais, Armagnac, and perhaps other localities in Guyenne, [3] but in Languedoc, Dauphiné, and Provence the prelates were strong enough to prevent any radical departures. [4]

Suffrage among the nobility was more extended than in the other orders. The

---

[1] For the elections of the clergy in Picardy see especially B.N., ms. fr. 3329, fols. 20-47v; ms. fr. 3953, fol. 2; ms. fr. 4812, fols. 8-19v; A. de Hauttefeuille and L. Bénard, *Histoire de Boulogne sur-Mer* (Boulogne-sur-Mer, 1860), I, 303-313, 337-338, 375-383; and Hector de Rosny, *Histoire de Boulonnais* (Amiens, 1871), III, 341-344, 382-383. For the Île-de-France, see *Convocation*, II, 242, 249-258; Arch. dép., Seine-et-Marne, B 130; and Arch. comm., Châlons-sur-Marne, AA 16. For Normandy, see Henri Prentout, *Les États provinciaux de Normandie* (Caen, 1925), II, 50-57. For Champagne, see "Documents inédits tirés des archives de Troyes et relatifs aux États généraux," *Collection de documents inédits rélatifs à la ville de Troyes*, eds. T. Boutiot and A. Babeau (Troyes, 1878), I, 25-198; T. Boutiot, *Histoire de la ville de Troyes et de la Champagne méridionale* (Troyes and Paris, 1873- 1875), III, 462-488, IV, 76-89, 162-163, 199, 218-221, 285-286, 304-307; *Documents inédits sur les États généraux tirés des archives de Vitry-le-François*, ed. Georges Hérelle (Paris, 1879), pp. 1-79 and related documents; B.N. ms. Champagne III, fols. 156-199v; Georges Hérelle, *La Réforme et la ligue en Champagne* (Paris, 1892), II, 86-96; and *Convocation*, II, 172-184.

[2] E. de Lépinois, *Histoire de Chartres*, (Chartres, 1858), II, 269-270. B.N., ms. fr. 26324, fols. 222-224. Ch. Croix, "Documents sur la ligue dans le bailliage de la Montagne: Les élections aux États généraux de 1588," *Annales de Bourgogne*, IX (1937), 308. Bibl. comm., Orléans, ms. 541, fols. 42v-46. Cauvin, pp. 13-47. Arch. comm., Blois, register for Aug.-Nov., 1576, July-Oct., 1614, Jan.-Feb., 1649 and Aug., 1651.

[3] Arch. comm., Agen, CC 150. Barbé, "Chronique," *Bul. du comité d'histoire et d'archéologie de la province écclesiastique d'Auch*, II (1861), 610-611. *Archives historiques de la Corrèze*, ed. G. Clèment-Simon (Paris, 1905), II, 328-337. Arch. dép., Vienne, C 608. Bibl. comm., Poitiers, ms. 304 (26). Abbé L. Lacroix, *Richelieu à Luçon. Sa Jeunesse—son épiscopat* (Paris, 1890), pp. 204-207. A Dupré, *Élections du clergé de Guyenne aux États généraux* (Bordeaux, 1893), pp. 7-11, extract from *La Revue catholique de Bordeaux* (Aug. and Sept., 1893).

[4] P. Gachon, *Les États de Languedoc et l'édict de Béziers, 1632* (Paris, 1887), pp. 1-22, and the documents cited in note 6 for Languedoc. Abbé A. Dussert, "Les États du Dauphiné aux XIVe et XVe siècles," and "Les États du Dauphiné de la guerre de cent ans aux guerres de religion," *Bul. de l'académie Delphinale*, 5th ser., VIII (1914), 292-299, and XIII (1922), pref. 10-18 respectively. Raoul Busquet, "Histoire des institutions," *Les Bouches-du-Rhône. Encyclopédie départementale* (Marseille, 1921), III, 448-544.

usual rule was for all nobles with fiefs to be convoked, including women and minors who sent proctors in the rare instances they chose to exercise this right. From the close of the sixteenth century there was a tendency to include nobles without fiefs in some places. They appeared in Périgord in 1614 and in Brittany at about the same time. No doubt many other localities could be added if our records were more complete. [1]

Languedoc and parts of Guyenne provide a notable exception to the procedure described above. Here the great majority of the nobles with fiefs were excluded from the electoral assemblies. The Wars of Religion and the troubles which followed the death of Henry IV did provide an opportunity for several more nobles to get themselves admitted to the assemblies of the estates of Velay and Foix, while during the course of the sixteenth century the number of those convoked from that order in Quercy increased from twenty-five to twenty-nine. The Fronde saw an effort by the nobles of Languedoc to get more of their number summoned, but the movement failed, and if anything, the magnates who held the twenty-two seats of the second estate in the provincial assembly were more firmly entrenched than ever by the end of our period. [2]

Royal and municipal officials who were nobles of the robe deliberated with the third estate even when they held fiefs. A few exceptions to this rule are known, but we would not be far wrong if we looked on the second estate as being composed of only those who wore the sword. By 1789 this situation had changed and the two types of nobility voted together for the deputies of the second estate, a fact which clearly marks the acceptance of the robe by the old nobility during the course of the century before the Revolution. [3]

Suffrage among the members of the third estate must be considered under two headings: the municipality and the countryside. Voting rights varied widely from town to town. In some places such as Amiens, Lyons, Dijon, Marseilles, Vienne, Agen, Saintes, Limoges, Toulouse, and indeed, in most of the towns in southern France the municipal officials controlled the elections of the deputies. [4] In other

---

[1] L. de Cardenal, "Les dernières réunions des trois ordres de Périgord avant le Révolution," *L'Organisation corporative du moyen âge à la fin de l'ancien régime* (Louvain, 1937), II, 119-120. Arch. dép., Dordogne, C. 14, no. 1; Armand Rebillon, *Les États de Bretagne de 1661 à 1789* (Rennes, 1932), pp. 83-87.

[2] G. Arnaud, *Mémoire sur les États de Foix, 1608-1789* (Toulouse, 1904), pp. 11-13; Étienne Delcambre, *Contribution à l'histoire des États provinciaux. Les États du Velay des origines à 1642* (Saint-Étienne, 1938), pp. 88-96; 143-166, 328-330, 412-447; Arch. dép., Lot, F 95; H.L., XIII, 307-343; XIV, 371-374, 380-382, 384-389.

[3] The mayor and some *échevins* of Poitiers and the mayor of Périgueux made good their respective claims to sit with the nobility of Poitou and Périgord. See Arch. dép., Vienne, C 608. Arch. comm., Poitiers, Carton 7, nos. 178 and 179. Bibl. comm., Poitiers, ms. 304 (26). Henri-François Ouvré, *Essai sur l'histoire de la Ligue à Poitiers* (Poitiers, 1855), pp. 68-71, extract from *Mém. de la société des antiquaires de l'Ouest*, XXI (1854), Arch. dép., Dordogne, C 14, no. 1. Cardenal, p. 120, n. 2.

[4] Arch. comm., Amiens, BB 33 for 1560, AA 16 for 1576; *Recueil des monuments inédits de l'histoire du tiers état (Col. de doc. inédits)*, ed. A. Thierry (Paris, 1853), II, 668-677, 851-866,

localities such as Paris, Villefranche-sur-Saône, Bourges, and Rouen, important bourgeoisie or selected notables from each quarter were also summoned. [1] Parishes in the towns of Melun, Le Mans, Chartres, Orléans, Anjou, Poitiers, Tours and some other places in Touraine sent deputies to the *bailliage* estates. [2] This procedure was almost universal in the Loire Valley region. Still other places as Troyes, Langres, and Blois made definite efforts to secure larger attendance in the elections during the sixteenth century. [3] In general, the towns in the north permitted far wider suffrage than those of the south and even where there were decided restrictions, those who desired to make suggestions to be included in the municipal *cahier* appear to have been free to do so. In Amiens, Beauvais, and Lyons the guilds were specifically requested to submit their complaints. [4] In Paris, Nantes, Lyons, and Blois boxes were set up to receive petitions from anyone. [5] Too often it

972-973, 1016-1017, 1036-1041, III, 5-10, 86-90; Arch. comm., Lyon, BB 81, fols. 316-334v; BB 82, fols. 19v-28v; BB 94, fols. 137-192; BB 121, fols. 165v-192; BB 150, pp. 273-313; AA 146; AA 147. Joseph Garnier, "Documents relatifs à l'histoire des États généraux du royaume, conservés aux archives municipales de Dijon," *Bul. du comité de la langue de l'histoire et des arts de la France*, I (1852-1853), 439-445. P. M. Baudouin, *Histoire du protestantisme et de la ligue en Bourgogne* (Auxerre, 1881), II, 181-183, 458-500. Louis Méry and F. Guindon, *Histoire analytique et chronologique, des actes et des délibérations du corps et du conseil de la municipalité de Marseille* (Marseille, 1847), I, 384-391. Pierre Cavard, *La Réforme et les guerres de religion à Vienne* (Vienne, 1950), pp. 198-202. Arch. comm., Agen, AA 44, AA 45. G. Tholin, *Cahiers des doléances du tiers état du pays d'Agenais aux États généraux* (Paris and Agen, 1885), pp. 11-12, extract form *Revue de l'Agenais, IX-XII.* Baron Eschasseriaux, *Études, documents et extraicts relatifs à la ville de Saintes* (Saintes, 1876), pp. 416-420. *Registres consulaires de la ville de Limoges* (Limoges, 1869), ed. Emile Ruben, II, 204, 220-222. *Inventaire sommaire des archives communales antérieures à 1790, ville de Toulouse* (Toulouse, 1891), ed. E. Roschach, I, 520, 527, 303-304, 333-334. G. de la Faille, *Annales de la ville de Toulouse* (Toulouse, 1701), II, 345, 409, 466-467. *Procès-verbaux des États généraux de* 1593 (*Col. de doc. inédits*) ed. A. Bernard, (Paris, 1842), pp. 796-797.

[1] *Registres des délibérations du bureau de la ville de Paris*, eds. Bonnardot, Tuetey, Guérin, and others, (Paris, 1883), V, 67-80, 84-87, 91-96, VIII, 9-21, X, 119-124, 129-131, 327-331, XVI, 28-98. *Registres consulaires de la ville de Villefranche*, eds. A. Besançon and E. Longin, (Villefranche-sur-Saône, 1912-1919), II, 236-237, 483-387, III, 44-45, IV, 311-313. Arch. comm., Rouen, A 19, fols. 415v-431v; A 20, fols. 382-385; 429v-430, 475v-478v, A 22, fols. 399v-411.

[2] Arch. dép., Seine-et-Marne, B 130. Cauvin, pp. 13-47. Lépinois, II, 269-270, 377-378. Bibl. comm., Orléans, ms. 541 (427), fols. 65-69. Jacques Soyer, "Les Députés du tiers représentant la ville et le bailliage d'Orléans aux États généraux de Blois en 1588," *Bul. de la société archéologique et historique de l'Orléanais*, XV (1908-1910), 437. Arch. comm., Anjou, BB 61, fols. 48-57. Albert Meynier, *Cahiers des gens du tiers estat du pays et duché d'Anjou en 1614* (Angers, 1905). Arch. dép., Vienne, C 608. Bibl. comm., Poitiers, ms. 304 (26). *Convocation*, II, 55-57, 81-83, 90-91, 99-102, 121-123. B.N., ms. n.a. fr. 9752, fols. 24-79v.

[3] *Convocation*, II, 67-68. Th. Pistollet de Saint-Ferjeux, "Langres pendant la ligue," *Mémoires de la société historique et archéologique de Langres*, II (1861-1877), 106. Arch. comm., Blois, register of 28 Aug. 1576.

[4] Thierry, II, 670-671, 851-852. *Inventaire sommaire des archives communales antérieures à 1790, ville de Beauvais* (Beauvais, 1887), p. 6, ed. by Renaud Rose. "Remonstrances, plaintes et doléances des habitans de Beauvais pour l'assemblée des estats de Blois, 1576," *Mém. de la société académique d'archéologie, sciences et arts du département de l'Oise*, I (1847-1851), 264-277. Arch. comm., Lyon, BB 81, fols. 316v-323, BB 82, fols. 19v-24; BB 94, fols. 147-149, 169v-170v; BB 150, pp. 275-278.

[5] Arch. dép., Ille-et-Villaine, C 2655, pp. 81, 122. Arch. dép., Lyon, BB 150, pp. 275-278,

was the oligarchy who decided which of these suggestions would find their way into the *cahier* and which would be forgotten, but at least an opportunity for self-expression was given.

Contrary to the slight increase in suffrage among the clergy and nobility, the number of those convoked to the electoral assemblies of the towns tended with some exceptions to decrease. The sixteenth century saw the bourgeois oligarchy slowly strengthen its hold over many municipalities and assume more and more the right of selecting the deputies to the Estates General. The reforms of Henry IV did little to change this situation, as he was more interested in reducing the number of local officials and strengthening the position of the representatives of the crown to ensure order than in bringing about a return to the larger more popular assemblies of an earlier day.

We have completed our summary of the activities in the municipalities and must now turn our attention to the elections in the rural areas. As early as the fourteenth century there was mention of the convocation of the *plat pays* in Normandy,[1] but it is doubtful if the term *plat pays* should be interpreted to include more than the small unfortified towns that did not have a charter of privileges. No absolutely certain evidence has been found of a large number of peasants being consulted in any jurisdiction in the Middle Ages or in the Estates General of 1484. In this year the typical *bailliage* assembly was composed for the third estate of the deputies from a few of the larger towns of the *bailliage*. Only four municipalities sent representatives to the electoral assemblies of Senlis and of Touraine and six to that of Amiens.[2]

By 1560 the rural parishes were included in Boulonnais, the *prévôté* of Paris, and probably in some or all of the preparatory elections in Normandy, the *bailliages* of Vermandois and Troyes, and the *plat pays* of Lyons. The villages were summoned to at least one preparatory election in Vitry-le-François in 1561.[3] In the election of 1576 the *bailliages* and governments of Montdidier, Amiens, Sens, and Chartres may be added to the places that permitted the peasants some voice.[4] By the Fronde

---

301. Arch. comm., Blois register for 29 Aug. 1576. The *cahiers* deposited in the box at Paris may be found at A.N., K. 675.

[1] Marcel Badout, "La Représentation du tiers-état aux États provinciaux de Normandie," *Mém. de l'académie nationale des sciences, arts et belles-lettres de Caen*, N.S. V (1929), 4-5.

[2] To say that peasants were not consulted in large numbers does not mean that only towns with charters were summoned. In 1308, for example, some non-chartered communities with fairs and market places participated in the elections. See *Documents relatifs aux États généraux réunis sous Philippe le Bel (Col. de doc. inédits)* ed. G. Picot, (Paris, 1901), introduction, p. 54. Viollet, pp. 31-58. Thierry, II, 422-423.

[3] Hauttefeuille and Bénard, I, 305. Rosny, III, 341-344. *Convocation*, II, 243-244. Prentout, II, 63-78. A Combier, *Étude sur le bailliage de Vermandois* (Paris and Lyon, 1874), pp. 86-88, 144-162. Boutiot and Babeau, 21-90. Boutiot, III, 462-471. Maurice Pallasse, *La Sénéchaussée et siège présidial de Lyon pendant les Guerres de Religion* (Lyon, 1943), pp. 194-213. Henri Jadart, *Les Remonstrances des habitants de Rethel et du bailliage de Vitry-le-François aux États généraux de Blois en 1588* (Paris, 1905), pp. 6-8, extract from *La Revue historique Ardennaise*, XII (1905).

[4] B.N., ms. fr. 3329, fols. 20-47v. Thierry, II, 852. Jolivet, "Recherches sur l'assemblée

the electoral jurisdictions of Ponthieu, Melun, Nemours, Perche, Orléans, Gien, Loudun, Poitou, La Rochelle, La Montagne, Auxerre, Basse-Marche, and Bas-Limousin may be joined to the list. [1] For many other places no precise documentation survives, and this fact prevents the list from being much larger.

One is struck by the similarity between the jurisdictions in which the peasants were consulted and those in which the curés were called. The parish priest and the peasants in his spiritual charge were convoked in most localities in the governments of Picardy, Champagne, Normandy, and the Île-de-France by the last of the sixteenth century. The practice of consulting the rural population was also followed in Burgundy in the *bailliages* of La Montagne and Auxerre, and in much of Orléanais. Further south, the convocation of the peasantry was rare, and one may say with assurance that they were consulted in a majority of *bailliages* only in the goverments of Picardy, Île-de-France, Champagne, Normandy, and Orléans.

There are several possible explanations for the increase in suffrage during the sixteenth and seventeenth centuries. It is likely, though no precise documentation is possible, that the Roman law principle of *quod omnes tangit, debet ab omnibus approbari* had some influence. This doctrine of "what touches all should be approved by all" was by no means taken literally as a justification for universal suffrage during the medieval period, for the practice was to emphasize the quality more than the quantity of those consulted, a fact which is clearly expressed in the medieval concept of the *maior et sanior pars*. This concept was specifically employed on numerous occasions in France during the era in which we are concerned in its French form of *le plus grande et sayne partie* to describe the number who attended the assembly of a town or the number of towns that sent proctors to the *bailliage* estates. Where further information is available we find in such instances that only a majority of the more important bourgeois were present, or only the more important towns were represented. [2]

Perhaps as a result of an increased study of Roman law by many royal officials, a more literal interpretation of *quod omnes tangit* came into use in some quarters

des habitants de Tonnerre," *Bul. de la société des sciences historiques et naturelles de l'Yonne*, XXX (1876), 217-247. B.N., ms. fr. 26,324.

[1] Ernest Prarond, *La Ligue à Abbeville, 1576-1594*, (Paris, 1868), II, 13-14. Arch. dép., Seine-et-Marne, B 130. *Inventaire sommaire des archives départementales antérieures à 1790, Seine-et-Marne*, ed. by C. Le Maire, IV, 26. Louis Duval, "L'Administration de la justice, la tenue des états provinciaux et les attributions du bailli dans le comté du Perche pendant les deux derniers siècles," *Bul. de la société historique et archéologique de l'Orne*, XI (1892), 100-113. Bibl. comm., Orléans, ms. 541 (427), fols. 13-30, 37v-40, 94v-98, 101-102v. B.N., ms. fr. 18,186, fols. 35v-36. M. du Moustier de la Fond, *Essais sur l'histoire de la ville de Loudun* (Poitiers, 1778), pp. 101-102. Lacroix, pp. 205-207. Charles Dagibeaud, ed. "Diaire de Jacques Merlin," *Archives historiques de la Saintonge et d'Aunis*, V (1878), 237-240. B.N. ms. fr. 18,187, fols, 135v-137. Croix, pp. 307-312. *Convocation*, II, 68-69. Raoul Mortier, *La Sénéchaussée de la basse-Marche* (Paris, 1912), p. 82. Clément-Simon, II, 343-353.

[2] C. H. McIlwain, *The Growth of Political Thought in the West* (New York, 1932), pp. 299ff. Gaines Post, "A Romano-Canonical Maxim, 'quod omnes tangit' in Bracton," *Traditio*, IV (1946); and "Plena Potestas and Consent in Medieval Assemblies," *Traditio*, III (1943).

about the middle of the sixteenth century, as is evidenced by the *bailliage* assemblies to revise and redact the customary law. During the medieval period the peasants had not been consulted at such times, though certainly they were deeply affected, but in 1539 the rural parishes were summoned to participate in the redaction of the customary law of Clermont-en-Beauvaisis, and after 1550 the idea that they should be convoked became almost universally accepted. Five years later Christophe de Thou of the *Parlement* of Paris was given the mission of presiding over such *bailliage* assemblies, and he continued this work until his death in 1582, by which time he had held many assemblies in northern and a few in central France in which the proctors of the peasants were included. The convocation of the rural parishes to the meetings to revise customary law not only reflected the ever present principle of *quod omnes tangit*, but also provided the idea, if not the necessary precedent, of their presence in the electoral assemblies for the Estates General. It should be noted that southern France was the region of written law. There, no assemblies to revise or redact the customs were necessary, and there the peasantry was almost universally excluded from participating in the elections. [1]

Perhaps the best example of what might be termed the conflict between the older and newer conceptions of *quod omnes tangit* is provided by the elections of the clergy in Châlons-sur-Marne in 1651. The lieutenant general who was the senior official present in the *bailliage* ordered the parish clergy to attend, and they came in such numbers that they overwhelmed the deputies of the ecclesiastical corporations. The latter protested and eventually boycotted the assembly, with the result that they were fined by the lieutenant-general. The corporations appealed to the *Parlement* of Paris to have the fine remitted and incidentally to order that in the future curés not be summoned. Before *Parlement*, one side argued that it was customary to convoke the curés and others said it was not. Of more significance was the stand taken by canons of the cathedral chapter, who were the leading defenders of the conservative position, that they were the principal priests of the jurisdiction and should with the rural deans speak for the first estate. The curés were merely "cadets", and to give each of them a vote equal to that of the proctor of the cathedral chapter was manifestly contrary to reason. When it came to the turn of a substitute for the *procureur général* of the king to speak, he pointed out quite correctly that there was no regular, uniform electoral procedure for France, but that it varied from place to place and for that matter from time to time in the same place depending on the circumstances. However, since the curés' interests were involved in the elections to the Estates General, it would be unjust to exclude them while permitting the seigneurs and deputies of the parishes to participate. On his recommendation the case was dismissed and the fine allowed. [2]

---

[1] J. R. Major, *Estates General of 1560* (Princeton, 1951), pp. 70-72.
[2] Arch. comm., Châlons-sur-Marne, AA 16. M. Hanra, "Notes relatives à l'histoire locale. Élection de députés aux États généraux de 1651," *Mém. de la société d'agriculture, commerce, sciences et arts du département de la Marne*, 2nd. ser. VIII (1904-1905), 255-268.

In addition to the newer interpretation of *qood omnes tangit*, the extension of suffrage for the third estate may be attributed to a bitter rivalry that existed between the municipal and local crown officials. The former were proud patricians who had long controlled the governments of the towns and the third estate of the *bailliage*. The latter were interlopers who appeared in large numbers in the course of the sixteenth century and sought to win control of the *bailliage* estates and even the municipalities themselves. The resulting struggle had powerful repercussions in the electoral history of France and is among the most neglected aspects of French social history.

Although the *bailli* was the senior local crown official, he was frequently absent from his jurisdiction during the sixteenth century, at which times it fell to the lieutenant-general to act in his stead. This officer, unlike his superior, was only a noble of the robe, and, supported by a host of subordinates, he was willing to go to extreme lengths to win political power and local prestige. As he determined, in the absence of the *bailli*, who should be summoned to the *bailliage* assemblies, he was in a position to add the smaller towns and the villages to the list of communities convoked if he felt that it would help him win support in his struggle with the municipal oligarchies of the larger localities. The inhabitants of these tiny communities were usually content to elect minor public functionaries or notaries, and these officials found it expedient to vote as their superiors directed. The peasant was indifferent to the merits of the struggle for power while the petty bourgeoisie of the small towns and *bourgades* had little reason to love the patricians of the nearby city. When they were elected to go to the *bailliage* capital, they were willing, more often than not, to fall into line.

One of the most flagrant examples of electoral manipulation occurred at Amiens in 1576. The *bailli* convoked the villages for the first time to take part in elections to the Estates General, though some sort of precedent had been established by the appearance of their proctors when the customs had been revised in 1567. If we can believe the charges of the municipal officials, twelve to fifteen interested individuals went from village to village and got themselves named as their deputies in informal or illegal assemblies in which they were given no instructions. When the *bailliage* estates met these persons were permitted to cast one vote for each village, while the deputy of the large and important town of Amiens was also allowed only one vote. It is not difficult to see who masterminded this electoral fraud when we note that the two deputies chosen to represent the third estate were both royal officials and that the *cahier* they took to the Estates General contained four articles designed to give them and their associates seats in the council of the town. The municipal officials hurriedly dispatched their own representatives to Blois, and they succeeded in presenting their remonstrances to the Estates General, though they were not given seats. In the future the crown ordered that the *prévôtés* of the *bailliage* be assembled and that there deputies be named to the *bailliage* estates. Each *prévôté*, rather than every village, was to have a vote along with

Amiens. Thus the king in council acted to protect the municipal privileges from its own officials.[1]

The lieutenant general of Anjou found it expedient to add the villages to those convoked in his jurisdiction in 1651. The traditional procedure called for the third estate to be composed of the seventeen magistrates of Angers, two deputies from each of sixteen parishes of the town, and one deputy from each of twenty other communities of the *sénéchaussée*. If this practice were followed, the lieutenant general and his fellow royal officials would be certain of defeat. He therefore ordered from eighty to a hundred outlying parishes to send proctors and gave them two votes each. By one means or another he managed to get the bulk of the new suffragists on his side. The mayor of Angers protested strongly against this innovation which greatly weakened the position of the town, and demanded that the traditional usage be followed. The rural parish deputies, on the other hand, argued that they made up the greater part of the province and should therefore have a heavy voice. The upshot of the dispute was a compromise in which both the mayor and the lieutenant general were named deputies and the petty bourgeois and peasants were accepted as participants in the assemblies of the third estate.[2]

The activities of the crown officials were a factor in leading to an extension in the number of localities convoked in Basse-Auvergne. There, thirteen privileged towns led by Clermont had traditionally spoken for the third estate of the province but the royal officials of the *sénéchaussée* who were located at Riom had long been jealous of this and other privileges. When an error was made at Paris and the letter ordering the elections for the Estates General at Blois in 1576 was sent to them, instead of to the leaders of the provincial estates at Clermont as was customary, the royal officials saw their opportunity and quickly ordered the three estates to meet at their seat. Perhaps realizing that their summons would be obeyed by few, if any, of those who usually composed such meetings, the officials at Riom added the *plat pays* to the list of those convoked. Some three to four hundred small towns and bourgades sent proctors to Riom, where deputies were named to go to Blois. Meanwhile, the *échevins* of Clermont had summoned representatives from the other twelve privileged municipalities and they too had elected deputies to the Estates General. The rival delegations appealed to the king, who ruled against his own officials in favor of the thirteen towns. In the future he did direct that some additional communities be consulted, but it was in 1588, when the quarrel between Clermont and Riom was renewed, before the king in council specifically ordered that the number of localities convoked be increased to nineteen. The crown had again acted to protect the privileged from a wholesale influx of the lesser

---

[1] Arch. comm., Amiens, AA 16, fols. 170v-171. Thierry, II, 851-866.

[2] A. Lemarchand, "Les Doléances des Angevins en 1651, mémoires inédits," *Revue de l'Anjou*, X (1885), 173-185. A. Debidour, *La Fronde Angevine* (Paris, 1877), pp. 170-181.

communities, but the activities of the local royal officials had nevertheless led to some increase in representation. [1]

There may well have been many other instances similar to those described above in which the local crown officials called on the unfranchised communities for support against the municipal oligarchies. In 1588 the proctors of the villages of the *bailliage* of La Montagne were summoned in usually conservative Burgundy and voted for the lieutenant general notwithstanding the opposition of the mayor and *échevins* of Châtillon-sur-Seine, the principal town of the jurisdiction. The municipal oligarchy was not content to accept the defeat given them and appealed to the *Parlement* at Dijon and to the Burgundian Estates General to reverse the election on the grounds that a royal official would not press the petitions they intended to make against the government of the king. Indeed, the lieutenant general was the son of the advocate of the king, the brother-in-law of the *lieutenant particulier* and of the clerk of the *bailliage*, and the uncle of the *procureur* of the king. Small wonder the mayor and *échevins* saw little chance, with him as deputy, of making known at Blois their complaints against the local administration. When the Burgundian *Parlement* and Estates General failed to annul the election, the magistrates of Châtillon dispatched one of the *échevins* to Blois, where he was given a seat along with the lieutenant general. [2]

The practice of Amiens and Châtillon of sending deputies direct to the national assembly when defeated in the *bailliage* elections by the royal officials was followed by many other towns. Even if we limit ourselves to the Estates General of 1576, 1588, and 1614, we can document that twenty-three towns on one or more occasions chose deputies who were admitted to the chambers of the third estate [3]. Still other towns like Amiens tried time and again for a seat without success. Not all these localities sought direct representation in the national assembly because of the activities of the local royal officials, but this was the most frequent motive found among the surviving documents. The fact that so many of their deputies were seated even though only two or three towns received direct summons from the king indicates clearly the lengths to which the royal council was willing to go to protect the privileged from its officials. Certainly the king did not support the activities of those who sought to increase the suffrage to secure their own ends at the expense

---

[1] M. Bergier, *Recherches historiques sur les États généraux et plus particulièrement, sur l'origine, l'organisation et la durée des anciens États provinciaux d'Auvergne* (Clermont-Ferrand, 1788) contains the bulk of the documents on the elections. B.N., ms. fr. 16,236, fol. 296. B.N. ms. fr. 16, 631, pp. 627-628. See also Gilbert Rouchon, "Le tiers États aux États provinciaux de Basse-Auvergne aux XVIe et XVIIe siècles," *Bul. philologique et historique du comité des travaux historiques et scientifiques,* (1930-1931), 165-189; and André Imberdis, *Histoire des Guerres religieuses en Auvergne pendant les XVIe et XVIIe siècles* (Riom, 1846), pp. 168-170.

[2] Croix, pp. 307-312. Gustave Laperouse, *L'Histoire de Châtillon* (Châtillon-sur-Seine, 1837), pp. 337-340.

[3] They are Paris, Beauvais, Langres, Lyons, Villefranche, Étampes, Orléans, Vendôme, Amboise, La Rochelle, Caen, Rouen, Châtillon-sur-Seine, Toulouse, Saintes, Bordeaux, Limoges, Nantes, Morlaix, Hybeix, Nortais, Marseilles, and Arles.

ELECTORAL PROCEDURE FOR FRANCE AND ITS IMPLICATIONS 143

of the upper classes. Here one finds no concept of divide and rule, but rather a strong determination to preserve the existing order in society. [1]

It is worthy of note that where their position can be ascertained, the nobility supported the bourgeoisie against the pretensions of the local crown officials. While the Estates General of 1576 was in session, several deputies of the nobility from Picardy brought the representatives of the town of Amiens into contact with the king when the municipality was in an unfortunate position as a result of the unfair electoral practices of the *bailliage* officials. Again, it was the nobility who thwarted the efforts of the *lieutenant criminel* of the *sénéchaussée* of Ponthieu to gain precedence over the mayor of Abbeville in the elections of 1588. That same year the Estates General of Burgundy, in answer to complaints like those of Châtillon-sur-Seine described above, ordered that in the future no royal official be named deputy by any of the *bailliages* of the province to the national assembly. Thus the other estates closed ranks with the bourgeoisie to save them from the machinations of the local royal officials, who alone were seeking to upset the long established privileges of the elite of French society. [2]

If, then, the activities of the local royal officials have to be accounted a major factor in the expansion of suffrage, it must not be denied that there was a demand on the part of the inhabitants of some of the excluded smaller towns and *bourgades* for representation in the electoral assemblies to the Estates General and in the regional estates that became particularly strong duting the Wars of Religion. The number of towns convoked in Forez was increased from thirteen to nineteen; in Berry the number went from six in 1561 to thirty-one in 1614; in the estates of Foix, from twenty-eight in 1520 to forty-five in 1693. A similar story could be told of Agenais and Périgord. The lesser towns of central and southern France, angered at heavy taxation, the sufferings of civil war, and, all too often, the overbearing selfish attitude of the larger towns, were determined to be included in the regional estates and in the electoral assemblies. Sometimes the smaller towns of this region managed to persuade the peasants to give them support in their search for recognition, but by and large the rural population remained indifferent. In the north where the small towns were already represented, they had no need to solicit the aid of the peasants, and the latter were content to remain aloof unless summoned by the local crown officials. [3]

---

[1] The much neglected registers of the *Conseil d'État* contain numerous examples of the crown supporting the privileged against its own local officials. See especially B.N. ms. fr. 16, 236 for the elections of 1588 and B.N. ms. fr. 18,187 and 18,188 for the elections of 1614.
[2] Thierry, II, 862-863; IV, 455-457. Arch. dép., Côte-d'Or, C 3069, fol. 247.
[3] J. B. Gallery, *Les États de Forez et les treize villes* (Saint-Etienne, 1914). Rouchon, pp. 165-189. Vicomte de Brimont, *Le XVIe siècle et les guerres de la réforme en Berry* (Paris, 1905), I, 228-231. Louis Raynal, *Histoire du Berry* (Bourges, 1847), IV, 21-26. *Recueil de pièces originales et authentiques concernant la tenue des États généraux*, eds. Lalourcé and Duval (Paris, 1789), IX, 1-2. These documents will hereafter be cited as *Pièces*. Arnaud, pp. 24-27. Arch. comm., Agen, AA 44, no. 3; AA 45; and CC 150. Louis de Cardenal, "Les États de Périgord sous Henri IV," *L'Organisation corporative du Moyen Age à la fin de l'Ancien Régime* (Louvain, 1939), III, 163-181.

Thus far we have dealt with those who attended and those who sought to attend the electoral assemblies to the Estates General; but what of those who did not want to participate? Their number was by no means insignificant and figures could be cited almost indefinitely to prove that only a minority of those who could vote went to the *bailliage* assemblies. One noble and the proxy of another represented their order in Touraine in 1484, three nobles attended in Berry in 1561, a dozen in Rouen in 1588, ten in Bordeaux in 1560, and twelve out of the twenty-seven summoned in La Montagne in 1588. The record of the upper clergy was a little better, but in those jurisdictions where they were convoked, a majority of the curés were usually absent. No less than 53 missed the electoral assembly in La Montagne in 1588. [1] Towns, when summoned, were likely to comply with the call, but probably in the places with a wide suffrage only a minority of those who could attend the municipal assemblies did so. At Orléans in 1588, 15 out of 17 *châtellenies* were represented, in Maine in 1576, 17 out of 27 communities obeyed the summons, but in the same year at Blois only 8 out of 20 did so. For Bas-Limousin in 1588 figures for the three orders reveal that 97 were present and 184 absent for the clergy, 90 nobles attended or sent proctors, 75 did not, 73 communities were represented, 93 were listed as failing to honor the summons. [2] When there was rivalry between several candidates, the turnout was sometimes much larger. Over four hundred nobles were reported to have attended the estates of Anjou in 1588, but in general one is rather surprised at the numbers who absented themselves during the Wars of Religion. The seventeenth century saw an increased interest in the elections which was marked by ever growing attendance in such provincial estates as that of Brittany. The *bailliage* elections in Rouen, which had been insignificant affairs during the Wars of Religion were so well attended in 1614 that not everyone could get into the hall reserved for the meeting. In the Fronde over two hundred ecclesiastics and 174 nobles were present, a far cry from the dozen who had deigned to vote for the latter order in 1588. Two hundred and eight nobles attended in Basse-Auvergne in 1651. [3]

The unspectacular figures of attendance, coupled with the demand for a voice by some of those who were excluded, brings us to a conclusion that we might well have divined in the beginning. There were many, even more than today, who were indifferent and did not avail themselves of the right to vote when they had it. Others were deeply interested in political affairs and would go to considerable trouble to vote and almost any length to obtain elected office. It depended on the

[1] Major, 48-49. Raynal, IV, 21-26. Arch. comm., Rouen, AA 20, fols. 382-385. *Archives hist. ... de la Gironde*, VIII (1866), 537-539. Croix, pp. 307-312.

[2] Bibl. comm., Orléans, ms. 541 (427), fols. 65-69. Soyer, pp. 437-438. Cauvin, pp. 13-47. Bibl. comm., Blois, register for Oct. 1. 1576. *Archives historiques de la Corrèze*, ed. G. Clément-Simon (Paris, 1905), II, 328-353.

[3] Arch. comm., Rouen, A 22, fols. 399v-411, 422v-433. *Formes observées en 1649 et pendant les années suivantes pour l'élection et la députation de certains citoyens du bailliage de Rouen aux États généraux de Royaume* (n.p., n.d.). See Bergier for documents on Auvergne.

VI

ELECTORAL PROCEDURE FOR FRANCE AND ITS IMPLICATIONS

individual, and no rule can be established beyond that the more important a person happened to be, the more apt he was to be interested.

Thus far we have discussed those who voted and those who did not, and now we must direct our attention to the relationship between the members of the three estates who actually attended the electoral assemblies. Did they elect and instruct their deputies together or did they vote apart? In either case, were they friendly and cooperative, or was there a class struggle that did much to undermine the position of the deputies when they stood before the crown?

In spite of a paucity of documents one can say with reasonable assurance that in 1484 in a majority of jurisdictions the three orders named their deputies together. An unchallenged statement was made to this effect in a heated debate during the Estates General, and studies on the individual provincial estates of the fifteenth century reveal that the three orders usually acted in a single chamber when they assembled for other purposes. [1]

Such evidence as we have suggests that in 1560 all, or at least a large majority, of the deputies from the governments of Brittany, Dauphiné, Provence, Champagne, Languedoc, Normandy, and Guyenne were elected by the three orders voting by head. For Picardy we can only say that the estates voted together in Boulonnais and separately in Amiens. Equally inconclusive evidence indicates that in the Île-de-France, Orléanais, Lyonnais, and Burgundy the three orders acted apart in a majority of the jurisdictions. By 1614 Picardy, Champagne, and Guyenne must be added to the list. Even Provence showed a tendency to slip into this category since only part of the deputation elected by her estates was chosen by a single order, but as in Marseilles and probably Arles voting continued to be in common, the region should be classified as being about evenly divided. [2]

Voting in the Estates General was done by governments after 1484, so that this change meant that whereas is 1560 seven ballots were cast by deputies representing the three orders, four by those standing for a single order and one in which they were about evenly divided, in 1614 the votes of only four governments were cast in the name of the three estates, while seven were voted by those chosen by a single estate and the one remaining government was again divided.

Was this change from a preponderance of the voting strength in the Estates General standing for the three estates of a locality to a preponderance representing local class interests brought about by a royal policy of divide and rule, by growing

---

[1] P. Viollet, "Élection des députés aux États généraux réunis à Tours en 1468," *Bibl. de l'École des Chartes*, XXVII (1860), 22-58.

[2] It is obviously impossible in an article to cite the sources for the elections in each *bailliage* in every government for every meeting of the Estates General. At this point I can only refer to the brief and inadequate discussion of the problem in my *Estates General of 1560*, pp. 42-48, 71-73. The failure of the three estates of Provence to elect all their deputies together in 1614 was caused by a delay in the assembling of the first two orders brought about by the death of the brother of the governor. Arch. dép., Bouches-du-Rhône, C. 10, fols. 376-400v; C 107, fols. 549-555. *Pièces*, VIII, 26.

social cleavage, or did it result from other causes? A review of the elections reveals that in Vitry-le-François and Troyes the three estates voted together in 1560, but that soon thereafter the orders began to act separately in both places. In each instance this change was marked by the introduction of a large number of villages to the *bailliage* assemblies.[1] To have continued to vote together would have exposed the nobility to being everwhelmed by the peasants of their own manors and they could have regarded such a possibility with little pleasure. Further circumstantial evidence is offered by our inability to find a single instance in the three governments of Champagne, Picardy, and Île-de-France or in the border regions in Burgundy and Orléanais, where in 1614 the villages definitely sent deputies to the *bailliage* assemblies that the three orders still voted together. The noble and the deputy of his village might vote together occasionally, as in the Boulonnais, but in the long run such practices tended to die, for though there is little evidence of a conscious class struggle during the sixteenth century, the age was far from equalitarian. In Normandy alone did the three orders continue to vote together when the peasants were consulted, but here there was a relatively complete system of preparatory elections, so that only a deputy or two appeared at the *bailliage* assembly from each viscounty to stand for the smaller towns and villages. The nobles who used preparatory assemblies much less frequently were in little danger of being overrun by so few. Their only problem was to attend in large enough numbers to outvote the delegations from such cities as Rouen.[2]

The *bailliage* of Alençon provides us with a further example of the difficulties of voting by head when large masses from the third estate were admitted. Here during the Fronde the nobles turned out in large numbers, and in preparatory assemblies elected deputies to go to the *bailliage* estates. For reasons not too difficult to imagine, the lieutenant general permitted the inhabitants of Alençon including artisans, to enter the assembly hall and vote individually, thereby completely overwhelming the handful of proctors of the second estate. The two candiates who were desired by the nobility of all the subordinate juridsictions were defeated and the lieutenant general was chosen. The king's council sustained the nobility and ordered that in the future the third estate should not be allowed to vote with the nobility. This is the only known instance in which the crown encouraged a separation of orders in the elections, and this step was undertaken to protect the privileged from the royal officials even though the deputies of the nobility were far less likely than the lieutenant general to have proved supporters of the government if the Estates General had been held.[3] One reason, then, for the separation of the estates in northern France was the desire of the first two orders

---

[1] Hérelle, *Documents... de Vitry-le-François*, 9-13, 86. Jadart, pp. 6-8. Boutiot and Babeau, pp. 21-90. Boutiot, III, 462-488. Mayer, XII, 327-334.
[2] Hauttefeuille and Bénard, I, 303-313, 337-338, 375-383. Rosny, III, 341-344, 382-383, 442-445. Prentout, II, 44-96.
[3] Odolant Desmos, *Mémoires historiques sur la ville d'Alençon* (Alençon, 1787) pp. 426-427.

VI

ELECTORAL PROCEDURE FOR FRANCE AND ITS IMPLICATIONS

to avoid being overpowered by the ever growing quantity of voters from the third estate. Where the number who attended the *bailliage* assemblies for this order was small, the three estates usually continued to vote together. Even where the peasants were convoked the clergy and nobility often retained the practice of acting in the same chamber as in Sens and Ponthieu in 1614.[1]

The above explanation is eminently satisfactory for northern France and for Haut- and Bas-Limousin where we meet with the separation of the orders and the presence of the proctors of the villages during the sixteenth century, but what of the rest of Guyenne and Burgundy where the estates also tended to separate, but where the peasant was rarely consulted? In the former, it seems to have become customary to convoke only the third estate during the sixteenth century to the meetings of the provincial Estates General which were concerned primarily with taxation.[2] This meant that in the local assemblies the third estate became accustomed to meeting and voting alone to chose the deputies to that body. Probably there was a tendency for them to continue this practice when the other orders were summoned. Even so, voting by order rather than by head was by no means as completely accepted in Guyenne as in the north. As late as 1614 all or part of the delegations of Comminges, Bigorre, Rouergue, Quercy, and perhaps Armagnac were elected by the orders together.[3]

Another situation that may have had some influence in bringing about the separation of orders grew out of the anti-clerical attitude of the secular estates in 1561. The king had requested that the three estates offer advice on how he ought to solve his financial difficulties and the lay orders seized this opportunity to recommend that part of the goods of the clergy be confiscated. An unusual electoral procedure was followed on this occasion. The *bailliage* estates chose deputies to attend assemblies of their government or province where in turn deputies were chosen to attend the Estates General. It was in these governmental assemblies that one can document the unfriendly attitude of the lay orders. In Languedoc and Champagne where the three estates had usually deliberated together the clergy found itself ostracized while the secular estates continued to act as one.[4] Perhaps some *bailliage* assemblies were divided for the same reason, and once the new procedure was accepted, it was difficult to change.

[1] *Convocation*, II, 61-62. Thierry, IV, 497-498.

[2] Historians have generally implied that the estates of Guyenne ceased to exist after the Hundred Years War, but judging by material found in the municipal archives of the region and above all in the archives of the subordinate estates of Comminges which have recently been transferred from Muret to the Archives of Haute-Garonne, we may suggest that the institution enjoyed a thriving existence during the 16th century. There is a crying need for a study of this least known of all the large regional assemblies of the old régime.

[3] *Pièces*, V, 18b, 20b. B.N., ms. Clairambault, 364, fols. 277-279. Arch. dép. Lot, F 96. M. A. Branet, "Les États d'Armagnac en 1631-1632," *Bul. de la société archéologique, historique, littéraire et scientifique du Gers*, XIV (1913), 168-183, 214-229, reveals that the secular estates of Armagnac were still deliberating together in the years indicated.

[4] Arch. dép., Haute-Garonne, C 2280, fols. 460-476. Boutiot and Babeau, I, 87-90. Boutiot, III, 462-488. A. Prévost, *Le Diocèse de Troyes* (Dijon, 1924), II, 344-345. Mayer, XII, 327-334.

Still another possible factor that admits of little proof is the example of the three estates deliberating apart in the Estates General in 1560 and thereafter. Certainly there must have been difficulties involved for a deputy, chosen to represent three orders and armed with the *cahier* of their complaints, when he found himself thrown into a national assembly in which his fellow deputies, chosen by the same constituents, deliberated elsewhere, and as early as 1560 this specific problem troubled the bishop of Vence. For this reason the ecclesiastical deputies of Guyenne, Auch, and Brittany found it advisable to insist that each of the deputies from their order consult the representatives from the other estates of their provinces so as "to be better instructed." [1]

Some of the above factors might serve to explain the failure of the three orders in Burgundy to name deputies to the Estates General together after 1484. In that year the Burgundian Estates General had won special permission to elect deputies rather than have *bailliage* elections, and the three orders had voted together. [2] In 1560 the same issue was raised, but this time the crown was able to stick to its request for *bailliage* elections. Almost nothing is known of the procedure used by the *bailliages*, but judging by the almost universal practice of voting separately which was in evidence in 1576, we may presume that in most instances the orders acted apart. It is certain that they had done so in 1561 when the Burgundian Estates General, along with the other provincial estates, had named deputies to the national assembly. [3] In 1576 and 1588 the provincial leaders sought to have deputies chosen by the three estates of Burgundy to represent "the body of the three estates," but they were successful only in the former year. [4] In the latter, the Burgundian Estates General appears to have been content to give approval to the persons elected and the *cahiers* prepared by the individual orders in each *bailliage*. Thus a semblance of provincial and class unity was preserved throughout the sixteenth century, but the major responsibility rested with the different orders in each *bailliage*. The most satisfactory hypothesis for explaining the change that took place after 1484 is that the abandonment of elections by province threw on the *bailliages*, which had no traditional estates, the necessity of naming deputies and that these jurisdictions by 1576 tended to follow the system of the separation of orders used in the national assembly. The failure of the three orders to act jointly in 1561 in the provincial estates was probably facilitated by the request of the king that each order decide how it could help the financial position of the king, a request that, as we have seen, tended to devide the secular orders from the clergy in

[1] *Pièces*, I, 139-141, 156.
[2] P. Pélicier, "Voyage des députés de Bourgogne à Blois, 1483. Élection des députés de la Bougogne aux États généraux de 1484," *Bibl. de l'École des Chartes* XLVII (1886), 357-369.
[3] Baudouin, I, 121-138, 156-170. *Négociations, lettres et pièces diverses relatives au règne de François II (Col. de doc. inédits)* ed. Louis Paris (Paris, 1841), pp. 652-653. Arch. dép., Côte-d'Or, C 3063, fols. 70-94, 112-116.
[4] Arch. dép., Côte-d'Or, C 3067, fols. 32v-47; C 3470, Henri III to Mayenne, Sept. 1, 1576; C 3069, fols. 237-257. Baudouin, II, 179-194. Henri Drouot, *La Première Ligue en Bourgogne et les débuts de Mayenne, 1576-1579* (Dijon, 1937), pp. 93-99).

other localities as well. Conflict between the orders appears only in the question of who should pay the deputies.

Whether the three orders voted together or separately is in itself no proof as to whether they were friends or enemies. Cooperation was possible when they met in different chambers, and bitter feuds could take place when they acted together. We must go further to explain the relations between the three estates. In 1561 there were places in which the secular orders cooperated against the clergy. This situation resulted from the great unpopularity of the Church at that time, but it can give little comfort to the advocates of a class struggle, for the clergy was drawn from both the lay estates. By 1576 and 1588 many catholics had rallied to the side of the Church and still others to the side of the crown. The struggle was one between these two Catholic groups and the Protestants. In 1614 and during the Fronde the issue was one between the royal and anti-royal factions. Such quarrels were deeply intermixed with local personalities and local issues, and they cut across class lines to such an extent that few indeed are the disputes that can be found that were between the orders except during the elections of 1561.

Most of the quarrels that can be cited grew out of the activities of the local royal officials, and usually it was the municipal leaders who formed the opposition. Occasionally there were disputes as to precedent between the various estates. In 1576 the *prévôt* of Paris gave the nobility seats on the right side of the chamber, and this led to protests from the clergy. [1] Even such a quarrel between the first two estates has few if any counterparts. The same year saw a disagreement between the councillors of Rouen and the chapter of that city over the location of the seats of the clergy, and a more significant one between the town and the nobility concerning who should be admitted to the assembly, an important point where voting was by head. [2]

The activities of the local royal officials occasionally caused quarrels with others than the merchant oligarchy. In 1649 the lieutenant general of Angoumois claimed the seat immediately to the right of the seneschal, but was successfully challenged by the dispossessed clergy aided by the nobility. [3] It was also during the Fronde that the lieutenant general of Alençon packed the assembly with his henchmen from the third estate so as to outvote the nobility and win the election. Certainly the most serious quarrel was at Chartres at the same time when the *bailliage* officials sought seats in the chamber of the nobility and were ejected by that order with some bloodshed. [4]

---

[1] *Journal d'un curé ligueur de Paris sous les trois derniers Valois*, ed. Édouard Barthélemy (Paris, 1866), pp. 176-178.

[2] Arch. comm., Rouen, A 19, fols. 415v-423v.

[3] B.N., ms. n.a. fr. 3378, fols. 302-304v. Dujarric-Descombes, "Mémoire de ce qui s'est passé en la ville d'Angoulesme à l'assemblée des trois corps de la province Angoulmois," *Bul. et mém. de la société archéologique et historique de la Charante*, ser. 6, V (1895), préf. 83-86.

[4] *Procez verbal concernant tout ce qui s'est faict et passé dans l'assemblée générale faicte à Chartres* (Paris, 1651). This pamphlet may be found at A.N., O¹. 350. Lépinois, II, 419-426.

Such episodes, however, can hardly be considered as indicating an underlying antagonism between the three estates, and with the rarest exceptions the ecclesiastic, noble, and bourgeois was a respecter of the privileges of others as well as a defender of his own. Only the local royal officials showed any tendency to foment change. Perhaps motivated by the Roman law principle of *quod omnes tangit* and more certainly by the desire to win control over the *bailliage* elections and the municipalities, this group of men did much to extend the suffrage. Most often their actions brought them into difficulties with the third estate, and only occasionally with the other orders. Except for their activities, even the historian who has long denied that there was an unusual amount of ill-feeling between the social classes in France would be amazed at how few and how petty were the disputes that can be found in the vast number of accounts of elections that have survived. The three estates may have had different views on certain matters in this or that *bailliage*, but they stood together as defenders of their mutual privileges and in this they had the unfailing support of king in council.

VII

THE PAYMENT OF THE DEPUTIES TO THE FRENCH NATIONAL ASSEMBLIES, 1484–1627[1]

THE deputies to the estates general and other national assemblies as the legal representatives of their constituencies were entitled to financial compensation for their services, just as was the proctor of the municipality or the syndic of the provincial estates who went to court in the interest of his locality. As attendance at court was a part of the feudal obligation to give counsel, the financial burden of such attendance during the Middle Ages normally was placed on the individual or on the constituency which had obeyed the call to name deputies. In England by the sixteenth century, however, the importance of parliament and the prestige given to those who served as deputies had become so great that, first for the counties and then for the boroughs, more and more persons could be found who were willing to serve without compensation. In a few towns of some wealth and importance where the deputation was named by a group of the leading citizens, the custom of paying one or two of their number to go to Westminster was perpetuated well into the Stuart period, the last known instance being in 1695. At a much earlier date poorer boroughs were willing to elect one or both their deputies from outside their jurisdiction in return for being freed from financial burden, and the invasion of the "foreigner" became one of the characteristics of the Elizabethan era. Many a gentleman who was unable to secure election by a county turned to some borough which was perhaps far from his residence and offered his services free, in return for the honor attached to being elected to parliament.[2]

Was the "foreigner" or local inhabitant who was willing to serve wholly or partly at his own expense a familiar figure in France? If so, we may presume that the estates general was regarded as an institution of prime importance from the standpoint of what it accomplished

[1] The research for this article was made possible by generous assistance from a Fulbright Fellowship, a Guggenheim Memorial Foundation Fellowship, and Emory University during 1952–54.

[2] J. E. NEALE, *The Elizabethan house of commons* (London, 1949), pp. 321–31; R. C. LATHAM, "Payment of parliamentary wages—the last phase," *English historical review*, LXV (1951), 27–50; A. F. POLLARD, *The evolution of parliament* (London, 1926), pp. 387–429; Edward PORRITT, *The unreformed house of commons* (Cambridge, 1909), I, esp. 151–203.

Reprinted by permission of The University of Chicago Press from the Journal of Modern History XXVII (1955). © 1955 by The University of Chicago.

VII

and for the prestige it gave to those who attended. If, on the other hand, few or none were willing to attend the French national assemblies without financial compensation, can we not legitimately conclude that the estates general was not regarded by the vocal elements of the population as an institution essential for the preservation of their liberties or for assurance of good government? To investigate the problem thus raised we must also familiarize ourselves with the established procedures for the payment of the deputies and determine the amount of the wages due them. This paper is written for the double purpose of discussing the problem and mechanics of the payment of deputies and of assessing the position held by national representative institutions in France.

A lively debate developed at the Estates General at Tours in 1484 on the question of the financial remuneration of the deputies. A representative of the clergy opened the discussion by pointing out that they had been assembled on the order of the king and had already spent two months at Tours incurring very heavy expenses all the while. He asked that they be paid wages in accordance with the custom. A deputy of the third estate from Troyes said that he, too, favored an indemnity but asked that the wages of the ecclesiastics and nobility not be paid by the people, who were already overburdened and oppressed. Should the poorest give alms to the richest? Should they pay the costs of those who did not represent them? The clergy of Poitiers had agreed to pay the deputies of their order from that *sénéchaussée* before their departure for the estates general. This praiseworthy action should be followed by all jurisdictions.

Philippe de Poitiers, deputy of the nobility of Troyes, then spoke with great eloquence and vehemence, for he had been deeply wounded by these words: "I would like the orator to tell me, my lords, if he thinks that the ecclesiastics and nobles of this assembly have brought no relief to the people, and if he imagines that his services and those of the deputies of the third estate have profited them more than the work of the clergy and the nobility. I strongly believe that he would not have audacity enough to affirm what to the eyes of all is most obviously false." Furthermore, the nobleman argued, why should the nobility be expected to pay the representatives of their order while the people pay for those of the third estate? The deputies of the three estates had generally been elected and empowered by the same assembly. They were responsible to the same group. Those who served for the third estate were no more tallageable than the deputies of the nobility because the former had been ennobled, or were bourgeois of free communes, or had privileges attached to their offices. The clergy were to pray for all, to advise, and to preach. The nobility were to protect everyone with their arms, and the people were to nourish and support the first two orders by their taxes and their agriculture. This arrangement was not devised to the advantage of anyone in particular, but to make it possible for everyone to advance, not in accordance with his own interests, but as the servant of the entire community. Did not the people always pay the deputies of the three orders in the provincial estates of Normandy and Languedoc? Let the natural order of things be followed and direct the people to pay all the representatives.

The advocate of Troyes and others wished to reply, but the chancellor who was present interposed, saying that the

FRENCH NATIONAL ASSEMBLIES, 1484–1627

privy council had spoken much of the indemnity of the deputies and would announce its decision on this subject before the end of the session. At this point in the conversation the deputies of the first two orders left the room, and the chancellor remarked that he wished that they would either surrender their wages or else be content to collect them from their respective estates because of the poverty of the people. Nearly all the deputies of the clergy and the nobility were rich enough to make this sacrifice without difficulty. Still, the common law sided with them, and the people must bear the entire burden. We see no evidence on this occasion of willingness of any of the deputies to part with the financial remuneration that was their due. Earlier in the same session some archbishops and bishops had protested against their failure to receive individual summons to attend the estates, but none of them appears to have taken advantage of an offer by the elected deputies to receive them, provided that they would serve without pay. It might be an honor to be a deputy to the estates general, but not honor enough to warrant financial sacrifices.[3]

Surviving documents indicate that the deputies of 1484 were often paid from the taille. We have the receipt that the Seigneur de Pigny gave the *receveur* of the tailles of the county of Poitou for the 300 livres he received for his services in the estates general and a similar document given another *receveur* by the *procureur général* of the three estates of Haute-Auvergne to acknowledge his payment as deputy. Some towns resisted the attempts to impose the taille on them, no doubt because of their privileges, and in Périgueux the *receveur* had to take the matter before the seneschal.[4]

The deputies of the third estate were most often paid by a levy on the more important towns and communities of the *bailliages*. A half-dozen municipalities reimbursed the representatives of the *bailliage* of Amiens. Laon contributed twenty livres toward the salary of one described as the deputy of the town, but the small amount concerned suggests that other municipalities also paid something. Troyes consented to give an advance to the deputy of the third estate of the *bailliage* but refused a similar request made by the representative of the clergy, with the suggestion that he refer his petition to his fellow-ecclesiastics. No wonder the representatives of Troyes played the leading role in the debate on the payment of the deputies during the session. Other examples could be given, though it must be confessed that too few documents on the payment of the deputies to the Estates General of 1484 remain to tell us all we would like to know.[5]

The next national assembly to which deputies were elected by *bailliage* was in 1560; and on January 30, 1561, the day before the final meeting of the

---

[3] Jehan MASSELIN, *Journal des états généraux de France tenus à Tours en 1484 sous le règne de Charles VIII*, ed. A. BERNIER ("Col. de doc. inéd." [Paris, 1835]), pp. 392–94, 406–8, 494–510.

[4] Archives nationales, K 648, fols. 92 and 115; Michel HARDY, *Inventaire sommaire des archives communales antérieures à 1790. Ville de Périgueux* (Périgueux, 1894), p. 251. I have converted all currency to livre and sous tournois, using the tables in J. S. C. BRIDGE, *A history of France from the death of Louis XI* (Oxford, 1921), I, 253–61.

[5] A. THIERRY (ed.), *Recueil des monuments inédits de l'histoire du tiers état* ("Col. de doc. inéd." [Paris, 1853]), II, 422–23; A. MATTON and Victor DESSEIN, *Inventaire sommaire des archives communales antérieures à 1790. Ville de Laon* (Laon, 1883), p. 74; T. BOUTIOT and A. BABEAU, "Documents inédits tirés des archives de Troyes et relatifs aux états généraux," *Collection de documents inédits relatifs à la ville de Troyes* (Troyes, 1878), I, 6–7.

estates, Charles IX issued an order to his *baillis* for the payment of the deputies, which transferred the burden from the unprivileged to all three orders. *Bailliage* assemblies were to be convoked both in connection with naming deputies to a new meeting of the estates general and to choose six persons from each estate to apportion the tax levied to pay those who served at the earlier meeting. This tax was to be divided among the clergy in accordance with the *décimes*, among the nobility according to the *arrière-ban*, and among the third estate according to the taille, except that the free towns were to be included. Thus the tax for the payment of the deputies was based essentially on income, for the *décime* was levied on the revenue of the benefices, the *arrière-ban* on the revenue of the fiefs, and the taille at least took into consideration the revenue of the individual. The procès-verbal of the division of the tax was to be sealed and sent to the privy council within two months.

For the remainder of the century the same system of raising funds to pay the deputies was employed, except that the local magistrates usually chose those of the three orders to help them divide the tax rather than have them selected by the *bailliage* estates. Only in 1560–61 did two meetings of the estates general come so close together that the electoral assembly of the latter could also be used to take up the question of the payment of the deputies of the former.

An order of the king in council dated March 26, 1615 for the payment of deputies who had just departed from the meeting of the estates general at Paris directed that the clergy determine the amount to be given to the deputies of their order and that the beneficies of each *bailliage* be assessed in accordance with the *décimes* they paid. The procès-verbal of the clergy indicates that the relative independence of the first estate in such matters was first granted in 1576, a step probably made possible by the establishment of the national assemblies of the clergy in 1561. All fiefs, including those held by ecclesiastics, were to be taxed to pay the deputies of the nobility. The *trésoriers de France* and the *receveur des tailles* were directed to assess and collect a tax based on the taille from all the towns and *plat pays* in each *bailliage* to pay the deputies of the third estate.[6]

Let us now turn to several of the individual *bailliages* and see more precisely how the directives of the king in council were carried out. The most detailed information we have is for the payment of the deputies of the *bailliage* of Vermandois to the Estates General of 1560. For some reason Vermandois did not take the necessary steps to pay its deputies in the electoral assembly for the Estates General of 1561 as directed but rather held a special assembly for this purpose in April 1562. The total amount that had to be raised was 2,393 livres, a figure which included not only the payment of the deputies of the three orders but also the costs of holding the *bailliage* assembly. The latter even involved compensation to some of those who attended the meeting, pay of messengers, and clerical fees. Each order was assigned the task of paying its own deputies and a part of the common electoral expenses.

[6] LALOURCÉ and DUVAL (eds.), *Recueil de pièces originales et authentiques concernant la tenue des états généraux* (Paris, 1789), II, 225, IX, 288–345; C. J. MAYER (ed.), *Des états généraux et autres assemblées nationales* (The Hague, 1789), VII, 390–99. Bibliothèque nationale, MS français, 18187, fols. 285v–87, contains the royal order for the payment of the deputies to the Estates General of 1614. Archives départmentales de Gironde, C. 3894, contains documents of the *trésoriers de France* relative to the payment of the deputies in 1614 in the goverment of Guyenne.

The amount levied on the clergy was subdivided among the five archbishoprics and bishoprics of the jurisdictions in accordance with the wealth of each. The *prévôté* served as the subdivision in which to divide the amount to be paid by the secular estates. Unfortunately, we do not have documents indicating the further subdivisions made of the charges for the ecclesiastics, but each holder of the fief was assigned his share of the sum levied on his *prévôté* for the nobility. The charges for the third estate were further subdivided among the deaneries and finally among the individual communities.[7]

Rarely do documents survive for more than one order in a *bailliage*. In pursuing the matter further, therefore, let us consider each estate in turn. As has been indicated, the royal orders directed that the costs of the deputations of the clergy be divided among the benefice holders in proportion to the amount of *décimes* paid by each. Our most complete information is for the *bailliage* of Orléans. Here a good many curés were seemingly excused from making payments for the delegation of 1560. For 1588 and 1614 the lieutenant-general of the *bailliage* was less neglectful and divided the costs among all those who paid the *décimes*, though the amount granted the deputies for the latter year was far less than that directed by the national assembly of the clergy. In Mâcon several hundred curés were among those who contributed toward the payment of their bishop, though none of them had been permitted to participate in the assembly which had elected him to attend the Estates General of 1614. All ecclesiastics in Bas-Limousin were called upon to pay their delegations for that same year.[8]

The roll of the *arrière-ban* in each *bailliage*, that is, the list of the fief holders who owed military service to the crown, formed the basis on which the tax on the nobility was levied. By the sixteenth century it had become customary for the vassal to pay a sum of money varying according to the estimated income of the fief in lieu of military service. To facilitate this levy, rolls had frequently been prepared giving the estimated revenue of the fiefs of a particular jurisdiction. From 1560 the rolls formed the basis for the division of the taxes to be collected to pay the deputies of the nobility. We have the roll with the amount assessed for the *bailliages* or *sénéchaussées* of Bas-Limousin and Vermandois for the Estates General of 1560, of Ponthieu and La Montagne for 1576, of Rouen for 1588, and of Périgord and Mâcon for 1614. These documents indicate that noblemen who held fiefs were not the only ones who were assessed. Widows and unmarried women who held fiefs also paid. Neither ecclesiastics nor princes of the blood were excepted. The Cardinal of Bourbon and the Prince de Condé paid for fiefs held in Ponthieu, and the Cardinal of Lorraine and the King of Navarre did not escape the tax collectors in Vermandois. Even foreigners failed to escape, as is evidenced by Genevese who held fiefs in the *bailliage* of Gex who were charged with part of the expenses of the delegation in 1614. Henry III specifically ordered that the costs of the Burgundian nobles in 1576 be divided among nobles and commoners who held fiefs, but under the Old Regime exceptions could always be found. A few months earlier the same king had excused

---

[7] A. COMBIER, *Étude sur le bailliage de Vermandois* (Paris, 1874), pp. 85–88, 142–62.

[8] Bibliothèque municipale, Rouen MS 967 (MS g. 167), No. 77; Bibl. mun., Orléans, MS 541 (427), fols. 32–35, 46; Arch. départ. Saône-et-Loire, C. 550, No. 27; G. CLÉMENT-SIMON, *Archives historiques de la Corrèze* (Paris, 1905), II, 366–70.

the men and inhabitants of Amiens who held fiefs from contributing to the costs of the delegation of the nobility on the grounds that among their privileges they numbered exemptions from the *franc-fief* and the *ban* and *arrière-ban*.[9]

The tax for the payment of the deputies of the third estate was divided among the parishes in accordance with the amount of taille levied on each and, theoretically at least, without regard to any privileges or exemptions. Among the few rolls that survive are those for Vermandois in 1560, where over 400 communities were assessed, and for the various Burgundian *bailliages* in 1576 and 1614. No community, however small, appears to have been purposely overlooked, even though it possessed no suffrage rights, as was so often the case in Burgundy and elsewhere. In addition to these few rolls, documents from literally hundreds of communal archives indicate the amount paid toward the expenses of this or that deputy.[10]

There were, needless to say, many variations in the procedure used to pay the deputies in different parts of France, but only a few of the more important ones will be considered here. The first place we naturally would look for exceptions is in the many jurisdictions in which the three estates voted in common by head rather than by order. In such places we would not be surprised to find the deputies paid by a universal tax or the taille, as in 1484. This surmise proves correct for Brittany, where the deputies of the three orders were paid by the provincial estates, which, of course, removed most of the burden from the clergy and the nobility. In other localities, however, where the three orders named their deputies together, each estate generally paid its own delegates. This was true in Provence in 1588, 1614, and was agreed on in principle in 1591, and in the *sénéchaussées* of Languedoc in 1576, 1588, 1614, and in the government of Languedoc in 1561.[11]

On the other hand, in Burgundy where the three estates voted separately, the clergy and nobility persisted in their efforts to place the burden on the third estate, as was done in 1484. A lively debate developed on this issue in 1561. The nobility argued that the delegation from their order would act for "the common good of the estates" and therefore that they should be paid by the estates. The third estate offered strong and successful protests against this point of view. In 1576 this difficulty arose again, and the king had to issue special orders for each estate to pay its own deputies. Apparently, the directive was not fully carried out, for in 1588 a complaint was made that several of the deputies had not been paid half their wages, and the Burgundian delegation of that year asked that

---

[9] COMBIER, pp. 150–55; CLÉMENT-SIMON, I, 87–96; A. de CALONNE, "Réparation entre les gentilshommes tenant fiefs nobles en Ponthieu de l'idemnité allouée à messire André de Bourbon Rubempré, délégué aux états généraux de Blois en 1577," *Mémoires de la société des antiquités de Picardie*, XIII (1873), 71–98; B.N., MS français, 5353; Arch. départ., Dordogne, C. 14, No. 1; Arch. départ., Saône-et-Loire, C. 550, No. 28; LALOURCÉ and DUVAL, IX, 301–2; THIERRY, II, 864–66; Arch. départ., Côte-d'Or, C. 3470 and C. 3471 for La Montagne; O. MOREL, *Documents sur le pays de Gex conservés dans les archives cantonales de Genève et de Lausanne* (Bourg, 1932), p. 32.

[10] COMBIER, pp. 155–62; Arch. départ., Côte-d'Or, C. 3471 and C. 3474.

[11] Charles de LA LANDE DE CALAN, *Documents inédits relatifs aux états de Bretagne de 1491 à 1589* (Rennes, 1908), I, 145; *Archives de Bretagne*, Vol. XV; Arch. départ., Ille-et-Vilaine, C. 2649, p. 151; Arch. départ., Bouches-du-Rhône, C. 3, fols. 12–13; C. 107, fols. 146–47, 554v; C. 5, fols. 40–40v, 335; Abbé de CORIOLIS, *Dissertation sur les états de Provence* (Aix, 1867), pp. 247–49; Arch. départ., Haute-Garonne, C. 2280, fol. 471; C. 2281, fol. 52–52v; C. 2283, fol. 231; C. 2286, p. 103; C. 2294, fols. 331v–33, 337–40.

this time their salaries be raised by a special tax on salt, a request which was granted by the king. It is probable that the deputies to the estates of the League were also compensated from the treasury of the provincial estates. In 1614 Burgundy and the adjacent territories returned to the system of each order paying its own deputies. Thus, in some parts of France where the three orders named their delegations together, each order paid its own deputies. In a few others, where the deputies were elected by their own estate, they were paid from a common fund.

Frequently in those jurisdictions where the lower clergy, the lesser nobility, the unprivileged classes in the towns, or the rural communities were denied suffrage rights, they were nevertheless made to pay part of the costs of the deputations. It is an oversimplification, therefore, to say that the deputies of the *bailliage* were paid by their constituents. Rather they were reimbursed for their services by a tax levied by royal command and, after 1484, generally falling on their order in their jurisdiction regardless of who had actually participated in their election. The fact that the representatives were paid by a special tax rather than from the usual revenue coming into the royal treasury made the people much more conscious of the costs of holding representative assemblies. They were likely to insist on large and specific benefits from the estates general before being willing to advocate its frequent convocation, and the failure of the institution to provide many useful results must be considered when we seek to explain its decay in France.[12]

The estates general, characterized as it was by *bailliage* elections, was not the only way the French rulers had of summoning the nation during the post-medieval period. The older system of convoking certain important individuals and deputies from the principal towns was employed occasionally, and a few municipalities—more than historians have realized—sent deputies direct to the national assembly even when the *bailliage* was designated as the basic electoral jurisdiction. In such cases the individual towns paid the entire costs of the deputation. Lyons compensated her deputies to the assemblies of 1468, 1483, 1506, 1560, 1576, 1588, and 1614. Amiens contributed toward the cost of the *bailliage* deputation in 1560, 1561, and 1576, but in 1588 and 1593 the town paid the deputies it had seen fit to send direct to the estates general. Such independence was liable to prove costly, for in 1614 Amiens was ordered to pay 50 livres toward the expenses of the deputy of the *bailliage*, even though the municipal officials had not participated in the *bailliage* elections and had again sent their own deputy direct to Paris. Troyes paid for its individual deputations in 1468 and 1516. Marseille paid for its municipal delegations in 1576, 1588, and no doubt on other occasions. Additional examples could be given in profusion.[13]

In the post-1550 period even delegations individually convoked appear to have received financial compensation for their services, and one is not surprised to find the crown trying to place this

[12] Arch. départ., Côte-d'Or, C. 3063, fols. 80v–86; C. 3469–C. 3472, C. 3474; LALOURCÉ and DUVAL, IX, 298–302, 307–16; Arch. mun., Bourg, AA. 12; Arch. départ., Saône-et-Loire, C. 550, Nos. 27 and 28.

[13] Bibl. mun. Lyon, MS 721, pp. 187–88, 191, and MS 722, fols. 51–52; M. C. GUIGUE, J. VAËSEN, and Georges GUIGUE, *Inventaire sommaire des archives communales antérieures à 1790. Ville de Lyon* (Lyon, 1887–1949), III, 259, 333; IV, 12, 122; Arch. mun., Lyon, BB. 94, fols. 162 and 169v; AA. 147; THIERRY, II, 676–77, 973, 1039–41; III, 10; BOUTIOT and BABEAU, I, 3–5, 24–25.

burden directly on the people. The Burgundian archives yield an interesting note concerning the payment of the first president of the parlement of Dijon for his services at the estates of 1558. In that year some of the towns elected deputies whom they paid without debate, but the first president was either a royal appointee or at best authorized by the local parlement. Nevertheless, the crown ordered that a tax be levied on every man and inhabitant of Burgundy to pay him.

Another interesting point relative to the payment of deputies to national assemblies arose in regard to the meeting of the notables in 1617 when no deputies were elected. Nevertheless, we find the *trésoriers généraux* of France in Provence seeking to get the provincial estates to vote 9,000 livres toward the costs of the meeting at Rouen. The estates refused, but the issue was raised again and again until 1622. Burgundy and Mâcon seemed no less displeased. Perhaps it was the opposition raised against this levy that led the king to assume the responsibility of paying those who attended the Assembly of Notables in 1626 without ordering a special tax.[14]

The controversy that so often occurred as to who should pay the deputies indicates very clearly that the expenses of having a delegation were regarded as serious. The clergy of the *sénéchaussée* of Guyenne would permit the Archbishop of Bordeaux to have an assistant deputy in 1614 only when assured that they would not be charged for the costs of both of them at any one time. Auxois was strongly opposed to the payment of the Burgundian delegation from a common levy in 1588 because the other *bailliages* had named more deputies. Foix decided to name only one deputy from each estate in 1614 because of the poverty of the province. There are instances of two or more *bailliages* naming the same deputy as an economy, though local pride sometimes rebelled against this practice, as in Comminges in 1576 when the three estates refused to elect the deputy chosen for the third estate of the *sénéchaussée* of Toulouse. Indeed, pride often so completely conquered avarice that *bailliages* named more than the requested number of deputies. The crown was well aware of the expenses required and used economy as an excuse to forbid the estates general of Burgundy to assemble for the election of deputies in 1560 and probably also as an excuse for ordering the election of the estates general of the nation to take place by government rather than by *bailliage* the following year.[15]

We face a difficult problem when we seek to judge whether the deputies were justified in their complaints at the costs of holding the estates and a still more difficult one if we try to ascertain whether the expenses had anything to do with the small demand on the part of the people for holding the estates general. The royal financial officials estimated the costs of indemnifying the deputies at more than 50,000 livres in 1484, but the

[14] Arch. départ., Côte-d'Or, C. 3469 and C. 3473; Arch. départ., Bouches-du-Rhône, C. 2069; CORIOLIS, pp. 251–52; Arch. départ., Saône-et-Loire, C. 551, No. 24; Paul ARDIER, *L'assemblée des notables tenue à Paris ès années 1626 et 1627* (Paris, 1652), pp. 228–33.

[15] A DUPRÉ, *Élections du clergé de Guienne aux états généraux* (Bordeaux, 1893), pp. 7–11; Arch. départ., Côte-d'Or, C. 3069, fols. 245–256v; G. ARNAUD, *Mémoire sur les états de Foix, 1608–1789* (Toulouse, 1904), pp. 1–40, 152–56; Arch. départ., Haute-Garonne, C. 3572, pp. 15–16; Louis PARIS (ed.), *Négociations, lettres et pièces diverses relatives au règne de François II* ("Col. de doc. inéd." [Paris, 1841]), pp. 632–33; Pierre de LA PLACE, *Commentaires de l'estat de la religion et république soubs les rois Henry II et François II et Charles IX* (1565), fol. 169.

assembly was willing to grant the crown only 1,200,000 livres each year for the following two years with one special supplement because of the coronation expenses. In short, the payment of the deputies cost a little more than 4 per cent of the amount that the estates thought they should give in taxes to the king. In 1614 Brittany paid her delegation to Paris 52,418 livres and 17 sous, but her provincial estates were not ashamed to offer the king a mere 200,000 livres for the year 1619. The amount of tax paid by individuals varied greatly. In Bas-Limousin in 1560, nobles paid anywhere from 2 sous to 25 livres, and in Vermandois from 9 sous to 25 livres. In Ponthieu in 1576 fiefs were assessed at from 9 sous to about 75 livres. Here figures indicating the estimated revenue of each fief reveal that each noble was forced to surrender about 4 per cent of his annual income. The revenue of the fiefs was probably underestimated, but Ponthieu was not one of the small jurisdictions and had had only one deputy. The burden must indeed have been severe in those *bailliages* which had two or more delegates. By 1614 we find the levy per fief varying as much as from 3 to 110 livres in such places as Mâcon and Périgord.[16]

The amount levied on the towns and parishes to pay the deputies of the third estate varied greatly. Laon paid 13 livres, 10 sous toward the costs of the deputation of Vermandois in 1560, but some rural parishes paid only 2 or 3 sous. The average levy on the more than four hundred communities of the *bailliage* was about 2 livres. Amiens was assessed 120 livres to pay its share of the wages of the deputies of that *bailliage* in 1576.

Vitry-le-François paid about 50 livres toward the cost of the deputation of the *bailliage* in 1588. Other examples could be given in abundance, but enough has been said to indicate that the French practice of spreading the cost of the deputations among the smaller towns and villages made the burden on the local capitals less severe than in those boroughs in England which still paid two deputies to the meetings of her parliament. On the other hand, in the case of the French clergy, nobility, and the inhabitants of the individual municipalities which elected deputies directly to the estates general, the burden tended to be far heavier, because, as will be indicated, the pay of the representatives was much higher in France.[17]

We are thus brought to a comparison of the pay of the deputies in England and France. In England the legal wage from well back into the fourteenth century had been 4 shillings a day for knights of the shire and 2 shillings a day for burgesses. This sum was certainly by no means adequate to pay the expenses of the deputies by the sixteenth century. A few localities gave more, but, as we have seen, the great prestige attached to service in parliament made it possible for the bulk of them to pay the legal wage or often nothing at all.

The official salary scale fluctuated widely in France. The kings in their ordinances for the payment of deputies in 1560, 1561, and 1576 specified no precise wages, though they did sometimes direct that the deputies should be paid as little as possible. Henry III limited the amount to be paid the delegates at the estates of 1588, and the ordinance speci-

---

[16] MASSELIN, pp. 509–11; Arch. départ., Ille-et-Vilaine, C. 2469, p. 151; COMBIER, pp. 150–55; CLÉMENT-SIMON, I, 87–96; CALONNE, pp. 71–98; Arch. départ., Dordogne, C. 14, No. 1; Arch. départ., Saône-et-Loire, C. 550, No. 28.

[17] COMBIER, pp. 144–62; Arch. mun. Amiens, BB. 43, entry of Oct. 24, 1577; Georges HERELLE, *Documents inédits sur les états généraux tirés des archives de Vitry-le-François* (Paris, 1879), p. 98.

fying the sum to be paid to the deputies to Paris in 1614 survives. In addition, we have the salary scale adopted by the clergy in 1576 and 1614 for their order. If we take representative salaries, when available, for those who attended the assemblies for which no legal limit was set, we can establish the accompanying table of comparative wages. With three known exceptions, those who attended the assembly at Rouen in 1626 received 600 sous per day. From this table it becomes clear that the legal wage of the French deputies of the nobility and the third estate varied between four and nine times their English counterparts in 1484 and that it had increased to from ten to fourteen times by 1614, despite the greater decline in value of the French currency.

For the most part, the *bailliages* paid the amount directed by the king or the national assembly of the clergy, but, as in England, there were many exceptions. In 1588 the *bailliage* of Orléans paid the deputy of the clergy 20 livres per day instead of 15, but in 1614 the same jurisdiction elected three deputies for the clergy rather than one, as earlier, and therefore felt compelled to be much less generous. Their combined salary ought to have been 9,180 livres, a tremendous burden, which was met by lowering the daily wage of the bishop from 24 to 12 livres per day and the other two deputies from 15 to 3 livres per day. The injustices of this arbitrary action were compensated by the saving of 6,120 livres. Other, though perhaps less extreme, examples could be given.[18]

Sometimes, instead of giving a deputy a fixed sum for each day spent at the assembly and traveling to and from it, a jurisdiction would offer only a small salary and expenses. A few of these expense accounts have survived, and it is of interest to study one of them. In 1588 Guy Hurault and Joachim Gervaise, two deputies of the town of Orléans, set out for Blois accompanied by two servants. Both Hurault and Gervaise were paid 30 sous a day for their services. In addition,

PAY PER DAY, INCLUDING TRAVEL TIME, OF DEPUTIES TO PARLIAMENT AND THE ESTATES GENERAL IN SOUS TOURNOIS

	1484	1560	1576	1588	1614
Knights of the shire (English)	18.8	32	34.3	38.4	41.7
Burgesses (English)	9.4	16	17.1	19.2	20.9
Archbishops			500		540
Bishops		200	400		480
Abbots, priors, deans, canons of cathedral churches		150	160–300	300 max.	240–300
Curés, priests, and other ecclesiastics			120		200
Nobles	75	150	?–400	300 max.	400
Lieutenant-generals and other important crown officials					300
Municipal officials of important towns	40–90	60–90	?–180	180 max.	260
Other deputies of the third estate					240

[18] LALOURCÉ and DUVAL, II, 225, 229, and IX, 288–345; MAYER, VII, 390–99; B.N., MS français, 18187, fols. 285v–87; Bibl. mun., Orléans, MS 541 (427), fols. 32–35.

they were allowed all their expenses, including transportation, wine for their boatmen on the Loire, a furnished room at Blois at $67\frac{1}{2}$ livres per month, a tip of 15 sous to the concierge of the hôtel de ville at Blois, where the third estate met, 12 sous, 6 deniers for Masses celebrated for their souls, and the wages of the servants at 10 sous each per day. The total cost of the deputation was about 1,420 livres, but the sum would have been greater had not Hurault fled from Blois the day of the assassination of the Duke of Guise, thereby remaining away 39 days fewer than his companion.

Occasionally, a community made some special gifts to their deputies. Lyons provided her representatives with some big hams in 1588, and Nevers sent a large cask of wine to Guy Coquille the same year, as though the vintages of Blois were not good enough for the eminent jurist.[19]

The actual as well as the legal wage was certainly far higher in France than in England, where few went to Westminster without incurring heavy financial losses. It is difficult to explain the wide difference in the pay scales between the two countries. Perhaps the cost of living was higher in France; yet surely the basic factor must have been the ability of the English constituencies to find satisfactory deputies at a lower rate. The greater desire of many Englishmen to serve in their national assembly is not only reflected by their willingness to accept a lower wage but also by the failure of the French candidates to provide any entertainment for their constituents, as was so often done across the Channel. Of even more significance was the almost total absence of persons willing to serve free in return for election. The only instance the writer has found in France of this nature is that of a royal official of the town and government of La Rochelle and Aunis, who in 1614 charged the sergeants who delivered to the parishes messages concerning the estates general elections to say that he wished to be elected and would pay his own expenses if chosen. He was selected as one of the three deputies of the third estate of the jurisdiction. The "foreigner," that is, the candidate from outside the jurisdiction, who offered to serve free in return for election appears to have been totally nonexistent in France, though there were no real legal disabilities to prevent such a practice.

There are several instances of deputies offering to serve free after election. The royal ordinance for the payment of the deputies to the Estates General of 1560 stated that archbishops and bishops were not to be recompensed because some of them had expressed willingness to forego any pay, a generosity which doubtless resulted from the strong feeling in many quarters against the prelates at that time. A bishop who was a deputy from Brittany was paid, nevertheless, and perhaps others also. In 1649 two deputies of the clergy of the *bailliage* of Chaumont-en-Bassigny after their election announced their intention to serve without pay because of the poverty of the benefices of the region. Their offer was to cost them little because this assembly was never held.

There are several instances of deputies who expressed willingness to serve for less than the normal wage because they had to go to court anyway, as in the case of a deputy of the town of Lyons

---

[19] Jacques SOYER, "Les députés du tiers représentant la ville et le bailliage d'Orléans aux états généraux de Blois en 1588," *Bulletin de la société archéologique et historique de l'Orléanais*, XV (1908-10), 435-47; Arch. mun., Lyon, CC. 1364; Abbé F. BOUTILLIER, *Inventaire sommaire des archives communales antérieures à 1790. Ville de Nevers* (Nevers, 1876), pp. 88-89.

in 1484, or again when a deputy agreed to serve for less than the usual wage in return for election. In 1614 the *procureur* of the town of Lyons wanted to be named assistant deputy to the provost of the merchants, and his request was granted on the condition that he would be paid only his expenses and his usual salary as *procureur*. He was denied only his special stipend as deputy—scarcely a sacrifice to be compared with that made by every deputy who made the trip to Westminster. But even such instances as these are extremely rare. Thus the deputy in France remained essentially the representative of his locality, where he was, with the rarest exceptions, a prominent resident and by whom he was paid for his service. A seat in the estates general was almost never desired enough for someone to offer to serve at his own expense, with the result that the French deputy never broke from his locality, as in England, or came to think of himself as representing the nation as a whole. The practice of free service, which had already begun in Tudor England and became universal after 1695, never really appeared in France.[20]

The French deputies may have been more fortunate than those in England in the amount they were supposed to be paid, but they more often had difficulty collecting. Generally a year or more was needed after the estates general had closed to collect the special tax to pay them, even when there was no dispute. The *bailliage* assembly to divide the tax to pay the deputies of Vermandois to the Estates General of 1560 did not even meet until April 1562. In 1589 it was reported that several of the deputies of Burgundy to the Estates General of 1576 had not been paid half their wages. Compiègne delayed ten years before paying her share of the salary of the deputy of the *bailliage* of Senlis to the second estates of Blois because she had little use for the League sympathies of the rest of the *bailliage*. The deputy of the nobility of the *bailliage* of Rouen in 1588 had to wait until 1608 for payment, and the repesentative of the nobility of Provence to Blois in 1576 was still seeking payment in 1581. Ten years elapsed before the heirs of the deputies of the nobility of Vermandois in 1588 could collect the salaries due them. Such examples could be multiplied almost without end.[21]

No doubt the difficulty of collecting salaries was at least one factor that led many to avoid election. Several courses could be followed by those who were named deputies. They could insist on an advance payment of part of what was likely to be owed them by the end of the assembly. This method was most successful where the provincial estates were to pay the deputies or where they represented a town. In both cases there was a local treasury which usually contained the necessary funds. Thus we find the deputies of the third estate of Provence getting advances in 1588 and 1591. In 1468 the delegates of the town of Périgueux received an advance, and those of Lyons in 1576. The delegate of

---

[20] LALOURCÉ and DUVAL, IX, 288–90; Charles DANGIBEAUD (ed.), "Diaire de Jacques Merlin," *Archives historiques de la Saintonge et d'Aunis*, V (1878), 237–40; LA LANDE DE CALAN, I, 145; Abbé MILLARD and Alphonse ROSEROT, "Procès-verbal d'assemblée des trois ordres du bailliage de Chaumont (Haute-Marne) pour les états généraux convoqués à Orléans en 1649," *Mémoires de la société académique d'agriculture, des sciences, arts, et belles lettres du département de l'Aube*, XLVII (1883), 321–45; Bibl. mun., Lyon, MS 721, pp. 187–88; Arch. mun., Lyon, BB. 150, p. 306.

[21] COMBIER, pp. 85–92, 142–62; LALOURCÉ and DUVAL, IX, 315–16; Bonnault d'HOUËT, *Compiègne pendant les guerres de religion et la ligue* (Compiègne, 1910), pp. 199–200; B.N., MS français, 5353; CORIOLIS, p. 248.

Amiens to the estates in 1593 was absent so long that the town thought it advisable to make several payments to his wife, who remained at home. Sometimes deputies found it necessary to write the *échévins* of their municipalities during the estates general asking for funds, saying that they had reached the end of their personal resources. Such measures were scarcely open to the deputies of the *bailliages*, since the special tax to pay them was levied only after their service was complete. Fortunate indeed were the deputies of the clergy of the government of Peronne in 1576 who managed to wrangle a small advance from those who assembled to elect them. Such good fortune was rare; by and large, the deputies were forced to provide for the costs of their service from their own funds with only the hope of eventual reimbursement to comfort them.[22]

Frequently the deputies on their return found it necessary to apply rather forceful persuasion to secure payment. In 1484 a deputy of the *bailliage* of Senlis refused to show his constituents a copy of the *cahier* the estates had submitted to the king until he was paid. More frequently appeals were made directly to the king or his officials. Since the taxes to pay the deputies were levied on royal orders, an appeal to the crown should have brought an end to their difficulties. Such was not always the case during the religious wars, however; it took four years and numerous official orders for the deputy of the third estate of the *prévôté* and *vicomté* of Paris in 1614 to get paid.[23]

Service in French national assemblies brought too little prestige to make it desirable for deputies to serve without pay, and any delights of being at court must have been considerably dimmed by the crowded living conditions in such small towns as Blois, where the French kings all too often assembled the nation. Many did not wish to serve, and those who were prevailed upon to do so frequently had to engage in long struggles for any sort of financial compensation. How different this was from the prevailing attitude toward a journey to the parliament at Westminster!

Only the feeling of great accomplishments by the estates general or the grateful expression on the part of the people for the sacrifices of those who served could compensate for so much inconvenience. Such gratification was almost never forthcoming, and it must often have seemed to the people that the only result of a national assembly was an ordinance that was not obeyed and the inevitable tax to pay the deputies. Pierre Robert summarized the feelings of many when he wrote that he was not sorry to have been too sick to attend the Estates General of 1614 for Basse-Marche, for "the deputies did nothing in return for the great expense they caused the whole province for which they received only the maledictions of the people."[24]

EMORY UNIVERSITY

[22] Arch. départ., Bouches-du-Rhône, C. 5, fols. 40v, 355; HARDY, p. 116; Arch. mun., Lyon, BB. 94, fols. 162, 169v; Arch. mun., Amiens, CC. 234, fol. 18; CC. 236, fol. 16; Abbé J. GOSSELIN, "La Ligue à Peronne," *La Picardie*, XVI (1870), 271.

[23] Jules FLAMMERMONT, *Histoire des institutions municipales de Senlis* (Paris, 1881), pp. 99–100; LALOURCÉ and DUVAL, IX, 317–28.

[24] Henri Auburgeois de LA VILLE DU BOST, *Histoire du Dorat* (Poitiers and Paris, 1880), p. 113.

VIII

The Loss of Royal Initiative and the Decay of the Estates General in France, 1421-1615,

In 1924 Professor Wallace Notestein read a paper before the British Academy in which he described how the members of the House of Commons won the initiative from the crown during the reign of James I (^{1}). It was a technical, detailed study of parliamentary procedure, but it was fraught with significance. He showed us how the Tudors ensured a cooperative Parliament through the activities of their councillors and how a combination of circumstances permitted the more independently minded members of the Commons in the early sixteen hundreds to escape the tutelage of the crown (^{2}).

During this period, Parliament learned to function efficiently as a result of procedures and precedents established and tested by constant use. At the same time, the English people came to look upon Parliament as a partner in the government so that when the great split came in the mid-seventeenth century, there was an institution capable of challenging the position of the crown, and though Parliament faltered badly in its first effort to govern, it was slowly able to assume control of affairs after 1688. The Tudor monarchs had unwittingly aided an institution that could and did provide an alternative to royal absolutism.

Let us now travel across the channel to France. Here we find the Valois-Bourbon monarchs struggling with much the same problems as their Tudor-Stuart contemporaries. Occasionally during the Wars of Religion and again in 1614 the kings turned to the Estates General, but at no point did that institution prove to be a satisfactory instrument for their policy. These opportunities were equally wasted from the standpoint of those who advocated a more important role

---

(^{1}) The research for this article was made possible by generous assistance from a Fulbright Fellowship, a John Simon Guggenheim Memorial Fellowship, a three year Faculty Research Fellowship of the Social Science Research Council, and Emory University. It was read in a slightly different form at the American Historical Association on December 29, 1956 in a session sponsored by the American Committee of the International Commission for the History of Representative and Parliamentary Institutions. I am indebted to my colleagues, Professors G. P. Cuttino, W. D. Love, and J. J. Mathews for reading and criticizing this paper.

(^{2}) W. NOTESTEIN, *The Winning of the Initiative by the House of Commons*, in *Proceedings of the British Academy*, XI, 1924-25, pp. 125-175.

VIII

for the representative institution in the government of the nation. The procedure used in the Estates General during this period prevented either the crown or the parliamentarians from exercising the necessary initiative to make it an effective institution. In France there was no alternative to royal absolutism save anarchy. Why had the Estates General become so ineffectual? It is necessary to turn back to the reign of Charles VII in search for the answer.

From the standpoint of royal initiative, the assemblies during the reign of Charles VII were of two general types: those that were held in the presence of king in council and those that were not. The former included both the assemblies of the three estates of the kingdom, or that part of it controlled by Charles, and of the three estates of Languedoïl. The latter consisted of the provincial, bailiwick, and other local estates ([3]).

Weak and indolent though he was, Charles VII held the initiative in the twenty-odd meetings of the Estates General and the estates of Languedoïl he held between 1421 and 1439. This statement is based on three facts. First, there were in the estates no revolts such as had occurred in 1356 when Étienne Marcel had challenged royal authority. The condition of France during this part of the reign of Charles VII was at least as bad as in 1356. Over half the country acknowledged a Lancastrian as its sovereign while Charles had neither money, troops, nor too certain a claim to the throne. Yet, the deputies did not revolt!

Second, Charles VII was able to push an unpopular kind of tax through seven different meetings of the Estates General, or the estates of Languedoïl, but except for the last meeting the provincial estates later forced him to accept instead an equivalent collected in the form of the more popular *taille*. It is therefore evident that the king controlled the Estates General well enough to get a disliked form of taxation approved, but did not control the subordinate provincial estates to the degree necessary to get their consent ([4]).

Third, Charles VII sometimes summoned the western provinces of Languedoïl to get consent to a particular tax of a fixed amount

---

([3]) There were a few instances in which Charles VII presided over the provincial estates, but it was impossible for him to be present at more than a small percentage of the meetings.

([4]) J. RUSSELL MAJOR, *Representative Institutions in Renaissance France, 1421-1559*, in *Studies presented to the International Commission for the History of Representative and Parliamentary Institutions*, XXII, Madison, 1960, pp. 25-45.

ROYAL INITIATIVE AND ESTATES GENERAL IN FRANCE 249

to fall on the bulk of the kingdom and then turned to the eastern provinces and there obtained consent for the identical tax, for the identical amount, to fall on the identical area. Thus in October 1424 the representatives from the western provinces met and voted a *taille* of 1,000,000 *livres* that was almost certainly intended to be collected from east and west alike, and then in November, the eastern provinces met and consented to the same tax in the same amount. Again in November 1426 the western provinces voted a *taille* of 120,000 francs and a hearth tax to be collected from the entire area. Then in December the eastern provinces voted the same two taxes in the same amount ([5]). It is evident that the king and his councilors could not go before one group of representatives and have them set a figure for the financial needs of the crown and agree on what form the intended tax should take, and then go before the representatives of the other provinces and get them to agree that the crown needed exactly the same sum to be collected by exactly the same tax, unless they held the initiative in at least the second assembly.

Charles VII kept the initiative in the Estates General in very much the same manner as the Tudors did a century later in England, but rather than piece together scraps of evidence from his various assemblies, let us describe the techniques used by his son, Louis XI, in the estates of Tours in 1468, for here there are several journals to aid us. Louis had summoned the three estates on this occasion to explain to them why it was imperative for the crown to keep the wealthy duchy of Normandy rather than give it to his brother, Charles. He saw to it that from their arrival at Tours until their departure, the representatives were carefully herded from place to place and from debate to debate by the spokesmen of the crown. Notices were placed on the gates and churches of the city directing the deputies to report upon their arrival to the royal clerk to verify their powers ([6]). The estates opened with brief talks by the king and several magnates and a two hour address by the chancellor, who explained the problems that would be created if Normandy were lost. During the three days that followed, with the royal clerk serving as secretary of the assembly, the councilors and other loyal friends of the king were called upon one after another to give

([5]) *Ibid.*, pp. 28-29.
([6]) ARCHIVES COMMUNALES, Rodez, BB 3, f° 52.

their opinion, and each in his own words explained why the king's brother should not be allowed to keep Normandy. By the time the representatives got the floor they had been sufficiently «brainwashed», or perhaps convinced, to accept in the presence of the councilors the royal policy, and the recommendations the three estates submitted at the end of the session were all that the crown could have wished. By the effective use of his councilors and his clerks Louis XI had turned a meeting of the Estates General into a propaganda weapon against his adversaries ([7]).

The very limited material available on the deliberations of the estates of Charles VII indicates that the same close relationship existed between the councilors and the deputies. They were in close contact before the estates opened and one of the lasts acts of the deputies before leaving was to obtain an order from the chancellery for their payment by their fellow townsmen. Even the king was expected to be present during a good part of the deliberations and the Bishop of Beauvais sharply criticized Charles VII for failing in this duty at the assembly at Orléans in 1439 ([8]).

Charles VII decided to abandon the Estates General and the estates of Languedoïl around 1440. In doing so he was not motivated by fear. He had effectively controlled the meetings for two decades during a time when he was very weak. He had every reason to anticipate doing so now that he was strong. Rather he abandoned the Estates General and the estates of Languedoïl because he no longer had need of them. In financial matters these two institutions served only to explain the need for money and to fix the amount and the nature of the tax in the hope of influencing the provincial estates to take favorable action, for the consent of these last assemblies had to be obtained as well before the money could be collected. Where there were no provincial estates, the consent of the privileged towns was required. Where there were great nobles, they had to be given a share in return for permitting the levy to be collected in their domain. Neither the provincial estates nor the towns hesitated to give less than what was asked or to insist on changing the nature of

---

([7]) MAJOR, pp. 54-58.

([8]) C. DE GRANDMAISON, *Nouveaux documents sur les États généraux du XV° siècle*, in Bulletin de la Société archéologique de Touraine, IV, 1877-79, pp. 139-155; G. DU FRESNE DE BEAUCOURT, *Histoire de Charles VII*, Paris, 1881-1885, I, pp. 356-365; II, pp. 577-601; III, pp. 434-452, 501-509; Pierre L. PÉCHENARD, *Jean Juvenal des Ursins*, Paris, 1876, pp. 198-207.

the tax. Thus in financial matters the Estates General and the estates of Languedoïl were useful only when it was necessary to apply additional pressure on the people to accept some form of taxation. By 1439 Charles VII felt strong enough to go directly to the provincial estates and the towns for consent without any preliminary propaganda. The victory at Orléans, the triumphant coronation at Reims, and finally the Burgundian alliance of 1435 had so changed his fortunes that final success seemed assured ([9]). Between 1439 and 1560 we know of only one occasion in which a full meeting of the Estates General was asked to vote a tax. In this instance, it might be added, the money that was voted had to be consented to by the provincial assemblies just as before ([10]).

There was certainly no reason for Charles VII to have preferred dealing with the provincial estates or the towns, for their deliberations were far more difficult to control than those of the national assembly. «When the representatives of the kingdom met, they were in his power. Persuaded by the royal councilors, impressed by the royal majesty, surrounded by the palace guard, and far from their homes, they rarely mustered sufficient courage to resist the king's desires. In the provincial estates and municipal assemblies, on the other hand, the reverse was true. The king was not present. In his place stood one or more royal commissioners who inspired little awe among the local leaders. There was no council to guide the deliberations and the initiative was seized by the members of the assembly who treated and bargained with their monarch rather than follow his lead. Secure in a fortified town or castle, surrounded by their friends, and far from the royal army, they did not hesitate to change the form of a tax, reduce the amount of the levy, or even refuse to vote anything at all. If they granted money, they were likely to request concessions in the same breath» ([11]). Thus it was the provincial estates and the privileged towns that were the true checks on royal taxation, and it is not surprising that Charles VII eventually abandoned a few of the former when he felt strong enough to collect the taxes without winning their consent.

The important thing, however, is that Charles VII *did* cease to convoke the Estates General and the estates of Languedoïl. If he and

---

([9]) MAJOR, pp. 34-39.
([10]) *Ibid.*, pp. 115-116. The meeting was the Estates General of Tours in 1484.
([11]) *Ibid.*, p. 38.

his successors had continued to summon them after 1440 as much as they had before, would not these institutions have become regarded in the minds of the people as playing an essential role in the government of the kingdom ? Might not procedures have developed that would have enabled the estates to function effectively, so that the deputies would have been in a strong position to challenge the crown during the time of division that occurred during the late sixteenth and early seventeenth centuries ? This is what was to happen in England a little later. Why could it not have happened in France ?

It is true that the period 1440-1530 was not as devoid of large assemblies as we have often been led to believe. There were only a handful of meetings of the Estates General, but the kings frequently summoned members of one or two estates to give advice on particular subjects. When ecclesiastical matters were under consideration, the clergy was convoked; when military, «the captains and chiefs of war»; when judicial or financial, the sovereign courts; when commercial, the deputies of the towns. The council and other royal officials were present and often various mixtures of the above groups attended. It is impossible to list all the meetings, but some idea of their frequency may be gathered from the fact that Louis XI held about ten assemblies of the deputies of the towns during a reign of twenty-two years ([12]).

These meetings were frequent until the middle of the reign of Francis I. They undoubtedly served to give the councilors experience in controlling deliberative bodies and to acquaint select elements of the population with the problems of government. On the other hand, their limited objectives and their very variety prevented the discovery of the more complex procedures that were necessary if a representative institution were to cope with the manifold problems of the sixteenth century. For example, our modern system of committees, so necessary for every type of deliberative assembly, could develop only if the same deputies were summoned over and over again to assemblies where it was necessary to deal with many different problems. In time they would then learn to break up into different groups to speed the deliberations; some might study taxation, others religious affairs, and still others legal administration. In this manner the deputies would become experts in this or that field and the work of the assembly would be greatly speeded. The limited

---

([12]) *Ibid.*, pp. 47-59, 117-140.

ROYAL INITIATIVE AND ESTATES GENERAL IN FRANCE

purpose of the meetings between 1440 and 1530, on the other hand, meant that there was no need to divide the work among those who attended. When a meeting was held to discuss the foreign currency problem, foreign currency alone needed to be considered. Furthermore, the wide variety of meetings meant that the same people were not called upon to work together year after year and that no one type of assembly ever became so firmly implanted in the minds of the people that they were likely to look upon it as sharing in royal authority. The assemblies of the clergy, the towns, the sovereign courts, and the great nobles so common during this period served more to keep alive the idea that the wise king acted only upon the advice of his leading subjects than they did to develop new deliberative techniques.

Even these assemblies were held less frequently after 1530, so that when a return was made to the use of the Estates General a generation later, the primitive procedure of the earlier period had been forgotten. It was necessary to start from scratch and build anew.

The first thing that strikes the historian as he studies the meetings of the estates beginning in 1558 and ending in 1615 is that the government had lost the initiative in the deliberations. No longer were the royal councilors able to direct the efforts of the deputies towards the preconceived solutions desired by the crown as had been done in the reigns of Charles VII and Louis XI. During the fifteenth century the government had been able to get national assemblies to vote for taxes, but in 1558 when the estates were merely asked to furnish a list of 3000 persons who could lend the king 1000 *écus* each at $8^{1}/_{3}\%$ interest, they balked, and only the enthusiasm brought about by the news of the capture of Calais led to a more cooperative frame of mind. In 1560 and 1561 the secular estates refused to vote taxes, and in 1576 and in 1588 they were equally recalcitrant ([13]). Thereafter, the crown did not bother to ask the deputies for financial aid. Meanwhile, the estates were making suggestions concerning every aspect of royal policy. They showed no respect for the prerogative and their *cahiers* which had been brief documents of specific complaints in the earlier age, now became

---

([13]) *Ibid.*, pp. 144-147. J. RUSSELL MAJOR, *The Estates General of 1560*, Princeton, 1951, pp. 97-114; J. RUSSELL MAJOR, *The Third Estate in the Estates General of Pontoise, 1561*, in *Speculum*, XXIX, 1954, pp. 460-476. Georges PICOT, *Histoire des États généraux*, Paris, ed. of 1888, III, pp. 32-85, 398-427.

lengthy proposals for a general reorganization of the state filling an entire printed volume for a single meeting (¹⁴). To restore a semblance of order in the estates of 1588, Henry III found it necessary to assassinate the Duke of Guise and to send a band of men into the chamber of the third estate in the hope of arresting the opposition leaders. The initiative had passed from the government just as it was to do later in England. Violence remained the only recourse of the crown.

Certainly one of the causes of the loss of royal leadership lay in the temper of the times. The deep distrust of ultra-Catholic and Protestant alike of the religious policies of the crown, coupled with political, social, and economic grievances, was sure to cause trouble in the Estates General even though the councilors of the last of the Valois had been as effective leaders as their predecessors.

A new method of choosing the representatives, however, was of equal importance, for it led to the assemblies being composed of men less favorably disposed to the crown and to procedural changes in the Estates General itself that blocked the effective exercise of royal initiative.

Until 1483 only the towns and chapters habitually elected deputies to the Estates General. The remainder of the clergy and the nobility who attended, did so by virtue of writs of summons sent them by the royal officials at the capital or their subordinates in the bailiwicks (¹⁵). The most important members of the two groups might well expect to be called by right, yet certainly the government had a degree of latitude among the others it chose. Beginning in 1483, however, the practice of holding elections in the bailiwick for all three estates was inaugurated, thereby giving the disaffected elements in the provinces the power to choose their own spokesmen. By 1561 there is evidence that the Protestants were engaged in block voting and other forms of electoral manipulation (¹⁶). In 1576, and especially in 1588, the Guise and the Catholic League showed a decided mastery of this highly important modern art. The situation could have been

---

(¹⁴) LALOURCÉ et DUVAL, *Recueil des cahiers généraux des trois ordres aux États généraux*, Paris, 1789, 4 vols.

(¹⁵) There were some exceptions to this rule for here and there instances have been found of provincial estates electing deputies prior to 1483. MAJOR, *Representative Institutions ...*, pp. 66-67.

(¹⁶) N. VALOIS, *Les États de Pontoise*, in *Revue d'histoire de l'Église de France*, XXIX, 1943, pp. 237-256.

mitigated only by the crown's taking an active part in the electoral campaigns, but it did not. Admittedly, there is instance after instance of local royal officials altering the electoral procedure to obtain the choice of a deputy favorable to the royal cause, but each time they were overruled by the king's council, so great was the crown's respect for the privileges of its subjects. Not one incident prior to the Fronde has been found in which an illegal election was allowed to stand even though the deputy so chosen was an outspoken advocate of the royal cause ([17]). In 1614 Marie de Medici did take her son on a well-publicized tour of the western provinces. This action, plus the ineptness of the opposition led by the Prince of Condé, made possible the election in that year of the only Estates General favorable to the government since the reign of Louis XI ([18]).

In addition to permitting the choice of deputies badly disposed towards the crown, the new electoral procedure led to confusion in the Estates General itself ([19]). Since it was the bailiwick that elected the deputies, the idea developed that each bailiwick should have the same vote. This in itself seemed just since the bailiwicks named various numbers of deputies depending on the whim of the electorate. Voting by head would have given a jurisdiction that had chosen three deputies for one estate three times the weight of its neighbor that had chosen only one. On the other hand, voting by bailiwick was more cumbersome than voting by head. The obvious solution to the difficulty was for the bailiwicks to elect the same number of deputies, and the crown soon recognized this fact. Beginning in 1576 the letters of convocation always specified that each bailiwick choose one deputy from each estate ([20]). Unfortunately, this regulation was rarely observed. Local pride often dictated the choice of more than the required number. The easiest way to keep two

---

([17]) J. RUSSELL MAJOR, *The Deputies to the Estates General of Renaissance France*, in *Studies presented to the International Commission for the History of Representative and Parliamentary Institutions*, XXI, Madison, 1960.

([18]) G. A. ROTHROCK, Jr., *The French Crown and the Estates General of 1614*, in *French Historical Studies*, I, pp. 295-318.

([19]) The only studies of the deliberative procedure of the French Estates General during the Renaissance are Lalourcé and Duval's introduction to *Recueil de pièces originales et authentiques, concernant la tenue des États généraux*. Paris, 1789, 9 vols.; Edmond CHARLEVILLE, *Les États généraux de 1576*, Paris, 1901, pp. 104-144. My general statements on deliberative procedure in the pages that follow can be substantiated here.

([20]) MAJOR, *The Deputies...*, p. 5.

VIII

rival candidates happy was to ignore the royal limitation and elect them both. Whatever the reason, of the ninety-nine bailiwicks that named delegations to the Estates General of 1614, only twenty-six complied with the royal order to send one and only one deputy from each estate. Clearly voting by bailiwick had to be continued if those jurisdictions that elected a large number of deputies were not to have an unfair advantage over those that observed the legal limit.

The decision to vote by bailiwick, however, led to other complications. France at this time was divided into twelve governments, but in three of them — Brittany, Dauphiné, and Provence — local loyalties were so strong that the inhabitants insisted that their deputies be chosen by their provincial estates in order better to preserve their integrity. It would be clearly unjust to allow the deputies from these governments no more voice than those of the bailiwicks in other parts of France. A solution was found by giving one vote to each government. To determine how the governments voted, the deputies from each met together. In the meetings for Brittany, Dauphiné, and Provence, voting was presumably done by head, but in the nine other governments, the deputies from each bailiwick had to be polled to determine the vote of the bailiwick and then the bailiwicks had to be polled to determine the vote of the government.

When it came time to prepare the *cahier* of the order, the deputies of the bailiwicks of each government met together to pool the *cahiers* they had received from their constituents. A *cahier* for the government emerged from these deliberations. Then, in turn, the *cahiers* of the various governments were combined to form the *cahier* of the order. Since the preparation of the *cahier* and voting were among the most time-consuming duties of an assembly, the deputies of this or that government spent more and more time working together. They found it advisable to choose their own president and clerk. They kept journals of their deliberations. Thus each estate became composed of twelve deliberative groups and the unity of action of the whole was difficult to maintain.

The Estates General of 1560, which saw the introduction of voting by bailiwick and government, also witnessed the separation of the orders. During the reigns of Charles VII and Louis XI the three estates had normally deliberated together, and even the brief separation of an order to discuss this or that matter appears to have

ROYAL INITIATIVE AND ESTATES GENERAL IN FRANCE

been exceptional [21]. In 1560, however, Charles IX ordered the three estates to meet temporarily in different chambers to prepare separate *cahiers*. When they had completed this task, they were to meet together again and choose a single speaker [22]. The Cardinal of Lorraine, who was the leading figure in the royal administration, sought this office, but religious passions and political rivalries were too aroused for the secular estates to accept his candidature. Likewise, efforts to get the estates to combine their separate *cahiers* into a single *cahier* to be enacted into an ordinance ended in failure [23]. Each order chose its own president, orator, and clerk and prepared its own *cahier* and petitions to submit to the crown. Efforts were made to get the three estates to act together in later meetings of the Estates General, but without success. From 1560 the Estates General consisted of three chambers and each of these chambers was divided into about twelve governments.

The division of the Estates General into three chambers and the division of each chamber into twelve governments meant that there were in all thirty-six deliberative units [24]. It would have been virtually impossible for the wisest and most experienced of royal councilors to have maintained the initiative in such a parliament even if there had been enough of them to attend the meetings of each of the thirty-six units, and the advisors of the late Valois-early Bourbon monarchs had only an average amount of wisdom and very little experience in dealing with representative institutions. Indeed, except for the opening and closing ceremonies, the councilors appeared in the chambers of the estates in 1560 and thereafter only to bring messages from the king. The deputies were left to do virtually as they pleased. The thirty year interregnum beginning around 1530 meant that there was no one who knew much about the control of assemblies when they were later revived. This inexperience was highlighted by the council at Fountainebleau in 1560 where it was decided to turn once more to the Estates General. The councilors saw clearly what use other monarchs in Europe were making of representative institutions, but they failed to grasp the

---

[21] MAJOR, *The Estates General of 1560*, pp. 79-80.
[22] BIBLIOTHÈQUE NATIONALE, ms. français 3159, f° 5.
[23] MAJOR, *The Estates General of 1560*, pp. 83-86.
[24] The clergy was sub-divided by archdiocese rather than by government in several meetings of the Estates General, but the result was the same.

role they themselves had to play to secure the desired results ([25]).

So it came to pass that the crown lost the initiative in France as it was to do later in England, but here the parallel ends. The very factors that had brought about a collapse of royal initiative in France prevented the assumption in its place of the initiative by the deputies. The system of voting by bailiwick and deliberating by government prevented the development of effective leadership on the floor. The English Parliament, it is true, broke up into committees and the use of these committees was one of the factors that led to the collapse of royal leadership, but there was this difference. The English committees were designed to study and make recommendations on particular subjects. They prepared and submitted individual petitions. Their formation speeded the work of the assembly and led to the development in Parliament of specialists in different areas. They trained the representatives for the assumption of a more important role in national affairs. The French governmental assembly, on the other hand, was composed of the deputies from a particular province, whose interests, loyalties, and prejudices reflected those of their region rather than of France as a whole. They felt it necessary to make recommendations on every sort of matter, and no specialization developed. Instead, each government duplicated the work of the other. The assemblies became longer, to the dismay of the crown, deputy, and taxpayer alike. At the same time the lack of specialization led to unwise recommendations and, more important, to the failure to develop experts on finance, administration, foreign policy, and the like among the deputies. They were not prepared to take the initiative when the crown could no longer hold it.

The result of the lack of leadership by either the crown or the deputies was confusion, delay, and lack of accomplishment. Sometimes hope ran high when the Estates General opened, but invariably by the time the final assembly was held the deputies and their constituents were disillusioned. More serious still was the disappointment of the officials who had advised the convocation of the estates. In place of sound advice, they had received selfish complaints; in place of devotion to the crown, they had seen only provincial loyalties and jealousies. From being advocates of these meetings, they became opponents. We have only to read the comments attributed to Cardinal

([25]) MAJOR, *The Estates General of 1560*, pp. 30-41.

Richelieu as he looked back on his experiences as a young deputy in the Estates General of 1614. The assembly his *Mémoires* declare, «had no other effect than to burden the provinces with the tax... to pay their deputies and to make it apparent to everyone else that it is not enough to recognize faults if one does not have the will to remedy them...» ([26]). Hence the great cardinal failed to turn to the Estates General when he came to power because he could forsee no useful results from its deliberations.

The history of representative institutions in France between 1421 and 1615 may, therefore, be divided into four periods. The first saw the crown exercising the initiative in the Estates General and the estates of Languedoïl but still having the regretful necessity of appealing to the provincial estates before taxes could be collected. The second period witnessed the virtual abandoning of the Estates General and the estates of Languedoïl, but the continued use of smaller deliberative groups of various types to give advice on specific matters. The crown maintained the initiative, but there was little development of procedure because of the different types and limited purposes of the meetings. A third period comprising the last half of the reign of Francis I and nearly all of that of Henry II saw a reduction in the number of these meetings, and the techniques of controlling assemblies were forgotten. The final period, therefore, was characterized by the loss of royal initiative, but this development found the deputies unprepared to assume a larger role. Confusion and lack of accomplishment became the rule. Neither the crown nor the people saw much occasion for the Estates General, and it was rarely convoked. As a result, the loss of royal initiative actually furthered the decay of the Estates General in France.

([26]) *Mémoires du Cardinal de Richelieu*, ed. H. DE BEAUCAIRE, Paris, 1907, I, pp. 367-368.

IX

HENRY IV AND GUYENNE: A STUDY CONCERNING THE ORIGINS OF ROYAL ABSOLUTISM[1]

The efforts of Henry IV and his principal minister, the Duke of Sully, to restore order and prosperity to France after the long and destructive Wars of Religion have generally been admired. Most historians have agreed, however, that they did not attempt to change the character of the monarchy, but rather were content to try to make the old system of government work.[2] It is my hope to throw doubt on this interpretation and to suggest that Henry and Sully consciously planned and began to implement changes that would have altered the nature of French government and society by undermining the provincial estates and through them the political position of the seigneural nobility and urban aristocracy. They were unable to make much progress in this direction in most parts of France because of the weakness of the crown, but in their dealings with the *généralité* of Guyenne they proceeded far enough to indicate that they desired to transform the Renaissance monarchy into a more absolute state.

---

[1] This paper was read at the meeting of the American Historical Association in December 1965. The material upon which it is based was gathered during a leave of absence in 1961-1962 made possible by a Social Science Research Council Fellowship and Emory University. To both I would like to express my appreciation. The following abbreviations have been used: "AC" for Archives Communales; "AD" for Archives Départementales; "BN" for Bibliothèque Nationale; "IAD" for *Inventaire sommaire des archives communales antérieures à 1790*.

[2] See for example Jean-H. Mariéjol, *Histoire de France illustrée depuis les origines jusqu'à la Révolution*, ed. E. Lavisse (Paris, 1911), VI, pt. II; Georges Pagès, *La Monarchie d'ancien régime en France* (Paris, 1946), and R. Barbiche, "Étude sur l'œuvre de restauration financière de Sully, 1596-1610," *École Nationale des Chartes, Positions des Thèses* (Paris, 1960), pp. 11-18. In a sense Poirson sees a reorientation of the monarchy, but in the direction of greater popular participation, not royal absolutism. Auguste Poirson, *Histoire du règne de Henri IV* (Paris, 4 vols.; 2nd ed., 1862-67). Exceptions, however, are Roland Mousnier, *La Vénalité des offices sous Henri IV et Louis XIII* (Rouen, 1945); and William F. Church, *Constitutional Thought in Sixteenth-Century France* (Cambridge, Mass., 1941).

The French Renaissance monarchy had been a decentralized state in which town councils and provincial estates had exercised numerous functions of government including, in many instances, the levying and collection of taxes. Even provincial governors and other royal officials had often been more the servants of their own interests or those of a powerful patron than of the king's. Upon occasion provincial estates and towns had claimed that they were unable to vote the taxes the king demanded, but then had given handsome presents to their governor, the secretary of state in charge of their province, and other royal officials to encourage them to persuade the king to accept their pleas of poverty. Clearly the French kings could never become absolute monarchs so long as this situation existed, but to alter it they had to find means to win the loyalty of the bureaucracy and to control the tax collecting machinery. By doing so they could not only deal a deadly blow at the landed and urban aristocracies that controlled the provincial estates and the towns, but also increase their own revenue without adding to the burden on the people. With more money a larger, more trustworthy army could be developed and royal patronage extended to insure wider support. At the same time, by preventing the provincial estates and towns from taxing as they pleased, an important source of revenue that had been finding its way into the hands of the great nobles would be removed. With less wealth the great nobles could afford fewer clients to do their bidding; with fewer clients they would be less dangerous to the king.[3]

It was one thing, however, to talk of winning the loyalty of the bureaucracy and breaking the power of the provincial estates and municipal governments and another thing to put such ideas into practice. Many public officials owed their

---

[3] For essays on the nature of the Renaissance monarchy and aristocracy see J. R. Major,, "The French Renaissance Monarchy as Seen through the Estates General," *Studies in the Renaissance*, IX (1962), 113-25; "The Renaissance Monarchy: A Contribution to the Periodization of History," *Emory University Quarterly*, XIII (1957), 112-24, reprinted in *The "New Monarchies" and Representative Assemblies—Medieval Constitutionalism or Modern Absolutism?* (Boston, 1964), 77-84, ed., A. J. Slavin; and "The Crown and the Aristocracy in Renaissance France." *American Historical Review*, LXIX (1964), 631-45.

posts to the kindly offices of a patron to whom they remained more loyal than to the king. Others felt themselves independent because they had purchased their positions and could not easily be removed. To attack the privileges of towns and provinces was dangerous and even dishonest, for Henry IV, like his predecessors, had promised to respect their privileges.

As a result, although all of Henry's close advisors wanted to see royal authority restored, there was a faction led by Chancellor Bellièvre who thought that this could best be done by winning the loyalty of the vocal elements of the population by respecting the traditional privileges of towns, provinces, and social classes. The people as a whole could be won by providing an honest, frugal government administered by a small number of dedicated officials who owed their positions to their ability and served at the king's pleasure.

The Marquis of Rosny, afterwards Duke of Sully, was the leader of the absolutist faction. He had entered the *Conseil des finances* in 1596 and had become its principal member in 1599. From this key position he attempted to spread his influence into other branches of the government. Exactly when the debate between the two factions began is not known, but by the close of 1605 Sully was clearly victorious and Bellièvre had been asked to surrender the seals of his office.[4]

Among the issues that led to the struggle between the two factions were whether the Paulette should be adopted making offices hereditary, and whether *élections* should be established throughout France in which royal officials, rather than those of the provincial estates and towns, would divide and collect taxes. Sully advocated both these measures. By making offices hereditary appointments could be freed from the influence of great noble patrons like the Duke of Guise, who had placed so many of his clients in the bureaucracy during the Wars of Religion that he had become more powerful in administrative circles than the king himself. By using royal tax collectors the crown could be freed from its financial dependence on provincial estates and towns.

---

[4] R. Mousnier, "Sully et le conseil d'état et des finances: La luttre entre Bellièvre et Sully," *Revue Historique,* CXCII (1941). 68-86.

Professor Mousnier, who has written such an admirable history of the sale of offices, has shown how the Paulette strengthened royal control over the bureaucracy and weakened the patron-client system. He has also proven by use of pamphlets that as early as 1614 contemporaries recognized that this had happened. Nevertheless, he believes that between 1602 and 1604 when the critical debate over the Paulette took place, Henry IV and Sully were motivated primarily by their desire to increase revenue. As evidence he argues that Bellièvre failed to mention the political motive for the Paulette when he attacked the proposal and that the crown had need of additional revenue.

Questions of motive, however, are always difficult to determine, especially when, as in this case, the two men who sponsored the measure left no contemporary evidence to explain why they acted as they did. Some years after 1605, Sully did tell Cardinal Richelieu that political considerations were of primary importance, but Mousnier attributes this statement to hindsight. He may, of course, be correct, but it is significant that Richelieu seems to have accepted it as true and the usually well-informed Jacques-Auguste de Thou attributed the Paulette to a desire to strike a blow at the patron-client system as well as to increase revenue. Furthermore, it is at least possible that Bellièvre's insistence that the Paulette would weaken royal authority was in answer to a claim made by Sully that it would make officials more loyal. Even if the effect of the Paulette on the patronage system was not discussed in the council, it may have been considered by Henry IV and Sully. An open attack in the council on the patronage system might have made the great nobles aware of how much the Paulette would endanger their position and have caused them to try to block the proposal. Mousnier is on firm ground when he states that Sully wanted to increase royal revenue, but the need was less compelling between 1602 and 1604 when the Paulette was a major issue than it had been before because the treasury was enjoying a surplus. That Sully was more anxious to increase royal power than to increase royal revenue is also suggested by his refusal to abandon the *élections* in Guyenne in return for reimbursement as will be shown below. Therefore, it seems probable that when Henry IV and Sully proposed to establish the Paulette and the *élections* between 1602 and 1604 they were motivated primarily by the desire to win control over the bureaucracy and the tax collecting machinery in the kingdom.[5]

Since the establishment of hereditary officeholding has been studied by Mousnier, the remainder of this paper will be devoted to the issues surrounding the creation of eight new *élections* in the *généralité* of Guyenne in January 1603, an act which was regarded by its sponsors as preliminary to the establishment of *élections* in the remainder of France.

The *généralité* of Guyenne, one of the largest in France, was created in January 1523.[6] During the reign of Henry IV, it included Rouergue, Quercy, Rivière-Verdun, Comminges, Agenais, Armagnac, Condomois, and Landes, where *élections* were established by the 1603 decree. In this region there were periodic assemblies of the three estates in Rouergue, Quercy, and Comminges, that had voted, divided, and collected taxes prior to the edict. In Rivière-Verdun, Agenais, Armagnac, Condomois, and Landes this task was done in assemblies attended by the deputies of the towns and communities, but rarely by the nobility and clergy. Périgord and the area around Bordeaux known as the *sénéchaussée* of Guyenne were also in the *généralité*, but *élections* had been established here prior to Henry IV's reign. The estates were rarely summoned in the *sénéchaussée* of Guyenne, but the three estates of Périgord met regularly until 1595 when, less than two years after their submission to the king, they ceased to be convoked, strong evidence of Henry's intentions in regard to the estates once he had established his own tax collecting machinery.[7]

---

[5] Mousnier, *Vénalité*, pp. 557-66. Jacques-Auguste de Thou, *Histoire universelle* (Basel, 1742), IX, 716. For Bellièvre's argument see "Contre la Paulette," *Revue Henri IV*, I (1906), 182-88. Jean R. Mallet, *Comptes rendus de l'administration des finances du royaume de France* (London, 1789), esp. pp. 194-95.

[6] L. Desgraves, "La Formation territoriale de la généralité de Guyenne," *Annales du Midi*, LXII (1950), 239-48.

[7] L. de Cardenal, "Les États de Périgord sous Henri IV," *L'Organisation corporative du moyen âge à la fin de l'ancien régime* (Louvain, 1939) III, 163-81. Other evidence of Henry's dislike of the provincial estates is not

IX

In addition to the assemblies of the estates in the individual provinces, there was an Estates General of the *généralité* and government of Guyenne which had met regularly since the closing years of Henry II's reign to deal with matters of interest to all the provinces.[8] Bordeaux did not participate regularly in this huge regional assembly, perhaps because as a *pays d'élection* it was less interested in its financial activities. As a result, leadership fell to the municipal officials of Agen, the next most important town in the region. It is through their activities and those of their deputies to court that the negotiations between the *généralité* and the crown can be best studied during the critical years of the reign of Henry IV.

The earliest clashes between the crown and the inhabitants of Guyenne grew out of the financial disorders that had arisen during the Wars of Religion. In 1597 the *Parlement* of Paris deplored the fact that financial officials were levying a third or half again as much as the king intended on some people while others, more favored, contributed nothing. Minor royal officials and other persons were illegally claiming exemption from the *taille*. To correct these evils the crown dispatched commissioners to a number of provinces.[9] Among them was Michel de Marillac, the future keeper of the seals and rival of Cardinal Richelieu, who was sent to Guyenne.[10]

---

lacking. Concerning a request from the town of Bordeaux that the estates of Guyenne be assembled, he wrote to Matignon in 1595: "... il me semble que le temps n'est pas propre pour faire telles assemblées, lesquelles ordinairment tendent plus à descharges mes subjects de despenses que à me fortiffier et assister en mes affaires; car chacun ne regarde pas plus loin maintenant que à sa commodité particuliere, de sorte que je veulx que vous vous passiés de la dicte assemblée s'il est possible et qu'elle soit remise en temps plus opportun, ..." Berger de Xivrey, ed., *Recueil des lettres missives de Henri IV* (Paris, 1848), IV, 343. On December 30, 1608 Henry told the deputies of the estates of Burgundy "Qu'ils lui parloient toujours des privileges du pays; que ces privileges n'étoint que pour faire des mutineries; que les plus beaux priviléges que les peuples pouvoient avoir, étoient quand ils étoient aux bonnes grâces de leur roi." Poirson, III, 14.

[8] J. R. Major, "French Representative Assemblies: Research Opportunities and Research Published," *Studies in Medieval and Renaissance History*, I (1964), 201-208.

[9] B. Barbiche, "Les Commissaires députés pour le 'régalement' des tailles en 1598-1599," *Bibliothèque de l'École des Chartes*, CXVIII (1960), 58-96.

[10] Barbiche did not mention Marillac's participation in the investigation and believed that Normandy was the only *pays d'états* to which investigators were sent. *ibid.*, p. 62. Marillac's biographer, Nicolas Le Fevre, sieur de Lezeau, said that Chancellor Cheverney sent Marillac to the *généralités* of Limoges and Guyenne. He was given virtual "carte blanche" to do what

No report of Marillac's mission to Guyenne has been found, but we know that he established contact with the three estates of Comminges in the spring of 1599. That October their deputy at Paris wrote that Marillac's initial report to the council had been unfavorable. To put Marillac in a friendly mood before the council consulted him concerning the provincial *cahier*, the deputy reported that he had promised that the estates would pay him 1000 *écus* to which he had some claim.[11]

The recommendations of the commissioners led to a long edict on the *taille* which was issued in March 1600, and to a series of measures directed specifically at Guyenne either because Marillac's report indicated that the situation was worse there than elsewhere or because the provincial estates were thought to be less able to defend their privileges than those in other parts of France.[12]

In 1600 and 1601 Jean de Martin, *trésorier général de France* at Bordeaux, was sent to the various provinces in his jurisdiction to hold the provincial estates, study tax collection, and verify local debts. He found that the provincial estates were needlessly burdening the people by the costs of their frequent meetings which they often held on their own initiative and by the sums they levied to support their own activities. He issued directives that struck severe blows at the independent position the estates had enjoyed. The length of their sessions, the number of representatives, and their daily renumeration were strictly limited. Meetings were to be called only with the express permission of the king and a limit was set on the amount that could be voted to support their legitimate activities. Hardly enough was allowed to pay the costs of holding the assemblies, sending deputies to

---

was necessary. Included in his orders were commissions to assemble the estates of Agenais, Rouergue, Quercy, Comminges, and Rivière-Verdun. BN, ms. fr. 14,027, ch. 2.

[11] AD, Hauté-Garonne, C 3764, nos. 7-10; C 3676, nos. 53-54. The estates of Agenais contacted Marillac during the winter of 1599. AD, Lot-et-Garonne, C 95, fols. 88V, 101.

[12] Barbiche, "Les Commissaires . . . ," p. 84. François-A. Isambert and others eds., *Recueil général des anciennes lois françaises depuis l'an 420 jusqu'à la Révolution de 1789* (Paris, 1821-33), XV, 226-38. Noël Valois, ed., *Inventaire des arrêts du conesil d'état, règne de Henri IV* (Paris, 1886-93), II, nos. 6094, 6114, 6117, 6151, 6159, 6164, 6263, 6294, 6344, 6465, 6479, 6488, 6491, 6511, 6543, 6575, 6577, 6610, 6611.

the king, and paying the debts incurred during the Wars of Religion. If enforced, the opportunity to make handsome presents to royal officials who supported their cause would be removed as well as many opportunities for graft and corruption.[13] On November 15, 1601, the king's council issued a number of decrees supporting Martin's orders. To prevent possible disobedience the council also ordered that henceforth the towns and parishes would turn the taxes they collected over to royal officials rather than to those of the provincial estates.[14] This act was soon followed by a directive sending two commissioners into the provinces with orders to study the tax records since 1585 in search of fraud and illegal exemptions.[15] The final blow fell in January 1603 when the edict was issued creating eight new *élections* in Guyenne.[16]

In evaluating the significance of this last act, one must examine the intentions of the crown. Since the offices in the *élections* were venal, it might be argued that the edict was a fund raising measure rather than one designed to break the power of the privileged classes and move in the direction of royal absolutism, just as Mousnier has suggested that the Paulette, which made offices hereditary, was initially designed to fill the royal coffers, not to undermine the patronage

---

[13] Martin was directed to visit the estates of Comminges, Rivière-Verdun, and Quercy in the spring of 1600. AD, Gironde, C 3873 bis, fols. 26v-27v. AD, Haute-Garonne, C 3680, nos. 1-16. His regulations for the estates of Quercy are at BN, ms. Clairambault 360, fols 12-14v. Sully praised Martin for his efforts. AD, Haute-Garonne, J 103, no. 97. In January and February 1601 Martin held the estate of Condomois, Armagnac, and Agenais. AC, Mézin, BB 2, fols. 65-73v; AC, Condom, BB 18; AD, Gers, E Suppl. 23,936, fols. 191v-94; AC, Isle-Jourdan, BB 2, fols. 52v-55. His regulations on the receipts and expenses in Agen are in AC, Agen, BB 17. An order of the king's council concerning the estates and taxation in Guyenne that was based on Martin's work was issued in Feb. 12, 1611. *Édit du roy, contenant revocation et suppression des huict bureaux d'élections, establis en la généralité de Guyenne par edict du mois de janvier 1603* . . . (Agen, 1612), p. 29-52. There are copies in AD, Lot-et-Garonne and BN, *Actes Royaux*, F. 46,923, no. 3.

[14] Valois, II, nos. 6630, 6639, 6641, 6643-50. AD, Gironde, C 3873 bis, fols. 10v-11v.

[15] G. Tholin, "Des Tailles et des impositions au pays d'Agenais durant le XVI⁰ siècle jusqu-aux réformes de Sully," extract from *Recueil des travaux de la société d'agriculture, sciences et arts d'Agen*, XIII (1875), 28-29. It is unfortunate that this significant work has been neglected by historians.

[16] *Edit . . . portant création et establissement de huict sièges d'eslections . . . de la généralité de Guienne* (Paris, 1603). There is a copy at BN, *Actes Royaux*, F. 46,912, no. 1.

system. The financial motive had evidently been paramount in the minds of Francis I, Henry II, and Henry III when they each in turn had established *élections* in Guyenne only to abolish them almost immediately when the provincial estates offered to reimburse the *élus* for the offices they had just purchased from the crown.[17] For example, in July 1581 *élections* had been created in Guyenne, but they had been abolished "forever" the following year in return for 70,000 *écus*.[18] At times the government frankly stated that it created offices to secure revenue as in January 1587 when it established additional posts in those parts of France where there were *élections*.[19] When Henry IV desperately needed money after the Spanish captured Amiens in 1597, Sully himself suggested that part of the needed sum be raised by creating and selling new offices. Included among the proposed financial positions were offices in the *élections*.[20] Therefore, only by a careful study of the actions of the crown and the leading citizens of Guyenne can it be determined whether the edict creating *élections* in January 1603 was intended as a move towards royal absolutism or merely as another stopgap measure by the Renaissance monarchy to obtain funds.

The decrees issued by the royal government between 1601 and 1603 caused a strong reaction in Guyenne. In the controversy that followed, Sully's desire to alter the nature of the Renaissance monarchy is revealed.[21] To defend their privi-

---

[17] AD, Haute-Garonne, C 3416; C 3804, esp. nos. 1-5, 8, 15, 41, 50, 51. In the 1550's the inhabitants of the villages of Comminges and a few other persons wanted royal tax collectors to avoid the expenses of holding the estates and perhaps for other reasons. C 3804, esp. nos. 6, 7, 9-14, 40, 50c. In their petition to the king's council in 1611 to obtain once more the abolition of the *élections*, the deputies from Guyenne cited five previous instances when *élections* in all or part of Guyenne had been suppressed. Their list was not complete. See pp. 17 and 75-78 of the printed edict of Feb. 12, 1611 cited in fn. 13. See also Tholin, pp. 26-27.
[18] *Edict du roy contenant révocation des édicts de création des sièges d'élections au pais de Guyenne* (Paris, 1582). Copies are at BN, *Actes Royaux*, F. 46,872, no. 8; and in AC, Agen, AA 17.
[19] *Edict du roy pour le restablissement des offices des bureaux d'élections cy-devant supprimez* (Paris, 1587). A copy is at BN, *Actes Royaux*, F. 46,884, no. 1.
[20] Sully, *Mémoires des sages et royales oeconomies d'estat . . . , Nouvelle collection des mémoires pour servir à l'histoire de France* (Paris, 1837), eds. J. Michaud and J. Poujoulat, 2nd sér., II, 248.
[21] Sully failed to mention this controversy in the *Mémoires . . .* probably, as Mousnier has suggested in regard to the Paulette, because he did not want to associate himself and or his master with these generally unpopular

leges which they clearly saw were threatened, the town councils, provincial estates, and Estates General of Guyenne swung into action. Efforts were made to block the royal edicts by winning favorable decisions in the sovereign courts in Bordeaux and Toulouse, by securing the support of Marshal Ornano, the king's lieutenant in Guyenne, and other powerful personages, and by sending one deputation after another to king and council.

The *consuls* of Agen secured Ornano's permission to summon the Estates General of Guyenne to meet in their town in November 1602. Once assembled, the deputies prepared a statement charging that the creation of commissioners to examine their tax records was a clear violation of their privileges and named two deputies to take it to court.[22] Aided by Marshal Ornano their suit was partially successful and on December 31 the decree was suspended by order of the council.[23]

The first round had gone to Guyenne. Anxious to show their gratitude and to insure further favors, Bayonne, Condom, Agen, and perhaps other towns each gave Ornano a fine horse.[24] Ornano, in turn, authorized the Estates General to meet in February and in May 1603 to name delegations to go to the king to secure the permanent revocation of the commissioners and the suppression of an unpopular tax.[25] To support their cause Ornano wrote letters to the king and the chancellor on January 25 expressing the satisfaction of the urban aristocracy of the region at the decision to suspend

---

measures. Mousnier, "Sully et le conseil . . .", p. 73, fn. 5; and *La Vénalité . . .*, p. 209, fn. 664. For this reason and because Sully left no extensive correspondence, his quarrel with Guyenne has been overlooked by nearly all students of the period including Poirson, Mariéjol, Barbiche, and Mousnier himself. There is little on the subject in the Bellièvre correspondence (BN, ms. fr. 15,890-15,911) probably because the chancellor was not directly concerned with financial administration. Furthermore, by the time the struggle reached its height in 1605 he had lost most of his influence. Jean P. Charmeil, *Les Trésoriers de France à l'époque de la Fronde* (Paris, 1964), pp. 360-61, mentions the edict creating the *élections*, but only a few local historians, especially Tholin, *op. cit.*, have recognized its significance.

[22] AC, Agen, AA 33; BB 40, fols. 132v-138; CC 116. AD, Dordogne, 5C 29, fol. 23-23v. Tholin, pp. 29-30.

[23] Valois, II, no. 7387. AC, Agen, BB, 40, fols. 143-144v.

[24] AC, Agen, BB, 40, fol. 148v-149.

[25] AC, Agen, BB, 40, fols. 145v-47; CC 116, procès-verbal of May 1603. AC, Mézin, BB 2, fols. 153v-154. For some relevant correspondence see also AC, Agen, AA 33.

the edict creating the commissioners and on July 19 he pleaded with the chancellor to look favorably upon the *cahier* of the estates.[26]

Once more victory went to Guyenne and on August 2 the edict on the commissioners was permanently revoked.[27] Joyfully the Estates General met in October to express the gratitude of the *généralité* in a tangible way. Taxes were voted to raise 6000 *livres* for Ornano, 1500 for his son, and 600 for his secretary. In addition, each of the successful deputies was voted 4500 *livres*, a handsome sum well in excess of the expenses they had incurred.[28] In November the Estates General met once more, this time to follow up its victory by trying to get the king to revoke the January edict authorizing the new *élections*. The support of the sovereign courts and the *trésoriers généraux de France* at Bordeaux was sought and a new deputation was sent to the king.[29]

This time the government stood firm. The *trésoriers généraux* at Bordeaux refused to permit the tax to be levied to reward Ornano and the others because the king had not given his authorization, the deputations to court met with little success, and in April 1604, the *Parlement* of Bordeaux verified the edict creating the *élections*.[30] Nevertheless, Guyenne continued to resist in the hope of getting rid of the new financial officials and preventing the actual establishment of the *élections*. The *consuls* of Agen arranged for the assistant syndic of Agenais to purchase one office for 3000 *écus* and frightened a less friendly officeholder so much that he abandoned his post.[31] In March 1604 the three estates of Comminges adopted regulations designed to reduce the costs of holding the estates in order to silence criticism in the province itself, but continued to levy illegal taxes with the result that they were rebuked by the king's council. Rivère-

---

[26] BN ms. fr. 15,897, fols. 339 and 351. *Archives historiques du département de la Gironde*, XIV (1873), 387-89.

[27] AC, Agen, CC 118, extract of the *cahier* of Aug. 2, 1603.

[28] AC, Agen, CC 116, procès-verbal of Oct. 11, 1603; BB 40, fols. 166-68, 191-92. BN, ms. fr. 18,168, fols. 17-18v.

[29] AC, Agen, BB 40, fols. 168v-169v; CC 116, procès-verbal of Nov. 18, 1603.

[30] AD, Gironde, C 3874 bis, fol. 135-35v, AC, Agen, CC 120, Bazas to Agen, July 24, 1604.

[31] Tholin, p. 32.

Verdun was likewise reprimanded.[32] The *trésoriers généraux* at Bordeaux reported to Sully in August 1603 that Rouergue was resisting new taxes and the following year the president of the *Parlement* of Toulouse wrote the king that the estates were stirring up trouble and preventing the decrees of *Parlement* from being executed.[33] A voluminous correspondence was carried on by the *consuls* of the towns in the hope of devising some means of defending their privileges and in the fall of 1604 it was decided that the individual provinces should send deputations to the king and council to seek the revocation of the edict creating the *élections* and other concessions.[34]

Agen's municipal officials chose their first *consul*, Julien de Camberfore, Sieur de Selves, to represent their town and the province of Agenais.[35] Selves arrived in Paris around the middle of December 1604 and quickly contacted the king who referred him to Sully and his council.[36] There followed a ten month battle between the powerful minister and the outspoken defender of municipal liberties. Their frequent engagements are clearly revealed by Selves' numerous letters to the *consuls* at Agen and by other sources. Neither Sully nor Selves were intellectuals and one looks in vain in Sully's utterances for learned explanations of royal prerogative such as James I was then regaling the elected representatives of the English people, and in Selves' for comments on the concept of popular sovereignty that had lately found so many defenders in France. Sully justified his acts in terms of the corruption of the estates and the welfare of the people; Selves in terms of tradition and privilege.

The contest between the two men was not as uneven as it may initially seem. Selves alone was nothing, but as the spokesman of traditional privileges and procedures he found many supporters both in the provinces and in the king's

---

[32] AD, Haute-Garonne, C 3686, nos. 16-17. Valois, II, no. 9305.
[33] AD, Gironde, C 3874, fols. 39-40v. BN, ms. fr. 23,198, fols. 288-95.
[34] AC, Agen, AA 33, Correspondance of 1604. AC, Condom, BB 18, esp. entries in October and November 1604.
[35] Selves's valuable correspondance has been utilized by Tholin, pp. 32-50.
[36] AC, Agen, CC 111, Selves to Agen, Dec. 21, 1604; CC 120, letters of Selves to the consuls of Agen, Dec. 1604; CC 123, Selves to Agen, Jan. 1, 1605.

council itself. Sully, on the other hand, owed his power solely to royal favor. His proud demeanor and fiery temper had won him many enemies whose numbers were augmented by his firm opposition to the graft and corruption that had lined the pockets of courtiers and officials for so long a time. In the early months of 1605 he felt that he was on the verge of disgrace.[37] Even when he was clearly master of the council, progress was slow. He never managed to have an edict issued establishing *élus* in the other *généralités* and they did not begin to function in all of Guyenne until 1609.[38]

Sully was thoroughly convinced that the officials of the provincial estates and towns were using their position to exempt themselves and their friends from taxation and to vote handsome sums for those who attended the estates, served as deputies to court, or performed other duties that might seem to justify reward. He was equally certain that large sums were granted to great nobles and royal officials in return for defending local privileges. Such practices, he thought, overburdened the people and denied necessary revenue to the crown. His information was derived from the investigations that had been held in Guyenne by financial officials, from reports from the *Parlement* of Bordeaux, and from disgruntled local inhabitants. In their first meetings in December 1604, therefore, Sully told Selves that the current financial administration in Agenais made the establishment of *élections* necessary and that most of the inhabitants of the province favored this step. Later Sully made revealing comments about the small revenue the king received from Agen and the heavy burden borne by the people, comments accompanied by a question of whether money was levied for gifts and local purposes, a question to which he well knew the answer.[39] This is not to suggest, however, that Guyenne

---

[37] Sully, III, 20-25, 34-40. Sully reported that his enemies accused him of disbursing royal funds in such a manner as to win the support of certain great nobles.
[38] Marc -A. -F. de Gaujal, *Études historiques sur le Rouergue* (Paris, 1858-59), II, 482.
[39] Selves's December 1604 letters from Paris are in AC, Agen, CC 111 and CC 120. His 1605 correspondance is in CC 123, including the Jan. 1 letter containing Sully's question concerning the gifts. Selves wrote of Sully's insistence that the *élus* were necessary on Jan. 12 and 30, Feb. 11, March 16 and 20, May 2, 18, and 20, and on other occasions. The most

alone was set aside for punishment. Sully made no attempt to hide the long range objectives of the crown. The king, he declared to Selves, "wants the *taille* to be levied in all of France in the same fashion." He specifically said that Languedoc, Dauphiné, and Provence were earmarked for *élections*.[40]

Sully evidently did not feel secure. Selves often reported that Gilles de Maupeou, intendant of finances, was the only member of the council who supported Sully on the *élections*. Villeroy, the influential secretary for foreign affairs, Sillery who was soon to become keeper of the seals, Forget de Fresnes, the secretary of state in charge of Guyenne, and other councillors told Selves that they did not believe that the *élus* were necessary.[41] Perhaps it was for this reason that Sully did all he could to discourage and frighten the deputies so that they would depart without submitting their petitions to the council. From the beginning he insisted that there was no chance that the king would revoke the edict creating the new *élections*. When Selves persisted in his mission, Sully threatened to throw him in the Bastille on the grounds that he had a faulty procuration. When this did not suffice, he threatened him with his cane, and when Selves finally managed to appear before the council, Sully stormed out of the room in anger.[42] Little wonder Selves arrived at the conclusion that "those who come here for the welfare of the

---

serious attack on the administration of the Agen *Consuls* was launched by the *procureur du roi* in Agenais. He claimed that he had been threatened by the *consuls* when he had tried to examine their financial records as instructed by the *Parlement* of Bordeaux. He sent a report to the king charging the *consuls* with financial disorders and abuses, charges which Selves was called upon to answer. AC, Agen, CC 122; CC 123, Selves to Agen, Feb. 15, March 3, and March 8.

[40] AC, Agen, CC 123, Selves to Agen, Feb. 11 (no. 13). See also letter of Jan. 30. This correspondance helps to confirm Richelieu's comment that Henry IV would have liked to establish *élections* in Languedoc. *Mémoires du Cardinal de Richelieu* (Paris, 1929), eds. G. Lacour-Gayet and R. Lavollée, IX, 302-303. Selves reported on April 6 that the crown wanted to treat Brittany in the same manner as Guyenne.

[41] AC, Agen, CC 111 and CC 120, Selves to Agen, Dec. letters, 1604; CC 123, Selves to Agen, March 3, 10, and May 14, 1605.

[42] AC, Agen, CC 123, Selves to Agen, Feb. 11 (nos. 12 and 13), March 3, 8 (no. 19), 20, and 27.

[43] *Ibid.*, Feb. 11 (no. 12).

people are hardly welcome."⁴³ "There is nothing so odious here," he wrote, "as syndics and deputies."⁴⁴

Since Selves and many other deputies braved his anger, Sully did all he could to discredit them and the cause they represented by obtaining letters and documents charging them with dishonest practices. He was not above tampering with the mail, Selves charged, and as a precaution the intrepid deputy usually entrusted his dispatches to friends going to Guyenne rather than to the post. He often repeated information given in an earlier letter and in several instances wrote twice the same day to insure that one letter would arrive safely.⁴⁵ When it became necessary to send very secret information to Guyenne around the first of April, the deputies from the *généralité* decided that one of their number should go in person.⁴⁶

Sully tried to discourage deputies from coming to court with petitions that might be favorably received by refusing to authorize payment for their services. Indeed, he even attempted to prevent assemblies from meeting to elect deputations to court. One of Selves's tasks was to try to get the council to authorize the tax voted by the estates in 1603 to reward those who had participated in the negotiations to secure the revocation of the edict on the commissioners. On January 22, 1605 the council decided to permit Ornano and his son to keep the 7500 *livres* that had been voted them, perhaps because they were fearful of offending a marshal of France at a time when his aid was needed in his restless government. The deputies, however, were not even permitted to receive compensation for their expenses.⁴⁷ Little wonder that

---

⁴⁴ *Ibid.*, March 10, 1605. For similar statements see letters of March 8 (nos. 18 and 19), April 22 and 29.

⁴⁵ Selves usually told the *consuls* how he dispatched each letter. He wrote twice on Feb. 11, and March 8.

⁴⁶ AC, Agen, CC 123, Selves to Agen, March 27 and April 6.

⁴⁷ BN, ms. fr. 18,168, fols. 17-18v. Vicose was later permitted to keep 1800 of the 4500 *livres* voted him, fols. 219v-220, but I have found no evidence that the other deputies were compensated for their expenses. AC, Agen, CC 123, Selves to Agen, Jan. 22, Jan. 30, Feb. 11, April 6, and June 22, 1605. For a brief but interesting account of how Vicose combined the roles of a royal official investigating financial matters in Guyenne and of a deputy of the estates defending local privileges, see D. Buisseret, "A Stage in the Development of the French Intendants: The Reign of Henry IV," *The Historical Journal*, IX (1966), 28-30.

as his mission extended month after month, Selves raised the question of his own payment.[48] He also found his efforts to get permission to have an assembly of the estates temporarily blocked by Sully.[49]

From the first, Selves clearly realized the threat that the establishment of the *élus* posed for the towns and estates. In moments when he despaired of success he punctuated his letters with such phrases as they want "to abolish the privileges of the towns in order to be able to do as they please, and remove the means of complaining." Or "Adieu liberties! privileges! Consular offices will no longer have their luster or power." Or again "They have created the *élus* in order to reduce the authority of the consulat .... If we do not take care, we will be consuls only to have the streets cleaned."[50]

On his arrival in Paris Selves had quickly recognized the advisability of joining forces with the deputies of the other provinces in Guyenne in order to have "a stronger battery against the canons of M. de Rosny."[51] Cooperation, however, proved difficult. Some deputies failed to recognize the serious threat that the *élus* posed to their privileges. Others like those from Rouergue and Quercy, preferred to try to persuade the sovereign courts in Toulouse and Montpellier to refuse to verify the edicts creating the new *élections,* a type of resistance not as promising for Agen because the courts in Bordeaux in whose jurisdiction it lay were less friendly. As a result, Selves cooperated closely only with the deputy from Condomois who found himself in a similar position.[52]

To accomplish his mission Selves soon saw that he would have to by-pass Sully and reach the king. To aid in this project he turned to the great personages of Guyenne and the court. Few of his letters fail to mention Marshal Ornano, the lieutenant general in Guyenne, whose aid Selves constantly sought and whose assistance he often received. It

---

[48] *Ibid.*, April 6 and Sept. 12, 1605.
[49] *Ibid.*, May 14, May 18, and May 20, 1605. Permission was, however, eventually granted.
[50] *Ibid.*, CC 123, Selves to Agen, Jan. 22, March 8, (no. 19), and March 10, 1605.
[51] *Ibid.*, Jan. 1, 1605.
[52] AC, Agen, CC 120, Selves to Agen, Dec. 1604; CC 123, Selves to Agen, Jan. 1, Feb. 11, March 3 and 8 (no. 19), 1605.

was Ornano who wrote the king and members of the council to secure a hearing for Selves when Sully wanted to send him away without presenting his petition, it was Ornano who sought permission for the estates to meet so that action could be taken against the *élus* and taxes voted for provincial affairs, and it was Ornano who warned the king that there would be popular disturbances in Guyenne if the *élus* were established.[53] Others Selves turned to included the seneschal of Agen, the secretary of state responsible for Guyenne, members of the council, lesser royal officials, and, of course, the king's mistress. Most of them probably expected a reward for their services although no one was so blunt as Nicolas de Netz, a counselor in the *Cour des Aides*. "Send a well-filled purse," Selves wrote on September 12, ". . . to pay M. de Netz because he has frankly told us that he will do nothing without money," a request that he repeated on October 17.[54]

Apparently Selves' instructions called for him to ask for the revocation of the edict creating the *élus* on the grounds that the *élections* had been abolished "forever" in 1582 in return for a substantial sum. He knew, however, that he would have no success unless the government was compensated for the revenue it anticipated from the sale of the new offices. It was probably to prevent him from making such a proposal that Sully tried to deny him access to the king and other councillors. The minister's efforts to prevent a financial offer from being made is the initial proof that he aimed at royal absolution, not additional revenue, for he knew how tempting a large sum would be to the other councillors and perhaps the king.

To circumvent Sully, Selves met with a group of the other deputies around the middle of March and prepared a plan that had to be kept so secret that it was agreed that one of

---

[53] AC, Agen, CC 123, Selves to Agen, March 8 (nos. 18 and 19), March 10, April 29, May 14, May 20, and July 11, 1605. *Mémoires authentiques de Jacques Nompar de Caumont, duc de la Force* (Paris, 1843) ed., LaGrange, I, 402-404. BN, ms. fr. 23,198, fols. 321-22. Many of Ornano's letters to the king and the chancellor supporting the desires of the inhabitants of Guyenne may be found in BN, ms. fr. 15,897, fols. 325-86; and *Archives historiques du départment de la Gironde*, XIV (1873), 352-438.

[54] AC, Agen, CC 123, Selves to Agen, January 5, 6, 22, Feb. 11 (no. 12), March 3, May 14, June 22, Sept. 12, and Oct. 17, 1605; CC 124, Verduc to Agen July 29, 1605. On Netz mission to Agen see CC 118.

their number would go to Guyenne to win the support of Ornano and their constituents rather than entrust their proposals to the mail. The plan called for getting Ornano's permission for the provincial estates to meet so that a definite financial offer could be made in return for abolishing the *élections*. Ornano was also to write the king telling him of the growing unrest in Guyenne. In this manner, the king would be confronted with a choice of adhering to his absolutist designs and of keeping the *élus* at the risk of rebellion, or of accepting a substantial sum of money accompained by a reduction of local discontent. It is true that some revenue would be achieved by the sale of the new offices, but as these officials would have to be paid salaries, this approach would be less profitable than accepting the offer of the estates.[55]

There was no doubt in Selves' mind that Sully would choose the road to absolutism. He therefore by-passed him and the council and made the offer to the king through the Countess of Moret, his current mistress. If she was successful, he warned the *consuls* on June 22, it would be necessary to give her "a fine present." Selves originally hoped for a reply in several weeks, but Sully's absence at a Protestant assembly and, perhaps, the indecision of the king and his other councillors led to a long delay. On August 23 Selves was recalled by the *consuls* of Agen, but he lingered on at court until October grasping at every hope of succes. Sully remained determined, however, and his influence on the king increased. Slowly resistance was stifled in the badly-divided provinces of Guyenne, the sovereign courts verified the necessary edicts, and the *élus* were appointed. By 1609 they had begun to collect taxes in all of Guyenne.[56]

---

[55] AC, Agen, CC 123, Selves to Agen, March 16, 27, April 6, 22, 29, May 14, 18, 20, and June 4, 1605. To persuade the consuls of Agen to accept the proposals of the Paris deputies, Selves pointedly told them in his letter of April 22 of a deputy sent by the *Parlement* of Bordeaux to protest against some tax farmers who Sully wished to send home without being heard, but the king, fearing an uprising, gave reasonable satisfaction. There was already considerable unrest in southwestern France because of the activities of some nobles and Protestants and the suffering of the agricultural classes. Mariéjol, VI, pt. 2, 4-5, 44-45, 66-72.

[56] Selves correspondance between June 22 and Oct. 17 is in AC, Agen, CC 120 and CC 123 except for some letters which appear to have been lost. Letters of Verduc, who joined Selves in Paris during the latter part of his mission and remained as Agen's representative after his departure,

HENRY IV AND GUYENNE 381

Selves and his fellow deputies had failed.[57] With the coming of the *élus* the Estates General of Guyenne became inactive,[58] and the provincial estates maintained a precarious existence by virtue of a royal decree permitting each of them to levy 3000 *livres* annually for local expenses, a sum too small to pose a threat to the crown or to justify for long the existence of the estates in the minds of the inhabitants.[59] Had

are at CC 124, along with letters from some deputies from other provinces in Guyenne. After Selves departure from court, most of the resistance to the *élus* was carried on by other provinces. The syndic of the nobility of Armagnac visited the estates of Comminges in Dec. 1605 and suggested that the provinces of Guyenne unite in an effort to block the establishment of the *élus*. Comminges sent a deputation to Ornano to seek his advice and assistance. AD, Haute-Garonne, C 3690, nos. 15-16. On Jan. 7, 1606, Ornano wrote the king telling him that the establishment of the *élections* was causing strong resentment in Guyenne because there was a tradition passed on from father to son that the *élus* would subvert their privileges, franchises, and liberties which had been preserved for so many years under the crown. The bourgeoisie and the inhabitants of the *plat pays* were especially fearful that they would be over-taxed because the *taille* was *réele*. He expressed fear that the edict would lead to unrest and, in conjunction with the seneschal and governor of Quercy, urged that the edict creating the *élections* be revoked. BN, ms. fr. 23,198, fols. 321-22. In 1606 the deputy of Comminges to court borrowed 10,250 *livres* as a down payment and purchased the offices in the *élection* in the name of the *pays* de Comminges for 25,250 *livres*. AD, Haute-Garonne C 3691 nos. 3-4; C 3692, nos. 53-54; C 3693, nos. 3-5; C 3694, nos. 1-6. Comminges still owned the offices when they were abolished in 1611. See pp. 25-26 of the printed copy of the edict of Feb. 1611 cited in fn. 13. Rouergue, Quercy, and other provinces continued to protest and in Dec. 1608 the *élus* were still not established in the first named province. *IAD, Aveyron,* ser. G, 89, AD, Aveyron, C 1903. In May 1609 the Estates General of Guyenne was permitted to meet once more to elect deputies to go to court to protest against the *élus*. AD, Gironde, C 3977. Valois, II, no. 14,891. AD, Agen, BB 40, fols. 368v-69v.

[57] Selves attributed his difficulties to the failure of the provinces in Guyenne to cooperate more closely. AC, Agen, CC 123, Selves to Agen, March 8 (no. 19) and March 12. He may have been partially correct because the Estates General of Guyenne had never been able to relegate the smaller estates to secondary status as the estates of Languedoc had its diocesan and seneschalsy assemblies. However, other rivalries lessened Guyenne's capacity to resist. The failure of the nobility and clergy to participate in many of the provincial estates must have weakened them. It is noteworthy that the most effective resistance was offered by the estates of Comminges and Rouergue where the three estates acted as a unit. To make matters worse the third estates of Agenais was then quarreling with the nobility over whether the *taille* was *réele* or *personnelle*. Part of Selves' mission was to support the suit at court. See AC, Agen, CC 123, Selves to Agen, Feb. 15; March 3, 6, 10, and 27. See also CC 108, CC 118, and CC 121. A similar dispute was a major factor in the establishment of *élections* in Dauphiné during the reign of Louis XIII. The towns in Agenais also quarreled among themselves and Selves devoted much of his time trying to thwart Villeneauve-sur-Lot's special deputy to court who was seeking a general levy on the region to repair a bridge. *Ibid.*, May 25, June 4, July 3, 11, Aug. 27, and Sept. 12; CC 120, Selves to Agen, Aug. 6, 1605. On this long dispute see also Valois, II, nos. 6212, 8721, 12,011, and 14,686.

[58] I have found no evidence of a meeting of the Estates General of Guyenne in 1605, 1606, 1607, or 1608.

[59] This decree of July 14, 1607 reaffirmed the rule regulating the estates

Henry IV lived or Sully remained the leading figure in the council, royal absolutism would have become firmly established in Guyenne at this time, but this was not the case. Henry was removed from the scene by the hand of an assassin on May 1610 and Sully resigned his principal posts in January 1611.

The regency of Marie de Medici has generally been interpreted as a disorderly period in which the crown unsuccessfully attempted to purchase the obedience of the great nobles at home and to establish friendly relations with Spain abroad. To me it was more than this for it marked the abandonment of Henry IV and Sully's attempt to establish royal absolutism and the return to the consultative tradition of the Renaissance monarchy with its respect for the rights and privileges of towns, provinces, estates, and social classes. No longer did Sully dominate the council; in his place stood Villeroy, Jeannin, and Sillery, three men who Selves had believed to be sympathetic to his cause. The new government tried to modify the Paulette[60] and in February 1611 revoked the edict of 1603 creating the *élections* in Guyenne in return for the provincial estates reimbursing the *élus* for the cost of their offices.[61]

There followed a period of increased activity for the Estates General and the provincial estates of Guyenne in spite of efforts of the crown to prevent a renewal of their past abuses, but a few years after Louis XIII personally assumed the reins of government, he reverted to the policies of his father. In September 1621 he ordered that *élections* once more be created in Guyenne. As a result the Estates General soon died and the provincial estates slowly decayed and finally disappeared during the course of the century. In July 1622 Louis issued an edict creating *élections* in Languedoc, but that province was temporarily saved through the intervention of its lieutenant general.[62] Both of these events

---

established by Martin in 1601. AC, Agen, CC 128; and Valois, II, no. 11,190.
[60] Mousnier, *La Vénalité* .... p. 568.
[61] The printed copy of this edict cited in fn. 13 also contains a copy of the *cahier* the deputies of the Estates General of Guyenne presented the council on Nov. 20, 1610 asking that the *élections* be suppressed.
[62] Major, "French Representatiive Assemblies ...," 201-208. *IAD, Haute-Garonne*, Sér. B, no. 420. Claude de Vic and Jean Vaissete, *Histoire générale de Languedoc* (Toulouse, 1874-1905), XI, 981.

took place before Richelieu came to power but at a time when Sully's lieutenant, Gilles de Maupeou, was the superintendent of finances in charge of Guyenne and Michel de Marillac, whose investigation of the financial abuses in Guyenne in 1599 had been partly responsible for the temporary establishment of the *élections* there a few years later, was one of the king's councillors with specfic responsibility for Languedoc.[63]

The assault on the provincial estates was renewed with unparalleled vigor between 1628 and 1630 when orders were issued creating *élections* in Dauphiné, Burgundy, Languedoc, and Province. The plan of Henry IV and Sully seemed about to be put into effect, but the Day of Dupes (November 10, 1630) led to a reversal of policy. Michel de Marillac, now keeper of the seals and largely responsible for domestic affairs, was dismissed. His victorious rival, Cardinal Richelieu, abandoned the effort to create an absolute monarchy and permitted Burgundy, Languedoc, and Provence to buy back their privileges just as the government of Marie de Medici had acceded to the wishes of Guyenne in 1611. Because of this act the dream of Henry IV and Sully was never fully realized. Even Louis XIV permitted the provincial estates to function in some parts of France.[64]

---

[63] R. Mousnier, "Les Règlements du conseil du roi sous Louis XIII," *Annuaire-bulletin de la société de l'histoire de France*, (1946-1947), p. 157.
[64] My suggestion that Marillac, not Richelieu, was responsible for the attempt to create the new *élections* has been anticipated by Mariéjol, pp. 405-406 and Pagès, pp. 104-105. In the hope of resolving some unanswered questions, I have begun a detailed study of the relations between the crown and the provincial estates during the first half of the seventeenth century. For bibliographical material, see Charmeil, pp. 359-74.

X

French Representative Assemblies: Research Opportunities and Research Published[1]

THE STUDY of representative institutions has always held an honored position in the English-speaking world. Bishop Stubbs was by no means the first to see in Parliament the basic ingredient for the constitutional history of England and during the last few decades Sir Lewis Namier and Sir John Neale have demonstrated how parliamentary history can be used as a means of studying the social and political structure of a nation. The work of Namier has already led to a reinterpretation of eighteenth-century England and that of Neale may in the long run have almost as much revolutionary significance for the Elizabethan age.[2] Little wonder that a group of English historians are now working on a monumental parliamentary history of their country.

Continental representative institutions have been less thoroughly studied in spite of the activity of the International Commission for the History of Representative and Parliamentary Institutions. This situation may result from the belief that the continental assemblies were less important than their English counterpart either because they often became inactive during the seventeenth century or because they functioned at the provincial rather than the national level. This situation is to be regretted because during the middle ages and the renaissance representative assemblies frequently played as important a role in continental countries as in England and they often provide valuable bases for studies on social and political structure. France is no exception to this rule and it is the purpose of this article to survey the existing studies of its local and provincial representative assemblies and to indicate source materials that provide the bases for further studies.[3]

1. The research for this article was done in 1961–62 by virtue of a Fellowship of the Social Science Research Council and a leave of absence from Emory University. I would also like to express my appreciation to the numerous French archivists whose unrivaled knowledge and unfailing courtesy made this article possible. To them it is gratefully dedicated.

2. Lewis Namier, *The Structure of Politics at the Accession of George III* (2 vols.; London, 1929); and *England in the Age of the American Revolution* (London, 1930); John E. Neale, *The Elizabethan House of Commons* (London, 1949); *Elizabeth and Her Parliaments, 1559–1581* (London, 1953); and *Elizabeth and Her Parliaments, 1584–1601* (London, 1957).

3. I have omitted the Estates-General and other comparable assemblies from

It is true that the techniques developed by the English parlimentary historians cannot be applied directly to the French provincial and local estates. The election of the deputies which Namier and Neale have studied to so much advantage in England is of little value because the clergy and nobility usually attended the French estates by right and the town councils generally named one or two of their number without argument.

On the other hand, the quantity of surviving documents on some of the individual provincial estates during the renaissance is far greater than for the English Parliament during the same period in spite of a dearth of diaries. The official nature of the French documents does

---

this survey because I am engaged in writing their history from 1421. For a summary chapter and references to the more important works on the earlier period see Ferdinand Lot and Robert Fawtier, *Histoire des institutions françaises au moyen âge* (Paris, 1958), II, 545–77. Attention should also be called to the various articles published in the *Studies Presented to the International Commission for the History of Representative and Parliamentary Institutions* and to P. S. Lewis, "The Failure of the French Medieval Estates," *Past and Present*, XXIII (1962), 3–24. I also plan to write a one-volume history of the provincial estates from the Wars of Religion to the reign of Louis XIV, but this study will not be of sufficient depth to remove the need for detailed studies of the individual institutions. References in this article to the archives and printed works are more complete for the renaissance than for the fourteenth and eighteenth centuries where I have neither done nor intend to do any research, but I have included some comments on these centuries in the hope of making the article more useful. There have already been several general studies of the provincial estates, but although those of F. Laferrière, "Mémoires sur l'histoire et l'organisation comparée des États provinciaux aux divers époques de la monarchie jusqu'à 1789," *Mém. de l'ac. des sciences morales et politiques de l'Institut de France,* XI (1862), 341–576; and Lucien Lachaze, *Les États provinciaux de l'ancienne France et la question des États provinciaux aux XVIIe et XVIIIe siècles. L'Assemblée provinciale du Berri sous Louis XVI* (Paris, 1909), are of sufficient length to be of value, they are not based on an adequate amount of research and were written before many of the studies on the individual provincial estates were published. Too brief, but more up to date and penetrating are H. Prentout, "Les États provinciaux en France," *Bul. of the International Committee of Historical Sciences,* (July, 1928); G. Dupont-Ferrier, "De quelques problèmes historiques relatifs aux États provinciaux," *Journal des Savants* (Aug.–Oct., 1928); Étienne Delcambre, *Les États du Velay des origines à 1642* (Saint-Étienne, 1938), pp. 5–10, 449–82; Émile Appolis, "Les États de Languedoc au XVIII siècle. Comparaison avec les États de Bretagne," *L'Organisation corporative du moyen âge à la fin de l'ancien régime,* II (1937), 129–48; and R. Doucet, *Les Institutions de la France au XVIe siècle* (Paris, 1948), I, 337–59. There are also accounts of the provincial estates in the various histories of French law.

make it difficult to discover the web of family alliances and personal enmities so characteristic of the age, but other types of sources can in part fill this gap. The official documents do, however, provide excellent opportunities to study the relations between the various social classes and between the estates and the *parlements*, financial courts, and above all the local royal officials. Most of the estates had syndics or other officials who looked after local administrative matters when they were not in session. From their activities much can be learned about how provinces were actually governed. In their debates and through their officials the estates dealt with every aspect of life from the building of roads and the support of postal services to the financing of educational institutions and the army. Studies conducted by the provincial and local estates to determine the basis for the division of taxes could be most effectively used by economic historians. The *cahiers* or petitions of grievances submitted to the crown after each session of the estates provide unrivaled sources for the study of public opinion and, if carefully used, insights into the actual conditions and problems of the locality in question. Statements of the poverty of a province, for example, should not be taken too literally when accompanied by requests for a reduction in taxes, but complaints about local royal officials and about the nobles purchasing nonnoble land suggest at least the growing importance of these classes.

The actions of deputies of the estates to the king in council can also be used to considerable advantage. These deputies often resided at court for months and their correspondence with local officials in their respective provinces and their reports after returning from their missions provide not only opportunities to study the relations between central and local government, but also insights into the policies and intentions of the royal councilors themselves. Ranke and many others have based their histories of the various European states largely on the reports of the Venetian ambassadors who had no direct contact with the internal affairs of the country to which they were accredited and often had little knowledge of its society, institutions, and culture. How much better it would have been if these historians had also used the letters and reports of the deputies of the estates, towns, and other corporate bodies who dealt directly with the royal councilors, financial officials, and judges of the sovereign courts. Most of their correspondence has been lost, but enough remains to be a major source for the history of France. Sometimes these deputies to court wrote of their contact with royal officials in general terms; a few, however, had no hesitation in naming those officials who were friends of provincial liberties and those who were exponents of an increase in royal power. Through their correspondence we can glean valuable insights into how and why the more absolutist and more centralized monarchy of Louis XIV replaced that of the consultative, decentralized renaissance.

There are those who scorn local history or at least relegate it to the local antiquarian who spends his evenings and holidays studying the past of his native town. Such an attitude is never justifiable, and least of all for France, a country that has never systematically published the records of its past, and one too large and diversified to be approached from the vantage point of Paris. Henry IV is the only French king after Charles VIII whose letters have been almost entirely published, and for his reign alone do we have an inventory of the acts of the king's council. It is true that the editions of the letters of Catherine de Medici, Cardinal Richelieu, and others are of help and that a summarized edition of the letters of Henry III[4] are now being published, but useful as these collections are they do not solve all the historian's problems even in the realm of political history.

Policy was frequently made at the local level in France especially before the reign of Louis XIV, and even when made at court, it was based largely on reports that came from local officials and other persons in the provinces. Thus the letters and reports a king and his council received are as important as those that they sent, but they have rarely been published, and then usually in relatively obscure provincial journals where they have all too often been neglected. Thus the absence of adequate published collections of documents severely limits the number of significant research topics that can be undertaken at the national level. One is left with a choice of summarizing the work of others or of choosing topics in local history based largely on archival material. The last will remain the most fruitful course until new local studies have provided a more adequate basis for synthesis or until calendars of state papers on the English model are published. Of the areas of local history that need to be exploited few provide as many and as important opportunities as the provincial and local estates.

There were representative assemblies in all parts of France, but in the northern and central provinces they rarely met after the reign

---

4. Michel François *Lettres de Henri III, roi de France. Soc. de l'histoire de France* (Paris, 1959), Vol. I.

French Representative Assemblies

of Charles VII except to ratify treaties, redact customs, or to elect deputies to the Estates-General.[5] As a result there seems to be little need for research on the individual estates of this region except for brief studies on the medieval period.[6] It is to the remainder of France where the surviving documents are more numerous that one must turn to find the best opportunities to study the provincial estates. But before beginning this survey, it would be best to make some general comments on the sources for the history of the estates.

Nearly all the provincial and local estates established archives during the late middle ages or the renaissance that were kept by competent clerks. Where these archives survive there is a superabundance of material for historical research. In general they are to be found in the departmental archives in the capital town of the province catalogued under series C. In addition, copies of the *procès-verbaux* of the assemblies and other documents were often prepared for the deputies to take back to their constituents. These documents have found their way into the other departmental archives in the province where they too are catalogued under series C, into the communal archives where they have generally been placed under series AA or CC, into the various collections of the Bibliothèque Nationale, and less often into the Archives Nationales where they have usually been placed in series K, KK, or H.

Another valuable source for the history of the estates may be found in the registers of the meetings of the town councils. Here the deputies of the third estate were chosen to the provincial estates and here they made their reports on the assemblies upon their return. These registers are in the communal archives under series BB. Additional documents may sometimes be found in other series and in special collections in the departmental and communal archives. Published or manuscript inventories are generally available[7] and the local archivists are

---

5. For a survey of the composition and procedures of the estates in this region and for bibliographical references on both the medieval and renaissance assemblies see my *The Deputies of the Estates General of Renaissance France* (Madison, 1960).

6. The only study of one of the provincial estates of this region from its origins until its demise based on an adequate amount of archival research is Joseph M. Tyrrell, "A History of the Estates of Poitou" (unpublished dissertation, Emory University, 1961). Another fruitful approach would be to study these estates collectively by reign as Antoine Thomas did for the assemblies in central France. See his *Les États provinciaux de la France centrale sous Charles VII* (2 vols.; Paris, 1879).

7. A list of the inventories has been published in *État des inventaires des*

both anxious and able to provide valuable advice. A few documents, especially those related to the nobility, are still in private hands, but they can sometimes be located and permission obtained for their use.

Other types of documents are also available for the study of the provincial estates. The acts and decrees of the king's council are essential and collections may be found in the Bibliothèque Nationale and Archives Nationales.[8] There, and in the Archives du Ministère des Affaires Etrangères are also located the correspondence and papers of many of the leading royal ministers including the reports they received from the provinces.[9] Other sources include the papers relating to the sovereign courts, the *trésorier généraux* of France, and other tax officials. They are located in the departmental archives in the former provincial capitals under series B and C. In the Archives Nationales, the *Trésor des chartes,* series J and JJ, are valuable for the medieval period and series G (especially G^7) on financial matters should be consulted by those who study the estates of the old regime. Much has been lost, but in most instances enough remains to form the basis for excellent histories of provincial estates.

Because of the valuable insights that could be obtained from the study of the provincial estates, there is need for many more histories of these institutions. Some provincial estates, such as those of Languedoc and Burgundy, seem to have been neglected in the post-medieval period because their archives are so rich; others because they are scarcely known to exist. Even when histories of provincial estates do exist, there are often opportunities for further research.

Archives Nationales, départementales, communales et hospitalières au 1er janvier 1937 (Paris, 1938); and *Supplément, 1937–1954* (Paris, 1955). In several instances I have relied on these inventories and have not yet visited the archives cited in this article. I have used the following abbreviations: AN = Archives Nationales, BN = Bibliothèque Nationale, AD = Archives Départmentales, AC = Archives Communales, *IAD* = *Inventaire sommaire des archives départmentales antérieures à 1789,* and *IAC* = *Inventaire sommaire des archives communales antérieures à 1789.*

8. See Noël Valois, *Inventaire des arrêts du Conseil d'État. Règne de Henri IV* (2 vols.; Paris, 1886–93).

9. See for example in the BN, Bellièvre Papers, MSS. fr. 15,890–15,911, and the Séguier Papers, MSS. fr. 17,367–17,412; in the AN, series H^1 on provincial administration, an important source for the estates during the old regime, and in the *Archives du Ministère des Affaires Étrangères,* the Richelieu and Mazarin Papers. Printed documents and secondary works on the provincial estates may be found at the BN under call numbers LK^{14} 1-.

French Representative Assemblies

Most of the studies on the estates have been theses at the *École des Chartes* or in law. The former are often published only in abstracts and the latter are generally organized on a topical basis and are devoted to describing the composition, procedures, and duties of the provincial estates during a given period, usually several centuries in length. This approach has its merits, but little sense of a chronological development emerges. Indeed, constitutional history in the English sense, that is, the day-by-day evolution of an institution as a result of the interaction between the crown and the people in an ever-changing political, social, economic, and intellectual milieu, can scarcely be said to exist in France in studies of the prerevolutionary period. There are, therefore, instances when there is a need to complement an excellent history of a representative institution written with the French topical-institutional approach with an English type chronological-constitutional study. The research opportunities in the field of the French provincial and local estates are therefore almost unlimited. Let us consider some specific examples.

Burgundy.—The estates of Burgundy usually met only once every three years, but when not in session its affairs were looked after by a *Chambre des Élus généraux* and a host of minor officials. The archives of the estates which are among the richest in France offer opportunities to study nearly every type of history from the renaissance until the Revolution.[10] Their great wealth has perhaps been a factor in causing historians to seek less time-consuming subjects and Billioud not unnaturally halted his excellent history of the relatively poorly documented medieval period in 1477.[11] Weill has investigated the estates during the reign of Henry III, but he based his work too narrowly on the *procès-verbaux* of the estates and his conclusion that the estates lost ground to the crown during the reign is open

---

10. Jean Rigault has recently published Joseph Garnier's introduction to the inventory of the archives of the estates located in AD, Côte-d'Or with an up-to-date bibliography. See *AD, Côte-d'Or, ser. C., introduction aux tomes III et IV* (Dijon, 1959). This introduction based on the classification of the archives of the estates suggests many of the topics that could be investigated using this material. Other departmental and communal archives in the province also contain material on the estates and AN, H¹ 98–217 should be consulted on the post-1670 period.

11. Joseph Billioud, *Les États de Bourgogne aux XIV° and XV° siècles* (Dijon, 1922). On the medieval period see also H. Prost, "Les États du Comté de Bourgogne des origines à 1477," *Positions des thèses de l'École des Chartes* (1905), pp. 115–22; and R. de Chevanne, "Les États de Bourgogne et la réunion du duché à la France en 1477," *Mém. de la soc. d'archéologie de Beaune,* XLIII (1929–30), 195–245.

to suspicion.[12] Drouot has written a brief account of the estates during the League in his monumental study of Mayenne.[13] Thomas' treatment of the estates during the reign of Louis XIV is useful in spite of its great age, and Dumont has published an excellent book-length article on the session of the estates in 1718.[14] Outside these works little has been done, although many historians have touched on the estates in their investigation of other subjects.[15]

There were five counties known as the *pays adjacents du duché de Bourgogne*. In two of them, Auxerrois and Bar-sur-Seine, taxes were collected by royal officials and there was no need for regular meetings of the estates, but in the remaining three the estates met at least every third year as in Burgundy. The most important of these estates, Mâconnais, was both *pays d'états* and a *pays d'élection*. Such a combination did not become unusual until the seventeenth century when the crown generally ceased to convoke the estates in those provinces where *bureaux d'élections* had been established to collect taxes. The survival of the estates of Mâconnais is probably to be attributed to the special privileges its officials had obtained in regard to the local royal tax officials and to its close association with the estates of Burgundy to whose meetings it sent a deputation. The estates of Mâconnais have been the subject of an unpublished thesis on the medieval period by Verdat[16] and of an administrative history of the seventeenth and eighteenth centuries by Roussot.[17] The archives of the estates[18] offer sufficient resources for a study of the estates during

12. G. Weill, "Les États de Bourgogne sous Henri III," *Mém. de la soc. bourguignonne de géographie et d'histoire*, IX (1893), 121–48.

13. Henri Drouot, *Mayenne et la Bourgogne, 1587–1596* (Paris, 1937), esp. I, 94–102. See also his *Notes sur la Bourgogne et son esprit public au début du règne de Henri III, 1574–1579* (Dijon, 1937); and with the collaboration of L. Gros his "Recherches sur la Ligue en Bourgogne, II. Matériaux pour servir à l'histoire des États royalistes," *Revue bourguignonne*, XXIV (1914), 47–239.

14. Alexandre Thomas, *Une Province sous Louis XIV. Situation politique et administrative de la Bourgogne de 1661 à 1715* (Paris and Dijon, 1844). F. Dumont, "Une Session des États de Bourgogne; la tenue de 1718," *Annales de Bourgogne*, V (1933)–VII (1935).

15. For some additional works see Rigault's, *Introduction*.

16. M. Verdat, "Les États du Mâconnais aux XIVe et XVe siècles," *Positions des thèses de l'École des Chartes* (1926).

17. Jean Roussot, *Un Comté adjacent à la Bourgogne aux XVIIe et XVIIIe siècles; Le Mâconnais, pays d'États et d'élection* (Mâcon, 1937).

18. The archives are at AD, Saône-et-Loire, C 462–C 772. See Roussot for other sources.

the intervening period and for a more chronological history of the estates during the old regime, but on the whole Roussot's study comes close to fulfilling these needs and there are other representative institutions that offer greater opportunities.

The three estates of Auxonne and Charolais met periodically and through their officials collected taxes, for in neither were there *élections*. The archives of the estates of Auxonne are rich enough to make possible a short study;[19] those of Charolais have already been exploited.[20]

There was a marked tendency for the duchy of Burgundy to absorb the *pays adjacents* during the seventeenth and eighteenth centuries. Auxonne lost its independent status in 1639, Auxerre in 1668, Bar-sur-Seine in 1721, and Charolais in 1751. The estates, where they existed, disappeared at the time of the union and the inhabitants were given representation in the estates of Burgundy. It was only with difficulty that the estates of Mâconnais maintained its independence until the Revolution. Apparently this centralizing movement originated among the officials of the Burgundian estates at Dijon and not from the royal officials at Paris, but it would be interesting to know more about the administrative problems and general climate of opinion that led to these changes.[21]

In 1601, France acquired Bresse, Bugey, and Gex from Savoy. These territories were incorporated into the government and the *généralité* of Burgundy, but their estates continued to meet until the Revolution in spite of some centralizing tendencies and the establishment of *élections* shortly after their conquest. The early history of these estates has been studied, but there is need for research of their activities after their final union with France.[22] Documents in the departmental and

19. The archives are located in AD, Côte-d'Or, C 7482–C 7513.
20. L. Laroche, "Les États particuliers du Charolais," *Mém. de la soc. pour l'histoire du droit et des institutions des anciens pays bourguignons, comtois et romands*, VI (1939), 145–94. The principal sources for the estates are at AD, Côte-d'Or, C 7519–C 7534; and AD, Saône-et-Loire, C 452–C 461.
21. F. Moreau, "La Suppression des États du comté d'Auxonne et leur réunion aux États du duché de Bourgogne," *Mém. de la soc. pour l'histoire du droit et des institutions des anciens pays bourguignons, comtois et romands*, II (1935), 189–94.
22. A. Tallone, "Les États de Bresse," *Annales de la soc. d'émulation et d'agriculture . . . de l'Ain*, LV (1927–28), 272–344, is a good study and includes a good bibliography. See also R. Pic, "Les anciennes assemblées provinciales de la Savoie et du Bugey aux XIIIᵉ et XIVᵉ siècles," *Le Bugey* II (1911–12), 627–35; and "Les États de Savoie, 1400–1601," *Le Bugey*, VI (1923–26), 387–407. On the post-1601

communal archives are adequate to support such a project.[23]

Dauphiné.—The representative assemblies of Dauphiné offer several opportunities for further research. Here there were a wide variety of representative institutions, none of which has been completely studied and some of which are virtually unknown except to a few specialists.[24] The most important of these institutions was the estates of Dauphiné. A. Dussert planned a three-volume history of this institution from its origins, but he died before completing the third volume. As a result there is still no chronological history of the estates for the post-1559 period and no description of its procedures and duties except for the middle ages.[25] To complete Dussert's work would be both a challenging and rewarding task.

---

period see "Observations au sujet des listes électorales de la noblesse du Bugey en 1651 et 1789," *Revue de la soc. littéraire, historique et archéologique du département de l'Ain,* X (1881–82), 218–21; R. Pic, "Les États du Bugey, les trois ordres, l'hôtel de Province 1761–1790," *Le Bugey,* I (1909), 113–18, 329–37; A. Vayssière "Les Archives de l'Ain. Assemblées du clergé de Bresse et de Bugey," *Annales de la soc. d'émulation et d'agriculture . . . de l'Ain,* IX (1876), 82–91, 329–37; and Louis Ricard, *Les Institutions judiciaires et administratives de l'ancienne France et spécialement du bailliage de Gex* (Paris, 1886).

23. The archives for the estates are at AD, Ain, C 886–C 990 for Bresse; C 991–C 998 for Bugey; and C 999–C 1025 for Gex. The archives of the *Intendance de Bourgogne* in AD, Ain, and in AD, Côte-d'Or also should be consulted. Some documents on the estates of this region have been published. Armando Tallone, *Atti delle assemblee costituzionali italiane dal medioevo al 1831. Serie prima, Stati generali e provinciali. Sezione quinta. Parlamenti piemontesi. Parlamento Sabaudo* (3 vols.; Bologna, 1928–29). Jules Baux, *Nobiliaire du département de l'Ain* (2 vols.; Bourg-en-Bresse, 1862–64); and *Mémoires historiques de la ville de Bourg, extraits des registres municipaux de l'hôtel de ville, de 1536 à 1789* (5 vols.; Bourg-en-Bresse, 1868–88), contain some documents.

24. André-Alexandre Fauché-Prunelle, *Essai sur les anciennes institutions autonomes ou populaires des Alpes-Cottiennes-Briançonnaises* (Grenoble, 1857), Vol. II, contains an account of the various representative institutions in Dauphiné, but it is not based on extensive archival research and is not of sufficient length to remove the need for further studies.

25. A. Dussert, "Les États du Dauphiné aux XIVe et XVe siècles," and "Les États du Dauphiné de la guerre de cent ans aux guerres de religion," *Bul. de l'académie Delphinale,* ser. 5, Vol. VIII (1914); and ser. 5, Vol. XIII (1922). Fortunately Dussert did publish several articles on the post-1559 period. They are: "Le Baron des Adrets et les États du Dauphiné (novembre, 1562–février, 1563). Essai d'organisation protestante durant la première guerre de religion," *Bul. de l'académie Delphinale,* ser. 5, XX (1929), 93–136; and "Catherine de Médicis et les États du Dauphiné. Préludes du procès des tailles et arbitrage de la reine-mère en 1579," *Bul. de l'académie Delphinale,* ser. 6, II (1931), 123–89.

X

It would be a challenging task because few relevant documents have been published and the archives of the estates became scattered before the Revolution. However, enough material may be found in the depositories at Paris, in the departmental archives of Isère, Hautes-Alpes, and Drôme, and in the various communal archives and libraries in Dauphiné to provide the sources for an excellent study.[26]

It would be a rewarding task primarily because there was an unusual social alignment in Dauphiné probably brought about by a famous dispute concerning the *taille*. In some parts of France the *taille* was *réelle*, that is, both noble and commoner paid the *taille* on the nonnoble land they held. In other parts of France the *taille* was *personnelle*, that is, the commoner paid the *taille* and the noble did not, regardless of the legal status of his holdings. In Dauphiné the matter was in dispute and for several generations there was a bitter quarrel between the three estates. At first the privileged were victorious, but as the nobility bought more and more land, up to one-half or even three-fourths in some localities, there was less taxable land upon which to base the *taille*.[27] At the same time the size of the royal demands grew rapidly. The inevitable result was a sharp increase in the *taille* assessed upon nonnobles. Led by their gallant syndic, Claude Brosse, the villages protested again and again to the king in council.[28] Failure followed failure until 1634, when the *taille* in Dauphiné was finally declared to be *réelle*, but already the three orders had become so divided that they had been able to offer no effective opposition when in 1628 the crown had suppressed the estates.

During the long struggle between the three orders, each had begun to meet in separate assemblies. The nobility had sought to strengthen its position by welcoming the *anoblis* and the royal officials of the

26. Dussert discusses the sources for the history of the estates in the introduction of each of his volumes. Since he wrote, the holdings of AD, Isère, have been greatly enriched. See Fonds Chaper, J 524^1–J 524^2; IJ 669, IJ 176, and IJ 177. At Paris attention should be called to the Richelieu Papers in the Archives du Ministère des Affaires Etrangères, MSS. 1546 and 1548, and to the pamphlets in the BN, esp. LK^2 661–LK^2 671 and LK^{14} 61–LK^{14} 65.

27. Pierre Cavard, *La Réforme et les guerres de religion à Vienne* (Vienne, 1950), p. 398. This excellent book will prove very useful to anyone studying representative assemblies in Dauphiné during the Wars of Religion.

28. A. Lacroix, "Claude Brosse et les tailles," *Bul. de la soc. départementale archéologie et de statistique de la Drôme*, Vol. XXXI (1897)–Vol. XXXIII (1899). This is a good study, but it is too narrowly based on the sources available at AD, Drôme, to be definitive.

sovereign courts into its ranks.[29] The third estate, on the other hand, was divided against itself because of the divergent interests of the towns and villages. It could not hope to hold its own against the nobility, and some individuals within the order probably welcomed two edicts of 1628 which substituted royal tax collectors (*élus*) for those of the estates and suppressed the estates.

The above facts are not too well established and the motivation behind the actions of the crown and the individual estates is largely a matter for conjecture. Still less well known is the *assemblée du pays* consisting of a handful of members from each estate that the crown turned to after the demise of the estates and that was still meeting as late as 1664 under the presidency of the bishop of Grenoble, or of the assembly of the ten principal towns of Dauphiné whose life extended at least until 1670.[30] The nobles proved to be the strongest defenders of provincial liberty and their efforts to thwart the royal will led to several decrees of the council forbidding them to meet and probably to a somewhat earlier death of their assembly.[31]

The *assemblée du pays* and the individual assemblies of the nobility and third estate should be treated in any history of the estates of Dauphiné because their activities were so interrelated, and the same is true with the assemblies of the individual *bailliages* of Dauphiné which seem to have met rather frequently. An exception to this statement should be made in regard to the assemblies of the Alpine *bailliages* of Embrun, Briançon, and Gap where there was an interesting hierarchy of representative institutions. At the bottom were the assemblies of the *escartons*. There were five *escartons* in the *bailliage* of Briançon prior to the treaty of Utrecht in 1713 when three were ceded to Piedmont, and three *escartons* in the *bailliage* of Embrun each with its separate assembly. The *bailliage* of Gap does not seem to have had any. The *escartons* were small, those in the *bailliage* of Briançon con-

29. One does not have to rely on circumstantial evidence for this statement. The idea was specifically voiced in a joint meeting of the nobility and clergy in 1627. AD, Isère, IJ 669.

30. Heavy reliance would have to be placed on the communal archives for these assemblies. For last-known meetings see AC, Grenoble, BB 111 and BB 112.

31. AD, Isère, has recently acquired the register of the deliberations of the nobility from May, 1602, to July, 1622; IJ 175. Additional material may be found in AD, Isère in l'Hôpital de Grenoble, H 357. For the quarrel between the crown and the nobility the archives of the Conseil des finances should be consulted. See for example, AN, E 24^A, fol. 360-360v; E 129^C, fol. 1-2; and E 134^C, fol. 197-198v.

French Representative Assemblies

taining only from four to twenty-one communities apiece. Each community sent deputies to the assembly of the *escarton*. Above the *escarton* there were assemblies of each *bailliage* and above the *bailliage* assemblies there was the assembly of the *trois bailliages des montagnes*. The assemblies of the *trois bailliages des montagnes* and of the *bailliage* of Gap appear to have ceased in the 1650's, but those of the other two *bailliages* and their *escartons* survived until the Revolution.[32] They provide an excellent opportunity to study the small Alpine towns and villages.

The Provincial Estates in Central France.—There were active provincial estates in all of the provinces of central France during the first half of the fifteenth century and these institutions have been the subject of an excellent study by Thomas.[33] Thomas, however, overemphasized the decline of the representative institutions in the region that took place during the reign of Charles VII. In Basse-Auvergne, Haute-Auvergne, and Forez there were estates that were active enough during the sixteenth and seventeenth centuries to merit special studies. By this time, however, the three orders had ceased to meet together except on rare occasions, and assemblies of the towns had assumed many of the duties formerly exercised by the three estates.

The archives in Forez are not rich, but there is one collection of documents that includes many *procès-verbaux*.[34] From this collection and from other sources Galley was able to compile an incomplete list of the assemblies of the nobility, the towns, and the three estates. His

32. There are some documents on the assemblies of the *bailliage* and of the *escarton* of Briançon in AC, Briançon, which have been exploited by Fauché-Prunelle II, 311–39, and others. The deliberations of Vallée du Queyras provide an excellent source for the assemblies of the *escarton* of Queyras and of the *bailliage* of Briançon during the seventeenth and eighteenth centuries. The assemblies of the *bailliage* of Embrun and of the *escarton* of Guillestre can be investigated during the same period through the rich archives of Guillestre. Especially valuable is BB 18, the deliberations of the *escarton* of Guillestre, 1591–1626. Paul Guillaume has written a brief account of the *escarton* in *IAC, Guillestre* (Gap, 1906), lviii–xci. The archives of the town of Gap provide the best source for the assemblies of the *bailliage* of Gap. All of the above sources contain material on the assemblies of the *trois bailliages des Montagnes* and all but AC, Briançon, are conveniently located in AD, Hautes-Alpes. Together they provide enough material for a doctoral dissertation if it were extended from the origins of the assemblies to the Revolution.

33. Antoine Thomas, *op. cit.* The text of this book, but not the documents, was also printed in the *Revue historique*, Vols. X and XI (1879).

34. AD, Loire, C 32. See also series B for references to the estates.

account of the assemblies themselves, however, is too brief and inadequate to remove the need for a new short study.[35]

In 1788, Bergier published a history of the estates of Auvergne and some documents collected by Dom Verdier-Latour.[36] His work was not devoid of merit, but it was hastily prepared, based on incomplete sources, and dedicated to supporting the pretensions of the town of Clermont-Ferrand at the expense of those of Riom. Rivière did not go much beyond Bergier and Verdier-Latour in his account of the estates in his history of the institutions of Auvergne.[37] Since that time Rouchon has written a penetrating article on the quarrel between the thirteen "good towns" of Basse-Auvergne and the *plat pays,* and Henry has pointed to the research opportunities provided by the estates.[38] Opportunities there are indeed for the departmental archives of Puy-de-Dôme and some of the communal archives contain rich resources.[39] Perhaps they could throw some light on why the "good towns" began to meet without the clergy and nobility, on the quarrel involving the town officials of Clermont, the royal officials of Riom, and the inhabitants of the *plat pays,* and on why meetings of the "good towns" became less frequent in the middle third of the seventeenth century and ceased altogether after 1680. On the last, the adverse comments made by the intendant Mesgrigny should be taken into account.[40]

Almost no work has ever been done on the estates of Haute-Auvergne.[41] As in Basse-Auvergne the clergy and the nobility ceased

35. Jean-B. Galley, *Les États de Forez et les treize villes* (Saint-Étienne, 1914).

36. Antoine Bergier and Dom Verdier-Latour, *Recherches historiques sur les États généraux et plus particulièrement sur l'origine, l'organisation et la durée des anciens États provinciaux d'Auvergne* (Clermont-Ferrand, 1788).

37. Hippolyte-F. Rivière, *Histoire des institutions de l'Auvergne* (2 vols.; Paris, 1874).

38. G. Rouchon, "Le tiers état aux États provinciaux de Basse-Auvergne aux XVIe et XVIIe siècles," *Bul. philologique et historique de comité des travaux historiques et scientifiques* (1930–31), pp. 165–89. P. Henry, "Note sur les États provinciaux de Basse-Auvergne," *Revue d'Auvergne,* LVIII (1944), 57–66.

39. AC, Clermont-Ferrand, Fonds Clermont and Fonds Montferrand are both exceptionally rich. Other communal achives such as those of Aigueperse, Riom, and Thiers should be consulted. In AD, Puy-de-Dôme, ser. C, are the records of the intendance of Auvergne in which there is some important material.

40. Mesgrigny's comments have been published by J.-B. Bouillet, *Tablettes historiques de l'Auvergne* (Clermont-Ferrand, 1842), III, 145–94. See esp. pp. 147–50.

41. Bergier's few comments are based entirely on the handful of documents

X

French Representative Assemblies

to meet with the third estate and the composition of the third estate itself underwent some changes during the sixteenth century. Meetings of the nobility were probably rare, but the third estate was active until about 1625 and met occasionally thereafter until 1693.[42]

Provence.—Provence had the usual wealth of representative institutions, the most important of which was the provincial estates, an aristocratic assembly in which the nobles without fiefs, the chapters, and the lower clergy were excluded and the urban patricians dominated the representation of the third estate. The participants in this assembly were among the most independent minded in France. They did not hesitate to negotiate with foreign powers or to reduce sharply the amount of the grants requested by their king. In 1630 they were threatened by an edict creating *élections* in their province, but it was only when the Prince of Condé was sent with a royal army that order was restored and they purchased the revocation of this and several other edicts at a price considerably lower than that asked by the crown. This very independent spirit, indeed, seems to have led to the demise of the estates, for the crown learned that the general assembly of the communities, an institution that consisted only of the *procureurs* of the clergy and nobility and the representatives of the communities that attended the estates, was much more pliable. After 1639 the estates were no longer convoked and the general assembly of the communities was used until the Revolution to consent to taxes that fell primarily on the third estate. Separate assemblies for the nobility and clergy of Provence also continued to meet, but the former, at least, were infrequently convoked and neither was especially important. In addition to the above institutions there were the usual diocesan assemblies of the clergy and assemblies in the twenty-three *vigueries* and *bailliages* into which Provence was divided.

This motley array of institutions has been studied by Busquet.[43] His work is excellent in most respects, but of necessity his account of

---

Verdier-Latour found for him in Clermont-Ferrand, and Rivière's brief statements come mostly from Bergier. However, see P.-F. Fournier, "Le Cahier de la noblesse de Haute-Auvergne aux États-généraux de 1614," *Revue de la Haute-Auvergne*, XXXII (1947–49), 117–21, and R. de Ribier, "L'Assemblée des États particuliers de la Haute-Auvergne en 1649," *Revue de la Haute-Auvergne*, VI (1904), 125–72.

42. AD, Cantal, contains very little, but there are a few documents on the estates in AD. Puy-de-Dôme ser. C. More valuable are AC, Aurillac, and AC, Saint-Flour.

43. R. Busquet, "Histoire des institutions," *Les Bouches-du-Rhône, Encyclopédie, Départementale* (Marseille, 1921), Vols. II and III.

each institution is too brief to remove the need for further research and he failed to use the rich resources of the Paris depositories. In addition, there is a description written near the end of the eighteenth century of how the estates functioned,[44] a study of the estates in the medieval period that has been published only in an abstract,[45] a volume on the general assembly of the communities that employs the institutional approach almost entirely for the period after the demise of the estates,[46] and a study of the *viguerie* assemblies that for the seventeenth and eighteenth centuries is admittedly only a description of the *viguerie* of Aix.[47] The rest remains to be done. The archives of the estates and of the general assemblies of the communities are rich as are some of the communal archives.[48] Research in this region would be of especial interest because here as in northern Italy noble and commoner often lived side by side in the towns and enjoyed frequent and friendly relations until social stratification became more pronounced after the middle of the seventeenth century.

Languedoc.—Languedoc was one of the largest provinces in France and it possessed one of the strongest and most aristocratic of the provincial estates. Attendance became more and more restricted during the late middle ages and in the eighteenth century only the twenty-three archbishops and bishops, twenty-three barons, and sixty-eight deputies from towns or dioceses could attend the estates where they deliberated together in a single house. The only serious attempt to write a complete history of this institution was published in 1818,[49]

44. Gaspard H. de Coriolis, *Dissertation sur les États de Provence* (Aix, 1867).

45. J. Denizet, "Les États de Provence depuis l'origine jusqu'à la réunion de la Provence à la France, 1481," *Positions des thèses de l'École des Chartes* (1920), pp. 5–17.

46. Bernard Hildesheimer, *Les Assemblées des communautés de Provence* (Paris, 1935).

47. M.-J. Bry, *Les Vigueries de Provence* (Paris, 1910).

48. The archives of the estates of Provence and of the general assemblies of the communities are at AD, Bouches-du-Rhône, Marseille. They are especially rich from about the middle of the sixteenth century. In the seventeenth century the estates and the general assemblies of the communities usually voted to publish their decisions. The largest collections of those of the general assemblies may be found in the BN and in the Bibliothèque Municipale at Aix. These *Abregé des délibérations* are very useful, but do not replace the need to consult the more detailed unpublished *procès-verbaux*. AN, H^1 1182–1362, is valuable for the eighteenth-century assemblies.

49. Baron Trouvé, *Essai historique sur les États généraux de la province de Languedoc* (Paris, 1818), Vol. I.

French Representative Assemblies

but since that time there have been two studies of the medieval period that explain how its organization and procedures developed,[50] one of an unusually high quality on the period around 1630 when the estates were threatened by the establishment of *élections* in the province,[51] and several articles.[52] Most of the archives of the estates, one of the richest in France, remain to be exploited. They provide a splendid source for nearly every type of history.[53]

There were also estates of the *sénéchaussées* and of the dioceses in Languedoc, but the former were so closely connected with the provincial estates that they ought to be studied together. The diocesan estates, on the other hand, must be treated separately, for while they were closely connected with the provincial estates, they often acted in local affairs and have separate archives. Some of these diocesan institutions were genuine assemblies of two or three estates; others permitted little or no participation by the clergy or nobility, but rather consisted of only the local bishop or his representative and the deputies of the communities. Of the former there have been studies of the estates of Vivarais,[54] Velay,[55] and Albi,[56] but they all end before or

50. Paul Dognon, *Les Institutions politiques et administratives du pays de Languedoc du XIII*e *siècle aux guerres de religion* (Toulouse, 1895); and Henri Gilles, "Les États de Languedoc au XV*e* siècles," *Positions des thèses de l'École des Chartes* (1952), pp. 51–54.

51. Paul Gachon, *Les États de Languedoc et l'édict de Béziers, 1632* (Paris, 1887).

52. See for example É. Appolis, "La représentation des villes aux États généraux du Languedoc," *Fédération historique du Languedoc méditerranéen et du Rouissilon, congrès de Rodez, 1958*, pp. 305–10; also in *Album Helen Maud Cam* (Louvain, 1960), I, 219–27; and "Les États de Languedoc et les routes royales au XVIII*e* siècle," *Studies Presented to the International Commission for the History of Representatives and Parliamentary Institutions*, XVIII (1958), 215–36.

53. The archives of the estates are at AD, Hérault, but there are many copies of the *procès-verbaux* and other documents both in Paris and in the various archives of the province. Particular attention should be called to AN, H¹ 748¹⁰–H¹ 1101, which contains some valuable documents such as the acts of the syndics of Languedoc. Documents have been published in Jean Albisson, *Lois municipales et économiques de Languedoc* (7 vols.; Montpellier, 1780–87); Cl. de Vic and J. Vaissete, *Histoire générale de Languedoc* (15 vols; Toulouse, 1872–92); and many other less important places.

54. Auguste le Sourd, *Essai sur les États de Vivarais depuis leur origines* (Paris, 1926); and *Le Personnel des États de Vivarais, 1601–1789, répertoire alphabétique* (Lyon, 1923). The archives of the estates are at AD, Ardèche.

55. Étienne Delcambre, *Contribution à l'histoire des États provinciaux. Les États du Velay des origines à 1642* (Saint-Étienne, 1938). The archives of the

just after the reign of Louis XIII. Companion volumes are needed to carry their stories up to the Revolution. In each case there is ample documentation to support the study. Two historians have written on the three estates of Gévaudan and a number of documents have been published.[57]

The remaining diocesan assemblies in Languedoc were of the latter type. There are studies of the estates of Alais[58] and Lodève[59] in the eighteenth century, of Castres[60] and Lavour[61] during the medieval-renaissance period, of Toulouse[62] during the seventeenth and eighteenth centuries, and of Rieux[63] throughout its history, but the remaining assemblies await their historian.[64]

---

estates are in AD, Haute-Loire. Some documents in these archives have been published in Antoine Jacotin, *Preuves de la maison de Polignac* (5 vols.; Paris, 1898–1906).

56. Elié A. Rossignol, *Petits États d'Albigeois* (Paris, 1875). The archives of the estates are at AD, Tarn.

57. J. Deniau, "Les États particuliers du pays de Gévaudan," *Soc. des lettres, sciences et arts de la Lozère. Chroniques et mélanges*, V (1930), 1–67. Atgar, *Les États du Gévaudan* (thèse de droit, Montpellier, 1957). I have not seen this last work and do not know whether it removes need for further study. The archives of the estates are at AD, Lozère. Numerous documents have been published. See especially F. André, "Procès-verbaux des délibérations des États du Gévaudan," *Bul. de la soc. d'agriculture, industrie, sciences et arts du département de la Lozère*, Vols. XXVI–XXXIII (1875–82); and Gustave de Burdin, *Documents historiques sur la province de Gévaudan* (2 vols.; Toulouse, 1846–47).

58. Jean Mazel, *Histoire administrative du diocèse civil d'Alais, 1694–1789* (Montpellier, 1936). Since Alais was not erected into a diocese with estates until 1694, there is no need for further research.

59. Appolis, *Un Pays languedocien au milieu du XVIIIe siècle, le diocèse civil de Lodève* (Albi, 1951); and "Une assiette diocésaine en Languedoc à la fin de l'ancien régime," *Comité des travaux historiques et scientifiques, section d'histoire moderne et d'histoire contemporaine. Notices, inventaires et documents*, XXII (1936), 5–58. These are the best studies of the diocesan estates.

60. Rossignol, *Assemblées du diocese de Castres* (Toulouse, 1878). The archives are at AD, Tarn, and would support an excellent study on the later period.

61. Rossignol, *Assemblées du diocèse de Lavour* (Paris, 1881). The archives are at AD, Tarn.

62. Thomas Puntous, "Les Assemblées de l'assiette dans le diocèse de Toulouse aux 17e and 18e siècles," *Rec. de législation de Toulouse*, V (1909), 185–225; and *Un Diocèse Civil de Languedoc: Les États particuliers du diocèse de Toulouse aux XVIIe et XVIIIe siècles* (Paris, 1909).

63. Jean Contrasty, *Histoire de la cité de Rieux-Volvestre et ses évêques* (Toulouse, 1936).

64. The archives of most of the remaining diocesan estates are in AD, Hérault,

X

Guyenne.—The representative institutions in the duchy, government, and *généralité* of Guyenne are the least known in France. Here there was an infinite variety of assemblies, but there is not a complete study of a single one of them. At the top of the hierarchy of representative assemblies was the provincial estates. These estates were rarely assembled during the middle ages and early renaissance. By 1556, however, the leading inhabitants of the region had become conscious enough of a community of interest to point out to Henry II that there were assemblies of the estates in each jurisdiction of the region to levy and collect taxes and to regulate other affairs, but that there was no assembly in which the estates of the entire region could meet together to deal with their common problems. Henry II recognized their grievance and on October 24, 1556, wrote the king of Navarre, his lieutenant-general in Guyenne, telling him to have the estates of every diocese and province of his government name one deputy from each order to attend an assembly to be held at a time and place of his choosing.[65] Thus a renaissance monarch authorized the creation of a representative institution whose deputies were drawn from a larger territory than any other in France with the possible exception of Languedoc.

The estates of Guyenne assembled at Bordeaux in September, 1557, but meetings do not seem to have become periodic until 1561 when the deputies began to play a major role in taxation. Between 1561 and 1605 there were over sixty meetings of the estates, but during the last years of the reign of Henry IV its activities declined considerably because that monarch, unlike most of his predecessors, had a profound dislike for representative institutions and did all he could to weaken their power. In 1603 he struck a blow at the smaller estates of the region by creating eight *bureaux d'élections* to assume their tax collecting duties. Whether Henry IV chose Guyenne as the place to begin his attack on representative institutions because he believed that they

---

AD, Gard, and AD, Aude, but those of Mirepoix are in AD, Ariège, those of Bas-Montauban are in AD, Tarn-et-Garonne, and those of Petit-Comminges are in AD, Haute-Garonne. Appolis has written several brief articles on the diocesan estates. See "Les compoix diocésains en Languedoc," *Cahiers d'histoire et d'archéologie* (1946), pp. 81–93; and "Les Assiettes diocésaines en Languedoc au XVIIIe siècle. Essai de synthèse," *Fédération historique du Languedoc méditerranéen et du Rouissilon*, XXVIIe et XXVIIIe *congrès, 1953–54*, pp. 115–24; also in *Anciens pays et assemblées d'états*, IX (1955), 53–65.

65. AD, Haute-Garonne, C 3796, No. 3.

were weaker (due to the failure of the clergy and nobility to participate fully in the provincial or in many of the local estates) cannot be said. His death in 1610 was followed by a return to the popular consultative traditions of the renaissance monarchy. The new *élections* were suppressed and the estates of Guyenne met about nine times during the following decade.

Soon after Louis XIII began his personal government, but well before Cardinal Richelieu became chief minister, the attack on representative institutions was renewed. *Bureaux d'élections* were once more created in Guyenne in 1621, meetings of the estates of Guyenne became exceptional, and apparently ceased altogether after 1635.[66] The local estates, stripped of their tax-collecting duties in the mid-1620's when the *élus* actually began to function, slowly waned until by 1680 there were no representative institutions in the entire area except for the diocesan assemblies of the clergy.

The estates of Guyenne is certainly worthy of a study because of the great area over which it operated, because it was the first to suffer from the more authoritarian character of the seventeenth century monarchy, and because it is the least known of all the large representative institutions in France. Unfortunately, only a few related documents have been published[67] and there are no archives for the estates. The historian who undertakes this task will have to search the various depositories at Paris and the departmental and communal archives of the region.[68] Enough could be found to provide the basis for an excellent book.

66. The meeting which the prince of Condé addressed at Bordeaux in November, 1638, was composed of the lieutenant-generals of the local *sénéchaussées* and not elected deputies. BN, MS. Dupuy, 869, fols. 87–91.

67. Most of the published documents are to be found in *Archives historiques du département de la Gironde;* see especially XXVIII (1893), 44–108, and XXXV (1900), 72–75, 192–208. See also Henri Stein, *Charles de France* (Paris, 1919), pp. 714–19; The assemblies of the clergy of the archdiocese of Auch have been studied; see A. Degert, "Les Assemblées provinciales du clergé gascon," *Révue de Gascogne*, Vol. LV (1914) –Vol. LXII (1926).

68. AD, Gironde, ser. C, contains the financial records of the *généralité* and provides a valuable source for the local and provincial estates from the late sixteenth century. For an account of the complicated changes of territory in this *généralité* see L. Desgraves, "La Formation territoriale de la généralité de Guyenne," *Annales du Midi*, LXII (1950), 239–48. Nearly all the departmental and important communal archives contain material, the most important being AD, Haute-Garonne, archives of the estates of Comminges, and AC, Agen.

French Representative Assemblies

At the time the *généralité* of Guyenne was created in 1523, Haut- and Bas Limousin, Périgord, and Lannes were *pays d'élections* and the *sénéchaussée* of Guyenne (Bordeaux and the surrounding territory) became one soon thereafter. Here the absence of tax-collecting duties led the estates to be less active than elsewhere and, except for the estates of Périgord, an article on each would suffice to relate their history.[69]

The estates of Périgord would be worthy of a short book although the efforts of Cardenal have made its last years fairly well known.[70] It was probably the first representative institution to feel the full displeasure of Henry IV, and after 1595 he did not permit it to meet again during his reign. The estates had an executive committee consisting of six members from each order that continued to meet at least until 1605[71] when its mandate expired. Henry IV refused to permit the three estates to assemble again to renew it or to elect new syndics. Thereafter, the three estates met only to elect deputies to the Estates-General. The surviving documents on the estates are not numerous, but enough remains to form the basis for an interesting study.[72]

The three estates of Quercy met regularly under the presidency of the bishop-count of Cahors until the mid-1620's when the *élections* were established. Deprived of its tax-collecting duties, the assemblies

---

69. On Haut- and Bas-Limousin see Thomas, *Les Etats provinciaux de la France centrale sous Charles VII*; and *IAD, Haute-Vienne*, ed. Alfred Leroux (Limoges, 1891), ser. C, pp. xxxii–xxxvi. For Lannes see Leon Cadier, *La Sénéchaussée des Lannes sous Charles VII, administration royale et États provinciaux* (Paris, 1885), extract from *Revue de Béarn, Navarre et Lannes*, Vol. III; and AC, Bayonne, Dax, and Saint-Sever. AC, Bordeaux, Bourg-sur-Gironde, Saint-Émilion, and Libourne, contain information on the assemblies of the three estates and of the towns of the *sénéchaussée* of Guyenne. AD, Haute-Garonne, should be consulted. A few documents have been published in *Archives historiques . . . de la Gironde* and other places.

70. L. de Cardenal, "Catalogue des assemblées des États de Périgord de 1376 à 1651," *Bul. philologique et historique du comité des travaux historiques et scientifiques*, XLIX (1938–39), 243–66; "Les États de Périgord sous Henri IV," and "Les dernières réunions des trois ordres de Périgord avant la Révolution," *L'Organisation corporative du moyen âge à la fin de l'ancien régime* (Louvain, 1937 and 1939), Vols. II and III.

71. AD, Dordogne, 5 C 29.

72. What remains of the archives of the estates is at AD, Dordogne, 5 C 1–5 C 29. See L. de Cardenal, "Note sur les archives des États de Périgord," *Bul. de la soc. historique et archéologique du Périgord*, XXXIX (1912), 145–52. AC, Périgueux, Bergerac, etc., contain material as do the Périgord MSS. in the BN.

became infrequent, the last-known one being in 1673. The archives of the estates are not rich, but Baudel's study is so mediocre that a short one-volume history is needed.[73]

Nestled between Quercy and Limousin lay the Viscounty of Turenne with its eighty-eight parishes and its two assemblies of the estates, both summoned by the viscount as feudal lord. Occasionally the two assemblies met together especially in the eighteenth century, but the more common practice was to meet separately to vote gifts for the viscounts. Only with the reunion to the crown in 1738 did these assemblies cease to meet. This interesting feudal survival has been the subject of two studies.[74] There is little need for further research.

The rich archives in Agenais, however, remain to be exploited. Here in the middle ages there were assemblies of the three estates, but during the course of the sixteenth century the more common practice came to be for the *consuls* or deputies of the towns and communities to meet alone to deal with taxation and other matters. Often the initiative in convoking the estates was taken by the *consuls* of Agen and they generally headed deputations to Paris and served as syndics of the *sénéchaussée*. The estates met several times annually until the early seventeenth century when both Henry IV and Louis XIII sought to limit the number of assemblies to about one a year. Even the edict creating an *élection* in Agenais did not bring the activities of the estates to an immediate end. There was, however, a notable decline in the late 1620's. Assemblies of the twelve principal towns came more and more to be substituted for the assemblies of the estates and even these appear to have ceased altogether after 1679. The archives of the estates of Agenais[75] are the richest in southwestern France and provide an admirable opportunity to study the activities of the bourgeois patricians of Agen in regard to the crown, the local royal officials, and the inhabitants of the smaller towns

---

73. M. J. Baudel, *Notes pour servir à l'histoire des États provinciaux du Quercy* (Cahors, 1881). There are a few documents at AD, Lot, especially in ser. F; and in the manuscript collection of the Bibl. Mun. de Cahors. AC, Cahors, Gourdan, Moissac, Figeac, etc., contain a little as do the BN and AD, Gironde, ser. C. A few documents have been published in Edmond Cabié, *Guerres de religion dans le sud-ouest de la France et principalement dans le Quercy* (Paris, 1906).

74. René Fage, *Les États de la vicomté de Turenne* (2 vols.; Paris, 1894). Jean Bressac, *Privilèges, libertés et franchises de la vicomté de Turenne* (Toulouse, 1922).

75. The archives are a part of AC, Agen, and are located in AD, Lot-et-Garonne. Additional material may be found in the communal archives in the area, some of which have also been transferred to AD, Lot-et-Garonne.

French Representative Assemblies

and communities. Tholin's writings suggest rather than fully exploit the possibilities.[76]

The clergy rarely attended the estates of Armagnac, but the other two orders met frequently until the mid-1620's when the *élus* assumed their tax-collecting functions. Meetings thereafter were exceptional. The *sénéchaussée* was divided into seven *collectes* and each *collecte* had its assembly that was usually attended by a few nobles and the deputies of the towns and communities. A least one of these little estates continued to function until the end of the seventeenth century. For Vic-Fezensac there are a large number of *procès-verbaux*[77] and for Bas-Armagnac there are several for the period 1632-1634.[78] The assemblies of the *collecte* of Auch could be studied through the registers of the deliberations of that town and for the seventeenth century the registers of Isle-Jourdain provide some information on the *collecte* of that name.[79] The estates of the viscounty of Bruilhois with its capital of La Plume, a hilltop community that was taxed on the basis of having only sixteen hearths, provides an opportunity to study the small rural communities. No *procès-verbaux* have been found, but the registers of the deliberations of the councils of La Plume and several other localities are rich enough to justify research from the late sixteenth century.[80] Both Isle-Jourdain and Bruilhois were part of the *aides* of Agenais and

---

76. G. Tholin, "La Ville d'Agen pendant les guerres de religion du XVIe siècle," *Revue de l'Agenais*, Vol. XIV (1887)—Vol. XX (1893); "Des Tailles et des impositions au pays d'Agenais durant le XVIe siècle jusqu'aux réformes de Sully," *Recueil des travaux de la soc. d'agriculture, sciences, et arts d'Agen*, Vol. XIII (1875); "Les Cahiers du pays d'Agenais au États généraux," *Revue de l'Agenais*, Vol. X (1883)—Vol. XII (1885); "Documents relatifs aux guerres de religion tirés des archives municipales d'Agen," *Archives historiques du département de la Gironde*, XXIX (1894), 1–282. For the earlier period, see T. N. Bisson, "An Early Provincial Assembly: The General Court of Agenais in the Thirteenth Century," *Speculum*, XXXVI (1961), 254–81.

77. They are in AC, Vic-Fezensac, now located in AD, Gers. See E suppl. 23, 985–23,987, for scattered *procès-verbaux* of the sixteenth and seventeenth centuries and above all E suppl. 23,936, which contains the *procès-verbaux* of the estates between 1598 and 1671. They are bound in a register, but are not in chronological order. Z. Baqué, "Vic-Fezensac au temps de la Fronde," *Bul. de la soc. archéologique du Gers*, XXXVI (1935), 40–53, has made limited use of this valuable document.

78. AC, Nogaro, AA 11. These archives in AD, Gers.

79. AC, Auch and AC, Isle-Jourdain, are now in AD, Gers.

80. AC, Layrac and AC, Fals, are in AD, Lot-et-Garonne, but AC, La Plume, is still in the commune.

206

also deputed to the estates of that *sénéchaussée*. Very little survives on the estates of Armagnac beyond what is in the *procès-verbaux* of the estates of the *collectes* and the deliberations of the councils of the towns, but there is probably enough on its assemblies and those of its *collectes* for a good book.[81]

The estates of Condomois, Bazadais, and Astarac should also be studied together because they were in the same financial jurisdiction. Very little is known about these assemblies, but it seems probable that the estates of Condomois divided the tax between the three localities in an assembly attended by the deputies of the towns of Condomois and the syndics of Bazadais and Astarac. The estates of Bazadais and Astarac then met separately to divide the tax between the parishes of their respective jurisdictions and to discuss other matters. Almost no *procès-verbaux* have been found concerning these meetings, but it is known that both the nobility and the third estate participated in Astarac. There were also estates in Albret that named deputies to the Estates-General, but in tax matters the individual towns deputed to the estates of Condomois or of Bazadais, depending on their location. As elsewhere the estates ceased to meet regularly soon after the edict was issued in 1621 turning the area into a *pays d'élection*.[82]

The estates of Rivière-Verdun consisted of deputies from twelve towns. Its archives have been lost and Contrasty has extracted what

81. In addition to the above sources a little material may be found in AC, Lectoure, ser. BB and CC. Published works are Paul Parfouru and J. de Carsalade du Pont, "Comptes consulaires de la ville de Riscle de 1441 à 1507," *Archives Historiques de la Gascogne*, XII (1892), esp. I, xvii-xxvi; A. Branet, "Les États d'Armagnac en 1631–32," *Bul. de la soc. archéologique du Gers*, XIV (1913), 168–83, 214–29; J. Duffour, "Députés de l'Armagnac aux États généraux d'Orléans en 1649," *Revue de Gascogne*, LX (1924), 31–33.

82. For Condomois, See AC, Condom, now located in AD, Gers. AA 16, containing twenty-two documents on the estates, could not be found when I was there. However, the deliberations of the municipal council are very detailed from 1588. The deliberations of the councils of Mézin, Astaffort, and Francescas located in AD, Lot-et-Garonne, are valuable from about the same time. For Bazadais the deliberations of the councils in AC, Réole, AC, Monségur, and to a lesser extent AC, Couthures (in AD, Lot-et-Garonne), contain material. For Albret the deliberations of the councils of Casteljaloux, Meilhan, Monheurt, Fieux, Moncrabeau, for the most part in AD, Lot-et-Garonne, contain material as do the deliberations of the council of Tartas located in AD, Lannes. For Astarac see Duffour, "Les États d'Astarac de 1582," *Revue de Gascogne*, ser. 2, VI (1906), 19–30.

French Representative Assemblies

there is of value from a variety of sources. Once more meetings ceased to be regular after the creation of the *élection,* the last-known one taking place in 1654.[83]

Mlle Darbin has just completed a thesis for the *École des Chartes* on the estates of Comminges. Her work, when published, will undoubtedly supplant previous studies, but the rich archives of these estates and the published documents drawn from them are of use to historians of the estates of Guyenne and of the neighboring smaller estates. As elsewhere the establishment of an *élection* in the 1620's reduced the role of the estates; assemblies became infrequent, the last-known one being in 1673.[84]

It is surprising that the estates of Rouergue has never found a historian.[85] All three orders participated actively in its proud history. In between the annual sessions the bishop of Rodez presided over numerous meetings of an executive committee of twelve elected by the estates to administer the affairs of the *sénéchaussée.* Regular meetings of the estates ceased with the establishment of the *élus* in the mid-1620's, the last-known assembly being in 1674. There were also estates in the Haute-Marche, the Basse-Marche, and the county of Rodez including four *châtellenies.* Sufficient documents may be

---

83. Contrasty, *Histoire de Sainte-Foy-de-Peyrolières* (Toulouse, 1917), pp. 198–210. See also Abbè Galabert, "Note sur les États de Rivière-Verdun," *Bul. de lo soc. archéologique du midi de la France,* X (1897), 105–10.

84. The archives of the estates are in AD, Haute-Garonne, C 3401–C 3807. Published documents on the estates include Jean Lestrade, "Les Huguenots en Comminges," *Archives historiques de la Gascogne,* ser. II, Vols. XIV, XV (1910–11); and "Cahiers des remonstrances des États de Comminges aux rois de France ou à leurs lieutenants généraux en Guyenne, 1537–1627," *Soc. des études du Comminges,* Vol. II (1943). See also B. de Gorsse, "Cahier documental concernant le pais et les États de Comminges," *Revue de Comminges,* XLVI (1932), 5–28; V. Fons, "Les États de Comminges," *Mém. de la soc. archéologique du midi de la France,* VIII (1861–65), 161–206; and L. Sahuqué de Goty, "Deux documents sur les États de Comminges et de Nébouzan ou rôle des assemblées provinciales sous l'ancien régime," *Revue de Comminges,* XIX (1904), 177–84.

85. Marc-A. de Gaujal, *Études historiques sur le Rouergue* (4 vols.; Paris, 1858–59); L. Guirondet, "Mémoire sur les États du Rouergue," *Mém. de la soc. des lettres, sciences et arts de l'Aveyron,* Vol. IX (1859–67); and L.-C.-P. Bosc, *Mémoires pour servir à l'histoire du Rouergue* (3 vols.; Rodez, 1797), are of very little value. H. Affre, *Dictionnaire des institutions, moeurs et coutumes du Rouergue,* (Rodez, 1903); and Jacques Bousquet, *En Rouergue à travers le temps* (Rodez, 1961), pp. 89–91, are helpful but much too brief.

found to support a study of these estates in the middle ages as well as the later period.[86]

The Estates in the Pyrénées.—The Pyrénées boasted a large number of representative institutions that survived until the Revolution. There is a certain unity to their history, for during the middle ages and renaissance most of the region belonged to the house of Foix-Navarre. The various estates came directly under the authority of the crown between 1589 and 1620 and were seriously threatened by the creation of *élections* in 1632. The following year they won a reprieve although limits were placed on many of their activities at the same time. The geographical similarity of the region and the historical parallels in the development of the estates offer an ideal situation for a comparative study. The value of such a work is enhanced by the fact that the composition of the various estates and their procedures varied greatly. In a microcosm one can study nearly every type of European representative institution. There were one-, two-, and three-house legislatures; there were some that were dominated by the nobility and others by the third estate. Some were very aristocratic with the lower clergy and the inhabitants of the villages being excluded and the lesser nobility being relegated to a secondary status. Other assemblies practiced an almost pure form of democracy. Two excellent comparative studies exist for the eighteenth century.[87] Sim-

---

86. The archives of the estates of Rouergue are in AD, Aveyron, ser. C. In view of the prominent role played by the bishop of Rodez, ser. G is of unusual value. AC, Millau, and AC, Rodez (cité), are especially valuable and AC, Rodez (Bourg), AC, Conques (in AD, Aveyron), AC, Saint-Affrique, and AC, Villefranche-de-Rouergue, contain material. Published documents include C. Couderc, "Notes sur les fastes consulaires de B. Arribat et documents sur l'histoire de Villefranche," *Mém. de la soc. des lettres, sciences et arts de l'Aveyron*, XIV (1893), 119–294; J Artières, "Documents sur la ville de Millau," *Archives historiques du Rouergue*, Vol. VII (1930); "Mémoire sur la tenue des États de Rouergue, écrit vers 1623, par Durieux, député du pays de Rouergue," *Bul. philologique et historique du comité des travaux historiques et scientifiques* (1885), pp. 23–27; and C. Valade, "Réunion des États de la province de Rouergue à Villefranche en 1649," *Mém. de la soc. des lettres, sciences et arts de l'Aveyron*, XVII (1906–11), 438–44.

87. Maurice Bordes, *D'Étigny et l'administration de l'intendance d'Auch, 1751–1767* (Auch, 1957), I, 254–303; and H. Jolly and H. Courteault, "Essai sur le régime financier des petits pays d'états du midi de la France au XVIIIe siècle," *Bul. de la soc. des sciences, lettres et arts de Pau*, ser. 2, LIV (1931)–LVI (1933). There are unpublished eighteenth-century documents for most of these estates in the AN, ser. H^1.

ilar works on the earlier, formative period of the estates would be of even greater interest.

There are also opportunities to study several of the estates individually. Other estates have already found their historian or cannot be studied because of a scarcity of documents.

The *bilçar* or estates of Labourd was one of the most democratic institutions in Europe. When the syndic thought it advisable, he directed, with the approval of a local royal official, the forty parishes in the jurisdiction to send a *jurat* to the estates at Ustaritz. Here the syndic presented propositions that required a solution, the *jurat* returned to his parish, assembled every head of a house to discuss the syndic's propositions, and then returned to Ustaritz to a second assembly to report the decision of his parish. The will of the majority of the parishes ruled. Unfortunately, few documents concerning this bizarre institution survive for the period prior to the eighteenth century and its historian has not been able to offer a satisfactory explanation of why the nobility and clergy did not participate or why the refer-back system was used in lieu of giving proxies to the *jurats*.[88]

The assembly of the third estate of Soule operated in a somewhat similar manner, but here the nobility and clergy seated together in a separate chamber were able to dominate proceedings. In 1730–1731 the third estate abandoned the refer-back system and the towns began to give their representatives proxies. The estates have been studied only for the eighteenth century, but there is insufficient documentation to support research on the earlier period.[89]

The dismemberment of the kingdom of Navarre as a result of the Spanish conquest left the small portion of that little country on the northern side of the Pyrénées without any estates. As a result a new institution, the Estates-General of Basse-Navarre, was created about 1523. It was divided into two chambers, one for the clergy and nobility and one for the third estate. The three orders often deliberated together, but they voted separately. Two estates could give the law to the third except in matters of finance when the third estate had the final say. Only the upper clergy was admitted, even the chapters

88. Étienne Dravasa, *Les privilèges des Basques du Labourd dans l'ancien régime* (Saint-Sabastien, 1952), contains a good study of the *bilçar*.

89. M. Etcheverry, "À travers l'histoire anecdotique de Bayonne et des pays voisins," *Bul. de la soc. des sciences, lettres et arts de Bayonne*, No. 22 (1937), pp. 107–18. N. Saint-Saëns, "Contribution à un essai sur la coutume de Soule," *Bul. de la soc des sciences, lettres et arts de Bayonne*, No. 34 (1940), pp. 85–97.

having no representation; but all owners of noble houses could enter. No distinction was drawn between the nobles because land in Navarre was alodial and a feudal hierarchy was almost nonexistent. Five towns named deputies directly to the third estate, but the remaining communities sent deputies to assemblies in seven *pays* or valleys where, in turn, deputies were chosen to attend the Estates-General. As these assemblies of the *pays* or valleys met frequently for purposes other than to elect deputies to the Estates-General, there were a goodly number of representative institutions in the tiny kingdom. These assemblies used the refer-back system and other procedures similar to the *bilçar* of Labourd except that the nobility was permitted to participate.

The archives of the Estates-General of Navarre are not especially rich for the period before the personal reign of Louis XIV, but Daranatz has been able to find enough material for a study of estates during the sixteenth century and Destrée has published one on the following period. Both accounts are good, but both rely almost entirely on the institutional approach and the reader emerges with little sense of the chronological development of the estates, a disappointing fact in view of the special relation between the little kingdom and the crown of France. Destrée describes the assemblies of the *pays* and valleys insofar as documentation permits.[90]

There were in a sense four orders in the viscounty of Béarn, some distinction being drawn between the barons and the lesser nobility. The estates, however, was divided into two chambers, one for the clergy, barons, and lesser nobles, and one for the third estate. Voting was done by head in the *Grand Corps*, or upper house, and by community in the lower, each individual vote being carefully recorded in the *procès-verbaux* of the estates. Thus for Béarn, almost alone among the provincial estates of France or for that matter of Europe, the historian can ascertain how each individual or community stood on each issue that was presented to the estates. A unique opportunity is thereby presented for a Namier-like study in which family, religious, and regional alignments are sure to play an important role. A

90. J. B. Daranatz, "Les États de Basse-Navarre au XVIe siècle," *Gure Herria*, Vol. III (1923), and Vol. IV (1924). Alain Destrée, *La Basse-Navarre et ses institutions de 1620 à la révolution* (Zaragoza, n.d.). To the above should be added F. Olivier-Martin, "La Réunion de la Basse-Navarre à la couronne de France," *Anuario de historia del derecho español*, IX (1932), 249–89. For specific data on the archives which are located in AD, Basses-Pyrénées, and for other published works see Destrée, pp. 447–63.

study of the relation between the estates, the house of Foix-Navarre, and finally the crown of France would also be of great interest because of the claims of Béarn to be a sovereign state and because of the powerful position the Protestants achieved there during the late sixteenth century.

The archives of the estates of Béarn are very rich for the renaissance and old regime, but this very fact has probably caused historians to be hesitant to study this period.[91] The continued use of Béarnais well into the seventeenth century and the unusually difficult handwriting in the *procès-verbaux* may have added to their reluctance. Cadier has written a good study of the medieval estates and he and Courteault have published some documents. Rogé has made additional contributions to this period.[92] Dartigue-Peyrou has published two volumes on Béarn between 1517 and 1572, but almost nothing has been done on the later period.[93]

The viscounty of Marsan was a part of the estates of Béarn until 1607 when a separate assembly consisting only of the third estate was established. In the eighteenth century it was further divided with one assembly for Mont-de-Marsan and the thirty-two neighboring parishes and one for the twenty-two or twenty-three remaining communities known as the estates of the *bastilles*. There is insufficient documentation to study these assemblies prior to the middle of the eighteenth century.[94]

---

91. The archives of the estates of Béarn are in AD, Basses-Pyrénées, C 679–C 1525. The *établissements* or complaints of the estates begin in 1436, the series of financial documents in 1487, and the *procès-verbaux* in 1558.

92. Cadier, *Les États de Béarn depuis leurs origines jusqu'au commencement du XVIe siècle* (Paris, 1888); and "Le Livre des syndics des États de Béarn," *Archives historiques de la Gascogne*, Vol. XVIII (1889). Paul Courteault, "Le Livre des syndics des États de Béarn," *ibid.*, ser. 2, Vol. X (1906). P. Rogé, *Les Anciens fors de Béarn* (Paris, 1908).

93. Charles Dartigue-Peyrou, *La Vicomté de Béarn sous le règne d'Henri II d'Albret, 1517–1555* (Paris, 1934), is an excellent general history of Béarn in the period indicated, but the estates is only incidentally treated. His *Jeanne d'Albret et le Béarn d'après les delibérations des États et les registres du Conseil souverain, 1555–1572* (Mont-de-Marsan, 1934), contains a brief description of the estates and many documents. See also Paul Raymond's introduction to *IAC, Basses-Pyrénées*, ser. C and D, (Paris, 1865), III, 58–138; and J. de Bertier, "Les Réceptions aux États de Béarn dans l'ordre de la noblesse," *Actes XIIIe congrès fédération des soc. académiques et savantes Languedoc-Pyrénées-Gascogne, Tarbes, 1957* (1959), pp. 157–61.

94. Henri Tartière, *IAD, Landes*, ser. A-F (Paris, 1868), Introduction, pp. 15–16.

The estates of Bigorre consisted of three chambers, one for each estate. Most of the clergy, including the chapters, were excluded. A distinction was drawn between the barons and lesser nobility, but the third estate was more democratic. Some towns and communities named deputies directly to the estates, others deputed to one of the assemblies held in five valleys where in turn deputies were named to the estates. The archives of the estates of Bigorre[95] contain little for the medieval-renaissance historians, but there was enough here and in other depositories to provide the basis for a good institutional study of the later period.[96] A chronological history would be of some value.

The estates of Quatre-Vallées had a single chamber that was composed of deputies of the third estate. In addition, there were active assemblies in each of the four valleys. The nobility sometimes sought, but with little success, to be included. The archives of the estates contain sufficient material for a history from the late seventeenth century, but it has very little for the earlier period except for some of the estates of the individual valleys, especially between 1622 and 1637.[97] To date almost no research has been done on these institutions.[98]

All three orders participated in the estates of Nébouzan, where they often sat in one chamber but voted apart. Not many documents

---

In AD, Landes, see esp. C 154. Abbé-Bessellère, "Étude sur la ville communale d'une petite ville dans le Marsan au commencement du XVIIIe siècle," *Bul. de la soc. de Borda*, XIII (1888), 304–6.

95. The archives are in AD, Hautes-Pyrénées.

96. Gilbert Pene, *Les Attributions financières des États du pays et comté de Bigorre aux XVIIe et XVIIIe siècles* (thèse, doctorat de droit, U. de Bordeaux, 1959). A copy of this thesis is at AD, Hautes-Pyrénées. It completely replaces Gustave Bascle de Legrèze, *Histoire du droit dans les Pyrénées* (Paris, 1867), pp. 70–92, and may be consulted for archival and bibliographical material on the estates.

97. The archives are at AD, Hautes-Pyrénées, C 279–C 349 bis. See C 284–C 288 for the assemblies of the individual valleys, 1622–37.

98. See Armand Sarramon, *Les Quatre-Vallées: Aure, Barousse, Neste, Magnoac* (Albi, 1954), pp. 282–86; F. Marsan, "Réglement des États du pays des Quatre-Vallées au XVIIIe siècle," *Bul. de la soc. archéologique du Midi de la France*, No. 19 (1896–97), pp. 136–42; Marsan, "La Déclaration du dixième et le pays des Quatre-Vallées en 1741," *Bul. de la soc. académique des Hautes-Pyrénées* (1927), pp. 89–93; and L. Ricaud, "Un Régime qui finit," *Soc. académique des Hautes-Pyrénées. Bul. local*, V (1901–4), 269–358, 367–448.

French Representative Assemblies

concerning this institution have been found and no one has attempted to write its history.[99]

All three orders also participated in the estates of Foix, but here they sat in one chamber and voted together. Not many documents on the estates have been found before the reign of Louis XIV, but there were enough to permit Arnaud to prepare an institutional study.[100] There were no provincial estates in Roussillon, but the estates of the valley of Andorra, so like those of the French Pyrénées before the Revolution, is still functioning today.[101]

Brittany.—There is still a need for further research on the estates of Brittany. The study of Carné[102] has some merit, but it was not based on an exhaustive use of the archives and is too brief and too outdated to answer many questions. Sée has published a long article on the estates in the sixteenth century, but he relied almost entirely on the institutional approach.[103] Only from 1661 is there a completely satisfactory history thanks to the efforts of Rebillon.[104] The archives of the estates of Brittany are very rich from about 1567 when the *procès-verbal* begins, and an excellent history could be written from the Wars of Religion until the personal reign of Louis XIV where Rebillon begins his work.[105] One would especially like

99. Most documents on the estates of Nébouzan are in AD, *Haute-Garonne*, C 3113—C 3117, and C 3253—C 3260. See also AD, Basses-Pyrénées, B 1391—B 1404. Published is a seventeeth-century account of the estates by Louis de Froidour, "Mémoire du pays et États de Nébouzan," *Revue de Pyrénées*, III (1891), 94–104, 387–428; J. Lestrade, "Documents inédits sur les États de Nébouzan," *Revue de Comminges*, XX (1905), 18–30, 57–70; Alphonse Couget, *Les États du Nébouzan tenus à Saint-Gaudens en 1743 et 1789* (Saint-Gaudens, 1880); and Ricaud, *Soc. académique des Hautes-Pyrénées. Bul. local*, V (1901-4), 269–358, 367–448.

100. The archives of the estates of Foix are at AD, Ariège, IC 50—IC 52, IC 189—IC 238. See also C. de La Hitte, "Lettres inédites de Henri IV à M. de Pailhès, gouverneur du comté de Foix, et aux consuls de la ville de Foix," *Archives historiques de la Gascogne*, Vol. X (1886); and G. Arnaud, *Mémoire sur les États de Foix, 1608–1789* (Toulouse, 1904).

101. Appolis. "Une Assemblée administrative sous un régime féodal dans le monde contemporain: Le Trés Illustre Conseil Général des Vallées d'Andorre," *Schweizer Beriträge zur Allgemeinen Geschichle*, Vol. XV (1957), 191–98.

102. Louis de Carné, *Les États de Bretagne* (2 vols.; Paris, 1862).

103. H. Sée, "Les États de Bretagne au XVIe siècle," *Annales de Bretagne*, X (1894–95), 3–38, 189–207, 365–93, 550–76.

104. Armand Rebillon *Les États de Bretagne de 1661 à 1789* (Rennes, 1932).

105. There is an unpublished study of this period in the library of the *faculté*

to have more knowledge of Richelieu's relation with the estates. He was governor of Brittany and displayed more interest in this province than others. One may suspect that such a study would reveal that the cardinal was less unfriendly to the provincial estates than has been imagined.[106] Rebillons' study of the sources of the estates of Brittany makes it unnecessary to mention them here.[107]

Normandy.—The estates of Normandy has the distinction of being the only important provincial assembly for which there is a history from its origins until its demise around the middle of the seventeenth century. In accomplishing this difficult task, Prentout was aided by the fact that the documentation had been reduced to manageable proportions through the loss of the archives of the estates and by the fact that he could utilize the work of Charles de Beaurepaire who had made several specialized studies on the estates and had published many volumes of documents.[108] Prentout's work is excellent in most respects. He employed both the chronological and institutional approach so that the reader is given a clear picture of the slow evolution of the estates and its relation to the crown as well as a view of its composition, procedures, and functions. Prentout's work does, however, have one serious defect. He relied too narrowly on sources specifically on the estates and neglected other related materials such as the unpublished correspondence of the royal officials and the rec-

---

des lettres in Rennes. It is Besnier, "Les États de Bretagne de 1598 à 1643." I have not yet seen this work.

106. See especially the Archives du Ministère des Affaires Étrangères, mémoires et documents, France, MSS. 1504–6.

107. Rebillon, *Les Sources de l'histoire des États de Bretagne* (Rennes, 1932). Special attention should be called to Charles de La Lande de Calan, "Documents inédits relatifs aux États de Bretagne de 1491 à 1589," *Archives de Bretagne,* Vol. XV (2 vols.; 1908–9). Since Rebillon wrote, several articles have been published in local journals on individual meetings of the estates.

108. H. Prentout, "Les États provinciaux de Normandie," *Mém. de l'ac. nationale des sciences, arts et belles-lettres de Caen,* N.S., Vols. I–III (1925–27). As Prentout includes a bibliography of the sources and published works on the estates of Normandy there is no need to repeat them here. However, special attention should be called to the eight excellent volumes of documents published by Charles de Robillard de Beaurepaire, *Cahiers des États de Normandie sous le règne de Charles IX; Henri III; Henri IV; and Louis XIII et de Louis XIV* (8 vols.; Rouen, 1876–91. Included are not only the *cahiers* of the estates, but other important documents. See also M. Baudot, "La Réprésentation du tiers-état aux États provinciaux de Normandie," *Mém. de l'ac. des sciences, arts et belles-lettres de Caen,* N.S., V (1929), 127–47.

ords of the king's council. This neglect is not very serious for the sixteenth century, perhaps, because the quantity of such material is not too great, but his failure to consult such huge collections as the Bellièvre and Séguier papers in the Bibliothèque Nationale and the Richelieu and Mazarin Papers in the Archives du Ministère des Affaires Étrangères seriously reduces the value of the last portion of his work. There is still need for a study that will provide a satisfactory explanation of why the provincial estates of Nomandy ceased to meet during the middle third of the seventeenth century.

The Estates in the Newly Acquired Territories.—During the reigns of Louis XIV and Louis XV the territory of France was expanded in the direction of the Low Countries and the Holy Roman Empire, and the island of Corsica was acquired. Nearly all the newly acquired provinces had estates. In some instances the French monarchy permitted them to continue to exist; in others it did not. An interesting study could be written explaining the factors that led to the divergent policies of the crown. In addition, there is still need for further research on some of the individual estates.[109]

There were several representative institutions in the territories acquired by France at the expense of the Low Countries. The most important of these was the estates of Artois. This institution has been the subject of an excellent study by Hirschauer from its origins until the French conquest in 1640.[110] For the next twenty-one years the estates was inactive, but it was revived by Louis XIV in 1661 and met frequently from that time until the Revolution. The archives of the estates offer a rich source for the study of the estates of this period.[111]

The estates of Walloon Flanders (or of Lille as it was sometimes called) was favorably treated by Louis XIV and met regularly

---

109. Since I do not plan to carry my own research on the provincial estates beyond the reign of Louis XIII, I have not visited the archives in the newly acquired provinces and have not made as careful a search for published works as I have elsewhere.

110. Charles Hirschauer, *Les États d'Artois de leurs origines à l'occupation française, 1340–1640* (2 vols.; Paris, 1923).

111. The archives are located in AD, Pas-de-Calais. There are two studies on the estates after the French occupation, but François Filon, *Histoire des États d'Artois depuis leur origine jusqu'à leur suppression en 1789* (Paris and Arras, 1861), is superficial; and G. Bellart, "L' Organisation et le rôle financier des États d'Artois de 1661 à 1789," *Positions des thèses de l'École des Chartes* (1956), pp. 23–28, is a descriptive study published as an abstract.

until the Revolution. Its activities have been the subject of a brief superficial study by Melun. A newer work exploiting the archival sources would be welcome.[112] The estates of Cambrésis was equally well treated by the French kings and has been better treated by the historians, no less than three studies having been made of its activities.[113]

The large and important provincial estates in the eastern territories acquired by France displayed less capacity for survival, although the vicissitudes of the Thirty Years War were often as much to blame as the French crown. The estates of Lorraine and Bar, for example, met for the last time in 1629, years before the French conquest. Duvernoy has provided us with an excellent study of the history of this institution until 1559, but except for an article on the assembly of 1626 nothing of value has been done on the last seventy years of the history of the estates.[114] The archives seem to provide ample sources for a study of this period and it would be of special interest to find out why the estates ceased to be convoked at the very time the existence of so many of the French provincial estates was threatened. There were also separate assemblies for the duchy of Bar.

The estates of Alsace underwent a crisis beginning in 1627, but the institution enjoyed a brief revival after the Thirty Years War when assemblies were once more frequent. The French acquisition

112. A. Melun, "Histoire des États de Lille," *Mém. de la soc. impériale des sciences, de l'agriculture et des arts de Lille*, ser. 2, Vol. VII (1860), ser. 3, Vol. I (1864), ser. 3, Vol. II (1865), ser. 3, Vol. IV (1867), ser. 3, Vol. VI (1868), ser. 3, Vol. VII (1869). There seems to be adequate material for a history of these estates in AD, Nord, ser. C, AC, Lille, AC, Douai, and elsewhere. For these and other estates of the region the Archives Générales du Royaume de Belgique and the manuscript collection in the Bibliothèque Royale de Belgique at Brussels should be consulted for the period before the French conquest and AN, H¹, for the period after the conquest.

113. Marc-R. Vilette, *Les États généraux du Cambrésis de 1677 à 1790* (Cambrai, 1950); A. Wilbert, "Les États du Cambrésis," *Mém. de la soc. d'émulation de Cambrai*, XXXI (1872), 247–308; and A. Durieux, "Les États provinciaux du Cambrésis," *Mém. de la soc. d' émulation de Cambrai*, XLI (1886), 131–245.

114. Émile Duvernoy, *Les États généraux des duchés de Lorraine et de Bar jusqu'à la majorité de Charles III* (Paris, 1904). R. Taveneaux, "Les États généraux de Lorraine de l'année 1626," *Annales de l'Est*, ser. 5, II (1951), 15–36. See these two works for bibliographical material. The archives of the estates do not appear to have survived, but the departmental archives, especially of Meurthe-et-Moselle, and the communal archives of the province contain many documents. Attention should also be called to the Lorraine collection in the BN.

X

French Representative Assemblies

quickly terminated its activity, the last meeting being in 1683. There is an adequate study of the estates of Müller.[115]

The estates of Franche-Comté had a long and active history that was abruptly terminated by the French conquest in 1674. Clerc has given us a somewhat romanticized chronological political history of its activities that could be improved upon.[116] His failure to describe how the estates functioned as an institution or to exploit the social-economic data that this institution provides opens further possibilities for research. Four volumes of documents located in the Bibliothèque Nationale have been published, and additional material may be found in AD, Doubs, and the communal archives of the province.[117]

The archives of the estates of Comté Venaissin are among the oldest and richest in France with registers of deliberations dating back to 1404.[118] The early history of the estates until 1594 has been studied by Girard and its final years, 1774-1791, by Mouret, but no one has yet exploited the rich opportunities offered by the intervening one hundred eighty years which saw several brief periods of French rule.[119]

The climate of opinion had changed so much by 1768 when France acquired Corsica that provincial estates were actually established on the island modeled somewhat after those of Languedoc. Villat has devoted some attention to this institution in his general study, but there seems to be an opportunity for further work both here and on an earlier representative assembly.[120]

Other Representative Institutions.—There are several other types of representative institutions that merit consideration, the most important of which was the general assemblies of the clergy. This institution was born at Poissy in 1561 and met periodically until the Revolu-

---

115. Friedrich W. Müller, *Die elsässischen Landstände. Ein beitrag zur geschichte des Elsasses* (Strassburg, 1907).

116. Édouard Clerc, *Histoire des États généraux et des libertés publiques en Franche-Comté* (2 vols.; Lons-le-Saunier, 1881).

117. Adolphe de Troyes, *La Franche-Comté de Bourgogne sous les princes espagnols de la maison d'Autriche. Les Recès des États* (4 vols.; Paris, 1847). See also A. Thiboudet, "Trois recès inédits des États de Franche-Comté," *Mém. de la soc. d'émulation du Jura*, Vol. XXXVII (1873).

118. The archives of the estates are in AD, Vaucluse (Avignon), ser. C.

119. Joseph Girard, *Les États du Comté Venaissin depuis leurs origines jusqu'à la fin du XVIe siècle* (Paris, 1908), extract from the *Mém. de l'académie de Vaucluse*, Vols. XXV-XXVI (1906-7). François Mouret, *Les Assemblées de pays du Comté Venaissin à la veille de la révolution française* (Nimes, 1952).

120. Louis Villat, *La Corse de 1768 à 1789* (2 vols.; Besançon, 1924-25).

tion to vote "free gifts" to the crown. It has been the subject of several collections of documents and many studies, the most important being those of Serbat, Blet, and Lepointe.[121] The assemblies of the clergy in the individual dioceses, however, have received scant attention and studies of several of them would be welcome.[122]

In view of all that has been said about the contributions of Calvin and Calvinism toward representative government, it seems strange that so little research has been done on the French Protestant assemblies where the reformer's influence was presumably most strongly felt. These assemblies were of two types, the synods and the political assemblies, both being organized at the national and local level. At the base of the synod was the consistory of the individual churches, above the consistories were the colloquies, above the colloquies were provincial synods, and above the provincial synods there was a national synod, each type of assembly being composed of both pastors and elders. Several collections of documents concerning the national synods have been published, but there is no detailed modern study of the national or local meetings.[123]

121. Louis Serbat, *Les Assemblées du clergé de France. Origines, organisation, développement, 1561–1615* (Paris, 1906). Pierre Blet. *Le Clergé de France et la monarchie; étude sur les assemblées générales du clergé de 1615 à 1666* (2 vols.; Rome, 1959). Gabriel Lepointe, *L'Organisation et la politique financière du clergé de France sous le règne de Louis XV* (Paris, 1923). For sources and secondary works see Blet, II, 433–49.

122. The *procès-verbaux* and other surviving documents on the assemblies of the clergy of the individual dioceses are generally in the departmental archives, ser. G. For an example of such a study see Appolis, "Les Assemblées financières du clergé dans un diocèse français au XVIIIe siècle," *Anciens pays et assemblées d'ètats*, XXIV (1962), 177–90.

123. The acts of the national synods have been published in English by John Quick, *Synodicon in Gallia reformata: or the Acts, Decisions, Decrees and Canons of those Famous National Councils of the Reformed Churches in France* (2 vols.; London, 1692); and in French by Jean Aymon, *Tous les synodes nationaux des Églises réformées de France* (2 vols.; La Haye, 1710). Élie Benoist, *Histoire de l'édit de Nantes* (5 vols.; Delft, 1693–95), contains many documents. The French Protestant movement in general has been studied by John Viénot, *Histoire de la réforme française des origines à l'édict de Nantes* (Paris, 1926); and *Histoire de la réforme française de l'édit de Nantes à sa révocation* (Paris, 1934). Jacques Pannier, *L'Église réformée de Paris sous Louis XIII, 1610–1621* (Strasbourg, 1922); and *L'Église réformée de Paris sous Louis XIII de 1621 à 1629* (2 vols.; Paris, 1931–32), are valuable for the periods indicated. M. Reulos, "Synodes, assemblées politiques des réformés français et théories des états," *Anciens pays et assemblées*

X

French Representative Assemblies

The political assemblies of the French Protestants have been nearly as neglected, for the often-cited work of Anquez is inadequate in many respects.[124] Fortunately, there are signs of renewed interest in these institutions.[125] The holdings of the departmental archives concerning the Protestants are on the whole disappointing,[126] but there are numerous and valuable manuscripts in the Bibliothèque Nationale,[127] the Paris library of the Société de l'histoire du protestantisme francais, and to a lesser extent the Bibliothèque Mazarine. Loutchitzki has published the *procès-verbaux* of the political assemblies for the period before 1570[128] and Barthélemy for 1620–1622.[129] Professor Gordon Griffiths is now preparing an edition of most or all of the *procès-verbaux* for the intervening years.

Conclusion.—There remain, then, many opportunities for research on the French provincial and local estates and on other types of assemblies. Even those whose interests turn more toward social-economic history can find much of value in the archives of the estates while those who lean more toward political-constitutional history can find no better place to turn. It is to be hoped that the estates will soon be made to yield their all too well-kept secrets of the French monarchy.

---

d'états, XXIV (1962), 97–111, rejects the idea that Calvinism deeply influenced the organization of French Protestant assemblies.

124. Léonce Anquez, *Histoire des assemblées politiques des réformés de France, 1573–1622* (Paris, 1859).

125. R. Kingdom, "Calvinism and Democracy: Some Political Implications of Debates on French Reformed Church Government, 1562–1574," *The American Historical Review*, LXIX (1964), 393–401. G. Griffiths read a paper before the American Historical Association in 1962 entitled: "Tradition and Reform in the Estates of France and the Low Countries in the Sixteenth Century."

126. There are a few exceptions. See, for example, AD, Gard, C 845, C 846, C 865, C 866, C 1919–C 1922, etc.

127. See especially *Nouvelles acquisitions françaises*, MSS. 7176–97, which contain a number of documents including the *procès-verbaux* of the general political assemblies from 1572 to 1625.

128. J. Loutchitzki, "Collection des procès-verbaux des assemblées politiques des réformés de France pendant le XVIe siècle," *Bul. de la soc. de l'histoire du protestantisme français*, Vol. XXII (1873), Vol. XXIV (1875), Vol. XXVI (1877), and Vol. XLV (1896). The *Bulletin* is also of value for the synods.

129. A. de Barthélemy, "Actes de la assemblée générale des églises réformées de France et souveraineté du Béarn, 1620–1622," *Archives historiques du Poitou*, V (1876), 1–473.

Reprinted from Studies in Medieval and Renaissance History, vol. 1, *by permission of University of Nebraska Press. Copyright © 1964 by the University of Nebraska Press.*

XI

The Crown and the Aristocracy in Renaissance France

THE historian has been so bewitched by the disappearance of the great feudal nobles in France during the early Renaissance that he has frequently lost sight of the fact that it was not the kings, but the aristocracy that profited most by their passing. This aristocracy consisted of three elements: the landed nobility, the upper bureaucracy and judiciary who were often nobility of the robe, and the bourgeois patricians of the towns, some of whom had been ennobled by the municipal offices they held.[1]

This article will deal primarily with the composition, economic position, and organization of the landed nobility, the most important element in the aristocracy. The landed nobility must be divided into a greater nobility and a lesser nobility. Some of the great nobles were from ancient families; others were new men who had been recently advanced by royal favor, for between 1515 and 1600 twenty-eight new peerages were created. Lesser titles were handed out with even greater generosity; Henry III alone erected fifty-five counties, marquisates, duchies, and principalities.[2] These great nobles were the true successors of the feudal dukes, for the governors who were sent to administer the duchies that had escheated to the crown were chosen from their ranks. These governors exercised, or sought to exercise, nearly every nonjudicial prerogative of the king. Thus, when Burgundy escheated to the crown, the king did not personally assume the duties of the former dukes; nor was centralized control established from Paris. Rather the provincial customs and institutions were left much as they were with a parlement replacing the feudal court and a governor the former dukes. Around these governors and other great nobles new centers of power emerged in every province, as will be indicated shortly.[3]

---

[1] Jean-R. Bloch, *L'Anoblissement en France au temps de François I*ᵉʳ (Paris, 1934), esp. 11–123.
[2] Roger Doucet, *Les Institutions de la France au* xvıᵉ *siècle* (2 vols., Paris, 1948), II, 462–63.
[3] J. Russell Major, *Representative Institutions in Renaissance France, 1421–1559* (Madison, Wis., 1960), 5–7. If the governor was frequently absent, his lieutenant generally assumed the leading role in the province.

The lesser nobles consisted of the old seigneurial nobility and a new nobility composed of nobles of the robe and the bourgeois—patricians of the towns or their immediate descendants who had purchased fiefs. Some historians have looked upon this movement from the town to the countryside as marking the growing ascendancy of the bourgeoisie. This is a grave error. Between the years 1000 and 1300 thousands of the most enterprising serfs flocked to the towns where many prospered, but one does not speak of this phenomenon as marking the rise of serfdom; it is correctly referred to as the rise of the towns. One does not insist that the serfs brought with them a "serf mentality" that pervaded the towns for centuries, or that they revolutionized urban economic activities by applying to them their knowledge of agricultural techniques. Is it not probable, then, that when many of the ablest and most successful burghers decided to move to the country and live as nobles during the Renaissance, they strengthened the landed nobility, that they adopted the mental attitudes of the class they were joining, and that their urban knowledge had a limited influence on agricultural practices?

It is true that the bourgeois purchaser of a fief was not immediately welcomed by his new neighbors. It was especially galling to a noble with an established family position to learn that he had become the vassal of an overrich merchant; at the Estates-General of 1614 the deputies of the nobility asked that nobles be excused from rendering homage in person to non-nobles who had purchased fiefs.[4] But the fact that the newcomer's nobility was challenged made it all the more necessary for him to abandon his bourgeois ways and live nobly in every respect. When Molière wanted to amuse the court of Louis XIV by satirizing the bourgeois gentleman, he did not depict him as the hardheaded, grasping businessman who was seeking to change rural society and rural economic practices; rather he created Monsieur Jourdain. Indeed, if the newcomers from the town had not been accepted sooner or later by the old nobility, the ranks of the second estate would have been very thin, for the number of families in Burgundy, and presumably in the other provinces, who during the Wars of Religion could trace their gentility back before the Hundred Years' War was small, and some of them had intermarried at one time or another with the bourgeoisie.[5]

[4] *Recueil des cahiers généraux des trois ordres aux États généraux* [hereafter cited as *Cahiers*], ed. Lalourcé and Duval (4 vols., Paris, 1789), IV, 193. For an example of trouble on this score, see Lucien Romier, *Le Royaume de Catherine de Médicis* (2d ed., 2 vols., Paris, 1922), I, 182–83.

[5] On ennoblement by prescription, see Bloch, *Anoblissement en France*, esp. 54–56. Historians who have studied the genealogies of noble families emphasize social mobility in the Renaissance. (See, e.g., Henri Drouot, *Mayenne et la Bourgogne* [2 vols., Paris, 1937], I, 30–33;

If one concedes that these newcomers must be considered part of the landed nobility, it becomes highly probable that this class was improving its economic position. It may be true that prices rose more rapidly in the sixteenth century than income from some landed estates, that some nobles were recklessly extravagant, and that others weakened their families by leaving part of their estates to younger sons, but it is also a fact that when a nobleman had to sell a fief, a purchaser, generally from the towns, was thereby enabled, sooner or later, to join the ranks of the landed aristocracy. Furthermore, the income per acre from land grew considerably,[6] and the aristocracy as a whole increased the size of its holdings. In this it was greatly aided by the enforced sale of a large part of the lands of the Church during the reigns of Charles IX and Henry III,[7] a little-known event that may have been nearly as significant as the sale of monastic lands in England. Income from Church lands that were not sold also found its way into the hands of the aristocracy as this class held nearly every bishopric and abbey in the kingdom. Even a dour Calvinist like the Duke of Sully drew about 45,000 livres per year from the abbeys he held in commendam.[8] Of importance also was the purchase by nobles of many peasant holdings.[9]

That it was possible for a noble to be frugal when the occasion demanded and to increase his income during the inflationary period of the Renaissance may be easily illustrated. The Count of Nevers, for example, reduced the size of his household in January 1468 because of heavy debts incurred by

---

Roland Mousnier, *La Vénalité des offices sous Henri IV et Louis XIII* [Rouen, 1945], 58–63, 506–41; Fernand Braudel, *La Méditerranée et le monde méditerranéen à lépoque de Philippe II* [Paris, 1949], 619–24; Pierre Goubert, *Familles marchandes sous l'ancien régime: Les Danse et les Motte, de Beauvais* [Paris, 1959], 16–19, 79–85, 131–37; Raoul Busquet, *Études sur l'ancienne Provence, institutions et points d'histoire* [Paris, 1930], 320–26; and J. Russell Major, *The Deputies to the Estates General of Renaissance France* [Madison, Wis., 1960], 147.) Édouard Perroy has found that of 215 noble families in Forez in the thirteenth century only 5 survived until the Revolution. He estimated that the average duration of a noble line was from three to six generations. There would, therefore, have been virtually no nobility if newcomers had not eventually been accepted into its ranks. (See his "Social Mobility among the French Noblesse in the Later Middle Ages," *Past and Present*, XXI [Apr. 1962], 31.) Claude de Seyssel, the leading theorist of the French Renaissance monarchy, recognized the existence of and the need for the practice of elevating members of the Third Estate to the nobility. (See *La Monarchie de France*, ed. Jacques Poujol [Paris, 1961], 125.)

[6] J. Russell Major, "The French Renaissance Monarchy as Seen through the Estates General," *Studies in the Renaissance*, IX (1962), 121; Braudel, *Méditerranée et le monde méditerranéen*, 624–37; Pierre Goubert, "The French Peasantry of the Seventeenth Century," *Past and Present*, X (Nov. 1956), 72.

[7] Victor Carrière, *Introduction aux études d'histoire ecclésiastique locale* (3 vols., Paris, 1934–40), III, 423–26; Ivan Cloulas, "Les Aliénations du temporel ecclésiastique sous Charles IX et Henri III (1563–1587)," *Revue d'histoire de l'église de France*, XLIV (1958), 5–56.

[8] Henri Carré, *Sully* (Paris, 1932), 356.

[9] Pierre Cavard, *La Réforme et les guerres de religion à Vienne* (Vienna, 1950), 392–98; Louis Merle, *Le Métaire et l'évolution agraire de la Gâtine poitevine de la fin du moyen âge à la révolution* (Paris, 1958), esp. 49–95.

war, the provision of a dowry for his sister, and other extraordinary expenses. Later, during the inflationary period, the dukes of Nevers managed to increase their income from 115,085 livres in 1551 to 466,260 livres in 1612. Hard times followed, and by 1626 the ducal income had been reduced to 319,260 livres, but expenses had been correspondingly cut to 311,373 livres. The ducal debt in 1625 amounted to only 91,000 livres, or about 30 per cent of the annual revenue.[10] Whether the dukes of Nevers were the exception or the rule will not be known for sure until there are many studies of the finances of noble families—a type of research apparently nonexistent in France today—[11] but numerous Renaissance châteaux throughout the country suggest that on the whole the income of the landed nobility, including the newcomers to its ranks from the towns, was on the increase, and that there were sufficient funds available for an aggressive policy.[12]

The structure and organization of the landed nobility cannot be adequately described until much more research is done, but two facts seem clear. First, the feudal system was still important and enhanced the power and prestige of the great nobles. The archives of the dukes of Nevers contained literally thousands of documents on the homage rendered them by their vassals throughout the Renaissance.[13] In their correspondence nobles constantly alluded to the lord-vassal relation. In 1583 one woman who had inherited two fiefs wrote the La Trémoïlles for permission to render liege homage by procuration, and another woman requested permission to mortgage three baronies. Other letters explain delays in rendering homage.[14] In 1572 young Henry of Navarre told his vassals to be ready to accompany him to La Rochelle and in 1580 informed a supporter that he was dispatching a nobleman "with fifteen or twenty of my gentlemen to help you make

[10] *Inventaire des titres de Nevers de l'Abbé de Marolles*, ed. Jacques Soultrait (Nevers, 1873), cols. 577–78, 528–29, 531. The Duke of Nevers was able to lend Henry III 100,000 livres in 1576 and 400,000 livres more in 1578. (*Ibid.*, cols. 524–25.)

[11] French historians have written many superb economic and social histories since World War II, but these histories deal with selected geographical areas, not noble families. There is also need for works comparable to John M. Bean, *The Estates of the Percy Family, 1416–1537* (London, 1958); Alan Simpson, *The Wealth of the Gentry, 1540–1660: East Anglian Studies* (Chicago, 1961); and Mary E. Finch, *The Wealth of Five Northamptonshire Families, 1540–1640* (Oxford, Eng., 1955).

[12] For example, a study of the construction and alteration of thirty-two châteaux in the Oise Department reveals that twenty-four were built or restored in the sixteenth and early seventeenth centuries, but only two during the period of economic decadence between 1643 and 1715. (Pierre Goubert, *Beauvais et le Beauvaisis de 1600 à 1730* [Paris, 1960], 534.)

[13] *Inventaire . . . de Nevers*, ed. Soultrait, esp. cols. 52–379. The documents are now lost. Other sources are too numerous to cite. Doucet agrees that the lord-vassal relation was widespread, but argues that it was declining. More likely it was being slowly replaced by the "new feudalism." (See *Institutions de la France*, II, 458, 468–74, and for archival sources, II, 487.)

[14] *Lettres missives originales du seizième siècle tirées des archives du duc de La Trémoïlle*, ed. Paul A. Marchegay (Niort, 1881), Nos. 193, 194, 205, 252.

Crown and Aristocracy in Renaissance France 635

war...."[15] The households of the dukes of Nevers were made up largely of their vassals, who were also to be found among those who commanded their towns and châteaux.[16]

Second, the old feudal system was complemented during the Renaissance by a patron-client relation, a system comparable with what the English have called the "new feudalism" or, less elegantly, "bastard feudalism." The "new feudalism" differed from the old in that the client did not render homage to the patron and the patron did not provide the client with a fief or in most instances with specified money payments at regular intervals. It was similar to the old feudalism in that it was an honorable relation based on mutual loyalty and interests. Under the "new feudalism" members of the lesser nobility, ambitious for advancement, often entered the service of a great lord. They might begin with minor posts in the lord's household or as men-at-arms in his *compagnie d'ordonnance,* but if they proved able and loyal they could aspire to important household positions, the captaincy of châteaux, or, through the favor of their patron, positions at court or in the royal bureaucracy. Other nobles preferred to reside at home, but dispatched their sons to their patron's château to serve as pages and to receive modest educations. The patron in return would either provide for the pages when they reached manhood or use his influence with the king to get them positions. When a patron summoned his clients to accompany him into battle, on a journey to court, or for some other service, he expected them to come clad in his livery, or at least his device, and with a suitable number of followers, depending on their rank. If a client got into trouble with the law, the patron was expected to use every means possible to prevent his being punished.[17]

Historians have generally assumed that this system was not formalized by a special oath or indenture,[18] but this view is incorrect, although further

---

[15] *Recueil des lettres missives de Henri IV,* ed. Berger de Xivrey (9 vols., Paris, 1843–76), III, 48–49, 311.

[16] Lists of the members of the ducal household in 1476 have been published in *Inventaire ... de Nevers,* ed. Soultrait, cols. 47–48. Jean de la Rivière, Antoine d'Avril, Hector Berthelon, and Étienne du Pontot were captains of towns and châteaux and holders of fiefs in the duchy. (*Ibid.,* cols. 414–15, 757; fiefs in the duchy are listed *ibid.,* cols. 795–874.)

[17] The patron-client system, or the "new feudalism," has never really been studied in France, but see the brief remarks in Romier, *Royaume de Catherine de Médicis,* I, 167–68, 208–22. For an account of Cardinal Richelieu's relation to his pages, see Maximin Deloche, *La Maison du Cardinal de Richelieu* (Paris, 1912), 327–62.

[18] See, e.g., Édouard Perroy, "Feudalism or Principalities in Fifteenth Century France," *Bulletin of the Institute of Historical Research,* XX (1943–45), 181. Bryce D. Lyon recognized the existence of contracts in France that were identical to the English indentures except that there was no retaining fee, but he apparently saw them as being of purely military significance. (Bryce Lyon, *From Fief to Indenture: The Transition from Feudal to Non-Feudal Contract in Western Europe* [Cambridge, Mass., 1957], 255–58.) However, retaining fees were paid

research will be necessary before it is known whether indentures were common or were only used occasionally. On April 8, 1429, for example, Gilles de Rais took a written oath to serve his powerful cousin, Georges de La Trémoïlle, against all seigneurs and other persons without exception until death.[19] No specific mention was made in this indenture of De Rais's obligation to bring his retainers with him in case of war or of La Trémoïlle's obligation to reward him for his services. These matters seem to have been clearly understood, however, for De Rais served his lord faithfully, and La Trémoïlle won for his twenty-three-year-old client the post of marshal of France three months after the indenture was signed. As this indenture was made just before the dawn of the French Renaissance, it would be well to cite another, dated near the end of this period.

We, duke of Rohan, promise to the queen mother on our honor to serve and defend her at the risk of our life . . . in whatever she will judge suitable to guarantee the king and his estate from the ruin which threatens them, binding ourselves from this hour never to leave the service of her majesty, but to follow her wishes in all things; her majesty having also promised us on the word of a queen to guarantee us from the evil that some will want to visit upon us in consideration of the above. Given at Angers, the 30th of May, 1620.

Henry de Rohan[20]

A rebellion, of course, followed.

Thus a "new feudalism" based on the ties of mutual loyalty between patron and client had come into being by the dawn of the Renaissance and continued to thrive well into the seventeenth century. In some respects it was more dangerous to the crown than the old feudalism because under the old feudalism the lord was limited in the number of his vassals by the

---

in France in the late Middle Ages, and indentures were often used for nonmilitary purposes. (B.-A. Pocquet du Haut-Jussé, "Les pensionnaires fieffés des ducs de Bourgogne de 1352 à 1419," *Mémoires de la société pour l'histoire du droit et des institutions des anciens pays bourguignons, comtois et romands,* VIII [1942], 127–50; André Leguai, *Les Ducs de Bourbon pendant la crise monarchique du xv* siècle* [Paris, 1962], 35.) It is difficult to study indentures in France without thorough archival research because in their publications French historians generally refer to any sort of contract between two nobles as a "treaty of alliance." Thus Leguai published an indenture and a treaty between two equals without drawing any distinctions between them. (*Ibid.*, 195–96, 201–202.) Historians of the Renaissance frequently refer to treaties between nobles, especially during periods of rebellion, and to one noble entering the service of another, but the actual contracts, if any, have almost never been published. Further research is badly needed on this problem, but it is my impression that indentures were used without retainer fees in Renaissance France much as William H. Dunham, Jr., describes them in England. (See his *Lord Hastings' Indentured Retainers, 1463–1483* [New Haven, Conn., 1955]. For the contribution of the *fief-rente* to the theory of *rentes*, see Bernard Schnapper, *Les Rentes au xvi* siècle* [Paris, 1957], esp. 43–44.)

[19] *Les La Trémoïlle pendant cinq siècles,* ed. Louis, duc de La Trémoïlle (5 vols., Nantes, 1890–96), I, 183. On this relationship, see also *ibid.*, 202–203, 226–29.

[20] Archives du Ministère des Affaires Étrangères, mémoires et documents, France, MS. 773, fol. 49.

number of his fiefs, or if the money fief be included, by the size of his treasury. Under the "new feudalism" neither fiefs nor specific payments were required, and the number of clients a lord had was limited only by his prestige, influence, and the popularity of his cause. When Condé raised his standard of rebellion at Orléans in the spring of 1562, the nobles who answered his summons were, with a few exceptions, not his vassals, but they named him as their chief and took an oath not only to obey him, but also "to hold ourselves in readiness as far as we are able in money, arms, horses, and other required things, . . . to accompany him wherever he commands, and to render him faithful service. . . ."[21] This document, which might be called a collective indenture, tied Protestant and other disaffected nobles to Condé and ushered in the Wars of Religion.

Most clients rendered faithful service to their patrons, and most patrons reciprocated by looking after their clients' interests, even to the extent of defending them from the king's justice. When in 1615 a seigneur of Marsillac violated the code and abandoned Condé's service to assume that of the Queen Mother, the angered prince told the sieur de Rochefort to punish him. Marsillac was beaten nearly to death, but the Queen Mother, highly incensed at the treatment meted out to her new retainer, demanded Rochefort's head. A bitter quarrel ensued between Condé and the Queen Mother in the presence of the King. The haughty Prince, while hiding Rochefort from justice, even had the effrontery to present his case against Marsillac to the parlement of Paris. Here he won some support, to the anger of the Queen Mother, but on Marsillac's recovery an apparent reconciliation between the two patrons was achieved. Rochefort continued in Condé's service, and the following year the young Prince got the King to give him the post of councilor of state and a gift of 36,000 livres.[22]

François de Bonne, duc de Lesdiguières, governor of Dauphiné, was willing to go to equal lengths to protect his clients from justice. He had established Marie Vignon, the wife of a silk merchant of Grenoble, as his mistress. This woman, not content with her role, conspired with a Savoyard colonel temporarily in Lesdiguières service to have her husband murdered.

---

[21] Jules Delaborde, *Gaspard de Coligny, amiral de France* (3 vols., Paris, 1879–82), II, 70–74.
[22] Henri, duc d'Aumale, *Histoire des princes de Condé* (7 vols., Paris, 1863–96), III, 42–45; *Négociations, lettres et pièces relatives à la conférence de Loudun*, ed. Louis Bouchitté (Paris, 1862), 788–89, 799. This post of councilor of state is perhaps a basis for Aumale's statement that Rochefort entered the King's service after this incident. (Aumale, *Princes de Condé*, III, 45.) More likely it was another case of a great noble's winning advancement for his clients. Note that two other clients of Condé were named councilors at the same time. (*Négociations*, ed. Bouchitté, 788.)

The deed was done, but the parlement of Grenoble mustered the courage to imprison the colonel. Furious at this affront the old duke returned to Grenoble and released his client, despite the concierge's argument that only an order from parlement could set the prisoner free. When the president of parlement protested, Lesdiguières sharply rebuked him for ordering the arrest without consulting him. In the end the colonel went free, and the powerful governor, instead of being punished by the king in council, was given a royal letter approving his conduct and a pension for his mistress. Two years later in 1617 Marie Vignon, plebeian-born widow of a silk merchant, achieved her ultimate goal of becoming the wife of Lesdiguières, marshal, duke, peer, and later constable of France.[23]

The above incidents were perhaps exceptional, but it is clear that the behavior of the great nobles' retainers was an object of concern to many. Special patrols had to be established at Tours in 1468 and 1484 during the meetings of the Estates-General with orders to arrest all unruly persons including the people of the princes and the king.[24] In the Estates-Generals of 1560, 1576, 1588, and 1614 the Third Estate included in its *cahiers* protests against the practice of gentlemen protecting from punishment those in their retinue who had committed misdeeds.[25] Royal ordonnances frequently forbade anyone to interfere with magistrates in the execution of justice, but to no avail. In the great ordonnance of 1629, near the end of the Renaissance, the crown had once more to prohibit nobles from protecting those wanted for crimes.[26]

Whatever the evils of the system from the point of view of the Third Estate, it had distinct advantages for the great nobles because it enhanced their prestige to have a large number of gentlemen in their service, and it gave them military power. Some nobles such as the Nevers and the La Trémoïlles relied primarily on their role as feudal lords supplemented by their positions as royal governors or lieutenant generals. As governors of Nivernais, the Nevers added the authority of the king to the wide powers they already wielded as dukes, and neither the inhabitants of the enclaves in the duchy nor the clergy could escape their authority. They owned and controlled a large number of castles and fortified towns which they gar-

---

[23] Charles Dufayard, *Le Connétable de Lesdiguières* (Paris, 1892), 375–79; Louis Videl, *Histoire de la vie du connestable de Lesdiguières* (Paris, 1638), 260–61, 297–99.
[24] Major, *Deputies to the Estates General*, 144.
[25] *Cahiers*, ed. Lalourcé and Duval, I, 324, II, 303–304, III, 224, IV, 311–12, 319, 322.
[26] *Recueil général des anciennes lois françaises depuis l'an 420 jusqu'à la révolution de 1789*, ed. François-A. Isambert *et al.* (29 vols., Paris, 1822–33), XVI, 272. For references to other ordonnances against maintenance, see Philibert Bugnyon, *Commentaires sur les ordonnances de Blois establies aux Estats generaux convoquez en la ville de Blois* (Lyon, 1584), 297–307.

risoned with captains and soldiers of their choice. In addition, they had a guard of archers and between 1615 and 1616 even a Swiss guard.[27] The La Trémoïlles, frequently lieutenant generals in Poitou and the surrounding provinces, were in an almost comparable position. In 1487 they had at least twenty-seven fortified towns and castles captained by their retainers, and in 1595 they raised from their lands five hundred gentlemen and two thousand foot soldiers at their own expense.[28] Other nobles such as the Montmorencys in Languedoc or the Guises in Burgundy used their posts as governors to establish large clienteles. Neither family owned a significant amount of land or had many vassals in their governments; thus it was necessary for them to rely on the techniques of the "new feudalism" to establish their position. Neither exercised powers as complete as the Nevers did in Nivernais, but the Guises drew strong support from Burgundy during the Wars of Religion. The biographer of one Montmorency has called him "the uncrowned king of southern France," and the provincial estates of Languedoc followed another Montmorency into rebellion in 1632.[29]

Cardinal Richelieu took advantage of his position as chief of the royal council to create a military establishment that consisted of a company of horse guards and a company of musketeers. Like the other great nobles, he insisted on personal fidelity. His intimate adviser, Father Joseph, is reported to have said that the cardinal wants "officers who will be faithful to him and only to him without exception and without reservation. He does not want those who serve two masters knowing full well he would not find fidelity in them. It is so rare to find men of this character that if it were necessary to buy them the Cardinal would pay their weight in gold."[30] That Richelieu found those who would serve him loyally even at the cost of incurring the hatred of the king's musketeers is well known to all readers of the romances of Alexander Dumas.

The situation would have been dangerous enough to the crown if the governors and other great nobles had drawn their clients entirely from the landed nobility, but they did not, and the "new feudalism" spread into the army, the judicial and administrative bureaucracy, and even into the towns. The much-vaunted army created by Charles VII was officered by the great nobles; even the mounted men-at-arms were generally of noble birth. Under

---

[27] L. Despois, *Histoire de l'autorité royale dans le comté de Nivernais* (Paris, 1912), 229–40.
[28] La Trémoïlle, *Les La Trémoïlle*, II, 108–10, IV, v; Charles Samaran, *Le Chartrier des La Trémoïlle* (Paris, 1930), 26.
[29] Drouot, *Mayenne et la Bourgogne*, esp. I, 102–19; Paul Gachon, *Les États de Languedoc et l'édit de Béziers, 1632* (Paris, 1887), esp. 87–91, 225–49; Franklin C. Palm, *Politics and Religion in Sixteenth-Century France* (Boston, 1927), 125–56.
[30] Deloche, *Maison de Cardinal de Richelieu*, 370.

such circumstances it is nearly certain that the great nobles assigned key subordinate positions in their companies to their vassals and clients and that the ambitious unattached noble in such a company soon found it advisable to adopt his commander as his patron. One is therefore not surprised to find that in the 1550's the lieutenant and the ensign in the Duke of Nevers' company were his vassals, and the guidon was a gentleman in his household.[31] The Duke of Mayenne had many clients in his company in Burgundy.[32] This situation led the great nobles to consider the royal troops they commanded as their own. These troops, although paid from taxes levied on orders from the king, wore the livery or device of their commander, and his colors became the company standard. Royal ordonnances encouraged this practice because in an age before uniforms it provided the best means to identify troops in battle and to place the blame on those who pillaged.[33] The primary loyalty of these troops was generally to their commanders whom they followed into revolt in many instances throughout the Renaissance. The king's army really consisted of the companies of such nobles as could be persuaded to support him, plus some hired mercenaries. Perhaps it was the unreliable nature of these French troops that caused the monarchs to entrust their personal safety primarily to Swiss and Scottish guards.

The great nobles exercised considerable influence over the appointment and behavior of royal officials in their fiefs. The dukes of Nevers had the right to name all royal officials in their territories, and when offices were made hereditary in 1604 in return for an annual fee, it was the dukes, not the king, who got the payments.[34] The counts of Laval had the privilege of naming royal officials in their lands,[35] as did some other important nobles. Governors were often able to win support from the royal judicial and administrative officials in their province, especially during the Wars of Religion, and their clients included town officials and leading ecclesiastics.[36]

---

[31] The lieutenant was the sieur de Givry; the ensign, the sieur d'Espeuilles; and the guidon, the sieur de Saint-Simon. (François de Rabutin, *Commentaires des guerres en la gaule belgique*. *Société de l'histoire de France*, ed. Charles Gailly de Taurines [2 vols., Paris, 1932–44], II, 123, 281.) One also notes that Gilbert de Chevenon who held the fief of Saint-Amand from Nevers joined the company as a man-at-arms (*ibid.*, I, 115–16) and that another vassal, La Brosse, was a member (*ibid.*, II, 147). Many other names could doubtless be added if a roster of the company were available. For an example of the intermixing of the gentlemen of the household with the company, see *ibid.*, I, 172–76.
[32] Drouot, *Mayenne et la Bourgogne*, I, 112–13.
[33] Gaston Zeller, *Les Institutions de la France au* xvie *siècle* (Paris, 1948), 310–11.
[34] Despois, *Autorité royale*, 273–76, 483–86. For a general account of the influence of the great nobles on the appointment of royal officials, see Mousnier, *Vénalité des offices*, 287–311.
[35] La Trémoïlle, *Les La Trémoïlle*, IV, 117–19.
[36] On the role of the governors, see esp. Gaston Zeller, "Gouverneurs de provinces au xvie siècle," *Revue historique*, CLXXXV (Jan.–June 1939), 225–56; Doucet, *Institutions de la France*, I, 229–44; and Drouot, *Mayenne et la Bourgogne*, esp. I, 73–77, 102–19, 293–313.

Crown and Aristocracy in Renaissance France 641

Great nobles also managed to place their clients in the judicial and administrative chambers of the central government. The practice was common by the time of Charles VI[37] and was continued by the nobility to the best of its ability in succeeding reigns. In 1540 one finds a vassal of the Duke of Nevers serving in the king's household.[38] Condé counted a president of the parlement of Paris among his loyal supporters during the minority of Louis XIII and got three of his followers named councilors of state in return for halting his rebellion in 1616.[39] The Duke of Rohan used his influence to get the governor of a town appointed to the king's household in 1617 and in 1620 sought to capitalize on this favor by having Marie de Médicis, his own patron, commission this old soldier to raise a regiment to aid in their rebellion.[40] The Guises were especially successful in the art of placement during the Wars of Religion. Indeed so great was the danger of the nobles penetrating into the government by getting appointments for their clients that the Duke of Sully later informed Cardinal Richelieu that the reason Henry IV made officeholding hereditary was to weaken the influence of the great nobles in the bureaucracy.[41]

One should not assume from the above that the great nobles exercised an all-powerful influence over the lesser members of the aristocracy. Often the reverse was more nearly true, a fact that can be best illustrated by a brief inspection of the relationship between the governors and the provincial estates. These estates, controlled as they were by the upper clergy, the nobility, and bourgeois patricians of the towns, regarded the governor as their agent at court. If they wanted a reduction in taxes, the suppression of newly created offices, or any other concession, they asked their governor to intercede with the king on their behalf. This the governor invariably did because the taxes to pay his salary and that of his military companies and guards were voted and generally collected by the provincial estates. A governor who was successful in winning special favors could expect further rewards. Thus in addition to voting Montmorency and members of his family their usual salaries and gifts, the estates of Languedoc in 1620 granted

---

The ambitions of the great nobles are indicated by the peace terms Mayenne suggested to Henry IV in 1594. (*Ibid.*, II, 362-63.) Indeed, governors became so powerful during the Wars of Religion that the Estates-General protested in 1588 and 1614. (*Cahiers*, ed. Lalourcé and Duval, III, 53, 140-41, IV, 200-201, 309-11.)

[37] Perroy, "Feudalism or Principalities," 181-85.
[38] *Inventaire . . . de Nevers*, ed. Soultrait, col. 54.
[39] Aumale, *Princes de Condé*, III, 53, 69; *Négociations*, ed. Bouchitté, 788.
[40] "Lettres adressées de 1585 à 1625 à Marc-Antoine Marreau de Boisguérin," *Archives historiques du Poitou*, XIV (1883), 349-54, 361-63.
[41] Mousnier, *Vénalité des offices*, esp. 63-66, 287-311; Cardinal Richelieu, *Testament politique*, ed. Louis André (Paris, 1947), 233-34.

him 30,000 livres in consideration of his extraordinary expenses, 132,000 livres to reimburse him for the cost of his troops used to suppress a recent uprising, and 10,800 livres for "his great services." The same assembly flatly rejected one royal request for 25,000 livres for five years to repair the bridge at Avignon and refused to do more than to promise to consider at their next meeting a second request for 400,000 livres.[42] Small wonder Cardinal Richelieu complained that the authority of the king was scarcely known in Languedoc.[43]

On the other hand, the ineffectual Duke of Guise enjoyed so little credit at court and in his government of Provence that the estates did not vote his salary or taxes to support his two companies in 1629 or 1630.[44] So important was it to have a governor with influence that in 1630 the three estates of Brittany petitioned the King to name Richelieu their governor, and a few years later Provence asked for his demented brother.[45]

The aristocracy sought to influence the crown through other officials. Royal commissioners sent to negotiate with the provincial estates invariably received payment, and the Secretaries of State, those confidential advisers of the king who dealt with the various provinces, were not neglected. The same assembly of the estates of Languedoc as cited above voted 1,500 livres for the King's Secretary of State who handled the affairs of the province and 300 for his assistant.[46] In 1599 the three estates of Comminges received a letter from their deputy requesting money for distribution at court to

[42] Archives Départementales [hereafter cited as AD], Hérault, procès-verbal of the estates of Béziers, May–June 1620. The 10,800 livres voted Montmorency were actually for his *ustinsiles des étrangers,* a company that the estates knew no longer existed. Other examples of gifts by the estates to governors are: Provence to Guise in 1601, 15,000 livres for his services (AD, Bouches-du-Rhône, C 9, fol. 20–20v); Burgundy to Biron in 1602, 10,000 *écus* in addition to his regular salary "in recognition of the favors and good offices he had rendered the province" at court (AD, Côte-d'Or, C 3016, fol. 465); Dauphiné to Lesdiguières in 1621, 18,000 livres and to his son-in-law, 6,000 (AD, Isère, I C 4, No. 45). Condé was fortunate enough to be assigned the task of negotiation with the estates of Burgundy and Provence in 1631 concerning the abolition of the *élus.* For his services he was voted 100,000 livres by the estates of both provinces. (AD, Côte-d'Or, C 3080, fol. 2v; AD, Bouches-du-Rhône, C 16, fols. 127v–128.) Provence also voted the two intendants 5,000 livres each. (AD, Bouches-du-Rhône, C 16, fol. 127v–128.)
[43] *Mémoires du Cardinal de Richelieu: Société de l'histoire de France,* ed. Robert Lavollée (10 vols., Paris, 1907–31), IX, 302.
[44] AD, Bouches-du-Rhône, C 16, fols. 66v–67, 127v–28v. In 1631 when the estates were in a desperate position Guise was voted 100,000 livres. (*Ibid.,* fol. 128v.)
[45] Louis, Comte de Carné, *Les États de Bretagne* (2d ed., 2 vols., Paris, 1875), I, 288; AD, Bouches-du-Rhône, C 108, fols. 105v–107.
[46] AD, Hérault, procès-verbal of May–June 1620. The estates of Provence voted the Secretary of State in charge of its affairs 800 *écus* in 1611 and his assistant, 200 *écus,* because of the importance of the affairs of the province being considered at court. (AD, Bouches-du-Rhône, C 10, fol. 263v.) The same amount was voted in 1612 and smaller sums thereafter. (*Ibid.,* fols. 336v, 404v; C 12, fols. 17, 51, 237, 281v, 354v–355; C 15, fol. 145v; C 16, fol. 96.) The estates of Burgundy voted the Secretary of State in charge of its affairs 15,000 livres in 1631. (AD, Côte-d'Or, C 3080, fol. 2v.)

ensure the preservation of their liberties, 1,000 *écus* being earmarked for Michel de Marillac who was already earning his reputation as an enemy of provincial liberties.[47] Secretaries and valets of important persons were sometimes remembered[48]; even the lowly historian did not escape notice. When the estates of Languedoc learned that the royal historiographer was planning to write a description of their province, they voted him 100 *écus* and promised him an additional sum if his book upon completion was found to be "useful." Enough mention was made of the privileges of the province at this point in the journal of the estates to leave no doubt in the mind of the most naïve member of our profession what kind of a book would be considered "useful."[49] Thus in Renaissance France the provincial estates levied taxes to pay royal officials to convince the king that they were unable to pay the taxes he requested and that their respective provinces had privileges that must not be overridden.

During the Renaissance about one-third of France did not have provincial estates that met periodically. In these provinces the landed nobility appears to have put direct pressure on its governors and patrons. The great noble who could not obtain enough concessions from the crown for his clients was faced with a choice of losing his influence over them or of revolting in the hope that the crown would purchase his submission. Thus, by rebelling, the Duke of Nevers increased his income from 401,003 livres in 1616 to 806,776 in 1617, but at the same time his expenses jumped from 400,345 to 808,520 livres, strong circumstantial evidence that the real winners of the revolt were his followers.[50]

The situation described above provides the basis for the contention that throughout the Renaissance the most powerful class was the landed nobility, just as it had been during the Middle Ages. This does not mean, however, that kings were necessarily ineffective. Just as the medieval king was the principal lord in the kingdom, so the Renaissance monarch was the greatest patron. The former governed with the cooperation of his vassals, the latter with the cooperation of his clients. To ensure this cooperation the king had at his disposal the highest offices of the Church, government positions, military commands, patents of nobility, and nearly every type of privilege. The great noble who wanted these things for himself or his clients usually found

---

[47] AD, Haute-Garonne, C 3676, Nos. 53–54.
[48] The estates of Provence frequently voted their governors' secretaries and servants money. (AD, Bouches-du-Rhône, C 10, fol. 404v; C 12, fols. 114, 236v, 277v–278, 354v–355.) The estates of Burgundy voted its governor's secretary 600 livres in 1605. (AD, Côte-d'Or, C 3017, fols. 37v–38v.)
[49] AD, Hérault, procès-verbal of the estates of Pézanas, Dec. 1597–Jan. 1598.
[50] *Inventaire ... de Nevers*, ed. Soultrait, col. 528.

faithful service the surest path to success. To make doubly certain, the king distributed pensions and the right to certain royal taxes on an annual basis to the great nobles. Thus royal control over the nobility was based largely on a vast patronage. The king who administered it wisely and fairly could hope for enough cooperation from the great nobles and their clients to make the system work. But if the king was a minor or was weak and the control of the royal patronage fell into the hands of a faction, those nobles who were excluded revolted.[51] There was no exception to this rule during the Renaissance.

The Wars of Religion made the dangers of the "new feudalism" all too clear to the crown, and beginning with the reign of Henry IV serious attempts were made to mitigate its effect. The first step was to free the bureaucracy from the influence of the great nobles. This was accomplished in 1604 by making officeholding hereditary in return for the payment of an annual fee. Eventually this enabled royal officials to become as independent of the crown as of the nobility, but so long as the right to have hereditary offices was challenged by other elements of the Renaissance aristocracy, the bureaucracy stood loyally by the crown except when the crown curtailed or threatened to curtail its privileges.[52]

The second step was to get control of the tax-collecting machinery so that the provincial estates would no longer be in a position to reward or punish royal officials. Henry IV began to move in this direction in 1603 when he issued an edict substituting royal tax collectors for those of the local estates in Guienne. This attempt had to be abandoned in 1611 during the regency of Marie de Médicis, but was renewed in Guienne in 1621 and elsewhere between 1628 and 1632. In some provinces the result was the abandonment of the provincial estates and the appointment of obedient royal tax officials; in others the provincial estates were allowed to continue to exist under careful scrutiny from the crown and with sharply curtailed taxing privileges.[53]

---

[51] On the use the king made of the great nobles to control the lesser nobles, see Romier, *Royaume de Catherine de Médicis*, I, 208–10; on the award of pensions, see Mousnier, *Vénalité des offices*, 407–409. I do not believe that either the army or the bureaucracy added much to the king's strength because both contained many persons who were loyal to the great nobles, and both were quite small by modern standards. (See Major, "French Renaissance Monarchy," 117–19.) It is true the size of the bureaucracy increased during the Renaissance, but this increase was caused as much by the desire to raise money through the sale of offices as by the desire to increase royal power. This is illustrated by the practice of having officials take turns performing the same duties. (Zeller, *Institutions de la France*, 138–40; Mousnier, *Vénalité des offices*, 25–28.)

[52] For an explanation of how the *droit annuel* strengthened the crown during the reigns of Henry IV and Louis XIII, see *ibid.*, 557–621.

[53] I am engaged in a study of the decline of the provincial estates during the reigns of Henry IV and Louis XIII and will offer evidence to support this paragraph at a later date.

The third step was to separate the mass of the Protestants from the great nobles. This was accomplished by persuading most of the great nobles to return to the Catholic fold during the seventeenth century and by the issuance of edicts granting a degree of religious toleration in 1598 and 1629.[54] The fourth step was to substitute intendants for governors as the principal royal officials in the provinces, an action that gradually took place after the middle of the seventeenth century.[55] The fifth step was to establish effective control over a large standing army by Michel Le Tellier and the Marquis de Louvois during the reign of Louis XIV.[56] The final step was to separate the great nobles from the lesser nobles, a process that took place gradually during the seventeenth century and was nearly completed by the creation of the court at Versailles where the great nobles laughed at jokes about the country gentlemen upon whom their power had formerly rested. In this manner, the "new feudalism" of the Renaissance became as much a part of the past as the "old."[57]

[54] The Edict of Nantes (1598) and the Edict of Alais (1629). By his abjuration Henry IV had already won the support of most Catholics.

[55] Roland Mousnier, "État et Commissaire: Recherches sur la création des intendants de province, 1634–1648," *Forschungen zur Staat und Verfassung: Festgabe für Fritz Hartung* (Berlin, 1958), 325–44. His recent "Note sur les rapports entre les gouverneurs de provinces et les intendants dans la première moitié du xviie siècle," *Revue historique*, CCXXVIII (Oct.–Dec. 1962), 339–50, indicates that the intendants were at first only the advisers and assistants of the governors. They did not supplant the governors in the provinces during the first half of the seventeenth century as was formerly thought.

[56] Louis André, *Michel Le Tellier et Louvois* (Paris, 1942), 277–427.

[57] The efforts of the crown to halt the practice of dueling and to demolish fortified châteaux have often been cited as weakening the nobility. Edicts against dueling, however, were designed to preserve the nobility, not to destroy it, and in the Estates-General of 1588 the nobles themselves asked that the death penalty be imposed on duelists. (*Cahiers*, ed. Lalourcé and Duval, III, 143.) Most nobles evidently did not regard the château-fort as a necessary ingredient for their power because from the dawn of the sixteenth century they generally preferred to build their châteaux in the more comfortable Renaissance style. During the rebellions between 1562 and 1629 many of the surviving château-forts as well as some recently fortified places fell into the hands of Protestants or lawless persons who resisted local officials and terrorized the countryside. This situation led the deputies of the nobility at the Estates-General of 1588 to ask that owners of fortified places guard them carefully to keep them out of undesirable hands. (*Ibid.*, 143, 148.) The deputies of the clergy and the Third Estate were more vehement and advocated demolition. (*Ibid.*, II, 77, 295–96, 308–309, III, 55, 228, IV, 314–15.) The provincial estates with the concurrence of the nobility often asked that forts be demolished. Thus in 1622 the estates of Béarn asked that all châteaux and other fortified places in Béarn be demolished except those at Pau and Navarrenx. (AD, Basse-Pyrénées, C 708, fols. 303–308.) The estates of Rouergue petitioned the King to destroy fortified places in 1596. (Archives communales, Millau, AA 12.) A similar request came from Provence in 1597 and was repeated many times thereafter. (AD, Bouches-du-Rhône, C 8, fols. 68v, 83v, 151–151v, 188v–189v, etc.) The estates of Burgundy did likewise in 1618, and among those compensated in 1631 for the demolition of a château was Cardinal Richelieu himself. (AD, Côte-d'Or, C 3017, fol. 203–203v; C 3079, fol. 6–7.)

XII

Noble Income, Inflation, and the Wars of Religion in France

IN THE MID-NINETEENTH CENTURY, Augustin Thierry argued in his famous *Essai sur l'histoire de la formation et des progrès du tiers état* that, from the revival of the free municipalities in the twelfth century until the meeting of the Estates General in 1789, the French third estate followed a "simple and regular" course in accordance with "one consistent plan" that led to the triumph of its ally, the absolute monarchy, and ultimately to the union of the three orders in June 1789. At that point "the family became complete," and for a moment the French appeared to have become a united nation. Thierry gave the clergy a nod and credited the nobility with "chivalry" and "military valor." "They knew how to die," he generously asserted,[1] but, as dying is an art that can be practiced but once, he did not assign them a very large role in determining the historical process.

Although Thierry insisted that the bourgeoisie was but one segment of the third estate, Marxist and non-Marxist historians alike soon began to depict France from the twelfth century to the Revolution as marking the rise of the middle class and a corresponding decline of the nobility. That it took the middle class so many centuries to rise and the nobility such a long time to die should have aroused the suspicions of perceptive historians. Nevertheless, when A. F. Pollard delivered his lectures entitled *Factors in Modern History* at the beginning of the twentieth century, he incorporated all of the traditional clichés. With the growth of commerce and industry, he argued, the middle class emerged and made its contribution to the establishment of the new monarchy, the founding of the British Empire, and nearly everything else that he regarded as good. "Where you had no middle class, you had no Renaissance and no Reformation," he confidently proclaimed.[2] At the same time the decline of the manorial system, the invention of gunpowder, the growth of nationalism, the emergence of absolute monarchies, and so on led to the decline of the nobility.

I would like to express my appreciation to Emory University, to the Institute for Advanced Study, Princeton, and to the National Endowment for the Humanities for the support that enabled me to write this article during 1979–80. I have benefited from conversations with John Elliott, Alexander Field, and John H. M. Salmon concerning certain problems my data presented, but the conclusions are my own.

[1] Thierry, *Essai sur l'histoire de la formation et des progrès du tiers état* (3d ed., Paris, 1855), viii, 188, xii. Thierry formulated his basic argument in the 1820s and published a version of his views in the *Revue des deux mondes*, May 1846, pp. 521–48, June 1846, pp. 722–41, March 1850, pp. 813–42, and May 1850, pp. 469–89.

[2] Pollard, in his *Factors in Modern History* (New York, 1907), 41.

Even fifty years ago, when Marc Bloch discovered that there was a seigneurial reaction following the Hundred Years War, he attributed it primarily to the middle class, who purchased land from noble and peasant alike. They, and not the nobility, took the lead in introducing bookkeeping and more advanced administrative methods into the countryside and in acquiring peasant holdings in order to re-create large estates.[3]

Today our admiration for the middle class has dissipated, and there would be little point in recalling the works of such historians as Thierry and Pollard had not their interpretation of noble irrelevance and inability to cope with changing circumstances persisted. The typical historian, with a mortgage on his house, payments due on his car, and several credit cards in his pocket still recoils in discovering that a noble borrowed money to remodel his chateau. If a noble provided his daughter with a larger dowry than his father had for his sister, it is taken as proof of fiscal irresponsibility rather than increased affluence. Such presumptions must be expelled from our minds if we are to understand the Renaissance nobility and approach its activities as we would those of other segments of society.

Robert Boutruche, the first of the post–World War II rural historians, laboriously catalogued the factors that reduced the nobility to financial impotence during the Hundred Years War. Devastation caused by that conflict, debasement of the currency, breakup of the manorial system, higher labor costs, and dismemberment of the patrimony among too numerous children reduced family income. At the same time, war, extravagance, and pious gifts conspired to keep noble expenses high. Boutruche recognized that some families sought to mend their fortunes, occasionally with success, but the financial picture of the nobility that he painted was bleak.[4] Subsequently, a number of local studies have been published that seem to confirm his findings.[5] Here and there someone has noted that the nobility partially recovered during the peaceful years of the Hundred Years War or that nobles did not fare too badly in regions that escaped the worst of the war, such as parts of Brittany and Auvergne,[6] but on the whole recent studies have reinforced the idea of noble decline, an impression that has been incorporated into surveys of the period.[7]

In 1966 French rural history took a great leap forward when Emmanuel Le Roy Ladurie published a study of the peasants of Languedoc; eleven years later

---

[3] Bloch, *Les Caractères originaux de l'histoire rurale française* (Oslo, 1931), chap. 4, sec. 3.

[4] Boutruche, *La Crise d'une société: Seigneurs et paysans du Bordelais pendant la Guerre de Cent Ans* (Paris, 1947).

[5] See, for example, Guy Fourquin, *Les Campagnes de la région parisienne à la fin du Moyen Âge* (Paris, 1964); Isabelle Guérin, *La Vie rurale en Sologne aux XIVe et XVe siècles* (Paris, 1960); Marie-Thérèse Lorcin, *Les Campagnes de la région lyonnaise aux XIVe et XVe siècles* (Lyons, 1974); Emmanuel Le Roy Ladurie, *Les Paysans de Languedoc*, 2 vols. (Paris, 1966); Guy Bois, *Crise du féodalisme* (Paris, 1976); André Plaisse, *La Baronnie du Neubourg* (Paris, 1961); and J. Tricard, "Les Limites d'une reconstruction rurale en pays pauvre à la fin du Moyen Âge: Le Cas du Limousin," *Études rurales*, 60 (1975): 5–39.

[6] Pierre Charbonnier, *Guillaume de Murol: Un Petit seigneur auvergnat au début du XVe siècle* (Clermont-Ferrand, 1973), 243–50; J. Kerhervé, "Le Domaine ducal de Guingamp-Minibriac au XVe siècle: Étude de comptes," *Mémoires de la société d'histoire et d'archéologie de Bretagne*, 55 (1978): 123–83; and Monique Chauvin-Lechaptois, *Les Comptes de la châtellenie de Lamballe, 1387–1482* (Rennes, 1977).

[7] Emmanuel Le Roy Ladurie, "Les Masses profondes: La Paysannerie," in F. Braudel and E. Labrousse, eds., *Histoire économique et sociale de la France*, 1, pt. 2 (Paris, 1977): 523–29.

he expanded his treatment to include all of France. In his hands population changes became the principal determinant of the historical process. Disease and war, he argued, reduced the population by about 50 percent between 1300 and 1450. The scarcity of labor compelled landlords to lower rents both in money and in kind, to reduce seigneurial dues, and to increase wages in order to attract and retain tillers of the soil. At the same time, declining demand reduced the prices of the products they had to sell. The result was a golden age for peasants and hard times for the lords of the manor. Then the situation was reversed. Between 1450 and 1560 the population doubled. Food prices soon began to rise rapidly because agricultural production failed to meet the needs of the growing population. Under such circumstances, the owner of a fief who exploited the domain himself, leased it for payments in kind, or used the sharecrop system could maintain his position. The owner who relied largely on monetary leases and dues paid in money continued to slide toward disaster. During the last four decades of the sixteenth century the Wars of Religion provoked a new crisis. Agricultural production dropped by about one-third, primarily because of the direct damage done by troops and the loss of livestock that reduced the amount of manure for fertilizer. This decline quickened inflation, although the population remained relatively stable.[8] This period of rapid inflation has generally been considered especially disastrous for the nobility.

The achievement of Le Roy Ladurie and other scholars of the *Annales* school has been remarkable; but they have failed to consider one aspect of the nobles' situation at the close of the Hundred Years War, and they have given us very little specific information about how the nobility fared during the inflation-ridden, war-torn sixteenth century. Unquestionably, the *Annales* historians' belief that the economic position of most noble families deteriorated drastically during the Hundred Years War is correct, but this deterioration was but one part of the picture. Just as the peasant had enlarged his holdings by acquiring the lands of deceased relatives during the period of depopulation, so the noble must have increased the number of his fiefs. Often he was able to incorporate vacated lands. In the county of Bigorre, for example, there were forty fiefs in 1313 but only eighteen in 1429. Twelve fiefs had disappeared because the villages on which they depended had ceased to exist, although the land, of course, remained. Ten fiefs had been acquired by six of the surviving eighteen seigneurs.[9] For the time being these eighteen seigneurs were in a difficult economic position, but they held what forty had shared only a century earlier. By waiting a generation or two for the rising population to bring down labor costs and raise rents and grain prices, would they not then have begun to prosper? This essay will test this hypothesis and ascertain how the nobility fared when the population stabilized and inflation worsened during the Wars of Religion. In making this study, I will rely on the financial records of the house of Foix-Navarre-Albret and available published evidence.

[8] Le Roy Ladurie, *Les Paysans de Languedoc*, and "Les Masses profondes," 483–865.
[9] Maurice Berthe, *Le Comté de Bigorre: Un Milieu rural au bas Moyen Âge* (Paris, 1976), 130–34. Some of the families of the eighteen seigneurs had not been in Bigorre in 1313.

WITH THE EXCEPTION OF THE VALOIS DUKES OF BURGUNDY, no French noble family accumulated as many fiefs during the late Middle Ages as did the house of Foix. Through marriage, purchase, and war the family acquired one lordship after another in southern France, including the kingdom of Navarre and the independent viscounty of Béarn. The problem of the counts of Foix was not to provide for a multitude of children in each generation but to produce an adult male heir. The demographic disasters of their age provided both a splendid opportunity to acquire more land and a serious threat to their existence. At length they, too, failed to produce a son, and in 1484 the daughter of the house married Jean d'Albret, heir to extensive lands in the southwest. The fiscal administration of this couple's descendants are largely the concerns of this essay.

The family owed its fiscal success during the Renaissance largely to Henri II d'Albret (1517–55). Henri did not need the bourgeoisie to tell him how to manage his estates. His grandmother's ancestors, the counts of Foix, had had their treasurers keep detailed records of their receipts and expenses as far back as the fourteenth century, and by 1460 their treasurer in the viscounty of Lautrec was totaling the entries at the bottom of each page in Arabic numerals.[10] For administrative supervision Henri turned to the crown for a model. In 1520 he established a *Chambre des Comptes* at Pau to audit the accounts of the financial officials in his numerous domains and to perform other duties. In 1527 he reduced its jurisdiction by creating a *Chambre des Comptes* at Nérac to supervise Albret, Armagnac, Périgord, Limousin, Rouergue, Fézenzaguet, Foix, Nébouzan, Lautrec, and Villemur. Some time after his daughter, Jeanne d'Albret (1555–72), married Antoine de Bourbon, Vendôme and other fiefs in the north were temporarily added to its jurisdiction. The *Chambre des Comptes* at Pau retained responsibility for Béarn, Navarre, Bigorre, Marsan, Tursan, and Gavardan. In the course of time many records have been lost, but no less than four thousand *cahiers* and *cartons* containing documents once held by the two *Chambres* still existed when an inventory of their contents was published in 1863. They provide one of the finest opportunities to study the financial position of a great noble family during the latter half of the sixteenth century.[11]

Henri d'Albret divided his counties, viscounties, and other domains among a number of treasurers, each of whom administered one or more of these jurisdictions. Each treasurer collected the money that was due from his jurisdiction, paid local expenses, and periodically turned over the surplus to a general treasurer. The accounts of all of the treasurers and of the officials who expended sums to support the royal household were verified annually by the appropriate *Chambre des Comptes*.

---

[10] For the medieval receipts and expenses of the viscounty of Lautrec, see Archives départementales, Pyrénées-Atlantique [hereafter, AD-PA], B1733–B1737. Unfortunately, Roman numerals soon replaced Arabic numerals in the page totals. For medieval accounts of other fiefs, see AD-PA, B1763–B1772, and series E, which was not part of the *Chambres des Comptes*.

[11] P. Raymond, ed., *Inventaire-sommaire des archives départementales antérieures à 1790: Basses-Pyrénées*, 1 (Paris, 1863): 10. There were some changes in the jurisdictions that the two *Chambres* administered after 1527. A few documents were destroyed or lost in a fire in 1908. I have only been able to sample the vast collection that remains. There is more than enough to support a good doctoral dissertation or, for that matter, a substantial book.

Noble Income, Inflation, and the Wars of Religion 25

There are difficulties in using these records. First, no one account summarizes all of the revenue the family received or all of the money that it spent. Gifts and salaries paid by the king of France do not always appear, and military expenses, except for the garrison in the powerful fort of Navarrenx and the salaries of a few captians, are not included in the dominal and household accounts (special treasurers dealt with troops during the Wars of Religion). Second, and perhaps more serious, treasurers kept records in order to account for the money that passed through their hands rather than to record profits and losses. Hence, money that remained in a treasurer's hands from the preceding fiscal year is listed as a receipt, and money turned over to the Albrets' general treasurer is counted as an expense. Money that was borrowed or derived from the sale or alienation of property and money that was transferred in from another account were also counted as receipts, just as the payment of a debt was entered as an expense. In ordinary times, the error incurred by considering the receipts from a domain as gross income is not large, and a comparison of the total receipts for a number of years quickly reveals the upward or downward trend of the gross yield. During the Wars of Religion, however, so much land was sold or alienated in some jurisdictions and so much money was transferred in and out of some accounts that the actual revenue can be ascertained only after an exhaustive study, if at all. The total "expense" is of no value, because it includes money transferred to the general treasurer and money spent at the direction of the Albret family that had nothing to do with the administration of the jurisdiction—that is, the total "expense" includes the net income.

The best surviving series of accounts is that for the independent viscounty of Béarn. Here the stewards (*baylies*) and notaries turned over, after deducting their expenses, the sums they collected from the individual subordinate jurisdictions to the treasurer of Béarn. Mills were leased for six years, but the tolls were farmed for more limited periods or collected by local officials. Careful management brought ever-increasing revenue until Béarn itself was invaded during the Wars of Religion. Officials were evidently proud of their achievement, for one of them recorded in 1539 that revenue from the domain had been increased by 2,000 *écus* "without doing an injustice to anyone."[12] Gross receipts that in 1530–31 stood at 12,856 Béarnais *écus* reached 38,461 *écus* in 1564–65, a threefold increase in thirty-four years (see Table 4, below).[13]

Receipts from the Albret domains in Périgord and Limousin increased from 10,566 *livres* in 1550–51 to 16,762 *livres* in 1573–74,[14] and their county of Fézenzaguet, whose gross receipts were 1,654 *livres* in 1561–62, was leased for 2,538 *livres* in 1569–70.[15] The treasurers of the southern fiefs—except those of Béarn, Navarre, and Foix—turned over 65,952 *livres* to the treasurer of the royal

---

[12] AD-PA, B246, as quoted in Charles Dartigue-Peyrou, *La Vicomté de Béarn sous le règne d'Henri d'Albret, 1517–1555* (Paris, 1934), 250.
[13] For an account of the administration of the domain, see Dartigue-Peyrou, *La Vicomté de Béarn*, 245–53.
[14] AD-PA, B1827, B1862. The fiscal year began and ended on Saint John the Baptist's Day.
[15] AD-PA, B1582, B1588. The fiscal year began and ended on Saint John the Baptist's Day.

TABLE 1
Receipts and Expenses in Navarre

Transactions[a]	1553[d]	1555[d]	1568[d]	1575[d]
RECEIPTS FROM THE				
PRECEDING YEAR	200	1,425[e]	3,064[f]	53
DOMAIN	5,017	4,478	1,781	4,800
ESTATES (DONATION)[b]	4,486	3,925	0	15,021
TOTAL RECEIPTS	9,703	9,828	4,845	19,874
PAYMENTS				
TO THE GENERAL TREASURER[c]	2,012	2,025	1,383	9,114
TOTAL PAYMENTS	7,542	9,137	4,787	19,130
AD-PA Source	B1412	B1414	B1415	B1417

[a] Figures for all of the transactions are in *livres tournois*. Payments in kind have been omitted.

[b] The donation voted by the estates was turned over to the treasurer of Navarre and included in his accounts. The estates made no donation in 1568.

[c] Payments to the general treasurer or other officials of the crown of Navarre were carried as expenses, but they represent a substantial part of the royal "profits." Some other payments were also made to persons not directly employed in Navarre and were, therefore, also part of the "profits."

[d] The fiscal year in Navarre was from January 1 to December 31, even before the adoption of the Gregorian calendar.

[e] The treasurer held 1,000 *livres* from the preceding year to pay debts contracted during that year.

[f] A large Catholic uprising in the fall of 1567 was not suppressed until the following year. A large sum was apparently transferred into the treasurer's account or left in his account in anticipation of a decline in revenue in 1568. In spite of this precaution, pensions and judges' salaries went unpaid.

household in 1556 and 85,039 *livres* in 1560.[16] There were, of course, occasional exceptions to the general upward trend prior to the most destructive stage of the Wars of Religion. Much of the domain in Navarre yielded fixed monetary payments, and an exceptionally high proportion of the receipts were derived from tolls. The result was a relatively static situation there, except when a rebellion reduced the receipts in 1568 or when the provincial estates gave more or less than their customary amount (see Table 1). Receipts from Armagnac appear to have stabilized, at least temporarily, before the Wars of Religion began, but destructive troops and alienations must have contributed heavily to the failure of the county to resume its growth during the latter part of the century (see Table 2).

The Albrets did not directly exploit the domain, nor did they rely heavily on the growing practice of turning their land over to sharecroppers. The payments they received in kind were of little importance. Instead, they preferred monetary leases, but, since these leases were nearly always for three years, their prices leaped upward with the demand for land; land rents rose even faster than grain

[16] AD-PA, B6, B8.

prices. The Albrets broke up their domain into segments that were small enough to permit aspiring peasants to compete for leases, a practice that led to more competitive bidding than there would have been had they catered to the affluent. In 1531, those interested in leasing domain lands in the viscounty of Lautrec were summoned to Carcassonne, but by 1549 the Albrets had realized that competition for farms would be greater if the auctions were held in various parts of the viscounty itself. The viscounty was therefore divided into eleven parts, and the approach of Albret agents to this or that segment of the domain was widely advertised.[17] The domain in the viscounty of Fézenzaguet was divided into a dozen or so segments before it was leased. Even so, two, and more often three or four, persons had to join together to make a successful bid in 1562, in 1565, and doubtless in other years. With rare exceptions the bidders were men without any form of title, not even that of judge, notary, or bourgeois of a small town. It is striking that only one group that obtained a parcel of the domain in 1562 managed to do so again in 1565. Had the demand for land forced land prices so high that the lessees of 1562 could not compete three years later, or had they learned their lesson? More likely, the price of land skyrocketed, because nearly every parcel of the domain was leased for more in 1565 than it was in 1562. In several instances, the rent more than doubled.[18]

Any attempt to study seigneurial revenue during the Wars of Religion is fraught with difficulties and dangers. On the one hand, the seigneur's need to borrow money, to sell or alienate part of his domain, and to transfer funds into an account was sometimes compelling. Since each of these transactions was considered a receipt, revenue seemingly rose rapidly at those times when the seigneur was in financial need. On the other hand, his revenue was likely to fall during the following years because his domain was smaller, although the yield from the remaining individual parts may have been larger. Then, too, the actual damage done by troops could obscure the secular trend. Of the lands of the house of Albret, the domain in Béarn provides the clearest picture of what would probably have happened had there been no war. The sovereign of the little state could not sell or alienate his domain without violating the privileges of his subjects, and its geographical location was removed from the center of the conflict. Here the receipts in 1584–85 were five times those of 1530–31 and over twice those of 1561–62, just before the Wars of Religion began. The one exception to the general upward trend occurred in 1568–69, when the conflict reached Béarn itself (see Table 4, below).

THE FIRST OF THE WARS OF RELIGION began in March 1562 and ended in March 1563. Jeanne d'Albret remained officially neutral, but her French fiefs were subject to the ravages of troops.[19] Military action was probably greater in the terri-

---

[17] Ibid., B1741.   [18] Ibid., B1583, B1585.
[19] For the war, see A. de Ruble, *Jeanne d'Albret et le guerre civile* (Paris, 1897); and Nancy L. Roelker, *Queen of Navarre, Jeanne d'Albret* (Cambridge, Mass., 1968), 186–207.

XII

TABLE 2
Revenue Received by the Treasurer of the County of Armagnac[a]

Jurisdiction	1555–56[b]	1558–59	1562–63	1569–72[f]	1574–75	1581–82	1595–96
Lectoure	2,385	2,470	2,666	2,606	2,850	3,279	2,197
Aurillac	2,840[c]	1,817[c]	2,769[c]	2,950[c]	1,887[c]	4,624[c g]	2,010[c]
Lomagne	1,300	1,200	1,241	1,500	1,516	1,328	1,258
Bruilhois	2,100	1,507	1,533	1,785	1,218	957	732
Fezensac	2,305	2,275	2,676	3,500	4,535	4,228	4,681
Pardiac	3,093	2,703	3,135	3,692	3,800	3,910	2,209
Eauzan	800	852	862	1,110	505	1,050	500
Rivière-Basse	435	468	481	610	675	597	300
Astaffort	122	124	75	100	161	—[h]	195
Tournon	310	333	375	380	610	508	450
L'Isle Jourdain	5,103	5,611	4,931	5,504	6,163	3,450	4,997
TOTAL	20,793	19,360	20,744	23,737	23,920	23,931	19,529
TOTAL RECEIPTS	26,059	—[d]	29,474[e]		30,019	26,856	28,110[i]
AD-PA Source	B2135	B1581	B1584	B1588	B1591	B1597	B1621

[a] All receipts are in *livres tournois*.
[b] The fiscal year was from one Saint John the Baptist's Day until the next.
[c] Aurillac also had an annual payment of 12 *pipes* of wine, which was used to pay part of the salary of an official.
[d] Total receipts are not available; some pages of the account are missing.
[e] Total receipts for 1652–63 include a 6,289 surplus from the preceding account.
[f] Figures represent the amount for which the domain was leased for the three-year period beginning in 1569.
[g] One payment of 4,047 *livres* was for the preceding year as well as for 1581–82.
[h] Astaffort was not farmed in 1581–82; the king of Navarre had assigned its revenue to one of his captains.
[i] Total receipts for 1595–96 include 7,906 *livres* that were held back from the account of the preceding year to meet expenses.

tory that the treasurer of Armagnac and Fézenzaguet administered. Here the land had been leased for three years beginning on Saint John the Baptist's Day in 1560. Hence, the war did not influence the amount for which the domain was leased, but it could have affected the ability of the lessees to meet their obligations. The total receipts from Fézenzaguet in 1562–63 came to 1,557 *livres*, only 93 *livres* less than in the preceding year of the lease.[20] A comparison of the receipts in 1562–63 with those of 1558–59 during the previous lease period reveals that, of the eleven fiefs into which Armagnac was divided, nine registered increases and only two registered losses, although the net gain came to only 1,384 *livres*. Especially surprising is Lectoure's gain, since the town was besieged and taken by the Catholics in one of the war's most important engagements in southwestern France (see Table 2).

Four years of nominal peace followed, but Jeanne's attempt to impose Protestantism led many of her Catholic subjects in Béarn and especially Navarre to rebel during the second religious war, which lasted from September 1567 to March 1568. Revenue from Navarre declined disastrously. The estates did not meet to vote their customary donation of over 4,000 *livres*; mills in the hands of the rebels yielded no income, and some tolls could not be collected. In all, Jeanne grossed less than 1,800 *livres* from her little kingdom instead of 8,500–9,500 *livres*, and this small sum had to be used to pay for repairs and other expenses. Her judicial officials and many pensioners went unpaid (see Table 1, above).[21]

Jeanne soon suppressed the rebellion, but her Catholic subjects remained discontented. Furthermore, the peace that followed between the rival factions was precarious at best. Under such circumstances, Jeanne realized that she could not hope to remain neutral and, at the same time, protect her lands when the next war began. She therefore decided to throw in her lot with her coreligionists in France, and in August 1568 she set out for La Rochelle. Charles IX retaliated on October 18 by ordering the seizure of all of her lands, and he dispatched the Baron of Terride to make good the royal threat. Terride entered Béarn on March 28, 1569. Pau quickly fell, and on May 24 he lay siege to the powerfully fortified town of Navarrenx. With Béarn almost entirely in his hands, Terride reorganized the government to insure Catholic control, confiscated the goods of the Protestants who had fled, and held a meeting of the estates to vote money to support his regime. On July 10, Jeanne countered by commissioning the Count of Montgomery to reconquer her lands, and by August 22, in a brilliant campaign, he had regained possession of Béarn.[22]

The financial impact of the two invasions was profound and clearly demonstrates what often happened when one side or the other took possession of a territory during the Wars of Religion. Terride proceeded to milk the viscounty of all that he could during the five months that he held sway. The domain lands,

---

[20] AD-PA, B1582, B1583. [21] *Ibid.*, B1415.
[22] Roelker, *Queen of Navarre, Jeanne d'Albret*, 268–71, 291–301; Pierre de Salefranque, *Histoire de l'hérésie de Béarn*, ed. V. Dubarat (Pau, 1929), 125–63; J. Russell Major, *Representative Government in Early Modern France* (New Haven, 1980), 249–50; and Nicolas de Bordenave, *Histoire de Béarn et Navarre, 1517 à 1572*, ed. P. Raymond (Paris, 1873), 150–290.

mills, and tolls yielded some money, and he pressured the towns and estates for substantial amounts. In all, he extracted over 18,000 *livres* from the war-torn viscounty, while apparently contributing nothing to the expenses of governing it.[23]

Following his victory, Montgomery restored Jeanne's loyal officials, including her treasurer of Béarn. Inasmuch as the fiscal year had begun on November 1, 1568, the leases and other arrangements had been made before Terride's invasion in March of the following year. Hence, the treasurer's problem was to collect the amounts that were due, but this proved to be impossible because the viscounty had been so thoroughly fleeced. With diligence he managed to gather 25,238 Béarnais *écus*, a third less than had been collected in 1564–65, and the estates did not meet again to vote the customary donation. Furthermore, large sums had to be expended to repair the mills and other facilities. As a result, Jeanne was able to draw only 6,365 Béarnais *écus* from the viscounty—that is, about a fourth of what she had received in 1564–65 (see Table 4, below).[24] Jeanne's victory did, however, enable her to confiscate the goods of the Catholic Church, which yielded about 80,000 *livres* annually. A conscientious Protestant, she used part of this sum to support the ministry and to provide salaries and student fellowships for the academy she had established, but she used funds not needed for these purposes to pay some of her officials, to strengthen the fortifications at Navarrenx, and to support the war effort.[25]

The invasion of her lands not only subjected Jeanne to a loss of revenue, but the need to support the Protestant army greatly increased her expenses. To raise money, she pawned her jewels and alienated part of her domain in Armagnac with the right of redemption (*rachat perpétuel*). The viscounty of Bruilhois brought her 10,000 *livres*, although she retained the rights of justice and the tolls. In such large transactions, noblemen often profited rather than villagers, who could only afford to bid for the right to lease small parcels of land. As a result of the alienations, Jeanne leased her domain in Armagnac for the three-year period beginning in 1569 for an amount approximately equal to what she could expect to receive in a single normal year (see Table 2, above). The civil war may have reduced the peasants' desire for land somewhat, but not enough to prevent them from offering a total of 2,538 *livres* to rent the domain in Fézenzaguet in 1569–70 and 2,507 *livres* per year in the two years that followed. In 1565–66 the total receipts of the viscounty had been 2,341 *livres*. Thus, in spite of the war, land rents were being forced upward.[26]

The third war ended in August 1570, but the conflict was renewed following the Massacre of Saint Bartholomew's Day two years later and continued, except for relatively short periods of peace, until the close of the seventh war in Novem-

---

[23] Terride evidently appointed Arnaud d'Esquille, who was treasurer of Navarre in 1568, treasurer of Béarn. Esquille was probably one of the Catholics who accepted the new regime, but, when his parents had his accounts verified by the *Chambre des Comptes* in 1576 following his death, they insisted that he had acted under duress. AD-PA, B258.

[24] AD-PA, B254, B257.

[25] Charles Dartigue-Peyrou, *Jeanne d'Albret et le Béarn d'après les délibérations des États et les registres du Conseil Souverain, 1555–1572* (Mont-de-Marsan, 1934), xcviii.

[26] Roelker, *Queen of Navarre, Jeanne d'Albret*, 311; and AD-PA, B1588.

ber 1580. Then in 1585 the war resumed and lasted until 1598, but mercifully peace was restored in the southwest in 1594. Under such conditions the financial drain on Jeanne until her death in 1572 and on her son, the future Henry IV of France, was almost continual. Béarn, which escaped direct involvement in any of the later wars, produced ever increasing revenue for its sovereign (see Table 4, below), but Armagnac, which lay in the path of the armies, was less fortunate. In 1574–75 and again in 1581–82, periods of relative peace, receipts compared favorably with earlier years. In 1595–96, the first year of peace in the region, the receipts from the eleven jurisdictions into which the county was divided actually dropped to prewar levels because of alienations. In fiefs such as Fezensac and Astaffort—in which there were few, if any, alienations—receipts had approximately doubled (see Table 2, above).[27]

An illuminating though somewhat misleading way to evaluate revenue is to consider the funds the general treasurer received from the great fiefs. Such receipts are misleading in two ways. On the one hand, expenses incurred by Jeanne and Henry were often paid by the treasurer of this or that county, a practice that reduced the amount available for payment to the general treasury. On the other, alienations could provide an abnormally large receipt for the year in which they took place and cause reduced revenue thereafter, until the domain was redeemed. These practices became more common in the later stages of the religious wars.

The first religious war (1562–63) evidently had little adverse effect on Jeanne's income. The receipts from her domain and the estates of Béarn that were turned over to her general treasurer came to 171,850 *livres*, as opposed to 127,315 *livres* in 1557–58. This growth is all the more remarkable in that the earlier account covered fifteen and a half months. Jeanne's decision to participate in the second, third, and fourth religious wars caused a sharp decline in receipts to 104,053 *livres* in 1572, primarily because she had been forced to alienate all or part of her domain in some counties, and the estates of Béarn did not meet to vote a donation. In 1575 and 1580 the accounts of the general treasurer included only that part of the domain that reported to the *Chambre des Comptes* at Pau, but the domain under its jurisdiction reported continual gains. There is no extant account of the revenue derived from the part of the domain that was under the jurisisdiction of the *Chambre des Comptes* of Nérac. It did yield some revenue, but Jeanne and Henry preferred to alienate the domain in this region rather than their lands further south, probably because it was more exposed. As early as 1566, the seigneurie of Peysac in the jurisdiction of the treasurer of Périgord and Limousin had been alienated to the benefit of the Bishop of Poitiers for 10,000 *livres*, and it still had not been redeemed in 1574. At least two other seigneuries had been surrendered to noblemen in the same region by 1573–74 in return for 10,000 *livres* each, and other lands were also alienated (see Table 3).[28]

---

[27] In the region south of Paris, rents in money also appear to have risen during the relatively peaceful years but often declined when the wars were at their worst; Jean Jacquart, *La Crise rurale en Île de France, 1550–1670* (Paris, 1974), 217.

[28] AD-PA, B1862; and Raymond, *Inventaire-sommaire des archives départementales*, 154–56.

XII

TABLE 3
Receipts of General Treasurer of Navarre, Béarn, and Other Domains

Jurisdiction	1557–58[b]	1564	1572	1575	1580	1585	1589	1595	1600	1605
Navarre	1,121	2,500	1,236	9,742	13,271	1,578	3,338	3,000	1,800	8,164
Béarn	10,076	36,642	46,295	43,577	49,356	56,564	38,901	25,719	26,181	41,300[q]
Estates of Béarn	19,440	19,410	—[c]	25,920	34,560	30,240	20,520	19,440	15,120	17,280
Foix & Pamiers	21,583	21,789	14,802	7,424	10,535	20,612	9,246	6,000	8,919	9,130
Bigorre & Barbazan	14,268	11,538	1,678	10,983	19,087	11,847	9,999	7,998	4,800	12,910
Nebouzan & Aspet	871	3,405	4,047	2,862	6,401	4,112	3,999	1,998	—	3,703
Marsan	6,571	4,486	2,552	6,150	6,196	7,677	8,178	2,832	5,280	9,362
Albret	19,265	20,110	15,580[d]	—[g]	—[g]	43,750	18,231	—	—	25,622
Armagnac	9,906	21,346	12,573[e]	—[g]	—[g]	19,240[i]	11,543	—	—	13,434
Fézenzaguet	647	1,882	900	—[g]	—[g]	2,830	2,083	—	—	1,144
Rodez	13,421	15,381	—[f]	—[g]	—[g]	10,130	—	—	—	14,333
Périgord & Limousin	8,583	10,476	4,390	—[g]	—[g]	17,053	2,419	2,936	—	—
Lautrec & Villemur	1,623	2,885	—[f]	—[g]	—[g]	240	—	—	—	700
TOTAL	127,315	171,850	104,053	106,658	139,406	225,873	128,457	69,923	62,100	157,082
TOTAL RECEIPTS[a]	151,247	191,520	118,762	136,477[h]	148,600	628,539[j]	466,450[k]	246,687[m]	489,539[o]	342,016[r]

EXPENSES	150,060	197,615	127,914	121,872	144,800	624,884	—[l]	339,290[n]	492,676[p]	298,774[s]
AD-PA Source	B143	B146	B148	B150	B155	B159	B163	B168	B171	B175

[a] Total receipts include revenue from sources other than those listed above. All receipts and expenses are in *livres tournois*.
[b] Because of the death of the treasurer, this fiscal year was from July 13, 1557 to November 1, 1558. All other years were from January 1 to December 31.
[c] The estates of Béarn did not vote a "donation" in 1572.
[d] The income from Albret in 1572 was low because the revenue from renting the mills had been alienated.
[e] The estates met on November 19, 1572 and voted 25,000 *livres*. Of this sum, 3,605 *livres* had been collected and were included in this total.
[f] There was no revenue from Rodez or from Lautrec and Villemur in 1572; perhaps it had been alienated.
[g] Receipts from the domain under the jurisdiction of the *Chambre des Comptes* at Nérac were not included in the account.
[h] Total receipts in 1575 included 16,000 *livres* from the Catholic clergy.
[i] The income from Armagnac in 1585 included a gift of the estates.
[j] Total receipts in 1585 included revenue from Vendôme and other lands in the north, loans, and some alienations in the south.
[k] Total receipts in 1589 included revenue from the domain in the north, the admiralty of Guyenne, and other sources.
[l] Some pages of the manuscript are missing for 1589, including those containing the total expenses.
[m] Total receipts for 1595 included small sums from northern domains, over 40,000 *livres* in sales and alienations, and 111,945 *livres* carried over from the preceding year to meet expenses that had been incurred but not paid.
[n] Expenses for 1595 included 137,362 *livres* in unpaid expenses.
[o] Total receipts for 1600 included small sums from northern domains, over 300,000 *livres* in alienations and the sale of wood, and 68,324 *livres* carried over from the preceding year to meet expenses that had been incurred but not paid.
[p] Expenses for 1600 included 256,085 *livres* used to pay creditors.
[q] Receipts from Béarn in 1605 included 10,000 *livres* from the Catholic clergy.
[r] Total receipts in 1605 included about 30,000 *livres* from northern domains and substantial alienations.
[s] Expenses for 1605 included 87,278 *livres* used to pay creditors.

TABLE 4
Price Indices and Receipts from the Domain in Béarn

Year	Paris Wheat Indices[a]	Toulouse Wheat Indices[b]	Toulouse Wine Indices[c]	Fiscal Year[d]	Béarn Domain Indices[e]	Béarn Domain Receipts[e]	AD-PA Source
1526–35	1.00	1.00	1.00	1530–31	1.00	12,856	B225
1533–37	0.83	0.73	0.72	1534–35	1.07	13,797	B229
1538–42	0.97	1.01	0.96	1539–40	1.59	20,388	B234
1543–47	1.41	0.87	1.10	1544–45	1.68	21,644	B238
1548–52	1.39	0.83	0.62	1550–51	1.78	22,907	B242
1553–57	1.21	1.44	0.76	1554–55	1.97	25,347	B246
1558–62	1.76	1.25	0.88	1561–62	2.31	29,678	B251
1563–67	2.60	2.07	1.41	1564–65	2.99	38,461	B254
1568–72	2.60	1.95	0.72	1568–69	1.96	25,238	B257
1573–77	3.56	3.13	1.40	1575–76	3.31	42,500	B262
1578–82	2.47	2.55	0.91	1579–80	3.24	41,648	B265
1583–87	4.45	2.86	0.94	1584–85	5.00	64,249	B271
1588–92	7.67	3.35	1.98	1589–90	7.09	91,067	B279
1593–97	6.12	3.87	1.23	1594–95	6.19	79,594	B286
1598–'02	3.23	3.08	1.23	1600	7.86	101,040	B294

[a] Calculated August through July; derived from Micheline Baulant and Jean Meuvret, *Prix des céréales extraits de la mercuriale de Paris, 1520–1698*, 1 (Paris, 1960): 243.
[b] Calculated for the calendar year; derived from Georges Frêche and Geneviève Frêche, *Les Prix des grains, des vins, et des légumes à Toulouse, 1486–1868* (Paris, 1967), 85–87.
[c] Calculated for the calendar year for local red wine; derived from Frêche and Frêche, *Les Prix ... à Toulouse*, 118–21.
[d] November 1–October 31; in 1600 the treasurer used the calendar year, but local officials continued to use the earlier practice.
[e] In Béarnais *écus* (1 *écu* = ca. 1.35 *livres tournois*), a parity retained throughout most of the period; Charles Dartigue-Peyrou, *La Vicomté de Béarn sous le règne d'Henri d'Albret, 1517–1555* [Paris, 1934], 299–302). The figures are for gross receipts in money; payments in kind have been omitted because they were relatively stable and came to less than 2 percent of the gross receipts. Accounting methods caused the receipts for 1589–90, 1594–95, and 1600 to be inflated.

The viscounty of Villemur was sold to Antoine de La Tour in 1583 for 18,856 *écus*, and in 1593 the baronies of Barbazan and Bégole were surrendered for 30,000 *livres*. Always the right of redemption was retained.[29]

The year 1585 marked both the close of nearly five years of relative peace and the beginning of a war that lasted until 1598. To prepare for the conflict, Henry alienated more of his domain and indulged in some borrowing to bring the total receipts from his hereditary lands to 628,539 *livres*. Thereafter, the receipts from his domain declined until the end of the war because it was smaller (see Table 3), and he curtailed the number of alienations. But the accounts of the general treasurer do not reflect the true state of income and expenditures during these years. As early as 1594 Henry repaid Lesdiguières, the Protestant leader in the Dauphiné, the sum of 94,500 *livres*, but he made new alienations through 1596 and, to a lesser extent, thereafter. Indeed, the general treasurer's accounts of 1600 and 1605 suggest that a period of refinancing took place—that old debts were paid and parts of the domain redeemed but that money for these purposes was often obtained by incurring new obligations. That there was an overall surplus by 1605 seems clear (see Table 3).[30]

Only part of a great noble's income came from his domain. Unless he was in disgrace, he held lucrative royal offices and often received pensions and other gifts. These sums usually do not appear in the accounts of the receipts of the domain, but they were an important part of the total income. Henri d'Albret drew 10,000 or more *livres* annually as governor of Guyenne. In addition, he received special gifts from the crown and from the provincial estates and towns in his governorhsip. Finally, he had the good fortune to marry the king's sister, which was worth 25,000 *livres* a year from the king, and she brought 10,000 more in her own right.[31]

THE EXAMPLE OF BÉARN SUGGESTS that a noble's income from his domain could increase throughout the sixteenth century, unless he alienated some of his lands or his property suffered serious damage from the wars (as was the situation in Armagnac). The critical question, however, is whether a noble's revenue rose as rapidly as the price of goods and services that he bought—that is, whether his real income increased. Prevailing scholarly opinion is that it did not, but in France and elsewhere this opinion has been based primarily on a comparison of noble income and grain prices, a practice that entails serious problems. In the first place, scholars have generally derived their price indices from the Paris grain market. Between the periods 1526-35 and 1578-82, wheat prices at Paris rose at about the same rate as those at Toulouse, but shortly thereafter they increased more sharply (see Table 4). By 1588-92 they were over twice as high in

---

[29] P. Raymond, "Extraits des registres de la Chambre de Comptes de Pau (XVI-XVIII siècles) d'après un manuscrit appartenant au baron de Laussat," *Bulletin de la société des sciences, lettres, et arts de Pau*, 2d ser., 1 (1871-72): 190, 260.

[30] Raymond, *Inventaire-sommaire des archives départementales*, B3165, B3194, B3199, B3407; and AD-PA, B168, B171, B175.

[31] Dartigue-Peyrou, *La Vicomté de Béarn*, 247; and Robert R. Harding, *Anatomy of a Power Elite: The Provincial Governors of Early Modern France* (New Haven, 1978), 135-42.

TABLE 5
Gouberville's Average Annual Expenses, 1549–63

Category	Cost		Percent
	Livres	Sous	
Clothes and Fabrics	51	5	28.3
Fruits and Sugar	0	15	0.4
Meat and Game	19	13	10.9
Fish	1	12	0.9
Spices and Salt	1	2	0.6
Beer for the Harvesters	0	6	0.2
Bread for the Harvesters	0	10	0.3
Candles	3	2	1.7
Legal Expenses	29	18	16.5
Travel Expenses	28	12	15.8
Wages	44	1	24.4
TOTAL	180	16	100.0

SOURCE: Emmanuel Le Roy Ladurie, Introduction to *Un Sire de Gouberville, gentilhomme campagnard au Cotentin de 1553 à 1562*, ed. A. Tollemer (Paris, 1972), xliii.

the capital as in the southern city. Undoubtedly, the difference reflects the consequences of the semi-siege that Paris endured between 1589 and 1593 and of troop movements that impeded grain shipments before and after that period. The use of the Parisian indices for the period roughly from 1585 to 1598, therefore, greatly exaggerates the rate of inflation. Nevertheless, gross receipts from the domain in Béarn increased more rapidly than Paris wheat prices except in the late 1580s and early 1590s, when gross receipts approximately kept pace with grain prices. Receipts from the domain clearly outperformed the Toulouse wheat market, the nearest locality for which grain indices are available. In the second place, prices in general rose more slowly than grain prices. Local wine in Toulouse actually sold for less during the period 1583–87 than it had during 1526–35, and it was only 20 percent higher during the period 1608–12 than it had been during the mid-1580s (see Table 4). Clearly, we must consider what a noble purchased with his income.

The requirements of great nobles, such as the Albrets, differed from those of typical country gentlemen. A gentleman counted himself lucky if he owned a fief or two. He probably produced nearly all of the food his household consumed either by the direct exploitation of all or part of his domain, by the sharecrop system, or by the payment of dues in kind. Guillaume de Murol, an Auvergne noble of the early fifteenth century, for example, produced all or nearly all of the grain he and his household of about twenty consumed. Furthermore, the value of the bread they ate came to only 22.7 percent of their diet, which in turn was only a little more than 60 percent of their expenses in money and in kind. Even if Guillaume had had to purchase his bread, it would have come to less than 14 percent of his total expenses.[32] About a century and a half later the Sire

[32] Charbonnier, *Guillaume de Murol*, 196–97, 205–06, 217–18, 233–34.

Noble Income, Inflation, and the Wars of Religion

de Gouberville also grew his grain and baked his bread. Only on special occasions did he purchase a higher quality bread from a baker. Bread was an infinitesimal part of his expenses. Over half of his expenditures between 1549 and 1563 were for clothes, fabrics, and wages (see Table 5). Available indices suggest that industrial prices rose less than half as rapidly as grain prices and that the wages of skilled workers rose more slowly still.[33] Gouberville also spent significant amounts for meat and game, travel, and legal expenses, but the prices of such things certainly did not keep pace with grain. Very likely, during most of the sixteenth century, the cost of living index for the typical country gentleman rose about half as fast as grain prices. If this is true, the country gentlemen prospered during most of the sixteenth century.

The expenses of great nobles, such as the Albrets, were more varied. It would be logical to assume that these nobles spent more on food than simple gentlemen because of their peripatetic way of life. Although they probably set aside enough land to support the permanent residents of each of their châteaux, substantial purchases were necessary when the duke or count arrived with his entourage of ladies, gentlemen, and menial servants. The Albrets were often accompanied in their wanderings by several hundred persons. Daily expenses for food, wine, feed for animals, lodging, and the like were recorded, totaled monthly, and entered in the household account as ordinary expenses.[34] In peaceful years, these expenses came to almost half of the annual outlay for the household, but efforts to economize reduced the proportion to little more than a third during the troubled war years (see Table 6). Household expenses, however, were but a small part of the Albret outlay, especially during the Wars of Religion; expenses for food were therefore only a minor part of the family's total expenses (see Table 3, above). The cost of most of the goods and services the Albrets purchased lagged far behind food prices. Indeed, their household and monthly expenses rose rapidly until 1565, reflecting the growing affluence of the family, but both dropped sharply by 1569 because of Jeanne's decision to participate in the war. Needless expenses were curtailed; and, by 1574, the household servants who were paid numbered hardly more than a fourth of the total in 1565 (see Table 6).

Even in their economizing periods the Albrets employed a large number of persons with diversified talents, who must have reduced the family's need to

---

[33] E. H. Phelps Brown and Sheila V. Hopkins, "Wage-Rates and Prices: Evidence for Population Pressure in the Sixteenth Century," *Economica*, n.s., 24 (1957): 289–306. The authors' source for France is not reliable, but their study shows so much correlation between wage and price movements in France, southern England, and Alsace that their estimates for France are probably fairly close to being correct. Using a base of 1451–75 = 100, they found that in 1601–20 the indices are as follows:

Index of	Alsace	Southern England	France
Prices of foodstuffs	517	555	729
Prices of some industrial products	294	265	335
Builders' wage rates	150	200	268

[34] Some of these "ordinary expense" accounts survive, but I have not examined them. See, for 1571, AD-PA, B18, B19; for 1572, *ibid.*, B23; for 1576, B26, B27; for 1577, B33; for 1578, B37; for 1579, B42, B43; and so forth.

TABLE 6
Accounts of the Treasurers of the Royal Household

Year[a]	Total Payments[b]	Ordinary Monthly Expenses[b]	Number in Household Paid	AD-PA Source
1556	64,879	30,340	171	B6[e]
1560	76,242	33,167	116	B8
1565	124,870	56,758	242	B13
1569	92,871	31,522	120[d]	B15
1574	51,990	28,266	61	B24
1583	59,751	34,429	77	B83
1588	102,643	38,775	75	B129
1596	293,056[c]	130,739	128	B140

[a] The fiscal year was from January 1 to December 31.
[b] All payments and expenses are given in *livres tournois*.
[c] I have omitted 83,888 *livres* carried over from the preceding account. The jump in costs was probably caused by Catherine's recall from Béarn in October 1592. She was apparently at court in 1596. To meet her expenses, Henry IV gave her 180,000 *livres*, which were added to the household account.
[d] Actually, 200 members of the household are listed, but only 120 were paid. A few are listed in other years who were not paid.
[e] This account is printed in part in P. Raymond, "Notes extraites des comptes de Jeanne d'Albret et de ses enfants, 1556–1608," *Revue d'Aquitaine et du Languedoc*, 10 (1866): 565–72.

seek the assistance of outside professionals and artisans. Its employees included clergymen, doctors, druggists, tailors, embroiderers, tapestry makers, pastry cooks, and potters as well as numerous ladies and gentlemen in waiting, household servants, cooks, and stable hands. A comparison of the wages paid to various types of employees in 1529, 1565, and 1596 reveals the striking fact that many remained unchanged, and in 1596 only the two *maréchaux des logis* and the two *aides en fourrière* enjoyed salaries that were more than 25 percent higher than those that their counterparts had received in 1529, despite two-thirds of a century of inflation (see Table 7). The 128 paid employees of the household in 1596 received an average annual salary that was only 24.2 percent more than that of the 136 employees in 1529. Part of even this modest increase must be attributed to the fact that a greater proportion of the employees held upper-echelon positions at the end of the century. It was fortunate indeed for the poorer employees that they ate at the Albret table.

Formulating a cost of living index for the Albrets or any other great noble family is difficult. They bought some food, but food was a very small part of their total expenses. They had many servants, but they made no attempt to increase their salaries commensurate with inflation. Their costs rose, but there is no reason to believe that the average price of the things they bought increased more than one-half or, at most, two-thirds as rapidly as grain prices. If this is true, the Albrets would obviously have prospered throughout the century had peace been preserved. From their accounts we see that, as their revenue increased in the peaceful years, they permitted themselves more luxuries and

TABLE 7
Paid Officials in the Households of Marguerite d'Angoulême,
Jeanne d'Albret, and Catherine de Bourbon

Office[a]	1529[c]		1565[d]		1596[e]	
	Number Employed	Average Salary[b]	Number Employed	Average Salary[b]	Number Employed	Average Salary[b]
Maîtres d'Hôtel	2	400	6	300	2	400
Écuyers	8	200	13	200	4	250
Dames & Demoiselles	5	360	9	322	10	360
Femmes de Chambre	5	80	13	80	7	78
Maréchaux des Logis	2	200	4	200	2	300
Fourriers	3	100	5	100	4	120
Contrôleurs	2	150	4	150	4	175
Médicins	2	300	5	400	1	400[f]
Valets de Chambre	5	110	25	100	10	120
Sommeliers	4	100	8	100	5	120
Aides à Cheval	12	80	23	83	5	80
Aides à Pied	4	25	5	25	7	50
Écuyers de Cuisine	2	110	6	100	2	120
Garde-Vaisselle	1	110	2	125	1	120
Fourrière	2	100	5	100	2	120
Aides en Fourrière	2	25	4	30	2	80
Portiers	2	60	1	20	1	50
Valet des Pages	1	20	1	29	1	20

[a] Officials not appearing in all three accounts have been omitted.
[b] All salary figure are in *livres tournois*.
[c] Abel Lefranc and Jacques Boulenger, eds., *Comptes de Louise de Savoie et de Marguerite d'Angoulême* (Paris, 1905), 67–77, 80–87. Where there is a discrepancy, I have used the first list.
[d] P. Raymond, "Notes extraites de comptes Jeanne d'Albret et de ses enfants, 1556–1608," *Revue d'Aquitaine et du Languedoc*, 11 (1867): 119–25.
[e] AD-PA, B140.
[f] One médecin, who received only 60 *livres*, has been omitted.

greater display. When they entered the Wars of Religion, they reduced needless expenses and devoted their resources to the military effort. When in 1572 it looked as though the marriage between Henry of Navarre and Marguerite of Valois would insure a period of peace, Jeanne spent 32,133 *livres* for jewels and other things for the wedding, although she had to borrow at least part of the money to make these purchases. But jewels were not a useless luxury. They could be transformed into cash in case the war was renewed more quickly than parts of the domain could be alienated.[35] She had mortaged her jewels before, and doubtless her son made good use of them in the years ahead.

[35] Raymond, "Notes extraites des comptes de Jeanne d'Albret et de ses enfants, 1556–1608," *Revue d'Aquitaine et du Languedoc*, 11 (1867): 182, 184.

Some may argue that the Albrets' ability to increase their revenues was atypical. It is true that, as sovereigns of Béarn and Navarre, they had the right to coin money and to ask the estates for donations. But they farmed the right to make coins for ever increasing amounts that paralleled the general growth of their revenues, and the donations of the estates of Béarn were not included in the domainal revenue.[36] Granted, in Foix and Armagnac, where the estates occasionally voted the Albrets a donation, and in Navarre, where they regularly did so, the sums collected were incorporated into the domainal revenue, but only in these lands did the sources of their income differ significantly from those enjoyed by other great nobles. Others may argue that Henri d'Albret was an exception, because in his later years he resided on his estates and took an interest in making them efficient, and that Jeanne, his daughter, and Catherine, his granddaughter (who served as Henry of Navarre's regent after 1577), were captives of the so-called Protestant ethic. Fiscal responsibility came naturally to them, and as women they had fewer expenses than men. The financial practices of other noble families must therefore be considered.

The finest extant records of any family are those of the La Trémoilles, and these records have been carefully studied by William A. Weary. The La Trémoilles had no more need to wait for the bourgeoisie to invade the countryside and teach them how to administer their estates than did the house of Foix-Navarre-Albret. During the lordship of Georges de La Trémoille, who is best known for his violence and intrigues during the days of Joan of Arc, a detailed memorandum was prepared on how the family's extensive estates should be managed. Special attention was paid to bookkeeping and the preservation of records. A century later, one of Georges's descendants, François de La Trémoille, was an equally vigorous administrator who extracted every possible *sous* from his tenants and even prepared his own legal briefs.[37] "Through marriage, purchase, and law-suit" such men as these managed to increase the number of their estates. In 1486, the family owned thirteen; in 1550, they had thirty-five.[38]

The La Trémoille family usually leased their land for three years, which provided them with ample opportunities to raise rents to accommodate inflation. They also made use of sharecroppers. The results were striking. Their average annual seigneurial income was 8,200 *livres* in 1486–96; by 1525–41 it had risen to 26,200 *livres*. Furthermore, the average salary and gifts the family annually received from the crown increased from 3,000 *livres* during the period 1486–88 to 18,200 *livres* during the period 1508–10. The La Trémoille fortunes occasionally took a turn for the worse, as, for example, when François had to provide for five sons and give dowries to two daughters. But, aided by several profitable marriages and, above all, by efficient administration, the general trend of the family

---

[36] In 1566, the right to coin money was farmed for six years at 5,000 *livres* per year; in 1579, at 5,500 *livres*; and, in 1585, at 7,000 *livres*; J.-Adrien Blanchet, *Histoire monétaire du Béarn* (Paris, 1893), 9–11.

[37] Weary, "Royal Policy and Patronage in Renaissance France: The Monarchy and the House of La Trémoille" (Ph.D. dissertation, Yale University, 1972), 33–58, 226–33, and "The House of La Trémoille, Fifteenth through Eighteenth Centuries: Change and Adaptation in a French Noble Family," *Journal of Modern History*, 49 (1977): "demand article."

[38] Weary, "Royal Policy and Patronage in Renaissance France," 36–37.

fortune was upward. In 1500, the family's revenues were the equivalent of 220 kilograms of silver; in the 1530s, 600 kilograms. A division of the estate and the Wars of Religion led to a drop to 430 kilograms in 1619, but a recovery followed. In 1679, the family income was the equivalent of 585 kilograms of silver and, in 1709, 710 kilograms.[39]

THE ALBRETS AND THE LA TRÉMOILLES were among the richest nobles in France. As such, they could and did employ a number of able men to handle their affairs. Thus, great nobles might have prospered even though they had been guilty of all of the follies historians have attributed to them. We must ask, therefore, how well nobles with less far-flung estates and fewer servants coped with inflation and war.

The Gascon baronies of Auzan provided their lords with 15,000 *livres* in 1454 and 86,000 *livres* in 1614.[40] The domain in the barony of Auneau near Chartres was subdivided into farms and leased to sharecroppers for about 4 *livres*, 8 *sous*, 6 *deniers* per *hectare* in 1551–60. In the seventeenth century it brought 12 *livres* per *hectare*, an increase that did not quite match the rise in grain prices but was more than enough to compensate the barons for the increased cost of the goods and services they actually bought. Furthermore, the domain consisted of only 699 hectares in 1560; a century later, because of the purchase of parcels of land, there were 1,100 *hectares* to support the noble lord.[41] Domainal revenue was, of course, closely related to land rents, and land rents increased about eightfold in the region around Paris between the reign of Francis I and 1670–75, far more than enough to compensate for inflation. Leases that were paid in kind approximately doubled during the sixteenth century. Picardy and the remainder of northern France followed a similar pattern, but rents in kind in Languedoc appear to have been more stable during the sixteenth century.[42]

In Normandy the demand for land led to a threefold increase in rent for parcels at Déville-lès-Rouen between 1480 and 1510 and from an eight- to tenfold increase at Hautot-sur-Dieppe between 1480 and 1550. The Norman counts of Tancarville rented their marshlands for grazing in 1459 for 300 *livres* per year. In 1498 they received 550 *livres*; in 1515, 900 *livres*; in 1521, 1,450 *livres*. Although leases were for nine or twelve years, the rents from their land grew from 110 *livres* per year in 1506 to 550 *livres* in 1554, after which the first War of Religion likely caused the drop to 493 *livres* in 1563. The total revenue from the county grew less rapidly because seigneurial dues stabilized; nevertheless, it increased

---

[39] *Ibid.*, 82, 205–06, 216, and "The House of La Trémoille."

[40] Ducruc, "Du revenue des baronnies d'Auzan depuis le XVe siècle jusqu'à la fin de l'ancien régime," *Revue de Gascogne*, 21 (1880): 482.

[41] J.-M. Constant, "Gestion et revenus d'un grand domaine aux XVIe et XVIIe siècles d'après les comptes de la baronnie d'Auneau," *Revue d'histoire économique et sociale*, 50 (1972): 165–202.

[42] J. Jacquart, "La Rente foncière, indice conjoncturel?" *Revue historique*, 253 (1975): 355–76; and B. Veyrassat-Herren and E. Le Roy Ladurie, "La Rente foncière autour de Paris au XVIIe siècle," *Annales: Économies, sociétés, civilisations*, 23 (1968): 541–55. Income did decline in the Paris region during the Wars of the League because the destruction made it difficult to collect rent.

from about 2,200 *livres* in 1460 to an average of 7,000 *livres* annually between 1540 and 1550, more than enough to compensate for inflation but not sufficient to restore fully the prosperity the counts had enjoyed before the English invasion in 1415.[43]

Around 1400 the Norman barons of Neubourg were making the most of their resources, but their income toppled following the English conquest in 1418. The yield from their fiefs, which stood at 739 *livres* in 1405–06, fell to 264 *livres* in 1444–45. The expulsion of the English was followed by a slow recovery that was initially made possible by an increased emphasis on livestock. Scanty surviving evidence suggests that rents and other revenues increased rapidly during the sixteenth century. In 1539, land was leased at 4 *livres* per acre, but in 1591 it brought three times that amount.[44] Here, as in Béarn, a noble's income from his domain could keep pace with inflation even during the Wars of Religion. He had only to refrain from alienating his land and to hope that plundering troops did not despoil his tenants so that they could not pay their rent.

Only with difficulty could an important noble avoid taking part in such a conflict, and, once committed to one side or the other, he was obligated to raise troops and support the cause. Lands had to be alienated and sometimes sold to pay soldiers. Most likely, the more cautious noble profited by the opportunity to obtain the proffered fief, for the peasant and the burgher were rarely in a position to engage in such large transactions.[45] Initially, a noble governor or commander may have suffered financially; in the long run, however, the crown compensated for most, if not all, of his expenses if he served the royal cause or paid him to desist if he fought under a rebel banner. In all, Henry IV gave at least 24,000,000 *livres* to League leaders in return for their acceptance of him as king.[46] Provincial estates and towns were more open-handed than usual when they felt threatened or sought a favor. Pillaging could be profitable, and more than one governor or commander helped himself to royal taxes. Matignon was said to have "entered Guyenne with 10,000 *livres* of rent and died having acquired 100,000 *livres* in the twelve years that he was governor."[47] His successor, Alfonso d'Ornano, a Corsican, had come to France in 1569 to seek his fortune, and he managed to leave his family well established in its new land. Gaspard de Saux-Tavannes reportedly seized 60,000 *livres* in the sack of Mâcon and, more certainly, made the family fortune in Burgundy. Blaise de Monluc slowly increased his wealth prior to the Wars of Religion, but his estate grew rapidly after that conflict began. He left his heirs a fortune sixteen times as large as that of his grandather. François de Bonne's early career coincided with the opportunities provided by the religious wars. Initially, he received only a few hundred

---

[43] Bois, *Crise du féodalisme*, 324, 320, 228, 231–33.

[44] Plaisse, *La Baronnie du Neubourg*, 225, 326, 339–43, 372–73, 539, 551.

[45] I base this statement on a casual inspection of those who acquired the fiefs that the Albrets alienated and on the list of those who engaged in land transactions with the dukes of Nevers; for the latter, see Harding, *Anatomy of a Power Elite: The Provincial Governors*, 228–30.

[46] J. Russell Major, *Bellièvre, Sully, and the Assembly of Notables of 1596*, Transactions of the American Philosophical Society, no. 64, pt. 2 (Philadelphia, 1974), 4.

[47] Harding, *Anatomy of a Power Elite: The Provincial Governors*, 135.

livres per year in rents; but by 1610 his annual income reached 121,699 *livres*, and he later became Duke of Lesdiguières and the last constable of France.[48] Great wealth was also amassed by Jean Louis de Nogaret de La Valette, who profited from royal favor to become Duke of Épernon; others similarly chose the court as the route to fortune during the reign of Henry III.

Unlike Monluc and Lesdiguières, the Nevers were very wealthy before the Wars of Religion began. They also committed every folly that historians have long attributed to the nobility as a whole. Expensive entertainment, gambling, large dowries, and conspicuous consumption were coupled with participation in foreign wars when no domestic conflict was available. One member of the family had to pay a ransom of 125,000 *livres*, and another revived the outmoded practice of crusading. Even biology appeared to be their enemy, for the Nevers failed to produce a male heir but had to provide large dowries for their daughters. At times, they could not pay their debts and had to sell extensive estates. Yet, in spite of everything, the family income, which stood at 115,085 *livres* in 1551, reached 446,260 *livres* in 1612. In 1550 the duke was worth about 2,000,000 *livres*, but after the male line became extinct in 1637 the family's immovable property was valued at 8,062,034 *livres*. Even after a debt of 2,500,000 *livres* is subtracted and inflation is taken into account, the family would appear to have more or less held its own.[49]

There were, of course, nobles who were punished for their folly. Louis de Lausignan, for example, built up a fortune through able and loyal service to the crown, but his son, Guy, lost substantial sums gambling, joined the Catholic League, and sought to become a spy for Philip II of Spain. In the end he reentered royal service, but neither he nor his son enjoyed Louis's success at court; and the family sank back into relative obscurity.[50]

Undoubtedly, a great noble who employed competent officials to manage his affairs could increase his fortune during the first half of the sixteenth century and could, even if the religious wars were costly to him, recoup his fortune after peace was restored.[51] Furthermore, the wars provided an opportunity for governors and troop commanders to make their fortunes, whether they chose the royalist cause or backed the rebels. But what of the typical noble who counted himself lucky if he drew several hundred *livres* from his lands when the Wars of Religion began? Since such nobles numbered in the thousands, to cite a few instances when they bought additional land or had to sell their diminuitive estates is insufficient to demonstrate that they were a rising or a falling class. Only a quantitative study can suggest their fate, and such a study exists for the nobles in the *élection* of Bayeux.

---

[48] *Ibid.*, 137, 149–52, 157; and Robert Forster, *The House of Saulx-Tavannes* (Baltimore, 1971), 1–5.

[49] Harding, *Anatomy of a Power Elite: The Provincial Governors*, 143–49; and J. Russell Major, "The Crown and the Aristocracy in Renaissance France," *AHR*, 69 (1963–64): 634. If 1625 is taken as the terminal date, there is no doubt that the family profited; its debt was then only 91,000 *livres*.

[50] Harding, *Anatomy of a Power Elite: The Provincial Governors*, 154–57.

[51] The fortunes of the peers increased after 1589; and the nobility as a whole prospered in the *élection* of Bayeux between 1639 and 1666, and probably over a longer period. See Jean-Pierre Labatut, *Les Ducs et pairs de France au XVIIe siècle* (Paris, 1972), 248–50; and James B. Wood, *The Nobility of the Élection of Bayeux, 1463–1666* (Princeton, 1980), 126–28.

The most striking thing about the nobles of Bayeux is how few of them had active military careers. Between 1552 and 1639, only 3 to 13 percent of them annually were in regular service. In those rare instances when the *ban* was summoned, the number of noblemen in the army varied from only 13 percent in 1568 to 38 percent in 1597, after the Spanish had taken Amiens. The exceptionally heavy turnout in 1597 resulted from the crown's decision to include in the feudal levy nobles who did not own fiefs and to impose heavy fines on those who failed to appear. Another notable fact is that the wealthier nobles predominated among those who became soldiers. "Almost three-quarters of the *élection*'s military nobility belonged to the richest half of the nobility, 43 percent (169 of 391) to the richest quarter alone."[52] Thus, poverty did not drive the nobility to arms. Most poor nobles remained at home, where they produced their own food and thereby escaped the worst effects of inflation. There is no reason to believe that their economic position was less favorable at the end of the Wars of Religion than at the beginning, provided that their lands had not been plundered too often.

Arguments that real noble income declined during the last part of the sixteenth century are based largely on evidence that there were many poor nobles at the end of the period and that nonnobles were purchasing fiefs. James B. Wood has demonstrated, however, that in the *élection* of Bayeux the proportion of poor nobles in 1639 was almost identical to what it had been in 1552 and that, although some commoners bought fiefs from nobles, nobles were more active in buying fiefs from commoners.[53] As a result, 87 percent of the fiefs in the *élection* of Bayeux belonged to nobles in 1562 on the eve of the Wars of Religion, 88 percent in 1597 at their close, and 93 percent in 1640. Nor did new nobles dispossess the old nobility. Indeed, the old resident nobility held 57 percent of the fiefs in 1552 and 62 percent in 1640, despite the unusually large number of patents of nobility that the crown sold during the Wars of Religion. In the long run, the nobility also increased its share of the revenue from fiefs. In 1552 and again in 1562, 8 percent of the income from fiefs went to commoners and unidentified persons. By 1587 their share had increased to 13 percent, but thereafter a decline set in. In 1597 commoners and unidentified persons received 11 percent of the income; in 1640, only 2 percent.[54]

In the vicinity of Paris, nobles who owned vast estates—such as the Montmorencys—and those who held court positions or received royal pensions managed to retain, or even increase, their holdings after the Hundred Years War. The scant surviving evidence suggests that they also increased their purchasing power but not to the extent that their financial position of the first half of the fourteenth century was fully restored. Lesser royal officials—that is, those in the sovereign courts and in finance—did penetrate the countryside and purchase some of the fiefs of the poorer gentlemen. The merchant, however, rarely partic-

---

[52] Wood, *The Nobility of the Élection of Bayeux*, 95, 82–84.
[53] *Ibid.*, 120–26. Wood has defined an old noble family as one that had been noble for a century or more.
[54] *Ibid.*, 145–49. There were 415 fiefs in the sample in 1562, 417 in 1597, and 487 in 1640.

ipated in this process; in other words, there was no "bourgeois conquest of the soil."⁵⁵ At Lyons, where the merchant rather than the royal official predominated, much of the land was owned by the Church, which prevented commoners from acquiring property before 1525. Not until the lands of the constable of Bourbon and, later, some Church property were put on the market did burghers begin to buy seigneuries. Local noblemen, who were neither wealthy nor numerous, were unable to compete.⁵⁶

In regions more removed from the great political and commercial centers, the old nobility probably fared as well as or better than they did around Bayeux. Normandy was perhaps the richest province in France, and the town of Bayeux, which boasted roughly 6,000 inhabitants, was more important than the typical local seat. To tap that wealth the crown sold or awarded no less than 74 patents of nobility in the *élection* between 1541 and 1598,⁵⁷ but in spite of this influx the old nobility, and the nobility as a whole, managed to hold its own.

Income from fiefs represents only part of noble revenues. Many nobles also managed to increase their income by the purchase of church and nonnoble lands. In 1569 the nobility bought over one-fourth of the goods sold by the clergy to meet royal demands in the twenty-two dioceses of the *généralités* of Paris, Champagne, Lyons, Berry, and Dijon. Other sales followed in these and other parts of France. In all, between 1568 and 1586 property worth 13,562,000 *livres* was alienated, much of which was not seigneurial.⁵⁸

More significant was the nobles' purchase of peasant land to round out their estates. After the Hundred Years' War the nobility of the Gâtine in Poitou took the lead in buying the scattered parcels of land belonging to peasants in order to form more consolidated farms, which they rented to sharecroppers on five-year leases. In the sixteenth century, nobles usually demanded payment of a specified amount of agricultural produce rather than a fixed percentage of the crop, as later became the custom. This practice favored the nobility, because crop yields fell toward the end of the century, a development that may explain why about 60 percent of the peasants abandoned their leases between 1570 and 1590. In Burgundy, the damage done by the Wars of Religion as well as indebtedness caused many peasants to part with their holdings and the common lands on which so many of them depended. In the Beauce the nobility, both new and old, acquired substantial holdings between 1543 and 1696.⁵⁹

The nobles' purchase of peasant holdings created a serious problem in prov-

---

⁵⁵ Fourquin, *Les Campagnes de la région parisienne*, 482, 465–82; Jacquart, *La Crise rurale en Île de France*, 66–85, 161–63, 245–47; and Veyrassat-Herren and Le Roy Ladurie, "La rente foncière autour de Paris," 549–55.
⁵⁶ Richard Gascon, *Grand commerce et vie urbaine au XVIᵉ siècle: Lyon et ses marchands*, 2 (Paris, 1971): 813–30.
⁵⁷ Wood, *The Nobility of the Élection of Bayeux*, 64.
⁵⁸ Le Roy Ladurie, "Les Masses profondes," 699–710. For purchases of Church lands in Languedoc, see his *Les Paysans de Languedoc*, 1: 362–71; and in Périgord, see N. Becquart, "Les Alienations du temporel ecclésiastique au diocèse de Périgueux de 1563 à 1565," *Annales du Midi*, 86 (1974): 325–33.
⁵⁹ Louis Merle, *Le Métaire et l'évolution agraire de la Gâtine poitevine de la fin du Moyen Âge à la Révolution* (Paris, 1958), 63–66, 91, 178–79; P. de Saint-Jacob, "Mutations économiques et sociales dans les campagnes bourguignonnes à la fin du XVIᵉ siècle," *Études rurales*, 1 (1961–62): 34–49; and J.-M. Constant, "La Propriété et le problème de la constitution des fermes sur les censives en Beauce aux XVIᵉ et XVIIᵉ siècles," *Revue historique*, 249 (1973): 373–76.

inces where the *taille* was *personnelle*, because such property was withdrawn from the tax digest and the difference was made up by increasing the burden on the remaining peasant holdings. In Dauphiné an exceptionally bitter dispute arose because the villagers were able to produce a legal argument that the *taille* was *réelle* in that region—that is, that the nobility and other privileged groups should pay taxes on the common land that they owned. During Henry IV's reign, the villagers gathered data to prove that from one-half to two-thirds of the tallageable land had passed into the hands of those who claimed to be exempt. Perhaps the peasants' figures should not be fully trusted, but the king's council recognized that they had a legitimate complaint. Finally, in 1634, after the dispute had raged for nearly a century, a decision favorable to the peasants was decreed.[60] In 1594 the third estate of Haute-Auvergne complained that the nobility had bought nearly half of the land owned by poor farmers. Thirteen years later the third estate of Forez and Beaujolais and the *plat pays* of Lyonnais asked the king to forbid the nobles to acquire rural property outside the jurisdiction of their justice and to make them either pay the *taille* on or surrender the lands that they had already bought. The king's council thought that the complaint was serious enough to warrant asking royal officials in the provinces to give their opinions on the request.[61]

As might be anticipated in provinces where the *taille* was *réelle*, the privileged sometimes sought to have it declared *personnelle* so that they would not be taxed on the nonnoble land they had acquired. The effort to redefine the *taille* surfaced in Agenais, Condomois, Provence, Languedoc, and probably elsewhere; the movement was most often spearheaded by royal officials and university faculties. In general, the effort failed because of the strength of tradition and because of the crown's realization that reducing the number of taxable acres was not in its interest.[62] The nobility, to its credit, did not press the issue vigorously, although by the eighteenth century nobles owned over half of the taxable land in parts of Languedoc. That the purchase of peasant holdings had become a national problem was brought forth during the Assembly of Notables of 1626–27, but a move to declare the *taille* to be *réelle* in all of France came to naught because those who attended were all among the privileged.[63]

THIS ESSAY HAS FOCUSED on the income nobles derived from land because land provided most of their sustenance. But, of course, this is only part of the picture. Many nobles profited greatly from the crown and the church and from invest-

---

[60] Major, *Representative Government in Early Modern France*, 76–80, 232–35, 326–32, 433–36, 481, 524–26, 531–32, 597, 614–16.

[61] Gabriel Esquer, ed., *Inventaire des archives communales de la ville d'Aurillac antérieures à 1790*, 1 (Aurillac, 1906): AA21; and Noël Valois, ed., *Inventaire des arrêts du Conseil d'État, règne de Henri IV*, 2 (Paris, 1893): nos. 11,232, 11,746.

[62] Major, *Representative Government in Early Modern France*, 65, 277–78; and Richard J. Bonney, *Political Change in France under Richelieu and Mazarin, 1624–1661* (Oxford, 1978), 365.

[63] Major, *Representative Government in Early Modern France*, 65, 503. Among the few who supported the proposal in the Assembly of Notables was Louis de Marillac, the brother of the keeper of the seals.

ments in mining, glass making, *rentes*, and trade. Some engaged in usury; of the 79,949 *écus* nine villages in the Rhône valley borrowed during the Wars of Religion, 39,040 *écus* came from the nobility, 31,856 from the bourgeoisie, 4,026 from the military, and 5,037 from persons of unknown origin.[64] Moreover, insufficient attention has been given to the economic problems posed by overly large progenies. With these limitations in mind and on the basis of the data now available, the following conclusions are justified.

1. The improved methods in accounting and exploiting the soil must be attributed to the nobility and its employees who adopted the new procedures before there was a significant bourgeois penetration of the countryside.

2. The income from the typical fief increased as rapidly as or more rapidly than grain prices until the Wars of Religion, because the nobility used short-term leases, usually of three to six years, that quickly responded to the growing peasant demand for land that was sparked by a demographic explosion.

3. The price of the goods and services that nobles purchased rose at about half the rate of grain prices, or possibly at two-thirds that rate in the case of the great nobles. As a result, the landowning nobility became more affluent. In all likelihood, its purchasing power more than doubled prior to the Wars of Religion. Therefore, insofar as nobles as a class had an economic motive for participating in the religious wars, it was to increase their already growing affluence. Truly poor nobles rarely took part. Even if they had desired to do so, they would have had difficulty buying the necessary equipment.

4. The domain continued to yield increased income during the Wars of Religion provided that the owner alienated little, if any, part of it and that it suffered little, if any, direct damage from the conflict.

5. Most important nobles who participated in the war had to borrow money and alienate part of their estates to pay their soldiers. Other nobles suffered from the depredation of troops and the loss of livestock that provided fertilizer for their land. Productivity declined and revenue temporarily failed to keep pace with inflation. The deleterious effects of the wars, which perhaps appeared as early as 1567 and became especially pronounced between 1585 and 1595, largely account for the contemporary literary evidence that the nobility was in economic decline near the end of the sixteenth century. There is no reason to believe, however, that the nobility lost its relative position, because merchants and government officials suffered as much and because some nobles managed to take advantage of the Wars of Religion to make their fortunes.

---

[64] Daniel Hickey, "Une Remise en question: Procès des tailles et blocage social dans le Dauphiné du XVIe siècle," *Cahiers d'histoire*, 23 (1978): 33.

6. The nobles recovered their economic position much more rapidly after the Wars of Religion than they did following the Hundred Years' War. Henry IV paid all or most of their debts by compensating friend and foe alike. The population was larger, and this assured low wages, a strong peasant demand for land to lease, and high prices for agricultural products, although the wartime peak was not maintained. Because of their purchase of peasant and, to a lesser extent, Church lands, the nobles' estates were more extensive than before.

La Noue's observation—"France is so populous and so fertile that what the war has damaged in one year is restored in two"[65]—is an exaggeration. Two years was enough time for the peasant to rebuild his cottage, replace his tools, and plant his fields, but it was not sufficient to rebuild the herds of livestock and to restore the fertility of the soil. This took place more slowly. Nevertheless, noblemen who owned a fief or two as well as the dukes and counts who held many were able to resume a march toward greater affluence, a process that had been only temporarily interrupted by the Wars of Religion.

[65] As quoted in Jacquart, *La Crise rurale en Île de France*, 254 n. 1.

XIII

**"Bastard Feudalism" and the Kiss:
Changing Social Mores in Late Medieval and
Early Modern France** During the late Middle Ages a new relationship between the greater and lesser members of Western European aristocracies emerged in which indentures were made to bind lord and client together but no fiefs were given or homage performed. Historians have explained why kings and magnates ceased to be able to provide fully for their social, political, and military needs by awarding fiefs, but according to Lewis, a leading authority on "bastard feudalism," it is not at all clear "why the idea of homage should have palled." The purpose of this essay is, first, to suggest that the failure to require homage in the new aristocratic relationship in France was caused by a change in the attitudes toward kissing; and then to address the question of whether this new relationship that has been given the derogatory name of "bastard feudalism" necessarily involved a decline in the loyalty that a man owed his lord. At times it has been necessary to draw heavily on historians of England because they have studied aspects of the new aristocratic relationship with such care.[1]

HOMAGE AND THE KISS DURING THE MIDDLE AGES At the base of the traditional feudal system lay the concept of vassalage as cemented in homage and fealty. The ceremony of homage varied, but, in its most common form, the vassal, without sword, belt, or spurs, knelt bareheaded, placed his joined hands between those of his lord, and declared that he was the lord's man in return for

---

[1] Peter S. Lewis, *Later Medieval France* (London, 1968), 200.

The initial research for this article was undertaken while the author was a member of the Institute for Advanced Study at Princeton. He is indebted to the Institute and to a sabbatical leave and a research grant from Emory University for the opportunity for uninterrupted research. He also thanks Thomas Burns, Natalie Zemon Davis, and Charles T. Wood for their critiques of earlier versions of this article.

Reprinted from The Journal of Interdisciplinary History *XVII (1987), 509-535, with the permission of the editors of* The Journal of Interdisciplinary History *and the MIT Press, Cambridge, Massachusetts. Copyright © 1987 by The Massachusetts Institute of Technology and the editors of* The Journal of Interdisciplinary History.

a specified fief. The lord then kissed the vassal on the mouth and said that he took him as his man. Fealty consisted of the vassal taking an oath of fidelity, most frequently upon the Gospels. As a result of this double ceremony, a contract came into being in which the vassal became obligated to give military and material aid and counsel to his lord. The lord in return was expected to provide his vassal with protection and maintenance that usually took the form of a fief.[2]

When the ceremony of homage evolved, kissing between unrelated members of the same sex and between the two sexes for non-erotic reasons was widely practiced. The early Christians were especially noted for their custom of kissing. Jesus reproached Simon the Pharisee for not kissing him when he entered his house (Luke 7:45). Paul often urged Christians to "Greet one another with a holy kiss" (Romans 16:16; I Corinthians 16:20; II Corinthians 13:12; I Thessalonians 5:26), and Peter enjoined them to "Greet one another with the kiss of love" (I Peter 5:14). Indeed, the kiss between men was so commonplace that Judas believed that he could use it to identify his Master without arousing suspicion.

The kiss of peace soon became part of the Christian liturgy. At first men and women kissed each other and Tertullian, one of the earliest Church fathers, expressed concern that pagan husbands would object to their Christian wives behaving in this fashion. What heathen, he queried, would suffer his wife "to slip into prison to kiss the fetters of a martyr? Or, for that matter, to salute any one of the brethren with a kiss?" Nor was the possibility that the kiss would arouse carnal desires lost on the early Christians. Clement of Alexandria complained:

> There are those that do nothing but make the churches resound with a kiss, not having love itself within. For this very thing, the shameless use of a kiss, which ought to be mystic, occasions foul suspicious and evil reports. The apostle calls the kiss holy. When the kingdom is worthily tested, we dispense the affection of the soul by a chaste and closed mouth, by which chiefly gentle manners are expressed. But there is another, unholy, kiss, full of poison,

---

[2] Marc Bloch (trans. L. A. Manyon), *Feudal Society* (Chicago, 1961), 145–162; François L. Gansholf (trans. Philip Grierson), *Feudalism* (London, 1952), 64–73; François Olivier-Martin, *Histoire de la coutume de la prévôté et vicomté de Paris* (Paris, 1922), I, 265–266; Paul Viollet (ed.), *Les établissements de Saint Louis* (Paris, 1881), II, 396–400; *ibid.* (1886), IV, 251–253.

counterfeiting sanctity. Do you not know that spiders, merely by touching the mouth, afflict men with pain? And often kisses inject the poison of licentiousness.[3]

Nevertheless, Paul's repeated injunctions were so clear that the kiss of peace, of salutation, and of friendship was preserved, but the danger of the liturgical kiss between men and women was diminished when the custom developed of having the two sexes sit on opposite sides of the church.

Little is known concerning the kissing practices of the Germanic invaders, but as Jones notes, "Gregory of Tours relates how the Frankish king Gunthramn sealed a pact with his nephew by kissing him, and how King Chilperich kissed his son Merovech and the latter's fiancée Brunichilde in swearing an oath that he would not try to prevent them from marrying." The only kiss in Beowulf, one of the oldest surviving works in a Germanic language, was between men. Bloch quotes a poem about a pre-Norman Englishman whose protector has died: "He dreams at times that he embraces and kisses his lord, and lays hands and head upon his knees, as he did in days gone by at the high seat whence bounty flowed." Examples from German literature between 1160 and 1220 are plentiful enough to provide some certainty as to current practices. Here Jones found that kisses between members of the same sex and between different sexes were largely restricted "to the conventional occasions of welcomes, farewells, reconciliations, and treaties." Erotic kisses were infrequent. In von Oberge's and von Strassburg's versions, when Isolde decided to forgive Tristan for killing her uncle, she kissed him as a sign of reconciliation and her father did the same.[4]

In many of the medieval love lyrics and in the songs of the troubadours, the kiss was treated as the ultimate reward that a lady could be expected to give to her lover. The first kiss that

---

3 Nicolas J. Perella, *The Kiss Sacred and Profane* (Berkeley, 1969), 12–18, 30; Joseph A. Jungmann (trans. Francis A. Brunner), *The Mass of the Roman Rite: Its Origins and Development* (New York, 1953), II, 321–332; Gregory Dix, *The Shape of the Liturgy* (Glasgow, 1945; 2nd ed.), 105–110; F. Cabrol, "Baiser," *Dictionnaire d'archéologie chrétienne et de liturgie* (Paris, 1924), II, pt. 1, cols. 117–130; Tertullian (trans. William P. Le Saint), *Treatises on Marriage and Remarriage* (Westminster, 1951), 29.

4 George F. Jones, "The Kiss in the Middle High German Literature," *Studia Neophilologica*, XXXVIII (1966), 196, n. 7, 195, n. 1, 204; Bloch, *Feudal Society*, 183; Eilhart von Oberge (trans. J. W. Thomas), *Tristrant* (Lincoln, Neb., 1978), 70–72; Gottfried von Strassburg (trans. Arthur T. Hatto), *Tristan* (Harmondsworth, 1960), 180–182.

Queen Guinevere gave to Sir Lancelot has been likened to homage in that "the lady held the position to the lover that in fuedal homage the lord held to the vassal . . . the act of amatory homage was modeled on the ceremony of the feudal contract of vassalage." The above analogy seems farfetched until we find Bloch arguing that when "the Provençal poets invented courtly love, the devotion of the vassal to his lord was the model on which they based their conception of the fealty of the perfect lover." He reproduced the twelfth-century seal of Raymond de Mondragon to substantiate his claim. Here we find the knight kneeling before his lady, his hands joined and placed between hers.[5]

Le Goff agrees that "in courtly love, the man is the woman's vassal and that an essential part of its symbolic system is the kiss." He regards this gesture, however, as not being relevant to an understanding of the ritual of homage because he believes that the kiss symbolized a basic equality between the participants. Women, who were considered inferiors, were not allowed to take part in the kiss. The evidence from courtly love he dismisses as being only an effort "to stabilize and coopt the 'feminist' movement of the Romanesque era." But before accepting this interpretation we must ask whether noble women were really excluded from the kiss.[6]

The bishop-elect of Carpentras placed the hands of an infant boy and his female guardian between his own when the former rendered homage in 1322, but he kissed only the infant. The text says that the bishop excluded the guardian from the kiss as a matter of decency, but Le Goff rejects this explanation in favor of one based on the presumed inequality of women. The dame d'Oisy anticipated the opportunity to kiss the handsome bishop of Cambrai when she did homage, but the latter, on hearing this, designated his bailiff to serve as his proxy, again in the name of propriety. The disappointed lady refused to accept this substitution and transferred her allegiance to the count of Artois. In both these instances it was presumed that the kiss would take place,

---

5 Perella, *The Kiss Sacred and Profane*, 84–123, 129. See also 268–269 for more details and for Perella's attack on Moshé Lazar's contention in *Amour courtois et fin amour* (Paris, 1964), that troubadour love was purely sensual in its goals. Bloch, *Feudal Society*, 233. See plate IV for Mondragon's seal.
6 Jacques Le Goff (trans. Arthur Goldhammer), *Time, Work, and Culture in the Middle Ages* (Chicago, 1980), 262.

CHANGING SOCIAL MORES 513

but the lord, who had taken vows of celibacy, refused in the name of decency. When the woman was doing homage in her own name, a lay proxy was provided to receive the kiss. When she was merely a guardian, only the infant was kissed. Le Goff cites no text stating that a woman was refused the kiss because she was inferior or any instances in which a layman refused to kiss a woman doing homage. Indeed, some ecclesiastics were less squeamish: the bishop of Langres kissed two female vassals when they did homage in 1328.[7]

During the high Middle Ages the ritual of homage doubtless varied as to time, place, and the individuals concerned, as it certainly did during the centuries that followed when the documentation is much richer. The preponderance of evidence, however, indicates that in France the usual procedure was for the lord and vassal, regardless of sex, to kiss on the mouth. Commoners did not participate in this part of the ritual.

The kiss in homage was given as "a sign of mutual fidelity," as a means "to confirm the promise of fidelity between two parties." The kiss was also used in the high Middle Ages to confirm other types of agreements, such as the gift of a piece of property, the renunciation of a disputed claim, and the making of a marriage alliance. Once again, if a monk and a woman were involved, the kiss on the mouth was omitted. Thus, when a married couple and their son made a donation to Saint-Aubin d'Angers, the monk who accepted the gift was kissed by the father and the son, but he refused to be kissed by the wife because "it was uncommon for a monk to be kissed by a woman," and he directed the lady to give the kiss to a lay proxy. In 1143, the viscountess of Turenne kissed only the hands of the prior of Obazine when she made a gift.[8]

The kiss may not have been part of the ceremony of homage in its earliest stage, although too few descriptions of the ritual

---

7 Ibid., 261. For the text of the document see Emile Chénon, "Le rôle juridique de l'osculum dans l'ancien droit français," *Mémoires de la société nationale des antiquaires de France*, VI (1919–1923), 145–146. Ibid., 147, n. 1. Chénon, who uncovered the descriptions of homage used by Le Goff and myself, cites a case in which a woman took her little great grandson to his lord, a layman, to do homage for him. When the lord laid claim to the kiss "according to the custom," the elderly woman refused and handed the child to the lord to be kissed. It was the *woman*, not the lord who refused; the kiss was considered by the lord to be part of the ritual. Ibid., 146, 145.
8 Ibid., 151, 135.

survive to enable one to speak with assurance. It was first recorded when the abbot-elect of St. Gall did homage to Otto I in 971 and it was firmly incorporated in the ceremony in France by the close of the tenth century. By then kisses had been exchanged for nonerotic reasons for centuries and it was but natural to include the practice in a ritual that was so important in binding society together.[9]

A NEW ATTITUDE TOWARD KISSING   In the late thirteenth century there was a change in the attitude toward kissing. The danger of kisses being exchanged by members of the opposite sex had been noted by the earliest church fathers. The stories of Lancelot and Guinevere and other romances of chivalry demonstrated clearly that the kiss could lead to unforeseen and disastrous consequences. More striking was a new attitude about the exchange of kisses between members of the same sex. During the ancient period homosexuality had been widely accepted. Even the early church fathers were more tolerant of it than might be expected. There was some tightening of the sexual code in the fourth, fifth, and sixth centuries, which may be attributed in part to a growing asceticism. The emperor Justinian outlawed homosexual practices, but neither the late empire nor the early medieval states were in a position to enforce such legislation, and the church was seemingly unconcerned. Indeed, there was a substantial increase in the amount of homosexual literature during the eleventh and twelfth centuries and prominent prelates were implicated. Not until the late twelfth century was there a concerted effort to stamp out homosexual practices and many years elapsed before it had a telling effect. Boswell suggests that this change in attitude was "probably closely related to the general increase in intolerance of minority groups apparent in ecclesiastical and secular institutions throughout the thirteenth and fourteenth centuries." Goodich sees the change as an outgrowth of the Gregorian reform movement. Whatever the cause, by 1300 homosexual practices were generally condemned by church and state alike, and kissing between members of the same sex that had once served as a sign of peace,

---

9 Le Goff, *Time, Work, and Culture*, 266, 362, n. 71; Robert Boutruche, *Seigneurie et féodalité* (Paris, 1968), I, 208–210.

CHANGING SOCIAL MORES 515

reconciliation, and agreement now became associated with homosexuality.[10]

This change in attitude toward kissing may explain why the English began to abandon the kiss of peace around the middle of the thirteenth century. It had long been customary for men to kiss men and women to kiss women as a sign of reconciliation just before communion, but this practice was now replaced by kissing a plaque on which was implanted a picture of Jesus or some saint. This practice gradually spread to the continent and the kiss of peace between Christians, that had been so meaningful as a token of reconciliation, ceased to exist in the liturgy of the Roman Catholic Church except in the form of a light embrace among the clergy. At about the same time, the kiss to seal the various types of contracts, which once had been very common, ceased to be performed.[11]

That a new attitude toward kissing had developed by the beginning of the fourteenth century is further suggested by the trial of the Templars. Philip the Fair and his advisers were anxious to discredit the Templars by every means at their disposal. They could hardly attack the order because a kiss on the mouth was included in the initiation, since it was also a part of the vassalage ceremony, but they were quick to couple mouth kissing with homosexual practices whenever the opportunity occurred. Thus, when Hugues de Pairaud was interrogated in 1307, he said that he had been kissed on the mouth when he had been inducted, but admitted that he had then been taken to a secret place where he had been kissed on "the lower part of his spine, on his navel, and on his *mouth* (italics mine).[12]

Kneeling also came under attack. When the ceremony of homage began to evolve, vassals had usually been ordinary freemen or even serfs. They did not object to kneeling humbly before their lord. The Carolingian monarchs had some noble vassals,

10 John Boswell, *Christianity, Social Tolerance, and Homosexuality* (Chicago, 1980), 61–266, 334; Michael Goodich, *The Unmentionable Vice. Homosexuality in the Later Medieval Period* (Santa Barbara, 1979), 39.
11 On the kiss of peace in Roman Catholic liturgy, see Jungmann, *Mass*, II, 321–332; Dix, *Shape of the Liturgy*, 105–110. Chénon, "Le rôle juridique," 136.
12 Georges Lizerand (ed.), *Le dossier de l'affaire des Templiers* (Paris, 1923), 40–41, 231. On the homosexual charges against the Templars, see Malcolm Barber, *The Trial of the Templars* (Cambridge, 1978), 61, 99, 147, 163, 165, 178, 190–192, 249; Boswell, *Christianity*, 295–298.

but they so far surpassed their subjects that they could impose such a ritual. By the close of the thirteenth century, however, a virtual revolution had occurred. Nearly all vassals had achieved noble status and these nobles had become conscious of their dignity, worth, and unity as an order. A pauper might kneel when he was about to receive alms, but for one noble to kneel before another noble was, as an eighteenth century jurist put it, "ridiculous." This opposition to kneeling before a noble was not extended to include kneeling before a king because, by 1300, the growing concept of royal sovereignty had exhalted the king above the magnates. Kneeling before the king provoked opposition only from such independent or semi-independent dignitaries as the kings of England and the dukes of Brittany. The situation was therefore ripe for an attack on these two elements of the ritual of homage as the Middle Ages began to draw to a close.[13]

CHANGES IN FEUDAL RELATIONSHIPS AND HOMAGE   Feudal relationships had already proved vulnerable to social changes, but the earlier adjustments had been made before the kiss had become suspect, and the ceremony of homage had gone unchallenged. When fiefs became hereditary soon after the inception of the feudal system, it became necessary to define the status of clergymen, widows, daughters, and minors who were unable to perform the services required of vassals. A man who held fiefs from more than one lord was faced with the problem of whom he should serve in case of simultaneous or conflicting demands. As a result, when oaths of fealty were taken, it became customary for the vassal to name one or more persons against whom he would not serve. By the late eleventh century, the economy was sufficiently developed for some lords to offer annual payments in money to those who would render them faith and homage. Thus the *fief rente* was established. The *fief rente* added to the flexibility of the feudal system because it enabled a great lord not only to expand his military force but also to extend his vassalage system into areas in which he owned no land.[14]

13 Henrion de Pensey, *Traité des fiefs de Dumoulin* (Paris, 1773), 39. For homage and vassalage, see Bloch, *Feudal Society*, 145–162; Le Goff, *Time, Work, and Culture*, 237–287. For the concept of the nobility as an order, see Georges Duby (trans. Goldhammer), *The Three Orders Feudal Society Imagined* (Chicago, 1980). For the kneeling pauper, see Natalie Zemon Davis, *Society and Culture in Early Modern France* (Stanford, 1965), pl. 4.
14 A complex jurisprudence gradually developed governing the responsibilities of a

At first, witnesses were present to testify that faith and homage were performed, but, by the thirteenth century, literacy had developed to the point that lords began to give their vassals letters describing the procedure that had been followed during the ceremony so that their right to the designated fiefs would less likely be challenged. Vassals, in return, repeated the ritual of faith and homage in writing in a document called an *avou*. Within forty days they were also expected to submit a detailed description of their fiefs called *dénombrements*. Finally, although the essence of faith and homage was an agreement between lord and vassal taken in person, long absence, sickness, old age, minorities, and other problems often made it necessary for one or the other of the two parties to be represented by proxy. As time progressed, personal convenience and, by the late Middle Ages, dislike of the ceremony itself replaced necessity. The kings delegated the authority to receive homage to their chancellors, bailiffs, seneschals, and other officials, and, during the reign of Charles VII, this delegation became the normal procedure for less important fiefs. Nobles also sometimes abandoned their insistence that homage and fealty be rendered in person.[15]

Since the vassal was expected to perform military service, there was from the start a problem of what to do with women and the clergy. Glanvill, writing in the late twelfth century, flatly declared that women could not do homage for this reason. Bracton relented, but new problems arose concerning the propriety of women participating in the ceremony. Around 1475, Sir Thomas Littleton took offense at a woman who did homage having to say "I become your woman; for it is not fitting that a woman should say, that she will become a woman to any man,

---

vassal's conflicting obligations. See, for example, Giovanni da Legnano (ed. Thomas E. Holland), *Tractatus De Bello, De Represaliis et De Duello* (Oxford, 1917); Honoré Bonet (ed. George W. Coopland), *The Tree of Battles* (Cambridge, Mass., 1949); Christine de Pisan (trans. William Caxton), *The Book of Fayttes of Armes and of Chyvalrye* (London, 1937); Pierion Belli (trans. Herbert C. Nutting), *A Treatise on Military Matters and Warfare* (Oxford, 1936). Bryce D. Lyon, *From Fief to Indenture* (Cambridge, Mass., 1957), 23–40, 147–244.

15   Olivier-Martin, *Coutume de Paris*, I, 256–277, 309–321; Léon Mirot, *Inventaire analytique des hommages rendus à la Chambre de France* (Melun, 1932), I, iv–x; Boutruche, *Seigneurie et féodalité*, I, 370–376. For examples of nobles using proctors to receive homage and fealty, see *Archives historiques de département de la Gironde* (hereafter cited as AHG), VIII, 515–516; XXVII, 489–492; Antoine Jacotin (ed.), *Preuves de la maison de Polignac* (Paris, 1905), IV, 430–432, 447–449, 510–512.

but to her husband, when she is married. But she shall say, I do to you homage, and to you shall be faithful and true, and faith to you shall bear for the tenements I hold of you, saving the faith I owe to our soveraigne lord the king." Years later such French jurists as Antoine Loisel, Pierre Hévin, and Henrion de Pensey quoted Littleton, who wrote in law French, with apparent approval. Abbots, priors, and other heads of religious communities, Littleton thought, who had given themselves entirely to God, should also be excused from saying "I become your man."[16]

The above changes demonstrated to everyone that aspects of the lord-vassal relationship could be altered and made it all but certain that, when kissing and kneeling fell into disrepute, there would be demands to change the ceremony of homage itself. The most outspoken and most quoted leader of the assault on homage was Du Moulin, who published an influential treatise in 1539. Simple homage, he insisted, implied no personal dependence. To kneel before a noble was ridiculous. One only knelt before a prince. The kiss was "indecent nay reprehensible," and not imposed by custom. The expression *la bouche et les mains* that was used to describe the ceremony of homage in many customs only meant that the mouth was used to promise loyalty, which was done with the hands joined. Furthermore, there was no precise form for the oath of fidelity.[17]

Splendid opportunities to study the efforts to alter the ceremony of homage so as to conform to the new social mores are provided by the redaction and reformation of the customs of the

---

16   William Holdsworth, *A History of English Law* (London, 1914; 2nd ed.), I, 305–306; G. D. G. Hall (ed. and trans.), *The Treatise on the Laws and Customs of the Realm of England Commonly called Glanvill* (London, 1965), 103; Samuel E. Thorne (trans.), *Bracton on the Laws and Customs of England* (Cambridge, Mass., 1968), II, 228; Edward Coke, *The First Part of the Institutes of the Laws of England; or, a Commentary upon Littleton* (London, 1794), I, sect. 87; Antoine Loisel, *Institutes coutumières* (Paris, 1846), II, 32; Pierre Hévin, *Coutumes générales du païs et duché de Bretagne* (Rennes, 1746), II, 542; de Pensey, *Traité*, 43. David Hoüard, an advocate in the Parlement of Rouen, was so impressed by Littleton that he published an edition with Littleton's law French in one column and a modern French translation in the other. Under each section he wrote a commentary. *Anciennes loix des françois, conservées dans les coutumes angloises, recueilliers par Littleton* (Rouen, 1766), 2 v. Coke, *Commentary upon Littleton*, I, sect. 86.

17   Charles Du Moulin, *Omnia Quae Extant Opera* (Paris, 1681), I, 129–130; de Pensey, *Traité*, 38–50; Olivier-Martin, *Coutume de Paris*, I, 311. Two centuries after Du Moulin wrote, Hoüard again insisted that the kiss was "indecent." *Dictionnaire analytique, historique, etymologique, critique et interpretatif de la coutume de Normandie* (Rouen, 1780), II, 354.

various parts of France and the commentaries of the jurists designed to interpret them. During the Middle Ages a few customs had been redacted—that is, transferred from the oral tradition to a written form—but the task did not begin in earnest until the early sixteenth century. In the latter part of the sixteenth century many of the customs were reformed. The redaction and the reformation of the customs was accomplished by holding large assemblies in which the three estates declared what the law was. There was popular pressure for change but, at the same time, it was difficult to depart much from the oral tradition during the redaction and still more difficult to make significant changes once the custom was in a written form. Nevertheless, because of omissions, vagueness, additions, and occasionally outright corrections, the customs were altered to meet the growing dislike of aspects of the ceremony of homage.[18]

When d'Ableiges described how homage was rendered in the town and provostship of Paris near the close of the fourteenth century, he specified that the vassal knelt before his lord and promised faithful and loyal service. The lord then took the vassal's hands between his own and kissed him on the mouth. When the custom was redacted in 1510, only the expression *la bouche et les mains* was used to describe the ceremony of homage. At that time the medieval interpretation of *la bouche,* meaning the kiss, almost certainly held sway. The phrase was repeated in the revised custom of 1580, but, later in the same document where more detail was given, the vassal was required to place only one knee on the ground and the kiss was omitted. It was in this form that the Paris custom was transplanted to Canada in the seventeenth century.[19]

Thus the custom itself was altered to reflect the changing social mores. A few commentators, antiquarians primarily,

---

18 René Filhol, *Le premier président Christofle de Thou et la réformation des coutumes* (Paris, 1937), 40–121.

19 Jacques d'Ableiges, *Le grand coutumier de France* (Paris, 1868), 273–274; Olivier-Martin, *Coutume de Paris,* I, 90–101, 265–266, 311; Charles A. Bourdot de Richebourg (ed.), *Nouveau coutumier général* (Paris, 1724), III, 1, art, 2; 4, art. 48; 30, art. 3; 35, arts. 63, 66. For a description of homage in Canada, see Francis Parkman, *The Old Régime in Canada* (Boston, 1902), 307–309. For the seigneurial regime, see Marcel Trudel, *The Seigneurial Regime* (Ottawa, 1967); Richard C. Harris, *The Seigneurial System in Early Canada: A Geographical Study* (Madison, 1966).

sought to retain the letter of the written custom. But the more common practice was to follow the lead that Du Moulin had given in 1539 and to insist that kneeling be reserved for liege homage to the king and that *la bouche* refer only to a verbal pledge of loyalty. De Ferrière went so far as to argue that the oath of fidelity was not necessary because private wars had been abolished in France and that it was useless for vassals to take oaths that they could neither keep nor execute. But he wrote this opinion after Louis XIV had reigned for many years.[20]

The customs in some other parts of France also underwent change. That of Melun required kneeling and the kiss when it was redacted in 1506, but when it was reformed in 1560 the vassal put only one knee on the ground and the kiss was omitted. In 1507, the custom of Amiens defined homage in terms of *la bouche et les mains,* but this phrase, indicating the kiss, was dropped when the custom was reformed in 1567. The kiss underwent a similar fate in Orleans to the delight of the commentator. The late medieval custom of Brittany specified a kiss on the mouth, but, by 1539, the custom prescribed the kiss only when one brother did homage to another. By the final reformation of the custom in 1580 this fraternal kiss was dropped and a bow replaced kneeling even when liege homage was performed. When the custom of Touraine was redacted in 1507, the kiss was required, but, when it was reformed in 1559, a partial reprieve was granted by removing this part of the ritual if the lord were represented by proxy. The Normans saw no need to describe the ceremony of homage when they redacted their custom, but when they reformed it in 1583 they were careful to limit the ceremony to the vassal placing his hands between his lord's. The representatives of the dukes of Aumale and Montpensier, the duchess of Longueville, and the count of Montaing had tried without success to require vassals to place one knee on the ground and to be bareheaded without arms or spurs, but they did not seek to preserve the kiss on the mouth. It was flattering to have nobles kneel before you, but the kiss was as repugnant to them as to their vassals. Some commentators sought to reduce the impact of the

---

20 See, for example, Louis Charondas Le Caron, *Coutume de la ville, prévosté et vicomté de Paris* (Paris, 1605; 4th ed.), fols. 3v–4. Olivier-Martin, *Coutume de Paris,* I, 311; Claude de Ferrière, *Corps et compilation de tous les commentateurs anciens et modernes sur la coutume de Paris* (Paris, 1714; 2nd ed.), I, 203–206, 959–972.

CHANGING SOCIAL MORES 521

ritual by limiting kneeling and the kiss to liege homage, or to deny that the king or even a noble need kiss a commoner when he did homage for a fief. As early as 1260, a noble claimed that he did not have to do homage to a commoner who had become his overlord, but the matter was not so easily resolved and the deputies of the nobility to the Estates General of 1614 pleaded not to have to do homage in person to a commoner.[21]

Most troublesome of all was the question of whether a woman had to participate in the kiss in doing homage. Lelet, René Choppin, and others followed Du Moulin in excusing women from the kiss on the grounds that it was not an essential part of homage, but more traditional jurists pointed out that women were almost never excluded in the customs and that they could no more dispense with this mark of obedience and fidelity than anyone else. Hoüard, who thought that it would be "indecent" for a woman to say "*I become your woman* (his italics)," failed to discuss women and the kiss. Buridan thought that for a woman to refuse to kiss her lord would be to hold him in contempt. It was not customary for men to kiss men, he argued, but it was for men to kiss women.[22]

In spite of a tendency on the part of a few to preserve some of the traditional aspects of the ceremony, the trend was clearly in the other direction. La Thaumassière alluded to "the ridiculous and superfluous formalities" of the old ritual. It would suffice if

[21] Bourdot de Richebourg (ed.), *Nouveau coutumier général*, III, 422, art. 134; 436, art. 24; I, 123, art. 24; 169, art. 20; IV, 252, art. 222; 309, art. 322; 382, arts. 333, 341; 607, ch. 13, art. 15; 652, art. 115; 64–65, art. 107; 122; Jacques Delalande, *Coutumes des duché, bailliage, prévosté d'Orléans et ressorts d'ueux* (Orléans, 1673), 75; Josias Bérault, *La coustume réformée du pays et duché de Normandie* (Rouen, 1620), 119: Gabriel Labbé, *Les coustumes générales des pays et duché de Berry* (Paris, 1607; 2nd ed.), 152–155; François Ragueau, *Les coustumes générales des pays et duché de Berry* (Paris, 1615), 131; Fourré, *Coutumes générales du pays et comté de Blois* (Blois, 1777), 130; Ferrière, *Corps et compilation*, I, 223; Jean Lelet, *Observations sur la coutume de Poitou* (Poitou, 1710), 200–202; Jean-Baptiste de Buridan, *Coustumes de la cité et ville de Rheims* (Paris, 1665), 133–135; Joseph Boucheul, *Coutumier général ou corps et compilation de tous les commentateurs sur la coutume du comté et pays de Poitou* (Poitiers, 1727), I, 329–330; Jean Mauduit, *Nouveau commentaire sur la coustume du pays et duché de Berry* (Paris, 1624), 185; Germain-Antoine Guyot, *Traité des fiefs, tant pour le pays coutumier, que pour les pays de droit écrit* (Paris, 1753), IV, 221–222; Olivier-Martin, *Coutume de Paris*, I, 124; Hévin, *Coutumes de Bretagne*, II, 542; Lalourcé and Duval (eds.), *Recueil des cahiers généraux trois ordres aux États-généraux* (Paris, 1789), IV, 193.

[22] Boucheul, *Coutumier général de Poitou*, I, 340; Loisel, *Institutes coutumières*, II, 32; Ragueau, *Les coustumes de Berry*, 133; Henry Basnage, *La coutume réformée du païs et duché de Normandie* (Rouen, 1678), I, 179–180; Hoüard, *Dictionnaire*, II, 354; Buridan, *Coustumes de Rheims*, 141–142.

XIII

the vassal took the oath "cap in hand." "Kids stuff," La Bigotière declared around 1700 in his commentary on the custom of Brittany, "the sort of thing that is done at the theater." Over a decade later another commentator on Brittany believed that the traditional form of homage "is rarely used today"; but he hastened to add: "we know of seigneurs who have required liege homage of their vassals in all the rigour of the article." Hévin, a generation later, urged that homage be abolished altogether because it was a "vain ceremony, and a pretext to vex his subjects without profit to His Majesty." Delalande took comfort in the belief that few lords required their vassals to assume the posture specified in the custom and Coquille, who thought that *la bouche* had signified the kiss in the ancient custom, believed that the kiss was no longer used in practice.[23]

From the sixteenth century, some customs permitted a vassal to present himself before his lord's domicile in his principal fief and announce in a loud voice that he had come to do homage. If neither his lord nor someone authorized to receive homage appeared, the vassal could kneel without hat, sword, or spurs and take the oath before a notary and other witnesses. Then, in some customs, he kissed the bolt of the door. The vassal might feel a little foolish in this procedure, but at least he escaped the humiliation of doing homage before another man. It was in this fashion and in accordance with the custom of Burgundy that Jean Baptiste Byon did homage on July 6, 1789.[24]

The French customs, therefore, provided increasing opportunities to escape the more humiliating aspects of homage, and most of their interpreters did all in their power to further this trend. It is necessary, however, to turn to the documents that actually described individual ceremonies to learn what occurred.

---

23 Gaspard Thaumas de la Thaumassière, *Nouveaux commentaires sur les coutumes générales des pays et duché de Berri* (Bourges, 1701), 136. René de la Bigotière is quoted by Jean Gallet, "Fidélité et féodalité: quelques aspects de la fidélité des vassaux en Bretagne au XVIIe siècle," in Yves Durand (ed.), *Hommage à Roland Mousnier: Clientèles et fidélités en Europe à l'époque moderne* (Paris, 1981), 118; Hévin, *Consultations et observations sur la coutume de Bretagne* (Rennes, 1734), 343; Delalande, *Coutumes d'Orléans*, I, 120; Guy Coquille, *Les coustumes du pays et comté de Nivernois*, in idem, *Les Oeuvres* (Paris, 1665), II, 87.

24 The procedure for doing homage in the absence of the lord and his authorized representative varied somewhat from province to province. See, for example, Bourdot de Richebourg (ed.), *Nouveau coutumier général*, III, 35, art. 63 for Paris; III, 496, art. 171 for Sens; III, 942, art. 20 for Berry; III, 1262, art. 380 for Bourbonnais. Boutruche, *Seigneurie et féodalité*, I, 380–382.

CHANGING SOCIAL MORES   523

In the early fourteenth century the archbishop of Bordeaux required his vassals to kneel and he kissed them on the mouth, but by 1530 a kiss on the cheek had become standard, although one and sometimes both knees were placed upon the ground. Perhaps the clerk who recorded the homage performed by Charles de Durfort in 1603 was not accustomed to the practices of the archbishop because he first recorded that the kiss was upon the mouth, but then replaced the offensive word by "cheek."[25]

Some noble families appear to have adopted a ceremony or at least a phraseology of their own. By the late sixteenth century the trade mark of the viscounts of Polignac had become the "kiss of peace" which they bestowed upon their vassals "after the fashion of nobles." Once we are told that such a kiss was planted upon the mouth. Always the vassal placed his hands between those of the viscount, but we are not informed if or how he knelt. In 1601 a vassal swore to follow the viscount in all wars and against everyone. Not even the king was specifically excepted. When the parish of Le Brignon did homage to the viscount in 1645, its inhabitants became his "liege men and subjects." In doing so they knelt on both knees, but the "kiss of peace" was not administered to these humble people.[26]

But the Polignac came from one of the most backward parts of France. Elsewhere the ceremony of homage was less impervious to change. Even the duke of Epernon, one of the haughtiest noblemen in France, permitted Pierre de Baritault to escape the kiss when he did homage in 1602. A woman who did homage to him in the name of her children in 1638 swore on the holy Gospels "to be forever a good, loyal and faithful vassal," but she neither knelt before nor was kissed by her now aged lord. Jean d'Anglade knelt bareheaded without belt or arms and placed his hands between the hands of his lord when he did homage in 1658, but although the document that recorded the event was written in Gascon, the ceremony was not so outdated as to include the kiss. Nicolas Fouquet, Louis XIV's celebrated minister, dispensed with the ceremony of homage but preserved his rights by having his vassals sign a statement acknowledging him as their overlord, and perhaps take an oath. Thus, by the early seventeenth century, the

25   AHG, XIII, 212–229; X, 174–175; XIII, 230.
26   Jacotin (ed.),*Preuves de Polignac*, III, 164–165; IV, 430–432, 446–449, 510–512.

kiss was falling before the onslaught of the jurists and public opinion. Homage was becoming an administrative matter.[27]

Homage did not cease altogether, however, because, if a vassal failed to perform this duty, the lord could legally take possession of his fief. Thus, in 1585, we find a woman asking Madame de La Trémoille, the former Jeanne de Montmorency, to delay seizing her lands on the grounds that her husband had twice gone to do her homage, only to find her absent. He was now away in the service of her son, the duke, and was not at the moment free to go a third time. Or again, in 1592, a nobleman protested to his lord that the reports that he was trying to avoid doing homage were false and that he was at his service. In 1613, the seigneur and dame of Bosjan tried to regain the lands of Frangi, Villeneuve, and Charni from the seigneur of Sarigny, because he had not done homage in the proper fashion. Among the procedural issues at stake was that Sarigny had failed to place both knees on the ground. In May 1617, the Parlement of Dijon sided in Sarigny's favor on the grounds that the Burgundian custom did not provide a "certain and precise form for doing faith and homage" and that he had met the essential requirements of the ritual. A similar dispute led the Parlement of Bordeaux to spell out in detail how liege homage should be done. In a decree of March 10, 1605, it stipulated that the vassal, bareheaded and without sword, belt, or spurs, should place one knee on the ground and, with his hands between his lord's, promise to be a good and faithful vassal and to assist him against everyone except the king. The lord would then raise the vassal and promise to be a good seigneur. The kiss was conspicuously omitted from the ceremony.[28]

In spite of a tendency on the part of the courts to side with the vassal on questions concerning homage, there were instances in which the lord actually seized fiefs. The dukes of La Meilleraye did so in 1673 and 1692, and there were a number of seizures

---

27 AHG, XLV, 540–542; II, 406–408; VII, 356–358; Gallet, "Fidélité et féodalité," 118–119.

28 Paul Marchegay and Hugues Imbert (eds.), *Lettres missives originales du seizième siècle tirées des archives du duc de La Trémoille* (Niort, 1881), nos. 205, 252; Pierre Taisand, *Coutume générale des pays et duché de Bourgogne* (Dijon, 1698), 97–100; Gabriel Davot, *Traités sur diverses matières de droit français à l'usage du duché de Bourgogne et des autres pays qui ressortissent au Parlement de Dijon* (Dijon, 1751), II, 263–264; Bernard Automne, *Commentaire sur les coustumes géneralles de la ville de Bourdeaus et pays Bourdelois* (Bordeaux, 1621), 479–480.

between 1694 and 1708, when part of the ducal lands reverted to the crown and were administered by royal officials. The dukes themselves were vassals of local lords for some of their lands, but they protected their pride by doing homage through procureurs. Indeed, homage by procuration appears to have become common in Poitou during the seventeenth century. At times both lord and vassal used proctors. Thus, in 1671, the procureur of the dame of Roquefeuil, bareheaded, with both knees on the ground and without belt, sword, or spurs, did homage in her name to Louis XIV, who was represented by his procureur. The oath on the Holy Gospels was administered, but the agents of the dame and the king saw no need to subject themselves to the kiss. The tie between lord and vassal had become totally impersonal. Homage in person, however, did not cease. In an elaborate ceremony in 1699, the duke of Lorraine rendered homage to Louis XIV for the duchy of Bar. Without hat, gloves, or sword, he knelt on a pillow and took the oath, but the kiss was conspicuously omitted. In 1775, the duke of La Trémoille did homage to Louis XVI, with the keeper of the seals serving as the royal proxy. In the description of the ceremony we are simply told that the duke assumed the "posture of a vassal," and are left to wonder what that posture was. Homage continued to be performed until it was abolished in the Revolution.[29]

The kiss in homage may have come under attack in England also; in the fifteenth century it was part of the ceremony, but by the seventeenth century it was a thing of the past. In 1429, John Nowell did homage to Thomas de Hesketh by kneeling bareheaded, placing his hands between those of the said Thomas, and saying: "Sir, I become your man from this day forward." When he had finished, Thomas kissed him. John then took an oath upon

---

29 J. Peret, "Seigneurs et seigneuries en Gâtine poitevine: le duché de La Meilleraye XVIIe–XVIIIe siècles," *Mémoires de la société des antiquaires de l'Ouest*, 4th series, XIII (1976), 36–38, 71, 74–75, 83–84. In Picardy, and no doubt elsewhere, fiefs were often seized for failure to submit *dénombrements*. Kristin Brooke Neuschel, "The Prince of Condé and the Nobility of Picardy: A Study in the Structure of Noble Relationships in Sixteenth-Century France," unpub.ms. (Brown Univ., 1982), 125. Philippe Lauzun, *Le château de Bonaguil en Agenais* (Agen, 1897; 3rd ed.), 124–125; Boutruche, *Seigneurie et féodalité*, I, 376–77, 380–382. For other examples of foreign princes doing homage for French fiefs, see Jean Dumont (ed.), *Corps Universel diplomatique du droit des gens* (Amsterdam, 1739), IV supplement, 393–395, 399–401. Louis de La Trémoille (ed.), *Les La Trémoille pendant cinq siècles* (Nantes, 1896), V, 146–147.

"a book." In 1439, when "a sekeness called the Pestilence" spread through England, the House of Commons petitioned Henry VI that those "holdyng of yow by Knyghtes service . . . in the doyng of thair said homage, may omitte the said kissyng of you, and be excused thereof at youre will, the homage beyng of the same force as though they kissed you, and have thair lettres of doyng of thair homage, and kyssyng of you omitted not withstondyng." The king approved this request. Around 1475, Littleton still prescribed kneeling on both knees with head uncovered and terminating the ceremony with a kiss. Less than a century and a half later Coke was to write: "if lords knew what benefit they may reape by receiving of homage and fealty, they would not neglect them." Homage had apparently disappeared altogether in England between the time of Littleton and the age of Coke, except in so far it was preserved in the coronation ceremony. Stone could write his monumental history of the aristocracy from 1558 to 1641 without even mentioning homage, although it was not until 1660 that homage and military tenures were officially abolished.[30]

30 David C. Douglas (ed.), *English Historical Documents* (Oxford, 1969), IV, 1117–1118. It is not the purpose of this article to study the homage ceremony in medieval England and I have gone only to the more obvious sources. Published documents are sparce, the evidence is contradictory, and the subject has generally been ignored by historians. It would be logical to assume that the Norman kings and barons used the same ritual in England as in Normandy. Unfortunately, prior to 1300, English jurists were more interested in the oath than the ritual and tell us little. Glanvill described only the oath; Bracton and the author of the *Fleta* were content to say that the vassal put his hands between the lord's. Neither kneeling nor the kiss was mentioned. In the latter, however, we are told that the vassal's hands were "uplifted" when he put them between his lord's. Hence the vassal had almost certainly assumed a kneeling position. This account of the ritual and very likely Bracton's are incomplete. Britton's treatise, written around 1300 at the request of Edward I, was essentially a reorganized, condensed version of Bracton, but he did stipulate that the lord should kiss the tenant. Again there was no mention of kneeling. A statute of Edward II, however, omitted any reference to the kiss or kneeling. But then again, Coke thought that the kiss and kneeling were a part of homage. *The Treatise on the Laws . . . Called Glanvill*, 104; *Bracton on the Laws and Customs of England*, II, 232; Henry G. Richardson and George O. Sayles trans., *Fleta* (London, 1972), III, 39; Francis M. Nicholas trans., *Britton: An English Translation and Notes* (Washington, 1901), 364; *The Statutes of the Realm* (London, 1810), I, 227; Coke, *The Compleate Copy-Holder* (London, 1641), 16–18. I am indebted to Mervyn James for the last reference. Foreigners sometimes commented on the English practice of men and women exchanging kisses of greeting and on parting, but apparently members of the same sex did not indulge. Lawrence Stone, *The Family, Sex and Marriage in England 1500–1800* (New York, 1977), 320–321; William B. Rye, *England as Seen by Foreigners in the Days of Elizabeth and James the First* (London, 1865), 90, 260–62; *Rotuli Parliamentorum*, V, 31; Coke, *Commentary on Littleton*, I, secs. 85, 94. Stone, *The Crisis of the Aristocracy, 1558–1641* (Oxford, 1965). Stone informed me that

CHANGING SOCIAL MORES

"BASTARD FEUDALISM" IN ENGLAND AND FRANCE   The lord-vassal relationship had long been inadequate to meet the military and administrative needs of kings and great nobles, and historians of England have made a great contribution by demonstrating the changes that were introduced to correct the deficiencies. In the reign of Henry I and earlier, the military household of the Norman kings included a number of persons who were neither vassals nor clerics. These men were retained by an annual fee and paid a daily wage when they were called upon to serve. Unlike the vassal, they could be discharged when their term of service expired. For this reason we find them being exhorted on the eve of a battle in 1124 "to fight for their reputation and for their right to continue to draw the king's wages and eat his bread." Since they served for a limited time, it made no sense for each of them to kneel before the king and declare that he had become his man. Homage was reserved for lifetime relationships. Some of these clients were reappointed year after year and, if fortunate, were eventually given fiefs for which they did homage. At this point the relationship became a lifetime one; the patron and client became lord and vassal.[31]

Initially, these non-feudal contracts for service had been verbal, but, by 1270, written contracts called indentures appeared. At first all of these indentures were for limited periods of time, but soon lifetime contracts also began to be made and the so-called "bastard feudalism" was born. The indenture was generally written on parchment, the copy retained by the lord being sealed and signed by the client and the copy retained by the client being sealed and signed by the lord. The new relationship was similar to the earlier one in the military household in that the client received pay for his services and did not do homage; it differed in that it was for a lifetime. The new relationship was similar to

---

he had never seen a description of how homage was performed (letter dated August 30, 1984). I can only speculate why the ceremony of homage ceased in England but was only modified in France. Perhaps the abolition of subinfeudation by the statute of *Quia Emptores* in 1290 and the decline in the value of feudal incidents so undermined the lord-vassal relationship in England that the ceremony of homage fell more easily before the onslaught of the changing social mores than in France where feudal relationships remained more viable. For England, see John M. W. Bean, *The Decline of English Feudalism 1215-1540* (Manchester, 1968).
31   John O. Prestwich, "The Military Household of the Norman Kings," *English Historical Review*, XCVI (1981), 1-35, quotation 11.

the *fief rente* in that it was for life and included financial payments; it differed in that no homage was done.[32]

The number of short-term and lifetime indentures rapidly increased following the outbreak of the Hundred Years' War. Edward III and his successors made individual contracts with a few nobles and captains to recruit specified numbers of troops for periods of one year or less. Thus, in 1369, John of Gaunt, duke of Lancaster, agreed to raise and lead "499 men-at-arms, 1,000 archers, 300 lances and bowmen . . . and 40 miners" for a period of six months in return for a specified sum. The duke in turn made contractual arrangements with his subordinates; but some of these contracts differed in one important respect from those of the king: many, although perhaps not a majority, were for life and obligated the clients to serve in peace as well as in war in return for an annual stipend. These clients usually resided in their own homes, but were expected to accompany their lord on his journeys and to render occasional service in his household, as well as to serve in his company in time of war. In addition to his permanent household and lifetime clients, a lord made temporary contracts when the need arose to expand his contingent in war or, in special circumstances, in peace. It was these temporary clients who were most often lawless and it was against them that late medieval legislation against livery was directed. The lifetime clients, however, evoked little criticism and it is with them that this article is concerned.[33]

Only a handful of the thousands of indentures that must have been made have survived, but, judging by the few that have done

---

32 There is a large literature on indentures and bastard feudalism. See, for example, Michael Prestwich, *War, Politics and Finance under Edward I* (London, 1972), 41–66; George A. Holmes, *The Estates of the Higher Nobility in Fourteenth-Century England* (Cambridge, 1957), 58–84; Kenneth B. McFarlane, "Bastard Feudalism," *Bulletin of the Institute of Historical Research*, XX (1943–1945), 161–190; idem, *The Nobility of Later Medieval England* (Oxford, 1973), 102–121; N. B. Lewis, "The Organization of Indentured Retainers in Fourteenth-Century England," *Transactions of the Royal Historical Society*, XXVII (1945), 29–39.

33 J. W. Sherborne, "Indentured Retinues and English Expeditions to France, 1369–1380," *English Historical Review*, LXXIX (1964), 720; McFarlane, *Nobility*, 102–107; N. B. Lewis, "Indentures of Retinue with John of Gaunt, Duke of Lancaster, Enrolled in Chancery, 1367–1399," *Camden Miscellany*, XXII (1964), 77–112. The sub-contracts of Sir Hugh Hastings in 1380 were for one year. Anthony Goodman, "The Military Sub-contracts of Sir Hugh Hastings, 1380," *English Historical Review*, XCV (1980), 114–120.

CHANGING SOCIAL MORES 529

so, it seems probable that they became less detailed as the responsibilities of the lord and his client under the new relationship became generally understood and accepted. At the same time, the amount that the lord agreed to pay was gradually reduced until contractually agreed upon payments were dropped altogether. Only two of the sixty-nine surviving indentures that William Lord Hastings granted between 1461 and 1483 specified money payments.[34]

The Hastings indentures provide our last opportunity to analyze the English contracts. In general, the retainer promised to serve Hastings in peace and in war in England for his entire life. He was to take Hastings' part in all quarrels except against the king and possibly other specifically designated individuals. When summoned he was to come with his men defensibly arrayed. In return Hastings promised to be a good lord and to help his retainer in all things as far as law and conscience allowed. Sometimes, but perhaps not always, the retainer also took a verbal oath; a sealed document with copies placed in the hands of lord and client alike seemed enough.[35]

As late as 1945, Perroy correctly declared: "We do not see yet very clearly how in France the princes developed their retinue; how they enrolled the services of the smaller nobility, how they built up private armies, how they paid the services of their retainers." He recognized that the English barons defined "the new relationship between patron and client, through contracts of retinue," but surprisingly believed that such contracts "do not seem to have existed on the other side of the Channel." Independently and almost simultaneously Lewis and I pointed to the existence of indentures in France, although Lewis appeared reluctant to use that term for the French contracts. More recently, Contamine has recognized that the *lettres de retenue* that the French kings used to raise troops during the Hundred Years' War were similar to the contracts of the English kings, except that the former were less precise and did not specify the duration of the contract, although probably it was for one month. Contamine, however, was interested in royal recruitment for the French army, and never analyzed

---

34 N. B. Lewis, "Indentures of Retinue," 80–82; William H. Dunham, Jr., *Lord Hastings' Indentured Retainers 1461–1483* (New Haven, 1955), 9.
35 *Ibid.*, 47–52, 123–138.

the contracts between the greater and lesser nobles, or indicated how the former used them to extend their power and influence.³⁶

In France, as in England, few indentures have survived. Only those made by Louis d'Orléans, the dukes of Brittany, and the counts of Foix have been found in sufficient numbers to form the basis for research on how a great noble made use of such contracts in a particular region. Lewis has studied them with care and has published a few Foix indentures made between 1358 and 1439. Following the French practice, he has preferred to label agreements between equals and indentures between lord and client as alliances, although he is well aware that there was a difference. There is justification for following the late medieval practice of referring to both types of contracts as alliances, but this terminology easily leads to confusion and may explain why French historians have not generally recognized the existence of indentures in their country. It therefore seems preferable to limit the term alliance to agreements between equals and to use indentures to describe the new non-feudal relationship.³⁷

The principal distinction between the lord-vassal relationship and the indenture system was that the vassal in the former ren-

---

36 Edouard Perroy, "Feudalism or Principalities in Fifteenth Century France," *Bulletin of the Institute of Historical Research*, XX (1943–45), 185, 181; P. S. Lewis, "Decayed and Non-Feudalism in Later Medieval France," *Bulletin of the Institute of Historical Research*, XXXVII (1964), 157–184; Major, "The Crown and the Aristocracy in Renaissance France," *American Historical Review*, LXIX (1964), 631–645; Philippe Contamine, *Guerre, état et société à la fin du Moyen Âge* (Paris, 1972), 64. Lyon, *From Fief to Indenture*, 258, has made the added point that the French contracts did not include a retaining fee.

37 These contracts are not indentures in the strict diplomatic sense of consisting of the copies of a contract having correspondingly notched edges; neither are Lord Hastings', but Hastings' contracts are usually referred to as indentures in the documents themselves. The modern meaning of the word had become accepted. In rare instances both the term "alliance" and the term "indenture" are used in the French documents. P. S. Lewis, "Decayed and Non-Feudalism," 157–184; idem, "Of Breton *Alliances* and Other Matters," in C. T. Allmand (ed.), *War, Literature, and Politics in the Late Middle Ages* (Liverpool, 1976), 122–143. On p. 141 of the latter Lewis publishes a contract containing the word "indenture." The Breton documents are unique in that the dukes rarely made a reciprocal promise to their clients. They seem to have used the contracts to bind men who were already their vassals more closely to them. Ibid., 132, 134–135. See also Michael Nordberg, *Les ducs et la royauté: études sur la rivalité des ducs d'Orléans et de Bourgogne 1392–1407* (Stockholm, 1964); Barthélémy A. Pocquet du Haut-Jussé, "Les pensionnaires feiffés des ducs de Bourgogne de 1352 à 1419," *Mémoires de la société pour l'histoire du droit et des institutions des anciens pays bourguignons comtois et romands*, VIII (1942), 127–150. Poquet du Haut-Jussé speaks of non-fiefed pensions, but as he publishes no complete documents, it cannot be ascertained whether these are indentures.

dered both homage and fealty, whereas in the latter the client only swore fealty, which he did by taking an oath on the cross or, more commonly, on the Gospels. So similar were the two that in several of the early Foix indentures the client placed his hands between those of his lord and the kiss was included. Only gradually did the new form completely replace the old. The Foix often promised to pay their clients a pension and occasionally provided an initial lump sum as well. Generally the arrangement was for life only, but sometimes specific arrangements were made for it to be continued during the next generation.[38]

From the latter stages of the Hundred Years' War until the end of the fifteenth century, there was a tendency for indentures in which the high nobility were the senior participants to become shorter, less specific, and more standardized. As in the case of Hastings' indentures, payment was rarely specified, although good lordship was certainly anticipated. Thus, in 1429, Gilles de Rais signed a written contract in which he swore to serve his cousin, Georges de La Trémoille, with all his power until death. He stated that he took this step because of the past favors that he had received and the courtesies that he anticipated. Although La Trémoille promised no specific reward in return, within three months he won for his twenty-three-year-old client the post of marshal of France.[39]

In 1451, Gailhard de Durefort promised "to serve, succor, and aid" Charles d'Albret and his children for life against everyone except the king and the dauphin. Homage was not performed and no reward was hinted at, but one was doubtless anticipated. The superstitious and ever-suspicious Louis XI was willing to forego liege homage if the occasion warranted, but fealty remained important to him. He insisted that Jean, count of Armagnac, swear in a document signed in 1465 to be loyal on everything that his fertile imagination could conjure up:

> I swear and promise by the faith and oath of my body, on my honor, by the Baptism through which I have been brought from the depths, on the peril and damnation of my soul, on the holy Gospel of God, and on the holy relics of the Chapel of the Palace

---

38 P. S. Lewis, "Decayed and Non-Feudalism," 162–168, 180–184. See also J. Quicherat, *Rodrique de Villandrando* (Paris, 1879), 319–320.
39 La Trémoille (ed.), *Les La Trémoille*, I, 183.

at Paris, . . . that I will serve and obey my lord the king always and forever, towards and against everyone, living and dead without any exceptions including my lord Charles his brother or anyone else. I will serve him moreover against mysaid lord Charles as against all others in whatever manner or quarrel that there be and with no exceptions whatsoever . . . I renounce all oaths, promises, seals, or alliances that I have formerly given, made or issued to anyone.

Louis, in return, promised to protect Armagnac from Charles, his brother, and all other persons. That same day, in a separate document, Louis returned to Armagnac the extensvie estates that had been taken from his father and grandfather. Thus in France, as in England, homage was dropped from the indenture in spite of its similarity to the *fief rente*.[40]

Can it then be, as has so often been argued, that the failure to include homage in the indenture signaled the fact that a client owed his patron less loyalty than a vassal did his lord? Or should we attribute the absence of homage in the new contractual arrangement to a change in social mores? The latter appears more probable. The evidence that the kiss and to a lesser extent the kneeling that was required in the ceremony of homage were unpopular in France by the sixteenth century is overwhelming. Evidence concerning the preceeding centuries is less voluminous, but the abandonment of the kiss to seal many types of contracts, the disappearance of the kiss of peace from the Catholic liturgy, the growing opposition to homosexuality, and the trial of the Templars all point to the fact that aspects of the homage ritual were unpopular when "bastard feudalism" was born in France. For a great noble to have insisted on the ritual of homage would have limited his recruitment efforts under the indenture system. He undoubtedly wanted to receive the same loyalty that he was entitled to under the lord-vassal relationship. The question is whether his wishes coincided with the social mores of the time.

---

40 AHG, VIII, 296–297. Pocquet du Haut-Jussé, "A Political Concept of Louis XI: Subjection instead of Vassalage," in P. S. Lewis (ed.), *The Recovery of France in the Fifteenth Century* (New York, 1972), 196–215; Godefroy and Nicolas Lenglet du Fresnoy (eds.), *Memoires de Messire Philippe de Comines* (London, 1747), II, 549. Charles d'Albret and Jacques de Nemours signed similar pledges. Charles Samaran, *La maison d'Armagnac au XVe siècle* (Paris, 1907), 398–400.

CHANGING SOCIAL MORES

THE LOYALTY OF A CLIENT   It would be desirable to make a quantitative study to determine whether a vassal was more likely to be loyal than a client, but the documentation that survives does not permit us to do so. One could cite many examples of loyalty and disloyalty on the part of vassal and client alike, but we have no idea of the total number of people involved or whether the few documents that survive are typical. One would assume that acts of disloyalty would be more apt to be recorded by contemporaries than instances when vassal or client behaved in the accepted manner.

Fortunately, from the latter half of the fourteenth century, treatises were written that provide insights into the contemporary mind. They dealt with such problems as "Whether the subjects of a baron are bound to aid their lord against the king," or, "If a baron is vassal to two lords who are at war with each other which should he help?" The authors who treated literally hundreds of such questions, drew no distinction between vassals and indentured knights. Bonet, probably the most widely read of these authors, insisted in *The Tree of Battles* that a knight "should be willing to die to keep the oath of his faith to his lord. I say the same of the knight in receipt of wages from the king or other lord, for since he has pledged to him his faith and oath he must die in defence of him and his honour." Knights "should keep the oath which they have made to their lord to whom they belong, and to whom they have sworn and promised to do all that he shall command for the defence of his land, according to what is laid down by the laws." "If a knight quits his lord in time of peace, whilst in receipt of wages, he should be condemned to go henceforth not mounted, but on foot like a sergeant." In time of war he should be executed.[41]

Bonet borrowed heavily from John of Lignano, but he himself was exploited by Christine de Pisan when she wrote on a similar subject. At least she gave more credit to her source than most because she tells us that Bonet appeared before her in a dream and told her to gather the fruit from his *Tree of Battles*. Having received the author's permission in this rather unusual manner, she proceeded to incorporate substantial portions of it into her *Book of Fayttes of Armes and of Chyvalrye*. Indeed, it was

---

41 Bonet, *Tree of Battles*, 136, 167, 122, 131, 132.

so self-evident to most writers that the hired soldiers owed the same loyalty to their captain as a vassal owed to his lord that they did not bother to discuss the question. Both were subject to the same "law of arms."[42]

The late medieval phase of the patron-client relationship has been given the pejorative name of "bastard feudalism" on the assumption that it was inferior to the traditional feudalism. In actual fact it was the traditional feudalism that was in a state of decay, and the patron-client relationship was invented in part to serve as a new way to tie the greater and lesser nobility together. Indeed, the dukes of Brittany appear to have used indentures to strengthen their fading ties with their vassals. Homage was not enough to insure loyalty; a written contract was needed. The belief that clientage ties were stronger than vassalage ties was expressed when Mézières wrote, around 1389, that a king need not worry about his officials doing homage to great nobles for the fiefs that they held from them, but he warned against permitting them to make public or secret alliances with the magnates. Meziérès, who was no stranger at the French court, then explained how such alliances lead to the corruption of justice and bad government.[43]

The weakness of feudal ties is also revealed by the efforts of kings and great nobles to tie their vassals more closely to their sides by creating orders of chivalry. In 1351, King John introduced chivalric orders into France by establishing the Order of the Star, and his unknightly descendant, Louis XI, brought the raft of medieval creations to an end when he founded the Order of St. Michael in 1469. In the intervening period, a number of great nobles created their own orders, the most famous being Philip the Good of Burgundy's Golden Fleece (1431) and René of An-

---

42 Da Legnano, *Tractatus De Bello*; de Pisan, *Book of Fayettes of Armes*, 189–191; Maurice H. Keen, *The Law of Wars in the Late Middle Ages* (London, 1965), 19–21. Keen informed me, in a letter dated May 28, 1983, that the two texts he has found "most useful on the subject of loyalty in the late middle ages in this kind of context" were Diego de Valera, *Ung petit traictyé de noblesse,* published by Arie Johan Vanderjagt in *Qui Sa Vertu Anoblist* (Groningen, 1981); and an unpublished manuscript entitled *Enseiegnement de la vraie Noblesse.* "*They clearly regard the feudal bond and the bond of the soldier as eminently comparable*" (italics mine). I would like to thank Keen for his assistance.
43 P. S. Lewis, "Of Breton *Alliances,*" 122–143. Philippe de Mézières (ed. Coopland), *Le Song du Vieil Pelerin* (London, 1969), II, 61, 350–355. Mézières' treatment of clientage is discussed in P. S. Lewis,"Of Breton *Alliances,*" 122–124.

jou's Croissant (1448). These orders undoubtedly were designed to serve a number of purposes, among them: to defend the true religion, to protect noble ladies, and to sponsor tournaments. But, in the minds of most of their creators, one of the greatest purposes was to bind their vassals more closely to them and to seek outside supporters. They put great stress on loyalty to the commander of the order and to one's sovereign lord, who was often one and the same person. Disloyalty and flight from the battlefield after the banners had been unfurled led to disgrace and expulsion from the order. The Burgundian dukes and René of Anjou found their order useful in drawing together the high nobility of their far-flung domains. Occasionally, a non-vassal would be inducted in the hope of attracting support from the outside, just as the fief rente and clientage was used, but this was a secondary purpose of the orders. Only three of the thirty-two knights who were members of René's Croissant in 1453 were not his vassals. So like clientage were these orders that the collar or other insignia of the members was often identical to the livery that clients wore.[44]

Thus, when the ties between lord and vassal weakened, the nobility invented clientage to assume its role in tying together the greater and lesser members of the aristocracy. Homage was not dropped because less loyalty was desired. Indeed, the purpose of clientage was to insure greater loyalty. Homage was dropped because the ritual had become unpopular as a result of the changing social mores in late medieval and early modern France. The problem now left to be resolved is the extent to which clientage was successful in restoring traditional loyalties and the length of time it was able to perform this function.

44 Malcolm Vale, *War and Chivalry* (Athens, Ga., 1981), 33–62; Keen, *Chivalry* (New Haven, 1984), 179–199; P. S. Lewis, "Une devise de chevalerie inconnue, créée par un comte de Foix," *Annales du Midi,* LXXVI (1964), 77–84; C. A. J. Armstrong, "Had the Burgundian Government a Policy for the Nobility?" *Britain and the Netherlands,* II (1964), 22–24.

XIV

The Revolt of 1620:
A Study of Ties of Fidelity

Shortly before midnight, on 22 February 1619, a man emerged from a window of the château of Blois and slowly began to descend a ladder. A bulky, middle-aged woman with a heavy box in her arms followed closely behind him. Four other men and another woman emerged next, and soon the party of seven was standing on the terrace more than sixty feet below the window. To reach the street they had planned a second descent by ladder, but the corpulent woman declared that she was too exhausted to go further. Her resourceful companions, however, managed to half lower her, half slide her down the embankment, and soon they were all standing in the street. Some passing soldiers took the woman for a whore, which caused her great amusement. The party then crossed the bridge over the Loire River but were momentarily consternated not to find a carriage at the appointed place on the other side. When they discovered it in a lane, they hurriedly shoved in the stout lady and took off down the road towards Loches, where Jean-Louis de la Valette, duke of Epernon, awaited them with an escort of 150 men. But before they had proceeded more than a few hundred yards, the stout lady had the carriage stopped. Her box was missing. Only after it had been recovered from a spot on the ground where the carriage had been waiting did she permit the party to proceed. In this fashion Marie de Medici, widow of Henry IV, mother of Louis XIII, escaped from Blois with a fortune in jewelry.

Marie had served as regent and as chief of council for her son

---

Research for this article was begun when I was a member of the Institute for Advanced Study at Princeton and on sabbatical leave from Emory University. Later I was assisted by a grant from the Emory Research Fund. I would like to express my appreciation to the Institute and to Emory for the research opportunities that they provided.

XIV

between 1610 and 1617, but in the latter year Louis had arranged through Charles d'Albert, his falconer, to have her favorite, Concini, assassinated. Louis, then only fifteen, had turned the direction of the goverment over to Albert and had heaped favors upon him and his friends. Albert became the duke of Luynes and acquired considerable wealth. Fearful of Marie's influence over her son, Luynes had confined her to the château of Blois and had removed Richelieu, the future cardinal, and other servants from her side. Sympathy for Marie, dislike of the upstart Luynes, and the desire to fish in troubled waters had led to the plot to free Marie and ultimately to the potentially serious uprising of 1620.

Neither the oft-told tale of Marie's escape nor the rebellion that was to follow has much importance in itself. What captures our attention is the series of events following the escape, which provide a unique opportunity to study the vertical ties of fidelity that were formed to bind Marie and her noble supporters together.

Richelieu was living in exile in Avignon when Epernon and Marie de Medici planned her escape from Blois, but on 7 March he received orders from the king to rejoin Marie at Angoulême, where it was hoped that he would exercise a moderating influence. It was in part through his efforts that Marie and Louis reached an agreement that spring. By its terms Marie was to remain free and have the right to appoint the members of her household and other officials. She gave up her nominal governorship of Normandy in return for full powers to rule Anjou with its important strongholds of Chinon, Angers, and Ponts-de-Cé. In addition, she was compensated for her expenses, and Epernon and her other accomplices escaped punishment. This reconciliation proved temporary. Louis continued to heap honors on Luynes and his friends, which infuriated those great nobles who received little or nothing of the royal largess. Marie herself felt neglected and longed for a more powerful voice in her son's affairs. Soon a new coalition was being formed to remove Luynes and to share more fully in the patronage of the crown.[1]

Epernon and his sons were, of course, part of the new coalition. They had become Marie's allies before her escape from Blois. At that time negotiations between Epernon and Marie had been carried on by agents who had had to travel in disguise.[2] No written alliance

---

[1] Gabriel Hanotaux, *Histoire du Cardinal de Richelieu* (Paris, n.d.), 2:265, 280-96, 301-20.
[2] The best contemporary account of these negotiations is by Epernon's secretary, Guillaume Girard. See his *Histoire de la vie du duc d'Espernon* (Paris, 1655), 302-13. See also Leo Mouton, *Epernon of Old France*, trans. E. Trotter (New York, 1935), 125-36.

XIV

THE REVOLT OF 1620

appears to have been made, perhaps because it would have been too dangerous to entrust the documents to agents who might be captured. When first approached, Epernon would do no more than inquire about what other support Marie had obtained and how much money she had. Satisfied on these scores, he, "believing that on the word of the queen, he was able to give his," committed himself to her cause.[3] To protect Epernon from Louis' wrath, Marie provided him with a letter the young king had sent her, saying that she could go where she pleased, and with another letter from herself requesting Epernon's assistance. This correspondence enabled Epernon to claim that he was only helping the queen mother to make a move her son had authorized. When Louis dispatched an ambassador to his mother after her escape, he instructed him to promise her "all the satisfaction that she wanted" in return for deserting Epernon; but she loyally refused.[4] Thus when Marie decided to form a powerful coalition to remove Luynes from her son's side in 1620, she had recently demonstrated that she could be a loyal mistress despite veiled threats and offers of substantial bribes.

Marie and her advisors quickly prepared a plan for military action, sought additional allies, and determined on an oath that would bind each adherent to her cause in return for her protection. The plan was both simple and revealing. Each of the magnates who rallied to her banner was to raise a prescribed number of soldiers and garrison them in towns. When sufficient forces had been mustered, Marie was to send remonstrances to the king and to the parlements. Only if her remonstrances were twice rejected were the troops to take to the field. Evidently Marie and her supporters hoped to overawe Louis and his advisors by a show of force. An actual battle was to be avoided if possible. Soon Marie had numerous supporters. They included Louis' illegitimate half brothers, Caesar, duke of Vendôme, and Alexander, the grand prior of France, and his cousins Louis, count of Soissons, and Henry, duke of Longueville. The dukes of Mayenne, Nemours, Retz, La Trémoille, Rohan, Roanès, Epernon, and other nobles of scarcely less rank joined the coalition. Most of western France from Normandy to the Pyrenees fell into their hands, and they hoped that Montmorency, the powerful governor of Languedoc, would also lend his support.[5]

---

[3] Girard, *Histoire du duc d'Espernon*, 307.
[4] Ibid., 338.
[5] Eusèbe Pavie, *La Guerre entre Louis XIII et Marie de Médicis 1619-1620* (Angers, 1899), 671-75. *Mémoires du Cardinal de Richelieu*, ed. Horric de Beaucaire (Paris, 1912), 3:37-48.

Epernon's adherence was of special value. As colonel-general of the infantry he had filled the royal army with his clients, and the officers of twelve of the king's companies in Champagne abandoned their posts because they preferred to serve him rather than the king. As commander of Metz, Epernon had a gateway through which he could bring in mercenaries from the Empire. As a mighty lord he had taken the precaution of procuring arms for ten thousand foot and six hundred horse following the assassination of Henry IV.[6] To swell her ranks further, Marie sent commissions to prospective commanders to raise troops on her behalf. Rohan dreamed of winning Protestant support and marching on Paris with sixty thousand men.[7]

Large sums were necessary, and Marie's treasurer, D'Argouges, was kept busy in Paris collecting debts owed to her and to her clients and borrowing what he could. Financial assistance was sought from abroad and jewels were pawned, but probably the largest source of revenue was the taxes seized from royal officials in the provinces the rebels controlled. By the end of June Marie had 2,273,000 livres in her treasury, an ample amount to insure that she could advance half the sum needed to pay the troops the magnates raised. They were apparently supposed to provide the other half.[8] It is, however, the oaths that Marie and her clients took that concern us most.

The initial plan appears to have been for Marie and the leading nobles to pledge their mutual loyalty in a single document that was dated 11 April 1620. It contains her signature and that of the dukes of Mayenne and Retz, with ample space reserved near the middle of the document and at the end for more names and signatures. To justify the rebellion, Marie claimed to be acting on the request of a majority of the magnates who shared her desire to protect the king from the perils that threatened him and to conserve his estate, which was in disorder. She promised not to enter into separate negotiations with the crown and to protect the magnates to the best of her ability. The magnates in return promised "to do all that she [Marie] will judge necessary to maintain royal authority and public tranquil-

---

[6] Girard, *Histoire du duc d'Espernon*, 334-35. Pavie, *La Guerre*, 579.

[7] For an example of a commission, see "Lettres adressées de 1585 à 1625 à Marc-Antoine Marreau de Boisguérin, gouverneur de Loudun," ed. Georges de La Marque and Edouard de Barthélemy, *Archives historiques du Poitou* 14 (1883): 361-63. Pavie, *La Guerre*, 134.

[8] Ibid. 144-49, 671-72. For d'Argouges' correspondence, see Archives du Ministère des Affaires Etrangères: Mémoires de documents: France, MS. 773 (hereafter cited as MS. 773), esp. fols. 41-42, 46, 47, 51, 62.

ity. And we swear on pain of the loss of our honor never to separate from her majesty, . . . and to employ our goods and our lives to guarantee her from harm."⁹

As the possibility of armed conflict increased, it was decided to prepare individual agreements that took the following form: "I Gaspard, Count of Colligny, Sr. de Chastillon, promise the Queen Mother on the loss of my honor to serve and defend her at the risk of my life. . . . Her majesty having also promised me on the faith and word of a queen to guarantee me from the harm that some will want to do me in consideration of the above."¹⁰ Louis Gouffier, duke of Roanès, and Henry, duke of Rohan, made almost identical pledges.¹¹ When Urban de Laval, seigneur of Bois-Dauphin and marshal of France, threw in his lot with the queen mother, at least one of his clients, Pierre de Champagné, sieur de la Motte-Ferchaud, signed a similar though slightly abbreviated pledge.¹² Thus the clients of Marie's clients took the oath and became her clients.

The first thing that strikes us about these four documents is that they were signed only by nobles. They were the individual noble's pledge to be loyal to the queen mother and they were to be kept by her or for her by one of her clients. Among these clients was Richelieu, in whose papers they are preserved today. It should be noted that each of the documents contained the phrase "Her majesty having promised. . . ." Marie, then, had also made a pledge. It may therefore be presumed that a separate, similar document bearing her signature was given to each noble for his protection, although none has been found. If the revolt failed, the worst fate that could befall the queen mother was the renewal of the genteel confinement at the château of Blois, whereas the nobles who assisted her risked loss of life and property. They would hardly have given a written pledge without receiving one in return.

The documents invite comparison with the indentures that were employed in the so-called "bastard feudalism"of the late Middle Ages.¹³ By that time the system of vassalage had proved in-

---

⁹ See Appendix A.
¹⁰ MS. 773, fol. 66.
¹¹ Ibid., fols. 44, 49. Hanotaux has published Rohan's pledge with minor changes. See his *Histoire du Cardinal de Richelieu*, 2:333, n. 1.
¹² See Appendix B. For Pierre de Champagné, see A. Angot, *Dictionnaire historique, topographique et biographique de la Mayenne* (Mayenne, 1962), 1:507-8.
¹³ There are many studies of "bastard feudalism" in England, the most detailed of which is William H. Dunham, Jr., *Lord Hastings' Indentured Retainers, 1461-1483* (New Haven, 1955).

adequate in many respects, and the indenture was adopted to provide the lord with the personnel he needed to meet his military, political, and social needs. An indenture was a written contract between patron and client in which the client swore to be faithful to his patron and to serve him against everyone except usually the king (and possibly some other persons), and the patron promised to protect and support the client. Initially some form of payment was prescribed, but gradually such stipulations were removed. Only two of the sixty-nine surviving indentures that William Lord Hastings granted between 1461 and 1483 specified a salary.[14] Indentures that were used to raise troops for military campaigns were often for a limited duration, but those associated with "bastard feudalism" were for life. They were generally written on parchment, the copy retained by the patron being sealed and signed by the client and the copy retained by the client being sealed and signed by the patron. The clients' copies have all disappeared; the patrons' copies have occasionally survived, because the patrons made better provisions to preserve their archives.[15] Thus in 1429, Gilles de Rais signed and sealed an indenture on parchment in which he swore to serve his cousin, Georges de La Trémoille, with all his strength until death because of past favors and future expectations. The indenture that La Trémoille presumably signed, sealed, and gave to Gilles de Rais has been lost, but within three months of the time when the agreement was reached he won for his twenty-three-year-old client the post of marshal of France.[16] Or again, in 1451, Gailhard de Durefort promised "to serve, succor, and aid" Charles d'Albret and his children for life against everyone except the king and the dauphin.[17]

The documents of 1620 differ from these indentures in that (1) they did not specifically reserve primary loyalty to the king, (2) they did not stipulate that the contract was for life, and (3) they were

---

Included in Appendix A are many indentures. French historians have largely ignored "bastard feudalism" and have been content to call the few indentures they have found "alliances." However, see the valuable articles by P. S. Lewis, "Decayed and Non-Feudalism in Later Medieval France," *Bulletin of the Institute of Historical Research* 37 (1964): 157-84; and "On Breton *Alliances* and Other Matters," in *War, Literature, and Politics in the Late Middle Ages,* ed. C. T. Allmand (Liverpool, 1976), 122-43. Lewis publishes supporting documents in both articles.

[14] Dunham, *Lord Hastings' Indentured Retainers,* 51.

[15] Indeed the largest collection of "indentures" other than Lord Hastings' are those that came to be preserved by the kings of England and France; that is, those of John of Gaunt, of the dukes of Orléans and Brittany, and of the counts of Foix.

[16] Louis, duke of La Trémoille, ed., *Les La Trémoille pendant cinq siècles* (Nantes, 1890), 1:183. It is noteworthy that Gilles de Rais did not reserve a higher loyalty for the king.

[17] *Archives historiques du département de la Gironde* (1866), 8:296-97.

written on paper and were signed but not sealed. The last distinction, however, may only reflect the growth of literacy, the high cost of parchment, and the increased use of paper. Indeed, a series of sixteenth-century royal ordonnances made the signature in lieu of the seal obligatory for private acts.[18] The idea that the signers owed their primary loyalty to the king, when in actuality they were revolting against him, was preserved in various declarations that they made stating that their goal was to preserve the king and his estate from ruin. "My status as duke and peer of France," Rohan explained, "obligated me for conscience's sake to reform the state."[19] Since no limit was set on the length of time the contracts were valid, they presumably remained in effect during the lives of the signatories or until they were abrogated. It should be noted that a vassal could renounce his allegiance and that the late medieval indenture could also be altered by mutual agreement.[20]

Whether the documents of 1620 were the product of a natural evolution from the fifteenth-century indentures or whether they were new creations to meet the needs of the moment can only be determined after a careful study has been made of noble alignments during the intervening period. The fact that to date no indentures have been found for this period is very suggestive, but it is not conclusive, because so many documents of this sort have been lost, and no thorough, informed search has been undertaken. The failure of nobles to mention indentures in their memoirs is not surprising. Rohan, the only memoir writer whose pledge of loyalty to Marie has survived, explained why he at first refused to aid her and later changed his mind, but he said nothing about signing a document.[21] Indeed, the noble memoir writers must also have rendered homage for their fiefs, but where do they tell us that they did so? Commonplace actions were not recorded, and the only documents most nobles tried to preserve were those concerning their social status and property rights.

Marie dispatched agents to many parts of France to persuade

---

[18] Paul Ourliac and J. de Malafosse, *Histoire du droit privé* (Paris, 1961), 1:106.
[19] Pavie, *La Guerre*, 140. See also Appendix A.
[20] F. L. Ganshof, *Feudalism*, trans. Philip Grerson, 3rd ed. (New York, 1961), 98-99. Marc Bloch, "Les Formes de la rupture de l'hommage dans l'ancien droit féodal," *Nouvelle Revue historique de droit français et étranger*, (1912), 141-77. Dunham, *Lord Hastings' Indentured Retainers*, 51.
[21] *Mémoires du duc de Rohan*, in *Nouvelle Collection des mémoires pour servir à l'histoire de France*, ed. Joseph F. Michand and Jean-J.-F. Poujoulat (Paris, 1837), 2nd ser., 5:515-16.

other nobles to subscribe to the oath of loyalty. Nor was the robe neglected. One of her clients won from Leroux de Bourgthroude, a president in the Parlement of Rouen, from his son, and his son-in-law, their "faith and word for the service of the queen."[22] Whether there was a formal oath on the Gospels or a written pledge is not known.

Another type of document may have been a factor in the revolt. On 10 January 1617, Caesar, duke of Vendôme, and Henry of Lorraine, duke of Mayenne, made a secret alliance with the avowed objective of freeing their youthful sovereign from foreigners who had taken possession of the government. They also sought to restore the recently imprisoned Henry II, prince of Condé, to his rightful place in the councils of the king. The two dukes bound themselves and their children to the alliance, and no time limit was placed on its duration. It was different from the previously discussed 1620 contracts in that it was a treaty between two equals. Neither duke was to serve, protect, or maintain the other, but they were to act in accord. It is not surprising, therefore, that when Mayenne fled from the court during the night of 27-28 April 1620 to offer his support to Marie de Medici, his ally, Vendôme, quickly followed.[23] During the three-year interval between the making of the alliance and Mayenne's unceremonious departure from court, Marie, his former enemy, had become a friend, and Condé, his former friend, had become an enemy, but the alliance between the two dukes had remained intact. The tie between them was probably paralleled by similar alliances between other nobles of equal status, for comparable agreements had been made between nobles for centuries. This agreement was unique in its contents only in the length of the explanation the two dukes provided to justify their union.[24]

The rebels of 1620 bound themselves together vertically by written pledges between the queen mother and individual nobles, and horizontally by formal alliances between individual nobles of equal status. The former contracts, as we have seen, bear a close resemblance to the indentures of the fifteenth century, and they are also closely related to the *maître-fidèle* relationship that has become so central to Roland Mousnier's interpretation of early modern

---

[22] Pavie, *La Guerre*, 163, n. 2.
[23] BN, MSS fr., 3802, fol. 37. I am indebted to Amanda Eurich for copying this document for me. Pavie, *La Guerre*, 106-12.
[24] See for example Lewis, "Decayed and Non-Feudalism," 179-80.

France as being a society of orders rather than a society of classes.[25] "The *fidèle*," Mousnier tells us:

> gives himself completely to the master. He espouses all the latter's ideas, inclinations, ambitions, and interests. He devotes himself to him utterly. He serves him in every way possible: he accompanies him, entertains him, speaks, writes, intrigues, and argues for him, fights, plots, and rebels for him, follows him into exile, helps him against everyone else, even against the king, against the state; if necessary, he gives his life for his master. In exchange for all of this, the master owes the *fidèle* first and foremost his friendship, his absolute trust, his confidence. He owes him food, clothing, maintenance, and protection in all the circumstances of life, even against justice, even against the head of state. He must see to the advancement of his *fidèle*, arrange a marriage for him, obtain offices and functions for him. If the master has rebelled and is making terms with the king, he must include stipulations on behalf of his *fidèles* in any treaty he signs.[26]

William Dunham could have used these same words to describe the *intended* relationship between Lord Hastings and his retainers in fifteenth-century England. The conspicuous difference between the late medieval and the seventeenth-century relationships, as seen by Mousnier, is that in the latter there was no signed and sealed indenture in which the client nearly always reserved a higher loyalty for the king.

But is this difference really so great? Richelieu was closely associated with organizing the revolt of 1620, and four of the indentures—or contracts, if one does not wish to apply this term to the agreements—found their way into his papers. A few years later, when Richelieu began to develop his own network of clients, his intimate advisor, Father Joseph, reported that the cardinal sought those "who would be faithful to him and only to him without exception and without reservation. He does not want those who serve two masters, knowing full well he would not find fidelity in them. It is so rare to find men of this character that if it were necessary to buy

---

[25] Roland Mousnier, *The Institutions of France under the Absolute Monarchy, 1598-1789*, trans. Brian Pearce (Chicago and London, 1979), 1, esp. 99-111. Mousnier provides a somewhat more detailed explanation of the vertical ties in *Etat et société sous François Ier et pendant le gouvernement personnel de Louis XIV* (Paris, Cours de Sorbonne, n.d.), 309-39. So important have these vertical ties become in Mousnier's interpretation that it was most fitting that they should have become the subject of a festschrift in his honor. See Yves Durand, ed., *Hommage à Roland Mousnier: Clientèles et fidélités en Europe à l'époque moderne* (Paris, 1981).

[26] Mousnier, *The Institutions of France under the Absolute Monarchy, 1598-1789*, 1:104-5. Mousnier uses *maître-fidèle* to describe the relationship between nobles of the sword and *protecteur-créature* to describe the relationship between participants of the robe. I am not sure that the robe and sword can be so neatly separated and have preferred to employ the terms patron and client to describe both relationships.

them, the Cardinal would pay their weight in gold."[27] Such high standards of fidelity may not have been habitually cemented by formal oaths, although oaths were taken on assuming many offices, but the moral requirement of loyalty was certainly present. Thus in 1658 Captain Deslandes offered his services to the powerful minister Nicolas Fouquet in a letter containing these words:

> I promise and give my fealty to My Lord the Procurator-General . . . never to belong to any but him, to whom I give myself and attach myself with the greatest attachment of which I am capable; and I promise to serve him generally against all persons without exception and to obey none but him, nor even to have any dealings with those whom he forbids me to deal with. . . . I promise him to sacrifice my life against all whom he pleases . . . without any exception whatsoever.[28]

With such written promises was there any need to require a formal oath on the Gospels or an indenture? No wonder Louis XIV took such precautions when he had d'Artagnan arrest his over-rich subject who had so many loyal clients.[29]

It is probable that a majority of the nobility never became the clients of any great lord. In the rare instances when a minor rural noble felt it desirable to have the support of someone in court, he could turn to a local magnate who might render him a favor in the expectation of some future service. Or he might apply to the leaders of the rival factions that surrounded the king. Thus on the eve of the Wars of Religion we find Picard nobles turning to both the duke of Montmorency and the duke of Guise.[30] When a noble did bind himself to a magnate, the ritual varied. Signed documents pledging mutual loyalty and protection could be exchanged if considerable danger was involved, which was the case in 1620. Here the distinction between the contract and the late medieval indenture was slight indeed. Or the client could take a formal oath or make a declaration of loyalty. Whatever the method used, the loyalty and service expected of the client and the maintenance and support required of the patron differed little from the late medieval code of "bastard feudalism." Fief owners, of course, had lords to whom they rendered homage. This vertical tie was still meaningful in 1620, but it

---

[27] J. R. Major, "The Crown and the Aristocracy in Renaissance France," *The American Historical Review* 69 (1964): 639.

[28] Marc Bloch, *Feudal Society*, trans. L. A. Manyon (Chicago, 1968), 450.

[29] Charles Samaran, *D'Artagnan capitaine des mousquetaires du roi* (Auch, 1967), 173-77.

[30] Kristen Brooke Neuschel, "The Prince of Condé and the Nobility of Picardy: A Study of the Structure of Noble Relationships in Sixteenth-Century France" (Ann Arbor: University Microfilms, 1982), 63-65, 79-82.

was becoming more a social and financial relationship than one requiring military service. Only one of the nine vassals of the duke of Epernon that have been fully identified served him in any capacity, but Epernon may have been instrumental in obtaining the positions that four of his vassals held in the royal bureaucracy.[31]

But how strong were the alliances between Marie de Medici and her clients? Her strategy had been to raise a large army and then negotiate with the crown from a position of strength. Experience had taught her that substantial concessions could be won this way and that the government would reimburse the rebels for the expenses that they had incurred. Had this not happened after her escape from Blois, when those who supported her cause were less numerous by far than they were in 1620? But the rebels reckoned without the king, who was now a year older, more experienced, and more determined than ever to assert his authority. In this Louis was abetted by Henry II, prince of Condé, who had recently been released from prison and was eager to revenge himself on the queen mother and on others who had been responsible for his confinement. Under these circumstances the timid Luynes had no choice but to acquiesce, and at dawn on 7 July, Louis departed from Paris with his guard of four hundred men and an improvised army of not more than six thousand. His first objective was to reassert his authority in Normandy, before the duke of Longueville, the governor, could consolidate his position. When the burghers of Rouen learned that the king was with the army, they threw open their gates, and on 10 July Louis entered the Norman capital with a scant five hundred men, the bulk of his small army still being far behind.[32]

The inhabitants of Caen were equally ready to welcome their sovereign, but the commander of the château, Prudent, was of sterner stuff, and his conduct tells us much about how a faithful client was supposed to behave. When Louis' valet-de-chambre, Cailleteau, summoned Prudent to surrender, he responded: "I cannot yield the château without the command of the grand prior who

---

[31] Nicholas Fessenden, "Epernon and Guyenne: Provincial Politics under Louis XIII" (Ann Arbor: University Microfilms 1973), 222. In the 1560s, on the other hand, Louis, prince of Condé, received considerable support from his Picard lands. Neuschel, *The Prince of Condé*, 126-36.

[32] There is a detailed account of the Normandy campaign in Pavie, *La Guerre*, 252-93. The principal published sources can be found in *Mercure françois, 1620* (Paris, 1621), 6:281-337; F. Danjou and M. L. Cimber, eds., *Archives curieuses de l'histoire de France*, (Paris, 1838), 2nd ser., 2:203-40; and Gabriel Vanel, ed., *Journal de Simon Le Marchand bourgeois de Caen 1610-1693* (Caen, 1903), 86-99.

entrusted its care to me." "But," Cailleteau replied, "are you not above all the servant of the king? Does not the château belong to him before anyone else? If you surrender to him with good will, we will offer you amnesty, and I will remain here as a hostage to guarantee this promise. But if you surrender it only to sheer force, know that you will be tried for the crime of lese majesty." Before this threat Prudent retorted: "I am indeed, in effect, the king's servant, who has placed me here through the intermediary of the grand prior, for whom I guard this place. If someone attacks me I am firmly resolved to hold out until the end and to die in the breach. I will surrender this place only when I see an order from the grand prior himself."[33] Rejected by the loyal Prudent, Cailleteau called out to the garrison, as he departed, that anyone who threw Prudent over the ramparts would be given ten thousand crowns.

Prudent's subordinates were less than enthusiastic about his stand, and as they watched the royal artillery being placed in position their doubts increased. Soon Prudent realized that his troops were becoming mutinous and that he could no longer count on them. Perhaps his own resolve was weakened when he became convinced that the king was conducting the siege in person. "I would rather die than oppose the first triumph of his arms,"[34] he declared, and he authorized negotiations. His emissary to the king asked that the ten thousand crowns be given to his garrison and that at the conclusion of the revolt the château be returned to the grand prior. Louis impatiently replied: "Go away, I do not treat with my subjects,"[35] but he did pardon the garrison and reimburse Prudent for the money he had spent to buy munitions to defend the château.

Once freed, the loyal Prudent set out to find the grand prior in order to justify his conduct. We do not know what took place at this meeting, but if the twenty-two-year-old grand prior was at all just, Prudent escaped censure. The grand prior had failed to send the requested aid and instructions to his commander while the royal army was closing in on Caen, and he played a most cautious role in

---

[33] Pavie, *La Guerre*, 284.
[34] Ibid., 288.
[35] Ibid., 289. Pavie gives a figure of 100,000 crowns for the amount that Cailleteau offered Prudent's soldiers if they would throw him over the ramparts and that Prudent asked the king to give his garrison, but most sources give 10,000 crowns, a more logical amount. See Vanel, *Journal de Simon Le Marchand*, 96, and *Mercure françois, 1620*, 6:312. Arnauld d'Andilly cites the much smaller figure of 10,000 livres. Eugène Halphen, ed., *Journal inédit d'Arnauld d'Andilly 1620* (Paris, 1888), 30.

the revolt, to the chagrin of Marie de Medici and her cohorts.³⁶ Prudent was not an experienced soldier. His full name was Prudent Michaut, but he was always referred to as Prudent or Monsieur Prudent. He was born in Châtillon-sur-Seine around 1565 and had been one of Mayenne's most influential agents in Burgundy during the League. With the restoration of peace, he had returned to Châtillon, where he was elected mayor in 1599. At some point he was appointed to the household of the duke of Vendôme, a natural child of Henry IV and the older brother of the grand prior. He apparently had become the tutor of the grand prior and in 1617 had been named commander of the château of Caen.³⁷ By all accounts his conduct had been more gallant and loyal than that of the professional officers and men under his command. Nevertheless, Prudent became the butt of jokes. Because his father had been a mason, he was judged to be "more familiar with the noise of hammers than of cannon." And in a play upon his name it was said: "To guard fortified places in the future one must choose madmen because Prudent men are worth nothing."³⁸ In any event, the mutual failure of lord and client was followed by the rapid collapse of resistance in Normandy. Longueville, who had shut himself up in Dieppe with three thousand men, capitulated, and the other Norman commanders quickly followed suit. The governor of Le Havre even sent the king four cannon notwithstanding the alliance he had with the grand prior of France.³⁹

Louis now turned towards Angers. Rohan urged Marie to withdraw to the south, where he, Epernon, Mayenne, and others had raised thirty thousand men, but Richelieu advised her to remain in her capital. He wanted to be the central figure in a negotiated peace. If Marie joined the magnates, there could be a serious war. When peace came, others would play key roles in the negotiations and his own rewards would be less. Militarily the decision to remain was disastrous. When the two opposing forces met four miles from Angers at the Ponts-de-Cé, the royal army was the most numerous.

---

³⁶ For Richelieu's comments on the behavior of the grand prior and Prudent, see *Mémoires du Cardinal de Richelieu*, 3:50, 56-57, 66, n. 1. See also Pavie, *La Guerre*, 290, n. 1.

³⁷ Henri Drouot, *Mayenne et la Bourgogne* (Paris, 1937), 2:75-77. Vanel, *Journal de Simon Le Marchand*, 53-54, 90, n. 2.

³⁸ Ibid., 291. *Mercure françois, 1620*, 6:314-15. For accounts of Prudent's conduct, see ibid., 286-314; Halphen, *Journal inédit d'Arnauld d'Andilly*, 29-31; Vanel, *Journal de Simon Le Marchand*, 90-97.

³⁹ Danjou and Cimber, Archives curieuses de l'histoire de France, 2nd ser., 2:217.

At this critical juncture the duke of Retz, who had signed the document pledging to defend Marie, decided to withdraw his troops because he had heard that peace negotiations were in progress. Under such circumstances he had no desire to risk his life. With ensigns flying and drums playing, he marched his fifteen hundred men from the field leaving a gap in the rebel line. Outnumbered, uneasy at fighting an army that included their king, and deserted, the remaining troops were easily defeated. It was 7 August. In one month Louis had conquered Normandy, secured a bridgehead over the Loire River, and routed the opposing forces. Marie and her court could have fled to the south, but on Richelieu's advice she chose to negotiate.[40]

Negotiations between the mother and the son had never really ceased. Shortly before the beginning of the Normandy campaign, Louis had offered many concessions to Marie's immediate household but had refused to pardon Mayenne and her other supporters. True to her agreement, Marie had rejected her son's offer because "she would rather die than commit so dishonorable an act."[41] Louis had countered on 28 July by declaring that those who served his mother were guilty of lese majesty.[42] Negotiations still did not cease, and the king showed a willingness to grant further concessions. Only after the victory at Ponts-de-Cé, however, was the crown willing to go as far as Marie desired. Mayenne, Rohan, Epernon and others had massed an army of thirty thousand men in the southwest, Marie still had five thousand men in Angers, and the Huguenots were restive. For three years the Béarnais had refused to obey a royal decree reestablishing Catholicism throughout Béarn and returning the church lands and revenues that Louis' Protestant grandmother had confiscated. Hence Louis decided to make peace with his Catholic subjects in order to compel his Protestant ones to obey. He could not fight both at the same time.[43]

Marie and her followers were given full pardons, captives were freed without ransom, offices were restored, salaries and pensions were paid for the period of the revolt, royal taxes that had been appropriated were written off, and Marie herself received six hun-

[40] Hanotaux, *Histoire du Cardinal de Richelieu*, 2:347-52.
[41] *Mémoires du Cardinal de Richelieu*, 3:36. For the negotiations, see ibid., 27-36. Pavie, *La Guerre*, 389-92.
[42] *Mercure françois, 1620*, 6:320-25.
[43] *Mémoires de Fontenay-Mareuil*, in *Nouvelle Collection des mémoires pour servir à l'histoire de France*, ed. Joseph F. Michaud and Jean-J.-F. Poujoulat (Paris, 1837), 2nd ser., 5:149-53.

dred thousand livres to pay her debts. The only losers were the taxpayers, who paid the expenses of both sides of the little war and suffered the depredations of the troops.[44] Nevertheless, Mayenne was reported to be disappointed; he received none of his anticipated profits from the adventure.[45]

The revolt of 1620 was of little importance in itself, but it does provide an opportunity to study the vertical ties of that day. Marie de Medici had proved to be a loyal patron; even in defeat she had succeeded in protecting those who had given her their fealty. In Prudent we have the faithful servant who did everything in his power to defend the château at Caen, which his master, the grand prior, had entrusted to him. But there was a dark side, because the rebels of 1620 did not always uphold the principles of fidelity. Thereafter, Marie always regarded the duke of Retz as a traitor, because he had withdrawn his troops on the eve of the battle of Ponts-de-Cé, and she never forgave Richelieu, her favorite client, when he transferred his allegiance to the king a few years later. All patrons were not so loyal as she was. The grand prior made no effort to aid Prudent, and her own son Gaston, duke of Orléans, was later accused of obtaining a pardon for himself from his brother but neglecting to insist that his followers be included in the amnesty.[46]

In the late Middle Ages when "bastard feudalism" was born in France, great nobles anticipated receiving the same loyalty from their clients as they did from their vassals. They did not require homage because the kneeling and especially the kissing parts of the ceremony had become unpopular. An indenture seemed an adequate insurance of loyalty. Honoré Bonet and the other Emily Posts of that day wholeheartedly agreed.[47] Indeed, the dukes of Brittany appear to have imposed the indenture system on their vassals to doubly insure their loyalty.[48] Since the patron-client system of the early seventeenth century evolved from the earlier "bastard feudalism," it is not surprising that loyalty continued to be stressed

---

[44] *Mercure françois, 1620*, 6:338-39. Pavie, *La Guerre*, 578-80. A temporary exception to the policy of restoring rebels to their positions was that the officers in the royal army in Champagne who had deserted their posts to join Epernon were at first not reappointed. They had been replaced and regained their positions only as vacancies occurred. Ibid., 579.

[45] *Mémoires de Fontenay-Mareuil,*, 153.

[46] Mousnier, *The Institutions of France*, 1:102-3.

[47] I have completed an article on this subject entitled " 'Bastard Feudalism' and the Kiss: A Study of the Changing Social Mores in Late Medieval and Early Modern France." In press.

[48] Lewis, "Of Breton *Alliances* and Other Matters," 122-43.

in this system. Indeed, Mousnier has argued that the patron-client tie was more important than the lord-vassal tie because it depended on a free choice. The latter relationship, based as it was on the ownership of fiefs, was determined by the chance of inheritance and must often have tied together lords and vassals who were incompatible.[49] Lords apparently found fewer of their servants among their vassals than from other sources, but the property tie caused vassals to avoid formal breaks. When Enguerrand VII de Coucy decided to serve Charles V of France against the English during the Hundred Years' War, he had to surrender his English fiefs.[50] Few vassals were willing to make such a sacrifice.

On the other hand, one should not exaggerate the strength of the tie between patron and client. It was based as much—or more—on self-interest as on personal affection. When a client felt that he had been inadequately rewarded or that his interests lay elsewhere, the tie was often dissolved. Thus in 1581, when the future duke of Sully wanted to follow the duke of Anjou to Flanders in pursuit of an inheritance, he temporarily severed his ties with Henry of Navarre with the latter's permission.[51] More often clients acted unilaterally in spite of their pledges. In 1562, for example, a group of nobles took an oath not only to obey Louis, prince of Condé, but also to hold themselves in readiness as far as they were able "in money, arms, horses, and all other required things, . . . in order to accompany him where he commanded, and to render him faithful service."[52] Although the pledge was to be in effect until Charles IX reached his majority, some nobles who signed it abandoned Condé during the first War of Religion.[53] In 1615 the seigneur of Marsillac left the service of Henry II, prince of Condé, to assume that of Marie de Medici, an act that caused him to be badly beaten by a Condé client and led to a bitter quarrel between the two patrons.[54]

There was another weakness in the system. In the Middle Ages the vassal had often made the king an exception when he swore loyalty to his lord, and the same concept of a higher loyalty was

---

[49] Mousnier, *The Institutions of France*, vol. 1, esp. 109-10.
[50] Barbara W. Tuchman, *A Distant Mirror* (New York, 1978), 301-4.
[51] Sully, *Les Oeconomies royales,* ed. David Buisseret and Bernard Barbiche (Paris, 1970), 1:89-95.
[52] Jules Delaborde, *Gaspard de Coligny, amiral de France* (Paris, 1881), 2:73.
[53] Neuschel, *The Prince of Condé,* 33-53.
[54] Major, "The Crown and the Aristocracy in Renaissance France," 637. Sharon Kettering cites many examples of clients shifting their loyalties in her forthcoming book to be published by the Oxford University Press and in an unpublished manuscript entitled "Patronage and Politics during the Fronde." I am indebted to her for sending me a copy of this paper.

present in the indentures when that period drew to a close. No such exception was specified in the patron-client relationship of the seventeenth century, but to an extent it nevertheless existed. One could rebel on the pretense of saving a king from his evil advisors if he was a minor, or even after a youth had technically reached his majority at the beginning of his fourteenth year. But if a king was old enough to join his troops in battle, it was difficult to preserve the fiction, and the rebel forces melted away. The majesty of kingship was becoming such that it overcame the fidelity that one owed to one's patron. Even the loyal Prudent could not withstand it.

APPENDIX A
A Contract between Marie de Medici and the Magnates, 11 April 1620

Nous Marie par la grace de Dieu Reyne de France et de Navarre, Mere du Roy, Voyans a nostre grand regret les desordres de l'Estat, et les perils ou se trouvent la personne du Roy nostre tres honnoré sieur et fils, et la maison Royale, recogneus et deplorez de la pluspart des grands du Royaume qui nous en ont fait scavoir leurs sentiments: Desirans comme nous avons contribué et la conservation de son Estat, apporter sous son autorité encore ce qui nous sera possible pour empescher les maulx dont il est aujourdhuy menacé. Promettons en parole de Reyne a nostre Nepveu le Duc de Mayenne, et a

[*Blank space left in the document, obviously so additional name could be added*]

de nous porter de mesme esprit et intention qu'eux pour faire sçavoir et cognoistre au Roy les causes des malheurs qui semblent inevitables s'il ne luy plaist y pourveoir promptement selon ses bonnes inclinations. Leur Promettons en outre de ne rien traitter sans eux en quelque sorte et façon que ce soit, et contribuer pour leur protection tout ce qui deppendra de nous sans nous pouvoir separer. Et Nous

[*Blank space left in the document, obviously so names could be added*]

Promettons a ladite Dame Reyne de faire tout ce qu'elle jugera necessaire pour maintenir lautorite Royale et la tranquilité publique. Et Jurons sur peine de la perte de nostre honneur de ne nous separer jamais d'avec sa Majesté. Protestans d'employer nos biens et nos vies pour la garentir des violences de ceux qui autheurs et Fauteurs des disordres dans lesquels ils s'accroissent outre mesure, veulent perdre et opprimer tous les gens de bien Faict a Angers le unziesme Jour D'Apvril Milsix Cens Vingt.

MARIE
Henry de Lorraine
Henry de Gondi de Retz

Source: Archives des Affaires Etrangères: Mémoires et documents: France, MS. 773, fol. 38.
Note: I have retained the original grammar, spelling, punctuation, and capitalization, but the microfilm I used leaves me in some doubt about several letters.

APPENDIX B
Indenture; Pierre de Champaigné, 26 April 1620

Je Sieur de la Motte Ferchault Gouverneur de Chasteaugontier, Promests a la Reyne Mere du Roy. sur la perte de mon honneur de la servir et deffendre au peril de ma vie, Au cas qu'elle juge ainsy que tout le monde fait, que ceux qui portez de mauvaise volonté envers elle peuvent tout aupres du Roy, la vueillent opprimer sous quelque pretexte que ce puisse estre. Sa Majesté m'ayant aussy promis en parole de Reyne de me garentir du mal qu'on voudroit me procurer en consideration de ce que dessus. Faict A Angers le vingtsix^{me} Jour D'Apvril Mil six Cens vingt

Pierre de Champaigné

Source: MS. 773, fol. 43.

INDEX

Abbeville: VI 143
Ableiges, Jacques d': XIII 519
Agen: III 36; VI 135; IX 368, 372-4, 378-80; X 204
Agenais: XII 46
   estates of: III 36; VI 134, 143; IX 367; X 204-5
Aix, viguerie of: X 198
Aix-en-Provence: IV 466
Alais, estates of: X 200
Albi, estates of: X 199
Albret, family: XII 37-8
   Charles d': XIII 531; XIV 396
   Henri d': XII 24, 35, 40
   Jeanne d': XII 24, 27-31, 39-40
Alençon, bailliage of: VI 146, 149
   François, duke of: V 702, 709
Alexander the Great: II 28
Alsace, estates of: X 216-7
Amiens: I 118; V 707, 709, 711-2, 715; VI 134-7, 140-2, 145; VII 219, 222-3, 225, 229; IX 371; XII 44; XIII 520
Andorra, estates of: X 213
Angers: VI 133, 141; XIV 392, 403-4
Anglade, Jean d': XIII 523
Angoulême: XIV 392
   Marguerite d': XII 39
Angoumois: VI 149
Anjou: IV 466; VI 136, 141, 144; XIV 392
   René of: XIII 534-5
Anne of Brittany: I 114
Anquez, Léonce: X 219
Aragon: I 124
Arles: VI 145
Armagnac: XII 24, 26, 28-31
   estates of: VI 134, 147; IX 367; X 205-6; XII 40
   Jean, count of: XIII 531-2
   Bas, estates of: X 205
Artois, count of: XIII 512
   estates of: X 215
Assembly of Notables of 1596: V 713
   of 1617: VII 224
   of 1626: VII 224, 226; XII 46
Astaffort: XII 31
Astarac, estates of: X 206
Auch: VI 148
   estates of: X 205
Aumale, duke of: XIII 520
Auneau, XII 41
Aunis: VII 227
Austria: III 40
Autun: IV 466, 473
Auvergne: IV 466; XII 22
   estates of Basse: VI 141, 144; X 195-7
   estates of Haute: VII 219; X 195-7; XII 46
Auxerre: VI 138
Auxerrois, estates of: X 190
Auxois: VII 224
Auxonne, estates of: X 191
Auzan: XII 41
Avignon: I 116; V 704; XIV 392

Bailliage, assemblies of: III 40. See under name of bailliage
Bar, duchy of: XIII 525
Bar-sur-Seine, estates of: X 190-1
Barbazan: XII 35
Barcelona: I 124
Baritault, Pierre de: XIII 523
Baron, Hans: III 29
Barraclough, Geoffrey: II 128
Barthélemy, A. de: X 219
Baudel, M. J.: X 204
Bayeux: XII 43-5
Bayonne: IX 372
Bazadais, estates of: X 206
Béarn: XII 24-5, 27-36, 42; XIV 404
   estates of: X 210-11; XII 32
Beauce: XII 45

Beaufremont, Nicolas de, baron de Sennecy: IV 468, 475
Beaujolais, estates of: XII 46
Beaune: IV 466
Beaupaire, Charles de Robillard de: X 214
Beauvais: VI 136
Bégole: XII 35
Bellièvre, Pomponne de: IX 365-6
Beowulf: XIII 511
Berard, Claude: IV 466, 472-3
Bergier, Antoine: X 196
Berry: IV 466; VI 143-4; XII 45
Bidache: I 116
Bigorre: XII 23-4
  estates of: VI 147; X 212
Birague, Chancellor: V 708-10
Blanchefort, Pierre de: VI 133
Blet, Pierre: X 218
Bloch, Marc: XII 22; XIII 511-2
Blois: VI 133-4, 136, 140-2, 144; VII 227-9; XIV 391-2, 395
Bodin, Jean: I 122
Bonet, Honoré: XIII 533; XIV 405
Bordeaux: IX 372; X 201
  archbishop of: XIII 523
  estates of: VI 144; VII 224; IX 367-8; X 203
  parlement of: IV 466; IX 373, 375; XIII 524
Bosjan, seigneur and dame of: XIII 524
Boswell, John: XIII 514
Bouillon, duchy of: I 116
Boulonnais, estates of: VI 137, 145-6
Bourbon, Antoine de: XII 24
  Charles, cardinal: V 709-10; VII 221
  Charles, duke of, constable of France: XII 45
  Catherine de: XII 39, 40
Bourges: IV 466; VI 136
Bourgthroude, Leroux de: XIV 398
Boutruche, Robert: XII 22
Bresse, estates of: X 191-2
Bretaigne, Jacques: IV 466, 473-6
Briançon, estates of: X 194
Brittany: I 114; IV 465-7, 470; V 712; VI 135, 145, 148; VIII 256; XII 22; XIII 520, 522
  dukes of: XIII 516, 530; XIV 405
  estates of: III 38; V 704-5; VI 132, 144; VII 222, 225; X 213-4; XI 642
Brosse, Claude: X 193
Bruilhois: XII 30
  estates of: X 205
Bugey, estates of: X 191-2
Burckhardt, Jakob: I 112-3, 116; III 27
Burgundy: I 114; III 30-31; IX 383; XI 631-2, 639; XIII 522, 524; XIV 403
  dukes of: I 113, 123; IV 466, 470, 473; XII 24
  estates of: III 36, 41; V 704; VI 134, 138, 142-3, 145-8; VII 222, 224; X 188-92
Buridan, Jean-Baptiste de: XIII 21
Busquet, R.: X 197
Byon, Jean Baptiste: XIII 512

Cadier, Léon: X 211
Caen: XIV 401-3, 405
Cahors: X 203
  university of: III 37
Cailleteau: XIV 401-2
Calais: VIII 253
Cambrai, bishop of: XIII 512
Carcassone: VI 133; XII 27
Cardenal, L. de: X 203
Carné, Louis de: X 213
Carpentras: XIII 512
Carsten, Francis L.: III 28
Castile: I 124
Castres, estates of: X 200
Cateau-Cambrésis: IV 461
Catherine de Médici: IV 463, 467-8, 470-6; V 708; X 186
Châlons-sur-Marne: VI 139
Champagne: IV 466; VI 134, 138, 145-7; XII 145; XIV 394
Champagné, Pierre de: XIV 395, 408
Charles V: XIV 406
Charles VII: I 113; III 30, 34, 40; VIII 248-51, 253, 256-7; X 187; XI 639; XIII 517
Charles VIII: I 113; II 31; X 186
Charles IX: IV 461, 467, 476; V 703; VII 220; XI 633; XII 29
Charles V, emperor: I 113; II 31; III 40-1

INDEX

Charles of France: VIII 249-50; XIII 532
Charolais, estates of: X 191
Chartres: VI 136-7, 149
Châtillon-sur-Seine: VI 142-3; XIV 403
Chaumont-en-Bassigny: VII 227
Chinon: XIV 392
Chivalry, orders of: XIII 534-5
Choppin, René: XIII 521
Claude of France: III 41
Clerc, Edouard: X 217
Clermont of Alexandria: XIII 510-1
Clergy, assembly of: III 31-2; IV 476; V 703, 710, 714; X 217-8
Clermont (Auvergne): VI 141
Clermont-en-Beauvaisis: VI 139
Clermont-Ferrand: X 196
Coke, Sir Edward: XIII 526
Coligny, Admiral: IV 471
Colligny, Gaspard, count of: XIV 395
Comminges, estates of: VI 147; VII 224; IX 367, 373; X 207; XI 642-3
Commynes, Philippe de: I 119, 122
Compiègne: VII 228
Comté Venaissin, estates of: X 217
Condé, Henry I, prince of: VII 221
   Henry II, prince of: VIII 255; X 197; XIV 398, 401, 406
   Louis I, prince of: XI 637, 641
   Louis II, prince of: III 33
Condomois: XII 46
   estates of: IX 367, 378; X 206
Contamine, Philippe: XIII 529-30
Contrasty, Jean: X 206
Coquille, Guy: XII 227; XIII 522
Corsica, estates of: X 217
Cossé, Marshal: V 702
Coucy, Enguerrand VII de: XIV 406
Courteault, Paul: X 211
Customs, redaction: I 115; III 35-6, 40; XIII 518-23
Damville, Henri de Montmorency de: VI 702-4
Daranatz, J. B.: X 210
Darbin (Marie-José de Naurois-Destany): X 207
Dartigue-Peyrou, Charles: X 211
D'Argouges: XIV 394

Dauphiné: I 115; IV 466-7, 474; VIII 256; IX 356, 383; XII 35, 46
   estates of: V 704; VI 132, 134, 145; X 192-5
Denmark: I 122
De Sayne: IV 466-7
Descartes, René: I 112
Deslandes, Captain: XIV 400
Destrée, Alain: X 210
Déville-lès-Rouen: XII 41
Dieppe: XIV 403
Dijon: III 39; IV 135; VII 224; X 91; XII 45
   parlement of: VI 142; XIII 524
Drouot, Henri: X 190
Du Moulin, Charles: XIII 518, 520-1
Dunham, William: XIV 399
Durefort, Gailhard de: XIII 531; XIV 396
Durfort, Charles de: XIII 523
Dussert, A.: X 192-3
Duvernoy, Emile: X 216

Edward I of England: I 121, 123
Edward III of England: XIII 328
Elizabeth I of England: V 703
Embrun, estates of: X 194
Empire, Holy Roman: I 122; II 18, 31
England: I 122; II 18; III 40; IV 463
   "bastard feudalism" in: XIII 527-30
   homage in: XIII 525-6
   parliament of: I 122; II 24; III 36; VII 217, 225-9; VIII 247, 249; X 183-4; XIII 526
Epernon, Jean Louis de Nogaret de La Valette, duke of: XII 43; XIII 523; XIV 391-4, 401, 404
Erasmus: II 18-21, 27, 30
Estates
   1506: III 41; V 713; VII 223
   1558: V 713; VII 224; VIII 253
   1575: V 699-715
Estates General
   1420: III 40
   1439: III 40
   1468: IV 469; VII 223; VIII 249-50; XI 638
   1484: III 30-1; IV 468-9; V 713, VI 132, 137, 145; VII 218-9; XI 638

(Estates General, *cont.*)
  1560: III 31; IV 462-3, 465-6; V 702-3; VI 132, 145, 148; VII 219-20, 227; VIII 256-7; XII 638
  1561: III 31; IV 460-76; VI 132; VII 220
  1576: VI 132, 141-3; VII 220; XI 638
  1588: VI 132, 141-2; XI 638
  1593: VI 132; VII 223
  1614: VI 132, 142, 145; VII 220; VIII 256, 259; XI 632, 638; XIII 521
  1789: I 116; VI 132, 135
  deliberative procedure: VIII 256-7
  electoral procedure: VI 131-50; VIII 254-6
  payment of deputies: VII 217-29
  why failed: III 30-1; IV 476; V 712-15; VIII 247-8, 250-2, 258-9
Estates, provincial: III 34-9; X 183-217. See under name of province

Faillaiseau, Jehan: IV 466, 469
Father Joseph (François Joseph du Tremblay): XIV 399
Fay, Sidney B.: III 28
Ferrara, cardinal of: V 708
Ferrière, Claude de: XIII 520
Feudalism, bastard (new): XI 634-45; XIII 509-35; XIV 394-9
Fezensac: XII 31
Fézenzaguet: XII 24, 27, 29, 30
Florence: III 27, 39; V 703
Foix: VII 224; XII 24, 25; XIII 530-1
  estates of: VI 135, 143; X 213; XII 40
Foix-Navarre, house of: I 113; X 208
Foix-Navarre-Albret, house of: XII 23-35
Fontainebleau, council of: IV 462; VIII 257
Forez, estates of: VI 143; X 195-6; XII 46
Fouquet, Nicolas: XIII 523; XIV 400
Franche-Comté, estates of: X 217
Francis I: I 113; III 41; VIII 252, 259; IX 371; XII 41
Francis II: IV 461; V 703
Fresnes, Forget de: IX 376

Frederick William of Brandenburg: I 124

Galley, Jean-B.: X 195-6
Gap, estates of: X 194-5
Gattinara, Chancellor: II 31
Gaunt, John of: VIII 528
Gavardan: XII 24
Germany: III 27-29, 31
Gervaise, Joachim: VII 226-7
Gévaudan: X 200
Gex, estates of: I 116; VII 221; X 191-2
Gien: VI 138
Gimont: V 704
Girard, Joseph: X 217
Glanvill: XIII 517
Goodlich, Michael: XIII 514
Gouberville, sire de: XII 36-7
Grand Prior of France, Alexander: XIV 393, 403, 405
Gregory of Tours: XIII 511
Grenoble: X 194; XI 637-8
Griffiths, Gordon: X 219
Guinevere, Queen: XIII 512, 514
Guise, family: V 702, 708; XI 639, 641
  Charles, duke of: III 38; IX 365; XI 642
  Francis, duke of: IV 463; XIV 400
  Henry, duke of: VIII 254
  Louis, cardinal: IV 475
Guyenne: IV 466
  estates of: III 34-5; V 704; VI 134-5, 145, 148; VII 224; IX 363-83; X 201-203; XI 644; XII 35, 42

Hautot-sur-Dieppe: XII 41
Henry II: III 34; IV 461; VIII 259; IX 368, 371; X 201
Henry III: I 122, V 701-15; VII 221, 225; VIII 254; IX 371; X 186, 189; XI 631, 633; XII 43
Henry IV: I 113, 123; V 702, 708-9; VI 135, 137; VII 221; IX 363-83; X 186, 201, 203-4; XI 634, 641, 644; XII 31, 35, 39-40, 42, 46, 48; XIV 391, 394, 406
Henry I of England: XIII 527
Henry VI of England: XIII 526

INDEX 5

Henry VIII of England: I 122-3
Henry, P.: X 196
Hesketh, Thomas de: XIII 525
Heunegrams, Jehan de: IV 466-7
Hévin, Pierre: XIII 518, 522
Hirschauer, Charles: X 215
Homage: XI 634-5; XIII 509-27, 531-5
Hoüard, David: XII 521
Huguenots, assemblies of: III 32; X 218-9
Hurault, Guy: VII 226-7

Ile-de-France: IV 465-7, 469-71, 474; VI 134, 138, 145-6
Isle-Jourdain, estates of: X 205
Italy: II 18; III 29, 39-40; IV 461

Jeannin, Pierre: IX 382
Jones, George F.: XIII 511
Justinian, emperor: XIII 514

La Bigotière, René de: XIII 522
Labourd, estates of: X 209-10
La Faille, Georges de: V 701
La Marche, estates of: III 30
La Meilleraye, dukes of: XIII 524-5
La Montagne: VI 134, 138, 142, 144; VII 221
Lancelot, Sir: XIII 512, 514
Landes, estates of: IX 367; X 203
Landtage: III 28
Langres: VI 136
  bishop of: XIII 513
Languedoc: I 114; IV 465-7, 470; IX 376, 382-3; XII 41; XIV 393
  estates of: III 35-7, IV 467; V 704; VI 133-5, 145, 147, VII 222; X 188, 198-200, 217; XI 641-3; XII 46
Languedoïl, estates of: VIII 248-51, 259
La Noue, François de: XII 48
Laon: VII 219, 225
La Plume: X 205
La Rochelle: VI 138; VII 227; XI 634; XII 29
La Thaumassière, Gaspard Thaumas de: XIII 521-2
La Tour, Antoine de: XII 35
La Trémoille, family: XI 634, 638-9; XII 40-1; XIII 524-5; XIV 393
  François de: XII 40
  Georges de: XI 636; XII 40; XIII 531; XIV 396
Lausignan, Guy de: XII 43
  Louis de: XII 43
Lautrec: XII 24, 27
Laval, family of: XI 641
  Urban de, seigneur de Bois-Dauphin: XIV 395
La Valette, lieutenant general: V 704
Lavour, estates of: X 200
Le Blanc, Guillaume: IV 466
  Robert: IV 467-8
Le Brignon: XIII 523
Le Goff, Jacques: XIII 512-3
Le Havre: XIV 403
Lelet, Jean: XIII 521
Le Mans: IV 466; IV 136
Lepointe, Gabriel: X 218
Le Puy: III 39
Le Roy Ladurie, Emmanuel: XII 22-3
Lesdiguières, François de Bonne, duke of: XI 637-8; XII 35, 42-3
L'Estoile, Pierre de: V 705
Le Tellier, Michel: XI 645
Lewis, Peter S.: XIII 509, 529-30
L'Hôpital, Michel de: III 31; IV 462, 470
Lignano, John of: XII 533
Lille, estates of: X 215-16
Limoges: VI 135
Limousin: XII 24-5, 31
  Bas-: VI 138, 144, 147; VII 221, 225; X 203
  Haut: IV 147
Littleton, Sir Thomas: XIII 517-8, 526
Lodève, estates of: X 200
Loisel, Antoine: XIII 518
Longueville, duchess of: XIII 520
  Henry, duke of: XIV 393, 401, 403
Lorraine, Charles, cardinal: IV 462, 475; VII 221; VIII 257
  Leopold, duke of: XIII 525
  estates of: X 216
Loudon: XV 138
Louis XI: I 113-4; III 34; VIII 249-50, 252-3, 255-6; XIII 531-2, 534

Louis XII: I 114; III 41; IV 474
Louis XIII: I 113-4; IX 382; X 200, 202, 204; XIV 391-3, 401-5
Louis XIV: I 113, 120, 124; X 714; IX 383; X 180, 190, 213, 215; XI 632, 645; XIII 520, 523, 525; XIV 400
Louis XV: X 215
Louis XVI: XIII 525
Lousse, Emile: III 29
Loutschitzki, J.: X 219
Louvois, François Michel Le Tellier, marquis of: XI 645
Low Countries: I 122; II 18
Luther, Martin: I 112
Luynes, Charles d'Albert, duke of: XIV 392-3, 401
Lyon: III 39; V 703-4, 706-7, 711; VI 135-7; VII 223, 227-8; XII 45
Lyonnais: IV 465-6, 469-71; VI 145
  estates of: III 39; XII 46
Lyonnais, Forez, and Beaujolais, estates of: V 704

Machiavelli, Niccolo: I 119; II 18, 26-31
Mâcon: VII 221, 224-5; XII 42
Mâconnais, estates of: VI 133; X 190-1
Maine: VI 133, 144
Mandure: I 116
Marcel, Etienne: VIII 248
Marie de Medici: VIII 253; IX 383; XI 637, 641, 644; XIV 391-5, 397-401, 403-8
Marillac, Michel de: IX 368-9, 383; XI 643
Marsan: XII 24
  estates of: X 211
Marseilles: VI 135, 145; VII 223
Marsillac, seigneur of: XI 637
Martin, Jean de: IX 369-70
Massol, Jacques: IV 466, 468, 471, 473
Matignon, Jacques de Goyon, count of: XII 42
Maupeou, Gilles de: IX 376, 383
Maxmilian, emperor: III 40
Mayenne, Charles, duke of: XI 640
  Henry, duke of: XIV 393-4, 398, 403-5, 407

Melun: IV 462-3, 466; VI 136, 138; XIII 520
Melun, A.: X 216
Mesgrigny, Jean de: X 196
  Jehan de: IV 466-7, 472
Metz: XIV 394
Mézières, Philippe de: XIII 534
Milan: II 27
Molière, Jean Baptiste: XI 632
Monluc, Blaise de: XII 42-3
Montaigne, Michel de: III 33-4
Montaing, count of: XIII 520
Montbéliard: I 116
Mont-de-Marsan, estates of: X 211
Montdidier: III 137; IV 466
Montgomery, Gabriel, count of: XII 29-30
Montmorency, family of: V 702; XI 639, 641-2; XII 44
  duke of: I 118, 120; IV 476; XIV 400
  François, duke of: IV 467
  Henry, duke of: XIV 393
Montpellier: IX 378
  university of: III 37
Montpensier, Louis, duke of: XIII 520
More, Sir Thomas: II 18, 21-4, 27
Moret, Jacqueline de Bueil, countess of: IX 380
Mortier, sieur de: IV 472
Mouret, François: X 217
Mousnier, Roland: IX 366-7, 370; XIV 398-9, 406
Mulhouse: I 116
Murol, Guillaume de: XII 36

Namier, Sir Lewis: X 183
Nantes: VI 136
Naples: II 27
Navarre: XII 24-6, 29
  Antoine, king of: IV 463, 468, 471
  estates of: X 209-10; XII 40
Navarrenx: XII 25, 29
Neale, Sir John: X 183
Nébouzan: XII 24
  estates of: X 212-3
Nemours: VI 138
  Henry, duke of: XIV 393
Nérac: XII 24, 31
Netz, Nicolas de: IX 379

Neubourg: XII 42
Nevers: VI 133; VII 227
  family of: XI 633-5, 638-41, 643; XII 43
  Louis, duke of: V 708
Nîmes: IV 467, 470
Nivernais: XI 638
Nobility, economic status: XI 633-4; XII 21-48
  numerical reconstruction: XI 631-3
  relations with crown: XI 643-5
Normandy: IV 466, 473; VIII 249-50; XII 41-5; XIII 520; XIV 393, 401, 403-4
  estates of: V 705; VI 134, 137-8, 145-6; X 214-5
Notestein, Wallace: VIII 247
Nowell, John: XIII 525

Obazine, prior of: XIII 513
Occam, William of: I 112
Orange: I 116
Orléans: IV 466, 468-70, 474; VI 136, 138, 144; VII 221, 226-7; VIII 251; XI 637; XII 520
  Gaston, duke of: XIV 405
  Louis, duke of: XIII 530
Orléanais: VI 138, 145-6
Ornano, Alfonso d': IX 372-3, 377-80; XII 42
Otto I, emperor: XIII 514

Pairaud, Hugues de: XIII 515
Paris: I 115; IV 463, 467; V 703, 706, 710, 712; VI 132-3, 136-7, 149; VII 223, 225-6, 229; IX 369; X 186, 191, 198, 202; XI 637; XII 35-6, 41, 44-5; XIII 519; XIV 394, 401
  parlement of: I 114-5, 121; III 32, 37; IV 468-9, 474, 476; V 707; VI 139; IX 368; XI 641
Patron-client relationship: XI 635-45; XIII 534-5; XIV 391-408
Pau: XII 24, 31
Paul, St.: XIII 510-1
Paulette: IX 365-7, 370, 382
Pensey, Henrion de: XIII 518
Perche: VI 138
Périgord: VII 221, 225; XII 24-5, 31
  estates of: VI 135, 143; IX 367; X 203
Périgueux: VII 219, 228
Péronne: VII 229
Perroy, Edouard: XIII 529
Peter, St.: XIII 510
Peysac: XII 31
Philip IV: I 113, 121; XIII 515
Philip the Good of Burgundy: XIII 534
Philip IV of Spain: I 124
Picardy: IV 466, 470-1; V 707; VI 134, 138, 143, 145-6; XII 41
Picot, Georges: V 701
Pigny, seigneur de: VII 219
Pisan, Christine de: XIII 533
Ploëmel: IV 467
Poissy: IV 463-4, 475-6
Poitiers: VI 136; VII 218; XII 31
  Philippe de: VII 218
Poitou: VI 138; VII 219; XII 45
Poland: V 702, 709
Polignac, viscounts of: XIII 523
Pollard, A. F.: XII 21-2
Ponthieu: VI 138, 143, 147; VII 221, 225
Ponts-de-Cé: XIV 392, 403-5
Portugal: I 124
Poulaim, Mathieu: IV 466-7, 469, 471, 473-4
Powicke, Sir Maurice: III 29
Prentout, Henri: X 214
Provence: I 114; III 38; IV 465-6, 469-71, 473-4; VI 134, 145; VII 222, 224, 268; VIII 256; IX 376, 383; XII 46
  estates of: III 38; VI 132; X 197-8; XI 642
Prudent Michaut: XIV 401-3, 405, 407

Quatre-Vallées, estates of: X 212
Quercy, estates of: III 37; VI 135, 147; IX 367, 378; X 203-4

Rais, Gilles de: XI 636; XIII 531; XIV 396
Rebillon, Armand: X 213-4
Reims: V 710; VIII 251
Renaissance Monarchy, characteristics of: I 112-24; II 17-31; III 17-41; IX 364-5

Retz, Albret de Gondi de: V 708
  Henri de Gondi de: XIV 393-4,
    404-5, 407
Richelieu, Cardinal: I 119-20; III 38;
  VIII 259; IX 366, 368, 383; X
  186, 202, 214; XI 639, 641-2;
  XIV 392, 399-400, 403-5
Rieux, estates of: VI 133; X 200
Riom: VI 141; X 196
Rivière, Hippolyte-F.: X 196
Rivière-Verdun, estates of: IX 367,
  374; X 206-7
Roanès, Louis Gouffier, duke
  of: XIV 393, 395
Robert, Jehan: IV 467-8
  Pierre: VII 229
Rochefort, William de,
  chancellor: VII 218-9
  sieur de: XI 637
Rodders, Michel: IV 466
Rodez: X 207
Rogé, P.: X 211
Rogier, Jehan: IV 467
Rohan, Henry, duke of: XI 636, 641;
  XIV 393, 395, 397, 403-4
Romans: V 704
Roque, William: I 467
Roquefeuil, dame of: XIII 525
Rouchon, G.: X 196
Rouen: IV 466; V 706, 710-1; VI
  136, 144, 146, 149; VII 221, 224,
  228; XIV 401
  parlement of: XIV 398
Rouergue: VI 147; XII 24
  estates of: IX 367, 376; X 207-8
Roussillon: X 213
Roussot, Jean: X 190-1

Saint-Aubin d'Angers: XIII 513
Saint-Gall, abbot elect of: XIII 514
Saint-Germain-en-Laye: IV 463, 467,
  473, 475; V 714
Saintes: VI 135
Salm: I 116
Sarigny, seigneur of: XIII 524
Sarrverden: I 116
Sault: I 116
Saux-Tavannes, Gaspard de: XII 42
Scotland: I 122
Sée, Henri: X 213
Selves, Julien de Camberfore, sieur
  de: IX 374-82
Senlis: VI 137; VII 228-9
Sens: VI 137, 147
Serbat, Louis: X 218
Seyssel, Claude de: II 18, 24-6
Sforza, Francesco: II 27
Sillery, Boulart de: IX 376, 382
Soissons, Louis, count of: XIV 393
Soule, estates of: X 209
Spain: I 124; II 27; III 40
Stone, Lawrence: XIII 526
Stubbs, Bishop William: X 183
Sully, Maxmilian de Béthune, duke
  of: IX 363-83; XI 633, 641; XIV
  406
Supersantis, Bernard de: V 710
Sweden: I 122

Templars, trial of: XIII 515, 532
Terlon, Claude: IV 467, 470
Terride, baron of: XII 29-30
Tertullian: XIII 510
Thierry, Augustin: XII 21-2
Tholin, G.: X 205
Thomas, Antoine: X 195
Thou, Christofle de: VI 139
Toulouse: V 707, 710-2; VI 133, 135;
  VII 224; IX 372, 378; XII 35
  estates of: X 200
  parlement of: IV 467; IX 374
  university of: III 37
Touraine: IV 466-7; VI 136-7, 144;
  XIII 520
Tournon, Cardinal: IV 475
Tours: III 41; IV 466; VI 136; VII
  218
Tristan and Isolde: XIII 511
Troyes: I 118; IV 466; V 706, 711,
  714; VI 136-7, 146; VII 218-9,
  223
Turenne, family of: III 33; XIII 513
  estates of: X 204
Turkey: II 28
Tursan: XII 24
Tuscany: IV 463

Ustaritz: X 209

Valencia: I 124
Valois, Marguerite de: XII 39
  Noël: IV 460, 470

INDEX

Van Dyke, Paul: IV 460
Velay, estates of: VI 135; X 199
Venaissin: I 116
Vence: VI 148
Vendôme, Caesar, duke of: XIV 393, 398, 403
Venice: I 119-20; III 27; IV 463; V 703
Verdat, M.: X 190
Verdier-Latour, Dom: X 196
Verguer, Claude du: IV 466, 473
Vermandois: IV 467; VI 137; VII 220-2, 225, 228
Versailles: I 120; XI 645
Vic-Fezensac, estates of: X 205
Vienne: VI 135

Villages, assemblies of: III 39-40
Villefranche-sur-Saône: VI 136
Villeneuve-d'Avignon: V 704
Villemur: XII 24, 35
Villeroy, Nicolas de Neufville de: V 207; IX 376, 382
Vitry-le-François: VI 137, 146; VII 225
Vivarais, estates of: X 199

Walloon Flanders, estates of: X 215-6
Weary, William A.: XII 40
Wolsey, Cardinal: I 120
Wood, James B.: XII 44